THE WEIDNERS IN WARTIME

Letters of Daily Survival and Heroism
Under Nazi Rule

Selected, translated, and introduced by
JANET HOLMES CARPER

*With translations from Dutch by Anthony Sluis
and a translation from Italian by Anna Rein*

WEIDNER FOUNDATION BOOKS

Paperback version copyright 2023 by Janet Holmes Carper
First published in hardback in 2020
All rights reserved.

This book may not be reproduced, in whole or in part, including illustrations and images, in any form beyond what is authorized by U.S. Copyright Law, and except by reviewers for the public press, without written permission from the John Henry Weidner Foundation for Altruism. All photographs, original documents, and source materials used, reproduced and translated in this book are by permission of the Weidner Foundation unless otherwise noted.

Weidner Foundation Books is a part of the John Henry Weidner Foundation for Altruism and serves to further the Foundation's mission of cultivating selfless and courageous action in the spirit of John Weidner and the Dutch-Paris escape line. For more information about the Weidner Foundation, visit www.weidnerfoundation.org

The Weidner Collection Series: *The Weidners in Wartime* is the inaugural publication in a new book series by Weidner Foundation Books featuring documents and memoirs about John Weidner and the Dutch-Paris escape line, with a particular focus on materials contained in the Foundation's Weidner Collection.

Series general editor: Ronald E. Osborn

Cover and jacket design by Terrill Thomas and Ronald E. Osborn

Cover images: Letter from Papa Weidner to Jean, Elisabeth, and Annette, with blue censor's mark, April 9, 1944 (The Weidner Collection); German paratroopers above Bezuidenhout neighborhood during the invasion of The Hague, May 10, 1940 (Fotocollectie Spaarnestad, Nationaal Archief).

Map of Occupied France by Ronald E. Osborn

Set in Garamond type by Weidner Foundation Books

Riverside, California
Printed in the United States

ISBN: 978-1-7346999-2-0

For Tom with love

Contents

	Foreword	i
	Preface	v
	A Note on the Translations	ix
	Who's Who in the Correspondence	xiii
	Map of Occupied France	xvii
1	The Weidners Before the War	1
2	"La Drôle de Guerre" – The Phony War	29
3	The Flight to Anduze	47
4	Daily Life in Occupied Paris	65
5	The Hague Rejoins the Conversation	87
6	The Encroaching War	115
7	A Party and a Wedding	161
8	Bombs and Refugees	195
9	The New Store	225
10	Resistance and Daily Life	255
11	An Engagement in The Hague	297
12	Escapes	319
13	"Serious Things Could Happen to Us"	351
14	Gaby	369
	Afterword	401
	Historical Timeline	407
	Sources	411
	Acknowledgments	413

Foreword
Marie-Claire Rolland

The book you are holding in your hands brings to life the daily existence during the Second World War of people I did not know, but whom I feel I have come to know. During the years from 1939 to 1944, a scattered family finds itself in Holland, France and Switzerland. The father, an Adventist pastor, and his wife and three children are of Dutch origin, but the children were born and raised in French-speaking countries, and French is the language of their letters. An intense correspondence among them faithfully reflects a period in which the daily struggles to survive loom large, and where travel is so difficult or impossible to arrange that their letters are the only means of communication.

These are authentic letters, never revised, never before translated, and read by few. That they have survived is a true miracle. Letters are most often lost or forgotten or thrown away when their news is no longer news. But Jean, the oldest son, kept the letters he received and made carbon copies of those he wrote.

Readers today who have not experienced this war must rely on documents and recollections of those who lived through it. But memories can be unreliable and even self-serving sixty years after the events. The Weidner family letters are primary sources, written day by day, raw documents, like contemporary snapshots of those years. The fight for life or survival was the lot of millions of civilians, and their road was long. Hunger, cold, lack of the barest necessities, separation from loved ones, long and anxious waits for news, loneliness, fear of catastrophe and tragedy which could come at any moment, constant check points, restrictions, and the burden of the Occupation—these are the concerns of the Weidners' letters.

Having myself been a little girl and then a young teenager during this war, the Weidners' experience seemed familiar in nearly every way. Reading their letters, I felt like a part of their world. I adopted them as members of my own family. I understood what they were saying, and I admired their strength and their uncomplaining courage.

The Weidner accounts make clear how preoccupying was the search for food. Of course we know that life is not possible without it, but one has to have known the deprivation of nearly everything to understand how degrading is the fight against hunger. I have never really gotten over my grief at seeing my mother waiting in line for hours to buy—if there were any left when she got to the head of the line—turnips or Jerusalem artichokes, vegetables with little nourishment. I felt intensely her humiliation. But the Weidners tell more often of the pleasure of finding food and of unexpected gifts, than complaining about daily hardships.

It was cold at home, and like Gaby Weidner, members of my family took refuge from the cold under the covers. Our teachers admitted to correcting their students' papers curled up in bed, flashlight in hand. We also wrote to friends on those government-issued pre-printed cards reserved strictly for family news. For us, too, travel was almost impossible. I remember overcrowded trains, often late, and the unforgettable railroad station which marked the border between the Occupied and Unoccupied zones. For Gaby, who is in Paris and whose parents are in The Hague, a visit might be possible, even across international borders, but should she go, she would risk being prevented from returning.

We too heard the aircraft guns, and they were louder than the planes, as Gaby points out. Our friends and neighbors too displayed the tricolors of the French flag on the July 14th national holiday, against regulations under the Occupation. We knew that telephone calls could be monitored, and we listened clandestinely to British radio. Letters were lost, prices mounted, and we grew suspicious of others and anxious for ourselves. Many around us were in poverty and miserable conditions like those Annette Weidner finds among her patients in The Hague. When two of my teachers arrived at the lycée wearing the yellow star, I felt unspeakable humiliation and shame that a country—my country—could act in so despicable a fashion.

The Weidners take note of the major happenings and injustices of the war, but only obliquely. When the Germans invaded Russia on June 22, 1941, my father could comment, "They are making the same mistake

FOREWORD iii

Napoleon made." But when the German invasion flounders at the battle of Stalingrad, Jean can only write that "Fischer," (the family code name for Germany) is really very ill and cannot last long. At the time of the attack on Pearl Harbor, Jean writes openly of "this Japanese-American war" but then theorizes about "Fischer's" possible future involvement in it. From The Hague, Mama Weidner writes "Now we see people that are really hungry." And Papa describes an Allied bombing as a "bowling game."

My own father could say what was on his mind, but the Weidners could not write about the events of the war. Their letters were sent via friends who were risking their lives if the letters were discovered and found to reveal anti-German thoughts. Letters from The Hague, sent by legal mail service, were read by the censors. Thus there are necessarily two levels of expression to comprehend in these letters: the transparent one, full of warmth and life, and the other one, which is mute and threatening. The latter is a constant presence and it cannot be erased, even when the letters tell of happy things like youth group outings, entertainment, or Jean's wedding.

There are silences that speak louder than words. Our occupied countries were gagged. We could not complain or protest. We could not revolt, except deep in our hearts.

The reader does not at first sense this shroud of silence because the parents and the young people all are full of tenderness and solicitude for each other and they maintain a kind of joyous affection which brushes aside what cannot be said. The family code of names for the major players in the war provides a further cover for their ideas and affords them the opportunity to mock the enemy behind his back.

The most mysterious person in this drama is Jean. There is no doubt that he is an attentive son, a generous and affectionate brother, and a dependable friend, but he is also an efficient member of the Resistance. He leads an escape network which helps Dutch refugees to reach Switzerland or Spain. Of this work he can say little, but he does describe to Gaby the work of "a friend of mine" who does things of this nature. Gaby understands perfectly that these activities are led by Jean himself.

There are no atrocities described in these pages, it is true. There is only an end, unexpected and unforgettable.

It is rare that such living testimony survives for posterity. That is why I am full of admiration and gratitude to Janet Holmes Carper who has read and translated an enormous quantity of Weidner family letters, which were often hard to decipher, written on old and brittle paper, and sometimes nearly illegible. Her well annotated selection speaks aloud in the voices of this family. This is an original and priceless contribution to history.

Marie-Claire Rolland
Inspecteur Général de l'Education Nationale
(Retired Inspector General of the French Ministry of Education)

Preface

John "Jean" Henry Weidner, Jr., a hero of the Dutch Resistance in France during World War II, rescued Dutch Jews and other refugees, including young men called up for work in Germany and Allied pilots shot down over France and Belgium. He personally guided many of them across the rocky Salève mountain on France's eastern border into Switzerland. He headed the Resistance network later known as "Dutch-Paris," which organized the escape route from The Netherlands, through Belgium to Paris and then to southern France and across borders to Switzerland or Spain. Incarcerated by the Gestapo, he managed to escape. After the war, he was honored by the governments of France, Belgium, Switzerland, The Netherlands, Israel, and the United States for his heroism, his bravery and his devotion to the cause of humanity.

John Weidner's Resistance work and that of his Dutch-Paris network have been expertly chronicled by research historian Megan Koreman in her book *The Escape Line* (Oxford University Press, 2018). It is the wartime correspondence of the Weidner family that is the subject of this book. Their intimately detailed letters describe the increasing difficulties of their lives in Holland and France as the war with Germany develops, first slowly, then with crushing violence. How the members of an ordinary family, separated by national and local barriers, deal with their fears and frustrations, as well as the occasional pleasures, is tellingly revealed in the correspondence of five prodigious letter writers.

The patriarch is "Papa" Weidner, Johan Heinrich Weidner Sr., a retired pastor of the Seventh-day Adventist Church. He and his wife Jeanne Linschoten-Weidner spend the war years in The Hague. With them is their youngest daughter, Anne Marie, "Annette," who is studying to be an assistant birth attendant and maternity nurse. Oldest daughter Gabrielle, "Gaby," is at this time in Paris, where she works as a secretary stenographer in the offices of the Seventh-day Adventist Church. John Weidner Jr., "Jean," is in Lyon, in France's Southern or "Unoccupied" Zone, where he both operates a fabric sales business and directs his Resistance network.

As the family members describe their efforts to lead normal lives, the pressures of war become ever more evident. Food and clothing are rationed, and finding supplies is a major preoccupation for everyone. Friends who live in the country can sometimes help Gaby obtain butter and eggs. She is a vegetarian as most Adventists are, so she can exchange meat rationing coupons for cheese. Jean sends Gaby potatoes, sugar, fabrics and money which she is able to share with her parents and Annette when communications are re-established after the early days of the war. "Passive defense" requires entire city blackouts in Paris and The Hague. Annette, called to assist at a birth in the outskirts of The Hague, must make her way on her bicycle through unlit streets. The threat of evacuation throws the lives of residents of The Hague into chaos, and early curfews in Paris limit the daily movements of Gaby and her colleagues. Eventually, there are bombing alerts and the loud reports of anti-aircraft guns.

Within France, written correspondence is extremely difficult. Letters between the Occupied and Unoccupied Zones must be sent by clandestine means, through friends and friends of friends. Only small government postcards are allowed for family correspondence. Letters from The Hague are limited to four sides of two pages and are read by the censors, who ink half-inch-wide gray-blue transparent streaks diagonally across the pages.

Disguising one's thoughts is essential. When writing about the progress of the war, Papa and Jean use names of people they know to represent opposing nations: "Arthur" represents England in the family code, "Arthur's uncle" is the United States, "Charlotte," is Belgium, and "Fischer" is Germany. They use more than one name when referring to themselves or each other. Sending postcards, which will be read by the censors, Gaby calls Jean by his middle name "Henri," and speaks of him in the third person. Another device the family uses when writing to each other about the war without raising suspicion is to express opinions which appear to support a German victory, or to imply that the Allies are losing the war. In one letter to Jean, Papa writes, "…according to Hitler, and Hitler never lies…"

PREFACE

Papa and Jean use this kind of code frequently, but Gaby does not, making all the more puzzling her occasional expressions of a kind of routine and seemingly unthinking anti-Semitism. "I know there are many Jews who deserve what is happening to them," she writes on June 29, 1942, "but still, there are some who are exceptions to the rule, and I think my doctor is one of those." It is possible, of course, that this could be her own code, writing opinions acceptable to the reader should her letter fall into the wrong hands. But since this kind of code never appears otherwise in Gaby's letters, it seems more likely that she simply follows society's pattern of routinely expressed anti-Semitism which would be unthinkable today.*

In the hundreds of letters in the Weidner family correspondence there are no clear references to Jean Weidner's Resistance work, except obliquely or when coded.

Amid the trials of the war years, the Weidners are sustained by their Seventh-day Adventist faith, whose Sabbath is observed from sundown Friday to sundown Saturday, "the Seventh Day" as also kept by observant Jews. Members of the Church call each other "Brother" and "Sister," follow the same strict dietary restrictions as Jews concerning "clean" and "unclean" meats (and are often vegetarians), shun alcohol and tobacco, and are pacifists and conscientious objectors, similar to Quakers and Mennonites. They may find security within their own world, as opposed to "The World" outside. They can look forward hopefully to the Second coming of Christ when all will join together in harmony and good will.

The letters of Papa. Mama, Gaby, Annette and Jean offer in moving detail a picture not only of life within a family, but of the daily experiences of all those in Occupied Holland and Occupied France where obtaining enough food is a struggle, everything is rationed and expensive, coal for

---

* Maarten Eliasar, whose father was a part of Jean Weidner's escape network, after reading a review of the diaries of E.N. Van Kleffens, Dutch wartime Foreign Minister in exile, [Riemans, Michael, *Majesteit, U kent het werkliche leven niet,* Vantilt, 2019] writes: "It becomes shockingly clear…how deeply anti-Semitism was embedded in those days." In light of Gabrielle's anti-Semitic expressions Maarten adds: "Even in Amsterdam, during the February 1941 general strike "Februaristaking" (the only official protest against the persecution of Jews organized by non-Jews during the war), the expression was 'blijf met je rotpoten van onze rotjoden af.' Freely translated, and excuse my French: 'take your f---ing claws off our f---ing Jews.' Although they weren't much loved, they were still 'ours'. So maybe Gabrielle's expressions can be seen in that light, without a fanatic anti-Semitic meaning."

heating is scarce, the winters are cruelly cold, and anxiety attends every action.

Separated by impenetrable national and political boundaries, in this dangerous time the Weidners are homesick for each other and war weary. But their letters reveal their courage, the strength of their faith, and their confidence in a future when they will all be together again in this world or the next.

The letters tell their own stories.

Janet H. Carper
Cornish, Maine
March, 2019

A Note on the Translations

Concerning the original pages and the style observed in the presentation of letters in this book

Shortly before his death in 1994, John Weidner and his wife Naomi worked to establish The John Henry Weidner Foundation for Altruism, dedicated to cultivating selfless and courageous action in the spirit of John Weidner and the Dutch-Paris escape line. The Foundation was at first centered in Lancaster, Massachusetts, and housed the Weidner Collection of historical documents, correspondence, photographs, and artifacts related to John Weidner's life and the Dutch-Paris escape line. Most of these materials, filling nearly 100 manuscript boxes, were collected and safeguarded by Weidner himself in the years after the Second World War before being entrusted to the Foundation. From the archives of the Foundation's Weidner Collection, the Editor has selected these letters out of the hundreds of wartime letters and postcards written by Weidner family members in French and Dutch and filed away since they were written over 75 years ago. They have not been translated before and have been read by only a few. Yet the typed or handwritten pages that circulated among the Weidner siblings and parents pack a lifetime into the few years they span.

Selections have been made within the letters, and the omissions are shown by three suspension points. Because the letter-writers themselves frequently use suspension points as the French do, to indicate unspoken surprise or indignation, the translator and editor has eliminated these in the translations to avoid confusion with the suspension points indicating omissions.

Within the letters' text the editor has also used brackets [ ] to insert brief explanatory notes not in the original letter. These may be useful to the reader. Longer notes appear in footnotes. Letters in Dutch have been translated by Anthony Sluis. The interview in Italian of Annette Weidner by Alberto Sbacchi was translated by Anna Rein.

Though the letter-writers nearly always write dates in the form of numbers, the dates of the letters in this book are given in words, to avoid confusion between French and English styles of expressing dates.

When the letter-writers save space by writing figures instead of spelled-out numbers in cases other than dates, the translator has left them in that form. The abbreviation for "Madame" ("Mme") is also retained.

Because of the very French nature of the letters from France, opening salutations remain in French, with only their first few appearances translated. For the same reason, John Weidner's French name "Jean" is always used in this book. Throughout his life in his correspondence with his many French and Dutch friends, he was always addressed in this way. His parents, however, often use some of the family nicknames for him: "Joop" (pronounced "Yope"), "Jopie," and "Poop." Gabrielle's family nickname is "Mies," which she uses as code for herself, just as she uses Jean's middle name "Henri" as her code name for him.

A few letters or parts of letters to the Weidners from other people have been included here, where they may clarify or explain. The letters to Jean from soldiers who were members of the youth group at the Paris Adventist Church tell of the aimlessness of the "phony war" in 1939.

It is a near miracle that this complete correspondence has survived. We have both sides of the conversations because Jean Weidner kept all the letters he received and he also made carbon copies of nearly every letter he wrote. He brought many large boxes of files with him when, after the war, he moved to California to set up a health food business there. The files in the Weidner Archive therefore contain his lifetime correspondence with European and American friends. Though he claimed to "hate to write," his letters are long, newsy, and full of details, though the reading is at times hampered by technical problems caused by shortages of paper, carbon paper, typewriter ribbons, fountain pens and ink.

Jean types most of his letters, for which any reader of the archives will be grateful, as his handwriting is at best a wavy line. He leaves no margins, nor does he divide his pages into paragraphs (perhaps to discourage the censors) where he occasionally hides comments about the war in his dense, single-spaced pages containing family news. He uses the carbon paper well beyond its useful life, leaving the print barely visible. His carbon paper sometimes folds, leaving the copy blank in one corner. Or the

A NOTE ON THE TRANSLATIONS

carbon paper is narrower than the width of Jean's overfull page causing missing words at the end of each line. Many of Jean's letters are typed on both sides of nearly transparent sheets of paper, making both the backward and forward texts equally visible and indecipherable on both sides. Typographical errors abound, and his words are sometimes spelled according to how they sound in French.

Gaby's handwriting is small, and clearly legible. When she types her letters, as a well-trained secretary-stenographer she never makes errors in French. But sometimes her worn-out typewriter ribbons leave little ink on the page. She uses her wider margins to write additional messages up the side and across the top of the paper.

Annette's thoughts tumble out in her bold and hasty scrawl peppered with ink blots from uncooperative fountain pens. Mama's letters are handwritten in Dutch and Papa's letters are typed at first in Dutch and later in French. He apologizes for his errors in French, but he never makes any.

—JHC

Who's Who in the Correspondence

Name	Also known as	Relationship
The Weidners		
Jean (1912-1994)	John, Henri, Joop (pronounced "Yope"), Jopie, Poop, Popie	
Gabrielle (1914-1945)	Miesje, Mies (diminutives of Gabrielle's second name, Hermien), Gaby	Jean's sister, two years younger than Jean
François (1916-1932)		Jean and Gaby's brother, two years younger than Gabrielle, who died at 16
Annette (1921-2004)	Anne-Marie, Madame Dumont, Maryse	Jean's younger sister, nine years younger than Jean
Papa (1881-1947)	Johan Hendrik Weidner	Father of Jean, Gabrielle, François, Annette
Mama (1885-1960)	Jeanne Linschoten Weidner	Mother of Jean, Gabrielle, François, Annette
Elisabeth (1915-d.?)	Elisa, Lizou, Lisa	Married Jean in 1942

Lykele Faber (1919-2009)	Ly, Li	Engaged to Annette in 1943

The Family's Secret Code

Arthur	England
Fischer	Germany
Charlotte	Fischer's fiancé, Belgium
Berthelot	Gestapo headquarters in Lyon
Monnier	Switzerland

Dutch-Paris Resistance Members

Hermann Laatsman	Mr. L.	Dutch Consul in Paris
Suzy Kraay	Erna	

Others

Julien Beaujolin	Gilbert Beaujolin	Jean's lifelong friend and first business associate
Madame Girou		Lay member and helper in the Adventist Church, Paris and Anduze

WHO'S WHO IN THE CORRESPONDENCE

Mémé Girou		Madame Girou's son
Oscar Meyer		President at the Paris Adventist Church
Paul Meyer		Adventist pastor in Lyon, brother of Oscar
Sister White (1827-1915)	Ellen G. White	Co-founder of the Adventist movement, writer, native of Gorham, Maine

Map of Occupied France

1   The Weidners Before the War

With strong roots in The Netherlands, yet with wide European experience, the Weidner family could live comfortably in a variety of cultures. They were as close-knit and mutually supportive when they were separated by tragic circumstances as when they were together before the war. Their Seventh-day Adventist faith both sustained them and brought them anguish and moral struggles, shared with each other especially in their letters during their years apart.

John Weidner's father, Johan Heinrich Weidner, Sr., born August 10, 1881, in Haarlem (Holland) was the son of a pastor in the Dutch Protestant Church. His mother died when he was three years old. As a young man, Weidner became interested in the tenets of the Seventh-day Adventist Church, much to his pastor father's chagrin. However, the son gradually persuaded his father to think as he did, and the father would have been converted to Adventist beliefs himself had he not died suddenly when Johan Heinrich was twenty-one years old.

Johan Heinrich Weidner continued his studies in Germany and then in England, and married Jeanne Gertrude Linschoten, herself from an Adventist family. He was named a pastor in Brussels, Belgium, where Jean Henri Weidner, Jr. was born a year after their marriage. Two years later came Gabrielle and then their second son François, two years after Gabrielle.

After his father's death in 1947, Jean Weidner Jr. writes, "Papa devoted himself body and soul to his ministry, which he loved. Salaries were very low and the early years were extremely difficult. ... Mama was a marvelous source of support and help. Since she didn't have enough money to pay for the tramway, she would walk to church on the Sabbath with her three children. When she was pregnant she had to clean the church sanctuary, as this was not covered in the budget." Throughout his youth, Jean seems to have been preoccupied with the fact that his parents worked so hard and had too little to show for it, and he often cited this as a reason he wanted to go into business instead of following in his father's footsteps and becoming a pastor. He wanted to be able to take care of his family and give his parents the comfort they deserved.

The senior Mr. Weidner's next pastorate was at Vevey in French-speaking Switzerland, and their baby sister Anne-Marie or "Annette," as her family called her, was born in 1921. Thus all four children were born and raised in French-speaking countries and considered their native language to be French. They struggled to learn the Dutch language, because their father fervently wished them to be Dutch and to retain the language of The Netherlands. Yet throughout his life, John Weidner Jr. maintained correspondence in French with many friends in France, Holland, Belgium and Italy, while retaining his Dutch citizenship even after many years of living in the United States. When writing to French friends he always called himself by his French names, "Jean," and "Henri", as we will do henceforth in this book.

Annette, too, was "homesick" for the French language during the war years in The Hague, where she was studying to be a maternity nurse. "I miss France so much," she writes to her sister Gaby in 1941. "The head nurse can't stand me. ... I get a sermon every time I make an error in Dutch." And when Annette breaks up with a boyfriend, she writes that among other drawbacks of marriage to the young man, "I would have to bring up my children in Dutch. Never to hear French anymore!"

From Switzerland, Papa was called with his family to serve on the faculty of the Adventist Seminary in Collonges-sous-Salève, in the Haute Savoie mountains in France only a few miles from Geneva, Switzerland. The school's buildings are nestled in a picture-book location just below the steep and forbidding cliffs of the Salève mountain. "Jean," John Weidner Jr., in particular seems to have regarded this period with nostalgic affection for the mountains he loved and learned to navigate, scaling the cliffs which towered above the Seminary, even though this dangerous exploit was expressly forbidden by his father. The knowledge of these cliffs and this mountain served him well later on, when he aided refugees escaping to Switzerland from the Nazi Occupation in France.

At the Seminary, "Papa" Weidner taught Latin, Greek and Flemish (Dutch) for twelve years. The Weidner children were students at the

Seminary. When she was fifteen, Gabrielle wrote to a former teacher, then living in Aigle, Switzerland. Her letter describes briefly her life at Collonges.

Gaby to Mademoiselle Widmer Collonges, May 13, 1929

Dear Mademoiselle Widmer,

I have been so slow to write to you, that I didn't dare to anymore. But as Papa is sending you a letter, I'll take this opportunity, knowing that you will forgive me for this long delay.

Don't think I have forgotten you! But time passes so quickly, and at the Seminary we don't have much vacation. We have so little time to do anything but study. Already I have been a student at the Seminary for two years, and my courses are: English II, Dutch II, French III, Geography II, Physiology, Bible II, Singing II, Organ II, Drawing and Sewing. My parents are satisfied with my grades.

We have been living in Collonges for 5 years now. But I still remember Aigle and our class. I often ask myself, "What became of so and so?" Do you still enjoy being in Aigle? I am very happy here, because I can take courses at the Seminary and live with my parents at the same time.

We'll be moving to a new house soon, in two weeks in fact. Our future house is half way between the one we live in now and the Seminary. We are all very happy about the move: first of all because it's closer, and then the house is nicer than this one. Do you sometimes go to Geneva? If so, we would be so happy to have you come and see us. You can take the tramway and it isn't far.

Now I must stop. By the way, if you see any of my former classmates, please give them my best.

With many memories and greetings,
Your former student,
 "Gabrielle"

The courses Jean Weidner took at Collonges included commercial studies, classics and theology. These choices no doubt reflected both his father's and his own hopes for his future.

In 1932 while the family was still based at the Seminary, François, the second son and third child, died of pleurisy and pneumonia at the Adventist clinic in Gland in Switzerland. He was sixteen and a half years old.

A mimeographed letter from his mother to friends of the family is written in Dutch on one side and in French on the other. The letter tells about François' illness and his last moments and describes the boy's life as "an example of many things: he was obedient, conscientious, ready to be of service, calm, always seeing things on the bright side." The letter ends with, "and that to which he often agreed during his illness also consoles his parents in their grief: 'God knows what he is doing.'"

After their studies at Collonges, oldest son Jean and next oldest sibling Gabrielle left the Haute Savoie mountains, but remained in France. In Lyon, Jean began his career as a businessman with his friend Gilbert Beaujolin, already a traveling salesman in textiles. Jean and Beaujolin had met at the Seminary, though Gilbert had left the school early to get himself started in business. Jean Weidner and Gilbert Beaujolin became lifelong friends.

During this time, Gabrielle is in Paris where she works in the bookstore and in the main office at the Adventist Church's headquarters at 130 Boulevard de l'Hôpital. She has chosen to enter "The Work" of the Adventists, rather than being in "The World." She lives on the top floor of the Adventist Church building, three floors above the sanctuary. She and the other church secretaries each have a small room whose door opens along a sunny corridor overlooking the Boulevard de l'Hôpital. All of the six rooms have a back window affording a view over Paris looking toward the Eiffel Tower. At the end of the corridor at the top of the spiral staircase, the secretaries have their own kitchen where they prepare their meals and can cook for their friends.

While on vacation in The Hague with her mother and sister Annette, Gabrielle writes to Jean, contrasting life in Holland, her own family's homeland, with life in France, which is much more of a home to her. Annette adds her own note on the last page.

In these two letters, both Gaby and Annette write anxiously about a near accident which Jean must have described earlier. According to Annette he was with Gilbert Beaujolin at the time and Beaujolin would have been driving, as it is only later, in January 1936, that Jean is preparing to get his license and his own car.

THE WEIDNERS BEFORE THE WAR

Gaby to Jean July 30, 1935

Bien cher Jean [Dearest Jean],

Mama told me that you were complaining about not hearing from me very often. It's very true, but the reason is that I almost never know your address, so I hate to send the letter home for them to forward, because it always takes a long time to reach you.

I had news of you through Mama and also in Papa's letter last week. It's really terrible to think of the accident you might have had! Mama got all emotional about it. I told her that she shouldn't cry, since after all, you were safe and sound, but she is very nervous and can't keep calm when she hears bad news. Maybe she'll get better as time goes on, but I think that François's death was a great blow to her which she still hasn't gotten over.

My vacation is going by too quickly, and I only have a few days left here. On Wednesday I'll leave for Brussels where I'll see Papa. I'll stay there until Monday or Tuesday. I am really supposed to be back at work on Tuesday morning, but I may take one more day. Last week the weather was pretty good, but not this week. The sky is always cloudy, and it rains from time to time. I do go to the beach, but as Anne-Marie's [Annette's] leg still hurts, I have to go by myself, and that's not as much fun. Although these days the waves are very big, so it's rather exciting to go into the water, even alone. I am not going to be able to accomplish my goal of learning to swim. I was counting on Anne-Marie to hold me up, but she couldn't. So I was thinking of taking lessons, but they don't give them on the seashore. And I was also hoping to sunbathe, but I was able to do it only once. It's really awful, because it's always cold here. Maybe that's why the Dutch character is so cold. Every time I go to the beach, I have to keep my coat on.

There is such a big difference between France and Holland, and especially between Paris and The Hague. I could never get used to living here all the time. Parisian women are much more elegant than the women here. In general the women are rather fat and they often wear hats that were in style 4 or 5 years ago. The Dutch are very curious. Every time we go out with Anne-Marie (who is walking a little since Sunday), people ask us what is wrong with her: the tram conductors, people on the beach, the neighbors, etc. In France they wouldn't dare. But there is one advantage, and that is that the Dutch men have better manners than French men, and girls can go out walking without hearing all the remarks they would hear in France. On Sunday afternoon, I was walking alone for an hour and a half, and I saw a lot of people, but not one said anything to me, while in Paris, the young men would have spoken to you ten times. But I still prefer to live in Paris. When will you come to Paris? I hope you can come to see me. ...

Anne-Marie and I share the great affection and feelings you have for Aunt Marie. I hope I will never be an old maid and if I do become one, I hope I won't be like her. I pity her but that doesn't help.

Your business must not be doing a lot now, but it will probably pick up again in one or two months. Do you still like this profession? You're probably glad about reducing your debt at the bookstore, but if you had a fixed salary of a thousand francs a month, it would be much more difficult to do it than it is now. I myself haven't been able to save any money, even though I often receive a little from home.

Anne-Marie wants to write you, so I'll save the other page for her. Good luck and be of good courage in your business. Many affectionate thoughts and kisses from your sister who is thinking of you, Gaby

Annette's addition to Gabrielle's letter is written in her big, bold handwriting. She refers to Jean's friend and business partner Beaujolin as "Julien." According to Madame Christiane Beaujolin, her husband's name was Julien Louis Beaujolin. "In 1940," writes Madame Beaujolin in 2009, "his friends, who didn't like the first name 'Julien', called him 'Gilbert.' And from that time on, his family and his old friends used either name!"

Annette to Jean   The Hague, July 30, 1935

Bien Cher Jean [Dearest Jean],

I haven't written you in so long, but there isn't much time during vacation, as I'm sure you understand. I had a wonderful time in Paris. It's amazing how much I love Paris; Paris, my home is Paris!! From Papa's letter I learned you had had an accident. Fortunately nothing happened to you or Julien. I had a small accident, too. The last day I was in Paris, I fell down and sprained my knee. 10 days in bed. But it's better now, and today I have been to the sandy beach already. Tomorrow I'll go to see Uncle Henri, with Gaby. I'm happy about that.

Today we got a letter from Papa saying that you are very nice and that you are becoming a pearl of a boy. This change is really wonderful. I hope that will operate in favor of your youngest sister, and that she will no longer have to take any of those punches, but instead get beautiful fabric for dresses (all that is a joke).

I hope that during the conference, you met a lot of nice girls that you like, as you are so choosy. Did you see the Royers? Do you think the two girls are nice? Does Rip still bite your slippers? Now I'll stop. Big kisses from your sister Annette

Things are a little too quiet for Gabrielle back at "130," the Adventist Church building where she lives and works. She's tired from her trip home from The Hague, and she's bored. She worries about her future. Selections from her seven-page letter to Jean.

Gaby to Jean August 7, 1935

Bien cher Jean,

I was so glad to get your nice long letter Friday afternoon. I left The Hague Friday morning. I was on the night 12:55 train and I was back to work at the office at 8 AM. I was able to lie down on the train as there was almost nobody there, but I couldn't sleep anyway. So I was very tired during the day. But I'm better now after a good night's sleep.

I was a little scared to go through customs because I had bought several things in Belgium, and now that the franc's value is so low, they are quite strict. You know how the women inspectors are always worse than the men, and of course I got a woman. I had a little problem about a blanket I had bought there. She called a customs man, but he said to her, "Oh, leave her alone." So she left and I was glad.

It's awfully quiet here. There are only three of us in the house. ... I get really bored, and I don't like to be alone, especially after getting back from vacation. ... You know I guess I'm not really cut out for a solitary existence. ...

Sometimes I'm afraid for myself, because I have been too lucky up to now, and I have never had any great troubles, and I tell myself that surely someday misfortunes will befall me. There are so many other girls who have not had all the advantages I have had. ...

Gaby, though uncertain of her own future, approves of the choices her brother has made.

Gaby to Jean Paris, August 21, 1935

... It's really nice of you to think the way you do of Papa and Mama and to want them to be proud of their children. They won't ever have much reason to be proud of me from any point of view, and I don't think I will ever be able to help them, because, as you know, in the Work, we are always paid very little. That's why it is much better for you to have another kind of position, as someday you will succeed in getting rich, while we can never put aside any money. But it seems to me you could soon think about getting engaged, as in one or two years, you could get married. You don't have to serve in the military as the French do, and I would think that in your travels you must meet some Adventist girls whom you like. Here in Paris I don't see any, otherwise I would tell you to make a little jaunt in this direction. But if you absolutely insist on marrying a Dutch girl, first you must go to that country. ...

In Gaby's own life, however, the question of possible suitors is complicated.

Gaby to Jean Paris, September 4, 1935

Bien cher Jean,
... For several days I've been in a pretty bad mood. You'll be amazed when I tell you why. For about three months there has been a young Adventist man here (age 27) who is here to learn French. But for the last few weeks he has been courting me, especially since last week. He comes to see me every day without any reason. He brings me flowers, etc. Last evening he arrived in the kitchen at 8 o'clock, saying he got the time wrong. He thought it was 8:30 and he was coming for the prayer meeting. After 10 minutes we had finished everything and we left. I brazenly left him alone in the kitchen. He is very nice, but I don't like him very much and could never marry him. He is a little timid and I'm a little sorry for him, but I can't do anything about it. I try not to be nice to him, and after the meeting I talked to everyone except him. I hope he'll get the picture, because if he

doesn't I'll ask Jenny to tell him to leave me alone. He comes from a rather good family and has a lot of money. But I just don't like him that much.

I'm telling you this, but maybe it's of no interest to you. Annette doesn't like him either and she already told me I shouldn't marry him (when she was in Paris a while ago). I haven't told Mama about it, but I will introduce this young man to her when she comes. He's not good looking at all. That's really too bad. Of course, that's why Annette doesn't like him.

Now I'll leave you as I have to go to the office. A thousand kisses from your sister who thinks of you every day.

Gaby

In her long and frequent letters (five in September and October) Gaby continues to share her thoughts with her brother Jean and gives him an account of her life in Paris. She works at the Adventist book store. She tries swimming lessons at the pool. She goes shopping with friends, "because it was pay day, and we take the first chance we get." In her letter of October 4, she wonders what to get for Jean's birthday and expresses her opinion about Annette's upcoming departure for England to be a nanny. She continues to have the same opinions of her would-be suitors. She worries about a possible war. (Italy has been making preparations for war in Africa, and on October 3, 1935, Italian forces invade Ethiopia.)

Gaby to Jean   Paris, October 4, 1935

Mon bien cher Jean,

... I took the opportunity to look at what I might get you for your birthday, as you will soon be 23 years old. I thought you might like some pajamas, as that's always useful. But I haven't bought anything yet, as I don't know if you need any. If you would like that, let me know as soon as possible, and that way I could buy them the first chance I get, as the department stores are rather far away, and I don't always have the time to go there. Tell me also what color you would like. If you would prefer something else, or if you would rather buy the pajamas yourself, tell me so frankly. But I wanted to get you something pretty, as you are always nice to me, and I want to do the same for you.

... I think Annette is awfully young to leave home. On the other hand, it is perhaps an opportunity that won't come again. It's sometimes so difficult to know what to do in life. I know something about that. Anne-Marie [Annette] may have told you something about my affairs of the heart. It is even more complicated than you think. Getting married to a husband I don't love is out of the question. I would be too unhappy, and so would he be. But at least for the moment I am not too worried because the British one still has to take care of his mother. But when his mother leaves next week, things will be different. ...

It is so terrible to think that there is war, I hope the League of Nations can fix it so that the war won't continue. It is so terrible to think of all those women, all those mothers who see their husbands and their sons leave without knowing if they will come back.

I'm so happy that your business is going well. It must be tiring though, to always be traveling. Do you manage to keep to your usual diet during your travels? When you eat in restaurants, you don't always get what you want. ...

And now I must leave you. I have a lot of work to do before the Sabbath begins. ...

I'm sending you lots of kisses,
        Gaby

On Fridays Gabrielle must finish her work or her letters before sundown when the Sabbath begins. The Adventist Church's Sabbath is Saturday. On Sundays there are outings with friends or the church youth group, and there is "collecting" or "ingathering", which involves the members soliciting from door to door from the public at large. They have permits to solicit, and the money collected is used for missions.

Gaby to Jean   October 18, 1935

... I go out every Sunday afternoon. I think it does me so much good when I go to the country instead of being in an office all the time. On Sunday morning the youth went out to do the autumn collecting. In the afternoon, Jenny and I went out with two young men from the church to the outskirts of Paris to the Parc des Sceaux. It was very pretty, very quiet. There is a little lake and we rented a rowboat for an hour. We took turns rowing. We had a lovely afternoon and we went walking afterward so that we didn't get home until 8 o'clock. But it helps clear one's mind from time to time.

You may know that there is a Scout group in Paris. They don't have uniforms yet, but that will come in a few weeks. They do outings every two weeks on Sunday. I try to join them in the afternoon. ...

Mama is not well. "Her heart is tired," Gaby writes, "but it comes from the thyroid, according to the doctor." Mama will enter the Adventist medical clinic in Gland, Switzerland for treatment. Papa will remain in their house in Collonges, near the Adventist Seminary, from which he can easily visit the clinic.

After taking his wife to the clinic, Papa accompanies his youngest daughter Annette to England, stopping in Paris on the way so that they can have a visit with Gaby. Annette will be a mother's helper in the family of a London Adventist pastor, Mr. Anderson. Mrs. Anderson is expecting her second child, and Annette will gain experience in the field she already hopes to enter, that of a maternity nurse.

It is Gaby's opinion that Annette is very young to be leaving home. In 1935, Annette is just fourteen years old, young indeed for a first sojourn abroad, but her first letter from London reveals a spirit of adventure and a maturity beyond her years. Annette's letter to Jean brings him her best wishes for his birthday.

Annette to Jean   London, October 11, 1935

Bien cher Jean,

I think it's time I wrote you if you are going to receive this letter in time for your birthday.

First of all, I want to wish you a happy birthday with much <u>happiness</u> (and by that I mean that you should have the happiness of having a wife who understands you and who is in accord with you), because you are 23 years old, or you will be, and you have to think about getting married.

I wish you good health also, etc. etc. and hope that you will get rich very soon (your dream ever since you were little).

But now you must be anxious to know how my trip went. Well, I left home on Monday evening. In Paris I stayed with Papa until Wednesday morning, and then we went to Dieppe. We traveled with Gaby's future mother-in-law Mrs. Overton, a short, fat, very funny woman. [Mr. Overton is one of Gaby's possible suitors, but his mother does not have the status of "future mother-in-law".] Everyone in the train compartment was laughing at her. In Dieppe I had my "baptism of water" on the boat, as it was the first time I ever went to sea. At the beginning the sea was calm but after an hour it was very bad and I was seasick. I advise you never to be seasick, it's really awful. And you see all those people vomiting. I had to stay below lying down for the whole crossing. And it smelled bad down there. You can't imagine how glad I was to arrive. I arrived that evening at the Andersons' and I began work the next day. My work is as follows: I get up at 7 o'clock. Then I light both fires, in the kitchen and in the dining room, then I clean the stove, and then I have breakfast. Then I do the dishes, make the three beds, I sweep the stairs, clean the rugs in the hallway, I polish the doorbell and the doorknob, and I dust in the bedrooms, I vacuum the rugs, sweep the kitchen, peel the vegetables for dinner, then I iron or do the washing, in the afternoon I clean the kitchen, the bathroom, then I clean my room, and then I have to go and get the little boy at school, which is a fifteen minute walk from here, and then I'm free for an hour, and then I must set the table and do the dishes, sweep the kitchen, then iron or do little jobs. Where I live the people are very nice. But the lady is going to leave Sunday to have her baby, and then I have to do everything myself, the housework, take care of the little boy, prepare the meals. It's preparing the meals that worries me, as it is not at all the same as in France. They don't eat very much here.

A potato, dry, without butter, a carrot, a tiny piece of cabbage or spaghetti. Often there's no dessert. Since I have been here there has been a pudding only three times. In the evening we have a little applesauce and three slices of bread that are so thin that they would equal one in France. I always feel as if I hadn't had enough after a meal. So Papa tells me to buy a pound of cookies every week.

Yesterday I got a long letter from Gaby. She gave me your address, and she told me she had a long letter from you. I hope you will also write me a long letter soon. ...

Papa left Tuesday morning and he is going via Belgium. Yesterday I received a card from Papa in Ostende.

Mama is better. I'm so glad. Poor Mama. It must upset her to have to be in bed all the time.

I'm beginning to be able to express myself in English now. In three months I will know English well.

Now I have to stop as I have to set the table, and this evening I have to do a lot of ironing.

I'll put this letter in the mailbox Saturday evening so that you get it Tuesday.

A big kiss from your expatriate sister exiled in England.
	Annette

c/o Mrs. Anderson
30a Bournville Road
Catford SE6
London

Friday evening.

Oh, Jean. It's terrible. The little baby died, and the mother is very weak and they fear for her life. Last night she had to go to the hospital, which is two minutes from here, and she was fine then. But at 10 o'clock the doctor came to tell Mr. Anderson that his wife was very ill and that they had to take her to another hospital. Mr. Anderson went there right away and he just got back now. The poor man was crying, and you can imagine how sad I was to hear the baby had died. They were waiting for it with so much joy. They already had suitcases full of clothes and everything was ready, Oh, no, it's so awful. But it's especially terrible for the parents. The poor mama who had made so many sacrifices, and who had so much pain. Fortunately the mother is a little better. She is in good health, and that is what will save her. They took some blood from Mr. Anderson's arm for his wife. And now he is alone in his room crying, and I am alone, but in the kitchen. I am so sad. That's why I am writing even though it's the Sabbath. I don't know what to do. I am so homesick. And now it won't be of any interest to me now because I only came because there was going to be a baby. And they probably won't need me anymore.

Oh, I don't know what to do tonight. I am so depressed thinking of the poor mother. Pray for her and for me, as it is my duty not to cry so as not to make them even sadder.

Adieu. Write me soon.
	Annette

When Papa writes to his children on October 20, 1935, from Collonges where he can be near Mama in the clinic, he does not yet know of the tragedy befalling the Anderson family in London. He writes in Dutch to Joop, Mies and Annette about Mama's slowly improving health, and changes to French in the same letter for Annette.

Papa to Annette   October 20, 1935

... And now, first a word in French to you, my dear Annette, "Miss Annette of London." What a shame we weren't able to see each other the day I left. I fully intended to surprise you that way. The lady was going to wake me at 7. She promised, but she didn't do it. So I woke up at 7:30, but alas! The half hour I was going to use to run to your house and back to take the train was already over. And to add to the sadness, at the station I heard that the train did not go through Catford; so I thought of my dear little doll who was watching for the train to pass, and thinking that Papa was in that one, and not seeing anyone waving from the window. What should I have done with the little roll that I promised you I would eat right after having waved to you? I ate it when I arrived at Ostende, thinking that you would approve under the circumstances. Did I do the right thing?

Ah, if you only knew how much Mama and I want to hear from that little London Miss. And already we are wondering when we will see you.

So, you're getting used to speaking English. I can just hear you saying, "Oh yes," and with an accent as if you have been born in London, and not in that city whose name begins with "L." [Lausanne] Are your hands still as delicate as usual? Or is the skin getting like that of an elephant? If so, watch out because an elephant trumpets— [Papa leaves out the rest of the French saying: "Un éléphant, ça trompe énormément" (An elephant trumpets a lot)]. And is the baby still making everybody wait for him? Do you have enough to eat by dipping into the extra supply? Because, you know, buy some more cookies or bananas or something else if you don't have enough, because we would never want you to go hungry as long as we still have a franc to spend. ... Please give my greetings to the Andersons and tell them I will write to them as soon as I can, but in the meantime I'm sending them a thousand thanks for their kind welcome. ...

Annette to Jean ("Jopie")   London, November 2, 1935
                                      8 o'clock in the evening

A. Weidner c/o Pastor Anderson
30a Bournville Catford SE6
London England

Bien cher Jopie,

You can't imagine how happy I was to get your long letter a few days ago. I really hadn't hoped to hear from you so soon, when I got up that morning at 7:30 and saw your letter. You can be sure I jumped at it to open it. The beginning of your letter made me laugh. I can't imagine having a bachelor brother. ...

I haven't much to tell you, as my life is pretty monotonous. It's not like you when you travel and see all the pretty scenery that I always dream of seeing in the South of France. ... But I'm writing you anyway, because otherwise, you would think I hadn't received your letter. I am very sorry you didn't receive my letter on your birthday, but then you had the unpleasant task of reading it a few days later. I have had the responsibility of the household for two weeks. I'm getting used to it now. But fortunately the Bible teacher, a very nice former missionary, comes almost every morning to help me cook dinner, because I don't know how to make all those good puddings which don't exist in France but which the English can't get along without. I am alone nearly every evening, as the Monsieur either goes to see his wife or has to give lectures. This afternoon he left at three o'clock and told me not to worry if he didn't come back this evening, as he would probably return tomorrow for dinner, as he had to go to the other end of London, and London is so big—

I put the little boy to bed early, as he was tired and now I am all alone.

I'm expecting a letter from Papa this evening. I've been expecting it all day, and I would be very sad if it doesn't come tonight.

You wouldn't believe all the work I have had. The little boy was sick for 10 days. It wasn't dangerous but he had a very bad cough, and he had stomach flu. So I had to take care of him, prepare the meals, keep the the house clean.

Fortunately we live all on one floor, because if I had to climb the stairs every time he called me—

One night I was alone and the little boy, whose name is Ian, had indigestion. His bed was covered with vomit and you know how sensitive I am, I can't stand that, and I was almost vomiting too. And I had to clean that all up and change the sheets. But it builds character. But he has been well for three days now, and I'm glad as now I go to get him at school which is ten minutes from the house, and that gets me out of the house a little, because during the ten days that he was sick, I only went out in the yard to get coal.

On Wednesday afternoon after washing the dishes, I went to the hairdresser to get a permanent and came home at 5:45. Then Mr. Anderson told me I could take the tram and go and see the stores, but I had to be back at 7:30 because he was going to see his wife. So I went to the department store to do a few errands. The department stores aren't like the ones in Paris. Here there are a lot of small shops. There are dress shops, hat shops, shops for toilet articles, etc. And they are much handsomer. There is a rug on the floor. You would think you were in a living room. Excuse my writing, but I have rheumatism in my back which bothers me so much I have to get up and walk every few minutes.

I am in the dining room. The fire is nice and warm and much more cheerful than in France, because one can see the fire and the coal, as in the old days.

Mrs. Anderson is better, but she has to stay in the hospital for ten days, and then she wants to go to the country, not far from London. She would like to take Ian and me. You see how nice they are since they want to take me to the country.

Then the monsieur will have to stay at home alone. But he says that's all right with him. And since I have done a lot of work lately, it would do me good to go to the country. But it isn't certain yet.

Yesterday he brought me some chocolate to console me because I hadn't received the letter, and because I had done such good work. Isn't that nice?

I am very sad that the baby died. I think I can stay on, because Mrs. Anderson will not have completely recovered for a while.

It's 9 o'clock. The mailman comes in 20 minutes. I am waiting impatiently.

You know, my eyes are acting funny now. For six months I have had sight in only one eye sometimes. It seemed as if my eyelid was moving and closing, and now both eyes are doing that and sometimes I have to sit down because everything seems to be spinning around me. Mr. Anderson thinks I need glasses. I think I'll get some advice from a doctor.

There's the mailman and there's a letter from Papa. I read Papa's letter, full of jokes as usual. I was sure I would get one tonight.

Papa tells me that Mama was able to get up for a half hour the day before yesterday, but they are still putting ice on her heart, and she will stay through November. Poor Mama. I will be so happy when she is well. Papa says he is sometimes very tired and depressed and that his heart beats very irregularly. I hope it will be better for him, but of course he is worried about Mama, and now he is alone at home, and Papa is like me, he doesn't like to be alone. But he wrote me that your business isn't doing too well and that you are going to come closer to him. He was very happy about that. You will be very patient with him, won't you, Jean. You won't argue with him, because he must be very upset now, and if he says something that isn't right, it would be better not to answer him. Gaby wrote me a long letter on Tuesday. Poor Gaby, she doesn't know what to do. She doesn't talk to you about it. So I don't know if I can tell you about it, but I want to. Her heart is hesitating between the two of them. Her heart draws her to René and her mind draws her to Overton, but she can't manage to love him. She says she is really unhappy, and that in the end she'll maybe be an old maid, or that she will end up marrying a third person, but there are so few young people in Paris, that she'll have to really think about it.

... You asked me what the British mentality is like. Well, I have a good impression of them. Not all the young men are blond. That's lucky because I only like dark haired ones. They are no more serious than Parisians. They are very helpful. But you wanted to know about the women. They don't use too much make-up, they sing very well, they are very, very helpful and don't spend too much money. The women participate in politics a lot, and there are policewomen in uniform.

In London Adventism is very advanced. There are a lot of churches and a lot of baptisms. Three weeks ago, Mr. Anderson's brother did 60 baptisms. They do advertising, they drive a carriage through the streets with the church's address on it. They put notices in the big newspaper like Paris Soir.

I can't tell you anything about politics, because it doesn't interest me. I'm not like you. You devour the newspapers. You know that there will be elections in England soon. ...

I'll stop now as it is nearly 10 o'clock and I want to go to bed, because I have to do the wash tomorrow.

A big kiss from your English sister who speaks English very well already and who is forgetting all her French.

    Annette
    XXXXXXXXXXXXXXXXXXXX
In English that means kisses.

In November Jean comes to Collonges to be with his father while his mother is ill in the Adventist clinic in Gland. Father and son appear to be getting along well without any of the the usual head-on collisions between these two strong and vibrant personalities. Annette, in an interview with Alberto Sbacchi nearly sixty years later, recalls the arguments between them. "My father was not very patient, and he would burst into a rage. Papa once said that Jean was the best son in the world from a distance, but they couldn't live together."

Jean to Gaby   Collonges, Friday afternoon, November 15, 1935

Ma bien chère Gaby,

    Papa was going to write you this afternoon, and then I would have written on Sunday. But Papa still has so much to do that he told me to write instead, and I hope he'll write for me on Sunday.

    First a little news from here. All is well. Papa is better and more encouraged. I too am very happy to be with my dear Papa. We are getting along very well and never fight. For that we're waiting for Mama to come home and be the referee. We're working hard on putting things in order here, and I'm working on the stamps a lot. At noon we eat at Madame Cattanéo's and in the evening we eat at home. Papa is a very good cook. We are like two bachelors who are trying to manage as well as possible. But Papa is encouraging me spiritually and we study the Bible every day, which does me a lot of good. ... We hope to sell a certain number of the stamps wholesale. That would help Papa to make ends meet, because on the material side, things are a bit tight. But it's already the 15th of the month and Papa gets paid at the end of the month. I've had a sort of flu for a couple of days, but it's nothing and I can't stay in bed as Papa wants me to. Papa is very good at giving advice to others when they are sick, but when he's the one, he won't follow anybody's advice. But it's not going to be serious. Already my cough is gone. So you see a little bit of what kind of life we lead here.

    Now about Mama. Papa went to see her on Sunday and Monday and I went yesterday. Mama is certainly better than the last time I saw her, but the progress is very slow, alas. It is really hard on her to remain lying down for so long without any change and without anything to do. Fortunately Papa goes to visit her often and from now on I will go to see her regularly every week. It's really difficult to pick the brain of the doctors. I think they are afraid of discouraging Mama and ourselves, but yesterday I virtually forced the doctor to tell me what was going on. Don't repeat what I'm telling you so that Mama doesn't get wind of it. Here it is. Doctor Muller and Doctor De Forest, whom I saw, both admitted to me that the cure wasn't making as much progress as they had hoped. Next week they are going to take Mama to Lausanne to see a specialist who has machines that they don't have at the Sanatorium. Then they will see exactly where the problem is coming from. It could be coming either from the heart or the thyroid gland. If it comes from the thyroid gland, they would have to operate. ... The outcome could be fatal, but that is not likely. If the operation is successful, Mama would make very rapid progress toward being cured. But if it is the heart which is sick, that is much more serious. But there is no immediate danger, and Mama can live for a long time, but living without being able to move is not possible for Mama. We must pray to God to save Mama and bring her back to us very soon. Prayers can save Mama, and we must use this means. God will hear us. Until now they have always placed ice on Mama's chest, but then she had the flu. ... Mama thinks a lot about her little Gaby and wants to see her. In a few weeks you will be able to see her, because in 5 weeks it will be Christmas, and time goes fast.

... We've had some good letters from Anne-Marie. She is very brave and the work will do her good, anyway I hope she won't tire herself out. If she were here with us, it would have been hard for her here as well, and for us. Now she'll be learning English, and that will always be useful.

I think that those who are against Scouting for the reason that it prepares one for the military are quite ridiculous, as you say, and I think they would do well to look to the beam in their own eye! ... That was funny what you told me about what somebody said about you. I think those who are so quick to criticize you and say mean things should damn well leave you in peace (pardon my language, but you know me). Anyway gossipers have always been the most narrow-minded and meanest people, and so one must ignore them and take the high road. ...

As for me, I am very serious and you certainly don't hear anything bad about me unless it's said in bad faith. I'll help my parents first and then I'll think about myself. But what about you? You haven't told me any more about your affairs of the heart. Maybe that's just as well as I would probably make jokes and laugh. You know me. But don't worry. Everything works out if we don't worry about love.

Now I must leave you my dear Gaby. I don't even need to say how much we think about you and that we pray for you every day and we are so happy to know that you do your work so conscientiously. That is the greatest satisfaction you could possibly give our dear parents. This week I will write to Annette, too. We look forward to hearing from you. I make so many errors when writing, but forgive me I am so busy as always. Be sure and hide my letter so no one can read it, otherwise what a reputation I will have!

Good-by, my dear Gaby. A thousand kisses from your brother and Papa.

Gaby answers this letter. She has received a package from Jean who is doing well in his business. She worries that she won't ever find a husband, because she will be 29 in four years, and then will be under the protection of St. Catherine, the patron saint of old maids.

Gaby to Jean   Paris, November 17, 1935

Mon bien cher Jean,

It's really very nice of you to have written such a nice long letter with so much news, and I was very happy to read it on the Sabbath, even though Mama's condition isn't much better. I could never have believed that it would take so long, and I think if the doctors were giving so little information, it was probably because they didn't know what to say and maybe because they didn't want to unduly alarm Papa when they saw he was so discouraged! The doctors can't very well tell what they don't know.

It's lucky you are at Collonges now and can cheer Papa up a little, as he seemed really sad. Is he really so broke? Of course it is impossible for him to live on his retirement pension alone, so I hope Papa will soon make a decision about the work he will do. Since up to now he has been a teacher at the Seminary, I think the Division will do something to help pay the expenses at Gland, as they can't fail to understand that it's impossible to pay everything. You know, there are times when I am really disgusted. I wonder why God allows our parents to have so many troubles. For the last few years one thing is hardly over before another begins. And yet, all their lives they have worked for God and sacrificed for the Work, and now that they are getting a little older, it seems to me that they should be able to rest a little and have a few pleasures. Sometimes it's a little hard to understand God's will and to resign oneself to it. But maybe later on we'll see what lessons are to be drawn from these trials.

The package of dresses came Friday afternoon. There were very few which fit me, as most were too small. But I found one which fit me very well. Of course it clings a little like all knit dresses, but it will stretch out when I have worn it for a while. I put it on this afternoon. A little later there is the meeting of the nomination committee of which I am a member this year and I hope I won't shock anyone. Unfortunately there are no young men on this committee, or I might make some conquests (this time I hope you aren't shocked, but I'm joking). I'm sending you the tag from the dress so that you know which one I chose. It is green with stripes. There was one I liked a lot, a brown suit. But I needed a dress which I can wear under a coat, and a suit would be more for spring. There was a also a jacket, but the skirt didn't match. Maybe Beaujolin made a mistake. I'm letting you know in case you were to have problems with it later. There were also one or two dresses whose belt was missing. If you want I can send you the package, or I can bring it at Christmas. But maybe that's not a good idea, because you might be able to sell one of them in the meantime. Anyway, tell me what you prefer that I do. ... I don't want you to give me the dress. It's really nice of you, but I know you need money, and that's why I want to pay you for it. ...

If I come to Collonges for New Year's, I'll tell you a little about my love life. For the time being I'm not in love with anyone and I'm a little cooled off about my two suitors. Maybe I'm wrong, but I don't want to encourage them too much if nothing is going to come of it. I think I'm going to end up an old maid. Fortunately I have four more years before I have to put on St. Catherine's cap.

As for you, it is really nice that you think first of our parents. But I hope that the day you at last find the right girl, you won't let that chance go by, because you won't have to get married right away and in two or three years things will probably be better.

Now I'll leave you and thank you again for your newsy letter. You can't imagine how glad I was to get it. Goodbye my dear Jean. Most affectionate kisses from your sister

Gaby

In her letter to Jean, Gaby is looking forward to being in Collonges.

Gaby to Jean   Paris, December 10, 1935

... What a shame that Mama can't be operated on yet, as this way she won't be at home when I'm there. But at least I'll arrange to go to Gland from time to time. And luckily there will be parties every night at the Seminary, so I'll have some entertainment. I will be so happy to see you all and especially you, as it has been so long since we have seen each other. Time goes quickly and in two weeks I'll be leaving. I'll leave Paris Thursday evening the 26th and I'll get back to Paris Sunday evening, January 5. ...

Today it snowed for the first time. But in Paris it doesn't last long and it becomes mud right away. I hope there will be snow at Christmas so I can do some luge-ing. I have to get some exercise, because in the last 6 months I have gained 6 kilos and I don't want that to continue. Of course I generally lose weight beginning in February every year. ...

Best kisses from your sister, Gaby

A few days later, Gaby again writes to Jean about their plans for gifts for the family. A sweater for Jean? Mama doesn't really need another nightdress. Maybe a bathrobe for Annette? But as customs charges are so expensive, Gaby will send some money and a small package for Annette in England via Mr. Overton (one of her suitors, the British one, whose attentions are not entirely welcome). And in only two weeks Gaby will be in Collonges, "if all goes as planned."

Jean to Gaby   Collonges, Friday, December 20, 1935

Ma bien Chère Gaby,

We were all so happy to receive your good news. Your card came yesterday. I was also happy to learn that you were definitely coming next Thursday. Papa left a little while ago (it's three o'clock in the afternoon) to go to Gland. He has to give a talk this evening and tomorrow, so he left early to prepare. Usually he goes only on Sunday and Monday. I'm going tomorrow. Sunday morning I'm going to Lyon and will get back Tuesday or Wednesday afternoon. Maybe I'll come back with Beaujolin. Here everything is fine. Papa appears to be more cheerful. Mama is fine from what we were able to find out. Operation will be soon. But we are seeing improvement and that is always encouraging. ... She will be so happy to see you. I'll be happy to see you too, as we have so much to tell each other. ... I am still looking for a car. I have applied for my driver's license and I'll probably take the test soon.

About the gifts. For Papa it's all decided, and we'll buy it in Geneva. ... For Annette, send the same amount for me that you are sending, I think it would be 10 Swiss francs. Send her a one-pound note if that still exists. For Mama, Madame Cattanéo said Mama didn't have any table napkins when she rented her apartment to those people from Monaco. What do you think, do you want to buy her some or do you want to wait until you're here and we can buy them in Geneva? If you write to Annette tell her that I bought some pretty little stamp tweezers which I will give Papa for New Year's as a gift from her. I think Madame Cattanéo will give me a pullover sweater for New Year's, so don't buy one. If you have already bought one, that's fine, because it will always be useful. We'll talk about all that later.

... I'm in a bit of hurry...and besides I don't want to tell you everything because then I won't have anything to tell you when you get here. ... We had a good letter from Annette. She is fine and shows a lot of courage. Papa wrote her yesterday. Papa takes the responsibility for Annette and I take it for you, and that way we divide up the family. ...

Bye for now, dear Gaby, and don't forget to bring me back my dresses, OK? You don't need to declare them at customs, I will take care of it. A thousand kisses from Papa who thinks about his daughter all the time and kisses from your brother Jean who is impatiently waiting for the moment he will see you. Forgive all my errors in French. I have forgotten all my French as well my typing, both fields of knowledge are very important, but as you know, I have a terrible memory.

Your old bro,
Jean

In his first letter to Gaby since the holidays, Jean refers to Gaby's English suitor as a "lord," a word French people often use when they are being scornful of an English person. Gaby must have been hoping that her potential suitor, Mr. Overton, would let her pay for the posting of the package to Annette once he reached England. The fact that he didn't makes her obliged to him in a way that she had hoped to avoid!

Jean to Gaby   Sunday, January 12, 1936

Bien chère Gaby,

Just a few lines to tell you we are fine. I am glad to know your trip went well. …

… But poor Gaby who wanted, yes who even hoped that this dear lord would have made her pay for the package to Annette, so now she is confused. Poor Englishman who is usually so stingy, how love must have changed him.

Nothing new here. The Ethiopian war is status quo. True, Ethiopia isn't exactly in the neighborhood. So I don't know what to tell you about. I'm getting closer to buying my car. Mr. Meyer from Geneva, Papa and I went to see my eventual car this morning, and Meyer thinks the motor is very good, and Petronie saw it Friday and also thinks it's good. So the time is approaching when I can try to break my neck (I forgot the "u") all alone on the main roads. [Jean uses the expression "casser la gueule" and leaves the "u" out of "gueule".]

Yesterday I went to see Mama, and Papa went too. She is getting very nervous. Someone has to be with her all the time. Papa will go continuously. He was there today also. He will go back tomorrow. I think that Mama will be operated on this week. I will give you other details as soon as I know them. …

Good-by, my dear Mrs. Overton, a thousand kisses from us all and particularly from your Citroën C4 (that's the soon-to-be-my car). …

Jean to Gaby   Sunday morning, January 26, 1936

Ma bien chère Gaby,

Friday I was in such a hurry I didn't have time to write you a letter, and I think you have probably received my card telling you I would write on Sunday.

First a few lines about our dear Mama. You know that she was operated on a second time about two weeks ago. They did two operations at the same time which makes three operations in all to date. They tied two of her arteries this time. The first time they only tied one. So they hope that thyroid gland won't get any sustenance and will dry up by itself. That's why the doctors said they would keep her under observation for 3 to 4 weeks to determine the results. If the gland continues to function too much, they will have to operate a 4th time to reduce the gland. I went see Mama yesterday, the Sabbath. Right now she is very nervous and cries a lot. Friday evening she had a spell from 7pm until midnight. And she says that the doctors had promised her that she wouldn't have any more spells after the operation, and here they are happening again. So now she is discouraged and doesn't believe anything they tell her. We try to encourage her and tell her that she will get well, but she has been told that for 18 weeks now and still no improvement. Her heartbeat is now 115 to 120, but that is even more than before the operation. ... She needs to have real faith that she will get well. ... Mama wants to come home. But if she were home, it wouldn't be any better, as she would have less care and she might be tempted to work. But let's not give up hope.

I think I'll be taking my driver's test tomorrow. Last Monday I failed it. But everybody failed it. They fail people because they need money. Anyway I hope to succeed this time. As soon as I get my license I'm leaving for the south. So this may be the last letter you'll get from me from Collonges. I'll write to you during my trip. I'll tell Papa to send you all my mail and you can forward it. Thanks in advance. ...

I'll leave you now, dear Gaby, as I still have a lot of work to do. Love from your brother and Papa who are thinking of you.

Jean is still in Collonges when he next writes to Gaby. In discussing her "affairs of the heart" Jean refers to the French proverb "Il faut ménager le chèvre et le chou," or "you have to humor both the goat and the cabbage," suggesting that we should never try to take a position on a subject being argued by two opposing parties.

Jean to Gaby   Collonges, Friday, January 31, 1936

Ma bien chère Gaby,

As you can see I haven't gone far. I have been waiting impatiently this week for an appointment to take my driver's test again, but nothing came. But I think I should be able to take it next Monday. If so, I hope to be able to leave Tuesday morning for southern France. I still have a few things to do. I just wrote to the Wibbenses in my pidgin Dutch, but that is better than nothing, oops, I mean nothing. [Jean misspelled he word "rien" (nothing) the first time he typed it.] That relieves Papa of some work. I also want to write to Aunt Christine and to Sister Groot. After that I'll be done; it's not a job I like doing.

Thank you for your letter which we were so happy to get. Papa and Mama send their love and they thank you for writing them so often and so regularly. Mama thinks of you a lot and hopes you are well.

So, in a few weeks, you have to make a decision about your love life. Let me give you a few bits of advice. First, one must never make hasty decisions in life. Time fixes many things. You must always humor both the goat and the cabbage and never decide in favor of one or the other. Either the goat will leave of his own accord, and you'll still have the cabbage. Or else the cabbage will rot and you'll still have the goat. Never listen to your heart, only your mind. There are some countries where polygamy is tolerated, so get some information from a geography teacher, and I'll pay part of your travel expenses as well as those of your 2 or, if necessary, your half dozen, husbands.

Here everything is fine. My car battery is dead, and that's something that time won't fix, but Mr. Lavergnat's battery charger will. Papa is well, and in good spirits and has a good appetite. The same goes for me, even my pockets are well supplied as I still have 20 francs and 10 liters of gasoline, enough to crash quite properly into a tree. ...

Mama is so brave and gentle that everybody really admires her. Now Papa has a frequent user's pass for the train. It costs him 25 francs for a month, going from Geneva to Gland and returning once a day. He'll also get a pass starting tomorrow for the tram between here and Geneva, and that costs twelve francs fifty for the same service. This way Papa can go back and forth between here and Gland more often, and that will encourage Mama a lot.

Beaujolin left on a sales trip a week ago. His business is going well, and I hope to go also and earn a few pennies. Now I'll leave you my dear Gaby, as I have a pile of work to do before the Sabbath. We're sending you all our love and many kisses especially from your Mama.

Your brother.

After twelve years at the Seminary, Papa Weidner has retired from the faculty at Collonges. He and his wife are located in Paris. Papa writes in Dutch to his son Jean in Lyon. In his letters, he discusses stamp collecting (both he and his son are avid collectors), gives financial and religious counsel, and tries to advise Jean about his relationship with Elisabeth Cartier whom Jean hopes to marry.

THE WEIDNERS BEFORE THE WAR

Elisabeth is a French girl who works for the French Consulate in Geneva and lives with her mother, a World War I widow, very possessive of her daughter. When the Weidners were all at the Adventist Seminary in Collonges, Elisabeth often came there from Geneva to hear the lectures of the Seminary faculty. In order to marry Jean, though, she must become an Adventist, and Papa wishes he could be of more help in teaching Elisabeth about Adventist beliefs.

A few excerpts from four of Papa's letters in 1938:

Papa to Jean   Paris, January 6, 1938

... You are having a difficult time with Elisabeth. But be of good courage. God has a hand in everything and that gives us peace of mind. You did not make the Ten Commandments, but He did, and He knew what is best for mankind. So if you cannot join with someone who can submit to that, then God will find a better way for you. ... Of course ideally it would be better if E. would tell her mother that she would obey God. But for that she is not grown up enough, and that is understandable. ... The more gently and patiently you handle such a situation, the more beneficial your influence will be. ...

Merci a thousand times for the weapons you sent me. [Jean had sent his father some razor blades.] But first I will use up the old weaponry and that will be one more time only. The imported stuff from Collonges will then have its turn. ...

Papa to Jean   Paris, January 13, 1938

... And now Elisabeth's case. ... God worked at her heart fruitfully. ... Now that we have <u>proof</u> that she let herself be led by God, we have to be careful not to make a mistake that could severely damage her spiritually, the danger being to make her a Saturday-celebrator too soon. (One can do that within 8 weeks if one pushes hard), but now she first has to get to know Jesus as her friend and redeemer, and if that is done thoroughly, then she can be taken to the Sabbath celebration. I am counting on your next letter to learn how things are and what she is going to do. Will her mother not allow her to stay with us in Paris for a week? Then Mama could get to know her better and I know that Mama has accurate opinions about people. ... Mama is also glad that you take advice from your parents. ...

... You should speak with her to find out her impression of Adventism. If her impression is unfavorable, then you should break away gradually. You should speak with her mother to find out if she is against Elisabeth going out with you or becoming an Adventist. If Elisabeth is sincere and wants to be further educated in Adventism, you should take measures to see that this is done. I can write her with some things she can think about. After that she will be changed. ...

Papa to Jean　　　　　　　　　　　　　　　　　　　Paris, May 10, 1938

... Have patience, my dear fellow, God also has so much patience with our weaknesses. But everything will come as long as you don't force it. ... I will write you more about these things and ask you about Elisa's baptism. I have a little plan for that ... she is only a lamb, she is no sheep as yet. But if you are a good shepherd, then she will turn into one for sure and will be a real support to you later."

Papa to Jean　　　　　　　　　　　　　　　　　　　Paris, June 30, 1938

... and when Elisa recognizes that you have a lot of patience with her, even if you have to start over twenty times to make something clear, then she will say to herself: "If Jean can stay so patient with the power of God, while he has such an energetic nature, then I can also learn to obtain the power through God to deal with my own weaknesses. ... "

Well, goodbye dear fellow, many kisses from all of us, also to E.
　　　Your Mama and Papa who think of you always.

2   "La Drôle de Guerre" – The Phony War

Hitler's armies are sweeping across Europe in 1939, scooping up "Lebensraum" as they go—Germany needs room to breathe and these are territories that really belong to Germany, the reasoning goes. But after Hitler's invasion of Poland, Great Britain and France declare war on Germany on September 3rd and mobilize their armed forces.

For the next eight months in Continental Europe there is no war. France has confidence that her Maginot Line on the eastern border will keep her safe from invasion. She sends her soldiers to guard it, and they do so, and wait, and wait for a war to happen.

During this time all the Weidners except Annette find themselves in Paris and not many letters are needed to maintain contact with each other. Annette is training to be a birthing and baby nurse in The Netherlands. Gabrielle still works at the Paris Adventist church. Eventually she will be promoted from the bookstore job to the position of secretary-stenographer in the main office.

The Weidner parents are part of the close-knit community at "130"— 130, Boulevard de l'Hôpital, the church's address. Jean Weidner is also in Paris at this time. He has sold his dress store in Lyon and in 1939 he establishes a wholesale textile business at 78 Rue de Cléry.

Jean is active in the "130" community and has taken responsibility for the youth group. According to later correspondence, this is a thankless job, as the group includes a number of rebellious young people who tend to dampen the enthusiasm of the rest of the members for learning, outings and other innocent pursuits.

But the war enters their lives, and many of the young men have been called up and are far away from the safety and comfort of the Paris church.

One of them, Joseph Gal, writes to Jean in October about his experiences in the French Navy during the non-war.

Joseph Gal to Jean Cherbourg, October 16, 1939

Dear Jean,

I received your letter which brought me much pleasure; yes, my dear Jean, you were really nice to write to me. For the moment all is well; I spent a good but calm month in a fort very close to Cherbourg, and we spent our days playing checkers and cards with neither hard work nor watch duty. But since October 9, we have changed our location and also our schedule. Now we have to be on watch, but that's the job. We are in a completely rural area among the cows. Everything is fine and we are well fed and in good health, and we can't complain...

I heard André Rancy had quite a serious accident, and that he lost a leg, poor André. He has had bad luck and I hope he is better now. Please give him my best if you see him.

You know, Jean, I try to be a good Christian, but here it's hard, if only because I don't drink my wine. There are those who think I am ill and therefore can't drink wine. In the Navy, you know, there's a lot of camaraderie, but when you act differently from them, it's not the same! Well, with God's help, I will certainly come out all right. ...

Perhaps the correspondence with Joseph Gal and others gives Jean the idea of reaching more of the absent members of the youth group. In December, he sends out a mimeographed letter to the former Youth Group members who find themselves under arms—puzzled soldiers waiting out the "Phony War." He includes news of many individual members of the youth group.

Jean to the youth group members December 1939

Dear Comrades from the Youth Groups,

We are sending you these few lines in the hope that they will reach you and will reaffirm the bonds of deep friendship which have always linked the young to our church. We think of you constantly, dear friends, who are scattered all over France and even abroad as a result of the war, and we think particularly of you, dear soldiers, who need so much moral and spiritual strength. Dear friends, please be assured that our hearts are with you and that we ask God's help for you every day. Through your letters, we can see that your feelings correspond with ours, which pleases us very much, and that we keep intact the star of brotherly friendship which guides us through this world in distress.

The beginning of September, instead of bringing us back together, has separated us even further. Many young people from the church have gone to all the regions of France, so that, out of about sixty members, we can now only count about twenty. We were profoundly disappointed; we would have liked to see you all again and take up our many activities. But we will keep alive our confidence in the future, and we are sure that we will all see each other very soon and tell each other about our experiences and begin again our fruitful and useful cooperation. ... But let us remember that whatever milieux and circumstances we find ourselves in, we must remain vigilant and never forget our life goal: the perfecting of character.

... Here in Paris we have returned to our regular activities: meetings every Sabbath afternoon, outings for Ingathering on Sunday afternoon, and during the week writing to our comrades. Alas, time is so limited, courses, work, Autumn Ingathering, studies, raid drills, everything keeps us busy and keeps us from writing as much as we would like. And yet, we think of you all the time, wondering what you are doing, if all is well, and if we will see each other soon...

And now here is some news of our young members. ... A few are here, five are continuing their studies here in Paris, Gabrielle Weidner is still here in the office, ... André Rancy is still in the hospital but hopes to get out soon. We are praying for you, André. ... as you can see the boys are in the minority, but never fear, we will be able to hold our own! ... in the armed forces "somewhere in France" are our friends Joseph Gal, ... Macdougal...Paul Fawer...Roger Guérin, and the others who are in every corner of France. ... Annette Weidner is in Holland and misses Paris very much. ... As for your servant, he is in Paris and writing you now, and could be called up at any moment which would oblige him to return to Holland.

... Our affectionate and brotherly thoughts.

Jean Weidner
President of the Youth Society, 130 Boulevard de l'Hôpital

Nearly two dozen responses to Jean's appeal for letters from the scattered young people are in the Weidner Archives. Parts of some of them give a picture of the lives of a few French soldiers in 1939 and 1940. Their handwriting is sometimes almost indecipherable and their French spelling and grammar sometimes wanting, but their spirits are high and they are hopeful. Georges Goldy is stationed at the Maginot Line. Selections from his seven-page letter:

Georges Goldy to Jean In the Armed Forces Somewhere in France
December 5, 1939

My dear Jean,

I was very glad to receive your letter and the church bulletin. I want to thank you for your letter, as I was happy to hear from you and the youth group. You can be sure that your words went straight to my heart and were very comforting.

In this war which has scattered us in all directions, despite the fact that we are, according to the formula presently in use, "Somewhere in France", we are separated from everyone, but not in our hearts and minds, across the miles. We soldiers think constantly of all of you who are behind the lines. ...

For me, life is still very monotonous, and I was used to a very active and varied life, rain and mud accompany us always, and this job is not always fun, and civilian life is better. But in a war you do all kinds of jobs, even the most unexpected ones, the ones that come to mind are: earthworks, artillery, sewing, police work, liaison work—I could cite dozens and dozens, but those will do. The food is more or less OK depending on the day, but personally I can't complain. Right now I am in the blockhouse and all we have to do is 24-hour guard duty. Whatever the weather, rain, wind, snow, we have to keep guard for two hours and woe to the poor guy who falls asleep and a patrol goes by, because then it's a military tribunal for him. ... sometimes we drink at least a liter of coffee. ... In our free time we read, mend and wash our underwear, listen to the radio, we sleep on straw, live a "vie de château" [like life in a castle] and stand in the trenches with our feet in the water.

Last Friday I had my baptism of fire, as we did hear shells whistling overhead, and we are all OK except for one who got a piece of shrapnel

"LA DRÔLE DE GUERRE" – THE PHONY WAR

in the cheek. It was over in a quarter of an hour. ... Georges Goldy, presently infantryman at the Maginot Line, waiting to become a civilian again.

A. Lams to Jean   Somewhere in France, December 12, 1939

Dear Jean,

    Thank you so much for the group letter that came the day before yesterday. I see you are in Paris. How are you? What are you doing in "the city of lights" with "blackouts"? Are you still a traveling salesman? It has been a long time since we have seen or heard from each other, and so I am eager to have a little more information, especially personal information, because in your long letter you don't talk about yourself. So often when I think about Collonges, I think about you! I so often admired you for your eagerness to help everyone. Many times you did errands in your Citroën, and didn't earn a cent, and you lost money on repairs. But what was the most striking to me about you was your frankness, you were never afraid to say what you thought. Even now I still have a feeling of gratitude toward you. You did so much for me: helping me to learn to drive, driving me to Annecy, taking Lucy and me to Geneva, etc.

    How is Miss Cartier? Maybe she has become Mrs. J. Weidner since your last letter? I will always remember the tête à têtes we had in chemistry class (Oh, now don't be jealous), and a certain expression too often used by Brother Evard and we couldn't stop laughing (and I don't even remember what the expression was) ...the good old times. Since I have been in the army, I have such nostalgia for Collonges. I'll get a leave soon, and I plan to spend three or four days at the Seminary. Something draws me there, but on the other hand, I am afraid that my sorrow at not finding my little fiancée there as in the old days, will be overwhelming. I love my little Lulu more and more every day. ...

    I am well. We spent three days at the front. I am a radio-telegraph operator, and I am very happy not to have a gun. Until now, God has protected me amid enemy shells and bullets. For a week I was at the observatory, close to the enemy. ... Right now we are in a kind of rest period. Since I am soon to have some leave, I am in good spirits.

    My brother is on a ship somewhere in China. My parents are in Troyes. My little fiancée is very brave, too. So everything is fine for us.

    Best greetings from your friend and brother in Christ.

A. Lams
Brotherly greetings to your sister.

Paul Fawer to Jean　　　　　　　　　　　　December 15, 1939

My dear Friend,

   Thank you so much for your letter. You cannot imagine what a pleasure it was to read. As for me, I have little news to tell you because in this fortress war, all we do is wait, and while waiting we set up living quarters as best we can. Little by little our barracks went from piles of hay in an attic to a comfortable living room with almost central heating, electricity, radio. In the morning they bring us juice in bed, and we made our beds with soft wood with stretched strings, and some even have box springs. This is to tell you that I am fine, and besides we take care of the road police, we have a car for 4 or 5 and we reserve the motorcycle for good weather. At the end of December or rather at the beginning of January, I will have ten days' leave, and I hope to have the pleasure of seeing you. Friendly thoughts from your old friend.
   Paul Fawer.

   Driver Paul Fawer
   Régentier Hautivre 4
   Canton 6
   Postal Sector 5548

Ernie Schaeffler to Jean　　　　　Château du Bas Mont, December 19, 1939

   … For the time being, I am in a quiet area. I spend most of my time in a little chateau on the banks of Mayenne. Right now it's nice and warm by the fire; our activity is much reduced at the moment by comparison to the previous weeks when tasks were keeping us busy for long hours. In the chateau, besides the offices, we have our mess and our officers are of an excellence above all possible praise. Reading is our principal occupation if there is no naval battle to entertain us. …
   Ernie Schaeffer

"LA DRÔLE DE GUERRE" – THE PHONY WAR 35

Roger Guérin to Jean   Camp Coëtquiden, December 26, 1939

My dear Jean,

    I hope you won't be too angry with me for being so late in answering your good and long letter which brought me much pleasure. The pleasure was all the greater as it was the first letter I received from longtime friends.

    True, several of them are, like me, billeted in France or elsewhere and a soldier's life, contrary to what one may think, does not always lend itself to a long and varied correspondence. There is a lack of the required comfort and tranquility. So, even though I am writing to you in an office (nothing like a civilian office!) and behind a typewriter, I am still being constantly interrupted either for the needs of the service, or by some indiscreet or rebellious trouble-maker. It's really amazing to see how certain people, once they become soldiers, forget the most basic principles of society! Well, that's only a minor misfortune. What is happening in the world right now is certainly more serious, and this is only a small consequence of it.

    Only four months have passed since the big white poster came to wrench us out of our normal existence. To me it seems as if we had been here for years, and God only knows how much longer we will be here. Of course being stuck in a camp deep in the Breton countryside is not the danger to be most feared! The most painful misfortune of all is to be something like 1000 kilometers from home.

    As you know I am in the offices of the French General Staff Headquarters, which, in cooperation with the Polish military authorities, is trying to form a new Polish Army. There is an impressive number of them here already, and they are apparently determined to avenge their martyred country. Most of them are good and courageous men, but the saying "drink like a Pole" is pretty much true, and a good many fights break out as a result.

    It would seem that until Spring the war is going to keep its present form of immobility and defense on both sides. If only it could stay that way and end up that way! But there are a few reasons to believe otherwise. Anyway, in my own case and that of all those of my same age here, there are plans to relieve us according to length of service, in order to send us under other skies somewhere in France, or elsewhere. There is some chance that this will not happen before the end of March, which is indeed a Spring month!!

Yesterday was Christmas, not a very merry Christmas, of course, which would have seemed terribly long if I hadn't had work to do in the office. I must tell you that I am going to be granted ten or so days' leave starting on the 30th, and anything which one looks forward to so much makes the time go more slowly. I would like to have been able to go through Paris to see my parents and visit 130, but it's impossible. I have to go through Bordeaux.

Thank you for the form letter with its news about the Paris Youth Group. I see that you are doing good things with it. It was an excellent idea to put you in charge of that activity. By the way, I think it was in cooperation with the youth group that a package was sent to the soldier I talked to Brother Wehrli about. On behalf of its recipient, I am sending my thanks to all those who took care of it. The soldier was very touched by this thoughtfulness towards him and talked to me with much emotion about the joy it brought him. Unfortunately, the poor guy hardly knows how to write and he has asked me to do it for him.

Thank you also for all the news. I hope that from time to time you can provide me with this pleasure. I hope that the war isn't interfering with your business too much. In any case you made a good choice to go into wool textiles. It seems that this is a business which works best right now, or the least badly in any case.

Let me in closing send you my best wishes for the year 1940. May all your dearest wishes come true concerning your union with the woman you love. I remember her well, and have excellent memories of her; she was a charming friend and good company. You have made a good choice, and I congratulate you. Since she also remembers me, please give her my best. Also, please give my greetings to all the friends at 130, as well as to your sister.

To you, my dear Jean, a cordial and brotherly handshake from your old friend, presently a French-Polish-Breton-Nîmes soldier.

R. Guérin

Roger Guérin
Colonel's Secretariat
S.C.I.F.
Coëtquiden Camp (Morbihan)

"LA DRÔLE DE GUERRE" – THE PHONY WAR

Pierre to Jean

Dear Jean,

I appreciated your letter so much and here I am to thank you with this letter. That was a good idea you had to send us news of everyone. Now we have more details about where our friends are.

I am writing this letter in the pharmacist's office where I was appointed secretary three days ago. It is a good job, and even though the salary is low, so is the work load, so no fears of meningitis for the moment.

We are billeted in a small town (somewhere in France) about ten kilometers from a border. We are very comfortable here. We are housed with families and I am happy to tell you that I myself am living in a nice house with a friend. The owners have gone to Normandy and there is only an old lady who takes care of the house, and even she lives in town and comes to visit only rarely. We do our own cooking on a beautiful stove which works at the touch of a button. We sleep in a cute bedroom. In short, we have become civilians again. This liberty is really wonderful. After more than three months of sleeping on straw, we had forgotten what civilized life was like, and it is like being reborn. We can shine our shoes, brush our nails and do all kinds of things that we hadn't been able to do for a long time. To undress at night and sleep on sheets, can you imagine? All we ask is that this last as long as possible, believe me. It's really restful not to hear the sound of guns any longer, and even though we like music, this type of drumbeat doesn't do anything for me.

In the town where I am, there is a Protestant service every Sunday. The service is led by two pastors. One is a civilian and serves the town and surrounding area, which has about ten families. The other is a military chaplain and does the Sunday service. There is a family where I sometimes spend an evening and it's always a pleasant way to spend time. I met Lams, the radio corporal who was at Collonges, you must know him. So in our division of 15,000 men, there are three of us who are Adventists, including MacDougal. You can see by what I have already told you that we can't complain. Life is good, and—I was going to say that the sun shines, but that isn't true as it rains all the time—it's the only unpleasant thing in this lovely countryside, but I think it's true everywhere.

Since the beginning of hostilities we have traveled a lot, and I like that. Wait a second, I'll get out my little pocket calendar and I'll tell you how many different places we have been in. There. It took me a while to find it, but you probably didn't notice. So I count 11 different areas in various departments. So we have been able to experience the mentality of the different provinces where we have been.

I'm going to stop my peregrinations now, and I still have a blank half page to fill. What shall I say?

Oh, this is it: I have beside me on the table a big barrel revolver like the ones the cowboys have. It weighs at least three pounds. It is used to set off the gas capsules in closed rooms. We will soon go through that. They make us go into to a hermetically sealed space and make us put on gas masks and the lieutenant sets off three gas capsules and we stay 5 or 10 minutes breathing the gaseous mixture and that way we identify the masks which let the gas through. But when your eyes itch and feel red and your throat is dry, it's a good excuse to go to the canteen and drink a few glasses to take away the disagreeable sensation of the gas.

So, now my page is filled and I am pleased with myself. My dear Jean, I send you my brotherly thoughts in friendship and ask you to give my greetings to all the young people for me, hoping to see you soon.

Pierre

T. MacDougal to Jean   January 10, 1940

Dear Friends,

It has been a little while since I received your letter addressed to the former Paris members now drafted like me. I wanted to write you something interesting and kept putting it off. But I think I'll tell you a little about my life since the beginning of the war. I hope it will interest you.

We have stayed in many villages and I don't even remember all their names. At least I can tell you that when we left the Reims area, around August 28, we took the train (trains for soldiers, and that means cattle cars) and we arrived in the Laon area near St. Gobain, famous for its manufacture of mirrors. In that time (as the Gospels say) I was in a company, that is, a soldier with a gun, cartridges, etc. We spent a week on a farm. The weather was beautiful. Every morning before practice, I went to do my religious meditations in the wheat fields admiring the little hills and valleys which are the charm of this countryside.

"LA DRÔLE DE GUERRE" – THE PHONY WAR

Then we left on buses, traveling by night at 15 kilometers an hour, to Lorraine, sleeping one night here and another night 60 kilometers farther on. In Lorraine we were on the front lines.

Life on the front lines is hard. During the day we dig holes 1 meter 80 cm deep to shelter us, and at night we keep watch. We can sleep for only a few hours and sometimes only one or two hours. We slept in the holes we had dug. We ate cold food. Of course, there were bombing raids also, and real ones, not movies. While I was there a French action took place and then an enemy counter-attack. I assure you it was no joke and we had to keep hold of ourselves.

After those days of fire we got back to having meals. We were just about at Craonne, the place of such terrible memories. It was the Chemin des Dames where so many died 23 years ago.

Here we are in the North where we are awaiting the next stage of our travels.

It is cold and we don't sleep in beds. Straw is our mattress and the tent cloth serves as our sheets. But we can't complain compared to those who watch and wait in the snow near Lierche-en-Lorraine and La Barre, etc. They must be frozen and they have to be very brave.

Dear friends in the Paris youth group, brothers and sisters in Christ, thank you for your prayers and remembrances of your brothers in the armed forces. You ask God to protect us all and to keep us united in the joy and affection which surrounds us and preserves us from evil. May we live the life of Jesus.

My best thoughts in friendship to you all and my best wishes for the year 1940.

T. MacDougal

Georges Goldy writes again and seems to take a naughty pleasure in describing military food, which includes meat, wine and rum. Most Adventists are vegetarian and do not drink alcoholic beverages, but Georges does not say that he avoids these when they are presented to him!

Georges Goldy to Jean   January 25, 1940

My dear Weidner,

    I'm answering your letter of the 11th of this month. ... About your being re-elected as President [of the youth group], that is very explicable. Who could have replaced you? Most of the young men have been called up, the others are too young, and you're the only one left, so you're the one to fill the presidency again. I think you were elected without any opposition, and in a unanimous vote, so here you are President for another year. ... I see you celebrated well at Christmas. We did, too, and if you're interested, I copied down the menus for Christmas Eve and New Year's Eve. Probably they aren't too different from yours. Réveillon [holiday banquet] of December 25, 1939: Choucroute garnie [sauerkraut and sausage], figs, a quarter of a liter of white wine, chased down with rum. At noon, ham, pork roast green beans, Swiss cheese cream. Chocolate éclair. A quarter of red wine, a quarter of champagne (demi sec from Vaugzes in Champaign). Porto cocktail. Coffee with rum. Beef in sauce, lentils, cookies, an orange, a quarter of red wine. New Year's: At noon, ham, pork chop, beans, cheese, a quarter of white and one of red wine. Evening: sardines, beef with mushroom sauce, blue cheese from Auvergne ... One of my pals who was supposed to go on leave heard about it only two hours beforehand. Everybody wants to command, and nobody wants to obey, it is complete chaos. We have a lieutenant who is commander of the company, and he is a great guy, but he is weak and the others do whatever they please. As for the Allies and the enemy, I couldn't care less. Chamberlain would do well to look after his umbrella. ... and Hitler his mustache and Goering his medals. The only thing we all want is to be left in peace once and for all, but is it possible!!!! ... Affectionate thoughts from your old Georges presently an infantryman on the line—O yes, the Line! What long fishing line is for you to guess/Maginot.

Another letter from A. Lams. In this letter, Lams refers to "Sister White". Ellen Gould White, 1827-1915, a native of Gorham, Maine, USA, was the co-founder of the Seventh-day Adventist movement.

"LA DRÔLE DE GUERRE" – THE PHONY WAR

A. Lams to Jean Monday, February 5, 1940

Dear Jean,

Thank you for your good letter of January 17, and for the "Youth Group Bulletin". ... Your letter did me so much good, and I see that despite all the difficulties, you haven't changed, and are still the optimist. Indeed, being the President of a youth group composed of phenomena like the ones I knew, is no small thing. But then, you will have all the more merit if you can succeed in leading those rebellious youth.

I am saddened and I suffer with you about the sacrifice you made in giving up Elisabeth. However, I approve of the courage you showed in making such a sacrifice as I am certain that you would not have been happy with a wife who doesn't share your faith. Sister White gave us very precise instructions on that subject. But who knows if Elisabeth won't some day think again really seriously about this question, and give herself entirely to God, out of convictions and not just out of love for you. I was afraid she would convert just because of you, but it seems that her love of the world was too strong. Dear Jean, try to console yourself, as you have the courage to do your duty, and our Celestial Father sees and understands your suffering and will guide you in the best way for you.

Thank you for all the news you sent from everywhere. I am so sorry that your sister Annette broke her arm. I think it was she that I went to get at St. Julien with your car in September 1937. If it was she, maybe she remembers me, and please give her my best wishes for a rapid recovery and convalescence.

Thank you so much for your offers of help. You are the same in your heart and you always love to be helpful. No, there is really nothing I need. I have enough pocket money, and I don't smoke, so I don't spend much. ... My spirits are good especially after my ten day leave which I had three weeks ago. I was able to spend 5 days at Collonges and had a wonderful time. Collonges is exactly the same as when I left it, except that there aren't as many students at the Seminary. ... I spent the other five days at my parents' home in Troyes. My parents were very happy to see me, and it had been six months since I had seen them. They are in good spirits, even though they have fewer commodities than in Sarreguemines. (I understand that this town had been heavily bombed.)

Please give my best wishes to all who know me in the youth group ... Your friend and Brother in Christ, A. Lams

Annette Weidner writes from The Hague for the Paris youth group's newsletter.

To the Youth Society of Paris   February 25, 1940

Dear Friends,

What a good idea to have a newspaper for the youth group. Congratulations. ... This precious newspaper will serve as a link for all the young people. I was glad to hear news from those newly evacuated or drafted. We will feel less alone now when a little messenger will arrive each month.

Here in The Hague, our youth group is quite large. There is a meeting every Friday evening. And yet, what I wouldn't give to be with you again. Now that the beautiful season is approaching, I remember the wonderful outings on Sabbath afternoon. What a joy it will be when we will all be together again, and maybe the present separation will encourage us to savor even more the bonds which unite Adventist youth.

I am glad to tell you that my arm has completely recovered.

I feel very much like an expatriate here in my own country. That might sound strange, but it's true.

I'll stop, my dear friends, hoping to see you soon, God willing. I am always with you in thought.

    Your Sister and friend "in exile."
    Annette Weidner

Excerpts from another letter from Georges Goldy with more ironic comments on military life and food:

Georges Goldy to Jean   In the Armies of the French Republic,
                                              One and Indivisible,
                                              Somewhere in France,
                                              in the Year of Grace 1940,
                                 the 28th of the month of February.

Dear Brother and friend,

Here I am back in military life, we're so used to it, that we can't get along without it. It's better than civilian life, and as they say, we always return to our first loves. You can't compare military life with civilian life.

We all have first class high quality modern comforts: judging by the bales of hay for beds, tables and chairs ... à la 6-4-2 [thrown together], electricity outages, central heating without coal, water when it isn't frozen, nonexistent gas, abundant and varied food, example: Monday beef with gravy, Tuesday boiled beef, Wednesday canned corned beef, Thursday salted beef, Friday, beef en daube [braised], Saturday b. with tomato sauce, Sunday, beef ragout, plus rice stuck together with paste, elastic noodles and macaroni, split peas in green sauce, lentils with pebbles, putty cheese, coffee made with sock juice, cement bread, and much, much more. ... I'd love to go into this as a career; I would have medals, stripes, a hat, and a beautiful uniform, a retirement pension. ...

Jean answers Roger Guerin's letter. He writes of "Mémé" Girou, who is quite a problem in the youth group. The same young man will become even more of a problem to society later on.

Jean to Roger Guérin   Paris, April 11, 1940

My dear Roger,

    I don't know how to apologize for having waited so long to answer your good letter of December 26, of last year. I must tell you that I am excessively busy 1) with my work, and right now life is not a bed of roses for a salesman because we have to work much more just to earn enough to keep from starving to death. As you, know, I am working with Maurice Guenin, and it's quite hard. 2) I am responsible for the youth group and I can assure you that with rebels like Mémé Girou it's no picnic. He has been sent home from everywhere, and nobody knows what to do with him. So now he's our problem. He's not a mean boy, but he has never learned either discipline or obedience. At the last Committee meeting, it was decided that he couldn't come to "130" for four weeks. Everything is fine with the other young people and in the Church Bulletin and the youth newsletter, you will get a little information about the youth here in Paris.

    Of course for you it's not a bed of roses either, and I know that in comparison with you I am privileged. I don't know how much longer that will be true, as I expect to be called up, and the waiting keeps me from making any definite plans. ...

You may have heard that a young student at Collonges who was 15 years old fell 200 meters while cliff climbing and was killed instantly. It's terrible. The Walter baby nearly drowned in the pool near the Chalet. Luckily his mother found him before it was too late.

I read your letter to the youth group and its details interested everyone. ... If you have time to write us a few more lines, we would be very glad.

... Arthur Vaucher wants to go to Belgium for a few days to see his fiancée. Yet another who wants to give up being a bachelor! Pretty soon I'll be the only one left of all the friends in our class at Collonges. But, that could change, and I'm not giving up! ...

My dear Roger, I'll leave you now and am sending my brotherly thoughts. I pray that God will protect you and keep you so that you can come back from this war safe and sound. We all think of you a lot, and we are with you in these difficult times.

A good handshake and greetings from your old friend who doesn't forget you.

Ch. Ratsimbason to Jean　　　　　　　　　In the Army, May 17, 1940

Dear Jean and friends,

I received your letter today, but with this war we don't get time to write often. ...

The moment is coming when war will break out everywhere.

But we are brave when facing the enemy. During the last two weeks the aerial bombing begins with the civilian population. It's a misfortune for the women and children that Mr. Hitler is not satisfied with the blood of combatants.

That is why we are going to fight to the end with the help of our courage and divine blessings.

Here at the front, things are calm right now, but the enemy's air activity is beginning to be terrible, and he is bombing the little villages and railways.

... Cannoneer Ch. Ratsimbason.

No. 89 2nd Group
11th R.A.L.C.
Postal Sector 5

"LA DRÔLE DE GUERRE" – THE PHONY WAR

So the war has begun, but as yet there is little evidence of it. In present-day France, World War II is called "La Guerre de '39-'45" (just as the First World War is referred to as "La Guerre de '14-'19"). But it is not until the end of May 1940, that the war really begins for France.

3   The Flight to Anduze

The Weidner parents move to The Hague in The Netherlands in 1939. As war approaches, the French authorities have been gradually changing their opinion about what categories of foreign nationals could remain in France. There is little consistency in these decisions, as they are made by local prefectures according to their own interpretations of national regulations.

Foreigners who have the best chance of being allowed to remain in France are those with jobs and/or family connections. Thus the Weidner parents must leave, while nothing prevents Gabrielle, an employee of the Franco-Belgian Division of the Adventist Church, from remaining at her post.

Gaby, writing in Dutch on March 6, to her parents and Annette in The Hague, reports that people seem to think that the real war—"the Big War," as she calls it—"will begin on the 15th, because Hitler always attacked on March 15th."

Jean still expects to be drafted by the Dutch Army and to be able to fight for his country. A note from Elisabeth Cartier reveals that she needs to know what his plans are. If Jean has "given Elisabeth up," as is suggested in A. Lams's letter of February 5, 1940, she may not quite see the situation that way, as the following letter from Elisabeth shows.

Elisabeth "Lis" Cartier to Jean   Geneva, June 13, 1940

Mon très cher Jean,

I'm writing you a few words in haste tonight. I am very worried about you, what have you decided? Will you stay in Paris? I would be very grateful if you would let me know. And Gaby? Now I want you to tell me if you need anything, I am still here. Please send me word right away. My dear Jean, I would write you again tomorrow, but I am anxious to know your decisions, I know you want to serve, but that doesn't mean you need to take risks.

I hope to hear from you as soon as possible. I beg you especially not to remain in the clutches of those Boches [Germans] if that situation arises; it would be better to run than to be their prey.

Adieu, Jean. Be confident and keep up your courage. I am with you. I pray God keep you and He will tell you my thoughts.

Lis [signature]

Little news arrives at first from the parents and Annette in The Hague. Jean has applied to the Red Cross for news of them, and a Red Cross form dated July 18, 1940 brings what may be the first news from the parents in a long time. It comes from the Dutch Red Cross, and the sender is J.H. Weidner (Papa) at Columbustr. 13 in The Hague (the Weidner parents' address) and is being sent to Weidner, Johan Hendrik at 130 Boulevard de l'Hôpital in Paris. Four lines at the bottom of the long form give the family news in Dutch: "All in good health. Finances better. Family in Utrecht and Antwerp healthy. Thinking of you." This form does not reach Paris until August 27, when no one in the family is there to receive it.

Since both Jean Weidner and his sister Gabrielle are in Paris until June of this year of 1940, few letters pass between them.

The month of May 1940, saw the end of the "phony war." German troops advanced through The Netherlands, Belgium and Luxembourg heading toward France from the north instead of from the East where they had been expected. The Maginot Line, so carefully constructed to block entry from the East, was of no use. In June, fearing the worst, thousands of people fled Paris and headed south,

At the Adventist Division, the staff also thinks it might be best to relocate in the South of France. On June 10, they pile records and personal belongings into a car whose designated driver is Jean Weidner, and lock the doors at 130 Boulevard de l'Hôpital.

The group arrives in Anduze, a historically Protestant city in the Department of Gard just south of the Cevennes mountains and north of the Mediterranean. Like most of the Parisians who survived the flight from Paris, they soon begin to arrange for their return home. Jean, who had abandoned his Paris textile business, goes back to Lyon to start again. Gaby's efforts to obtain authorization to travel to Paris and return to her job are complicated by the fact that she is not French.

THE FLIGHT TO ANDUZE

A series of Gaby's letters to Jean in Lyon tell of the frustration and red tape she encounters.

Gaby to Jean   Anduze, August 1, 1940
                                                                      Thursday morning

Mon cher Jean,

I was very happy to get your letter already yesterday as I hadn't expected one before today. Fortunately, you were able to get enough gas to get back to Lyon.

Here everything has been quiet. Mémé left yesterday morning for Nîmes and will get back this evening. We asked him to get information about repatriation of refugees, but guess what, yesterday morning, going to the town hall with Lisette, we saw a notice which said that all refugees going to Paris, Seine, or Seine et Oise [departments in the Paris region] should report without delay to the Reception Center in Nîmes for their repatriation.

We both took the 12:30 bus and arrived in Nîmes at 2:30. But at the Reception Center we were told that foreigners didn't yet have the right to return to the Occupied Zone. But for the French there are trains nearly every day. But it isn't much fun to take these trains. At least when I looked at all those people waiting who were eating and sleeping in the courtyard, I said to myself that I wouldn't particularly enjoy traveling with them. To take a train where you pay for the ticket, you have to have a certificate of mission. From the Reception Center they sent me to the Chamber of Commerce, saying I could get a mission certificate there. But from there I was sent to the Prefecture, because at the Chamber of Commerce they were only dealing with commercial and industrial company executives. At the Prefecture they told me I had to wait, as for the moment the German authorities are allowing only French citizens to be repatriated. Lisette and I were very discouraged when we took the bus back at 5 o'clock. Always this problem for foreigners. I assure you Papa and Mama are lucky to be in their own country. It is sad to think that everybody else can go home but we have to wait here until when, I wonder?

I'm going to write to Brother Wehrli to ask him for an attestation that I am employed by the bookstore and that I need to return. It could always help. Can you go to the Consulate for me? Maybe they can tell me what I must do to get back. ...

I'm sending you a few letters which came for you, but I took off the envelopes to make them lighter. ...

I'm thinking of going to do the canvassing in Nîmes with Lisette, because I can't sit around and do nothing for much longer. But we are going to ask Brother Guerin if it is safe going together, being both foreigners.

Lisette is really worried because she thinks she has lost a thousand franc note that Marthe gave her before she left Alès. I wondered if she had hidden it somewhere in the room when we arrived, but she doesn't remember anything about it and we looked everywhere. There is only one hope left, and that is that Marthe might have taken it back, so Lisette is waiting impatiently for a letter from her. If not, that would be a real blow to her. I hope it will turn up.

It seems that correspondence with Paris is stopped for a few days. But I think it will start up again very soon. I think Marthe did the right thing by returning to Paris, but it would have been better if she had come back to get her things and especially the office things and gotten a train a few days later from Nîmes if there wasn't one from Alès. We can check 30 kilos in addition to hand baggage. But some say that we have to be able to carry it all by ourselves. I'll see. I have a lot to do before I'll be on my way.

... My affectionate kisses.
    Gaby

P. S. I am really beginning to worry about our parents, and I'm going to write to Brother Tissot to find out if they have heard anything since the last card.

I got a letter from Renée Wagner. It took them 5 days to reach Melun by barge. Then they went back to Paris on foot and it took them 2 days. Her husband is a secretary-translator. He has a very good job.

Your letter was opened by the censors.

Gaby writes Jean again on the following day. Though she is still in Anduze, she writes on the letterhead "Sign of the Times" of the bookstore of the Paris Adventist Church, where she works. The group has brought office supplies from "130."

THE FLIGHT TO ANDUZE

Gaby to Jean

LIBRAIRIE LES SIGNES DES TEMPS
130 Boulevard de l'Hôpital (13th)
Anduze, August 2, 1940

Mon cher Jean,

Today I got your letter of July 31 which brought balm to my soul, because the Consul said that Dutch people can return to the Occupied Zone. For several days communications have been cut off, and since mail doesn't even get to Paris, I think there aren't any passenger trains either.

At the same time as your letter I got one from Brother Meyer telling me to come and spend Monday and Tuesday in Brignon, as he has a lot of correspondence. I'll be able to discuss useful arrangements with him, but I think he will be in complete agreement that we should go to Paris at the first opportunity. I suppose that if I can go back to Paris, Lisette can also. In any case, Brother Meyer will have gone to the Swiss Consulate and will have information.

It would be a real problem if I couldn't get a direct ticket to Paris, because I was planning to check part of my baggage, especially my case of provisions. Well, I'll see. I could leave some of my things with Sister Girou [Mémé" Girou's mother] but I'd much prefer to take them myself. ...

I also got a letter from Sister Lanarès telling me that Pierre is a prisoner in the Yonne [department in the Paris region], as you already knew. ... She has had no news of René since the beginning of June. ...

It's really nice of you to want to send me some butter, but I'm afraid it will be melted by the time it arrives, and by then I might not still be here. In today's newspaper, they say that there is plenty of butter in Paris. So I'll eat some there. Also bread isn't rationed and I can get all the flour I want. As for my provisions, I could have done with a little less, but they won't be wasted and maybe I'll be glad to have them when the rationing cards are established. ...

I'm glad to know that business is good. ...

Where are you staying?

Greetings to everyone. Best thoughts from your sister.

   Gaby

As planned, Gaby has gone to Brignon, about 30 kilometers from Anduze, to help Brother Meyer with the accumulated church correspondence.

Gaby to Jean   Brignon, August 7, 1940

Bien cher Jean,

I'm still in Brignon where I'm staying three days instead of two. It's a nice change. ... Sister Habéry is doing the cooking, and I have helped some. There are 8 of us at the table.

Your card came before I left, as it arrived Sunday. Maybe there will be some mail for me in Anduze. But since we can't write to the Occupied Zone, there must not be much.

I'm glad to have the provisions, because now with the ration cards we can't get much of anything. But what bothers me is to have to take everything to Paris. But Brother Meyer advises me to wait a little while to see if Sister Girou is going to leave soon. It would be so hard to travel with all my baggage, and going in a car would certainly be easier. Sister Girou is waiting for an answer from her husband. He applied for a pass to France and one to Portugal. He'll take whichever one he gets first. So if he goes to Portugal, Sister Girou won't wait for him, and we can leave. ...

   I hope to see you in Lyon before I return to Paris. I wrote to Brother Tissot in Berne, to find out if they had heard from our parents. If they haven't, we have to do something through the Red Cross. I hope your sales trip through Savoie went well. Many kisses. Gaby

Arrangements to travel to Paris in the Girou car are becoming more complicated. Mémé Girou (the troublemaker in the Paris youth group) is impatient and fights constantly with his mother, and his father's plans have not been clarified.

To reach Paris from Anduze Gaby will have to cross the Demarcation Line which splits France horizontally through its middle into "Occupied" and "Unoccupied" zones. On June 22, 1940, just after the group from "130" headed South to Anduze, France's weak and elderly leader had signed an Armistice with the German occupiers. He then abandoned Paris to the enemy, moving his government to Vichy in the Southern or "Unoccupied Zone."

Gaby to Jean   LIBRAIRIE LES SIGNES DES TEMPS
                                                                      130 Boulevard de l'Hôpital (13th)
                                                                                Anduze, August 9, 1940

THE FLIGHT TO ANDUZE

Mon bien cher Jean,

Today I got your letter of the 6th and I hasten to answer as you are leaving on your sales trip next week. ...

Mémé is going to Alès next week to apply for returning, because here we can't get the authorization. You have to go to Alès. I think Brother Meyer will travel with us to Paris. It still depends on when Brother Girou returns. But there will almost certainly be room for us. Mémé has had enough of being here and wants desperately to leave.

So we plan to leave, unless there are unforeseen circumstances, on Thursday the 22nd of this month and very early in the morning, and we think we can be in Paris by Friday. We won't be going via Lyon but via Moulins. So I won't see you. ... I'll try to take all my baggage in the car, but it's too bad I don't have a suitcase. That would have simplified things as there is room on the roof. But if it doesn't work I can always send it through the railroad station. But I think we can make it work. Tell me where I can write you next week and before we leave. I hope that when I get to Paris we can still correspond between the two zones, as I would be terribly sorry to be completely separated from you. I am really worried about our parents. ...

Mémé is going crazy here. He has endless disputes with his mother. He is really lazy. Even Lisette has had enough of him!

It's hot here and that's very tiring. ...

I see that you listen to the radio all the time. We are expecting restrictions. But I'm not too worried about it. Madame Girou promised to sell me the potatoes from Marolles, and as soon as I get to Paris I'll start getting some provisions.

In Paris there are no silk stockings. Even here there are hardly any, and when new ones come in, they are almost double the price. Luckily I bought several pairs last week. I think I'll buy some cloth for a winter dress, too, if I can find something nice. That will be an expense, but I can catch up later. There is almost no wool material left in Paris.

I am glad that Elisabeth can do things for you. I keep wondering if she will ever get baptized. It's too bad that someone nice couldn't take care of her in Geneva.

Good luck in your business. I hope that you can soon buy yourself a lighter colored suit that will keep you cooler.

My dear Jean, I'm sending my best kisses.
      Gaby

Gaby to Jean

LIBRAIRIE LES SIGNES DES TEMPS
130 Boulevard de l'Hôpital (13th)
Anduze, August 18, 1940

Mon bien cher Jean,

I wanted to write to you this week, but I didn't know where to reach you as you were on tour. ... When I am in Paris I won't be able to receive your letters, and if I can't hear anything from home either, I will be very lonely. Let's hope we can soon correspond between the two zones, and also that I can write to Holland from Paris. I still have had no answer from Brother Tissot. So I think it would be a good idea for you to ask Elisabeth to apply to the Red Cross to get information.

This week: a real blow. Tuesday evening Sister Girou said she might stay here and Wednesday she told us she won't be going back to Marolles but that she wants to wait for her husband here. We told her that it was not nice of her to tell us at this late date. Guess what she claimed: that this had always been a possibility and we were the ones who had misunderstood, and that she has said all along that if her husband returned and had a lot of baggage she wouldn't be able to take us all. ... You were right: they can't be depended on, and Lisette came right out and told her that. ... The reason she doesn't want to return to Paris is that several people have told her she doesn't know what it's like there. But Mémé has had enough of being here and since she doesn't want to go back to Marolles, he wants to go to his sister's in Morocco. His mother doesn't want him to and that makes endless arguments. Today Lisette went to close the door to their room, saying that if they wanted to argue so loudly they could at least close the door. I'm so sick of being here. ...

Believe it or not, my box weighs 60 kilos. We weighed it. I'm going to Alès tomorrow and I'll be able to buy a suitcase. ...

Lisette is very happy with her yarn which she is knitting with. We did a lot of work last week; she made me a brown velvet dress and pajamas. I worked on it too, and Madame Daunis sewed everything on the machine. Now all I need is a coat for this winter. I hope I can find one, if not I'll wear the old one, if I still have my trunk, of course!

I am so happy your business is going well, and that you could buy yourself some underwear, you really needed some. Buy yourself some pajamas too, if you can. I had to laugh when I read that you were selling widows' veils. Now we have seen everything! But I can see that you are not afraid of work and that you will always come out on top.

Lisette is writing to Brother Meyer to tell him her situation, and she is having trouble because the inspiration doesn't come. She is not very good at correspondence and doesn't know how to express herself. To each her own talents! Anyway, she certainly knows how to wield a needle. Few are as clever as she. ...

I am using my last sheets of letter paper. Forgive me if they don't look very fresh. I can't buy a new tablet before leaving, but I'll have to buy something small tomorrow.

Yesterday was my birthday. I really thought you would forget, but I was so glad your long letter arrived on that day. If only I could have received a letter from home, that would have been the greatest gift I could have received.

I don't need to have a certificate of repatriation made. The Town Hall was willing to do that. That works for car travel, but not for the train.

If I get back to Paris I will find your underwear and I'll send it to you as soon as I can send packages. Or else I'll wait until someone is going to Lyon. ...

Do you think food rationing cards for pasta, rice, fats, exist everywhere in France? Mémé says that in the Occupied Zone one isn't supposed to use them, but that would surprise me.

No, I won't get to Holland any time soon. I would have to be very sure I could get back. I don't like listening to the radio. So many bad things are said about our former Allies. I wonder how it will all come out. If Germany is too slow, it will be too late to attack this year, and that will take us into next year. I'd rather it be over this year.

Now I must stop. I hope you have the strength to read this letter all the way through. ...

Affectionate kisses,
    Gaby

The next day Gaby writes from Alès, about 15 kilometers north of Anduze, where she must have bought the smaller pad of paper she is writing on. Lisette and Pastor Oscar Meyer, President of the Adventist Division in Paris, are both Swiss and therefore have similar foreigners' problems to those of Gaby, who is Dutch.

Gaby to Jean   Alès, August 19, 1940

Mon cher Jean,

We're in Alès where I had some errands to do, and we are taking the opportunity to get information at the sub-prefecture.

We were told that for the moment foreigners can't return to the Occupied Zone. As a matter of fact neither can the French, at least not by ordinary trains, even if they have an order of mission. But that will be fixed shortly. They can return by road. They told us that we could always try to leave, at our own risks and perils, but that we might be sent back. In any case, there is less risk by the road than by train. ...

They told us it's better to go via Lyon than via Clermont. They turn back fewer people there. ...

I just wrote to Brother Meyer in Toulouse to update him and ask him if I should try to leave through Lyon or wait for him. I would rather travel with him, as there would always be someone to help me and he knows German.

I was able to buy a large suitcase, so on that score I am all set. ...

I forgot to tell you that Sister Girou made me some little cakes for my birthday, and they spelled out the words "Bonne Fête" [Happy Birthday]. She decorated the Sabbath table very nicely. It was very nice of her. It's too bad she is so hard to get along with in so many ways. Lisette gave me a little bottle of cologne. I didn't have any more, as I had just run out.

We are at the Post Office where it is nice and cool. Much better than outside. Lisette went to her Consulate in Lyon. I told her she could always try to see if they could help her with her return. Such a shame that Sister Girou doesn't want to return, as we would have had fewer risks. But I don't talk to her about it anymore, as I don't want her to be able to say later that she came back as a favor to us. ...

Now I'll stop and we'll go and get a glass of lemonade as we are very thirsty.

Je t'embrasse bien fort [I kiss you really hard].
        Gaby

P.S. Did I tell you that I got a letter from René who saw the Koukoutches while going to church in Montpellier. Mr. K. had another nervous breakdown and is hospitalized near Montpellier. I think he collects them!

THE FLIGHT TO ANDUZE

Gaby to Jean   Anduze, August 23, 1940

Bien cher Jean,

... I wonder what is happening on the other side of the zone line. It's really mysterious that we aren't allowed to correspond. I've been told that the Germans did that for some kind of revenge. But you can't believe everything you hear.

I'm glad you sent me a piece of soap the day you left, as I only had one left and you can't do much with 125 grams. I'm all set for sugar, and fortunately I had several kilos of rice and pasta thanks to you who are always wanting me to have enough provisions. But as soon as I'm in Paris I'll try to buy a little more. I can't buy it here anymore because of the problem of transporting it. ...

Lisette wishes she had bought more yarn in Paris, as it was much less expensive than it is here. She is making a pretty little jacket with the yarn you sold her here. ... Maybe I'll make a long-sleeved pullover for myself this winter or I'll ask Madame Steinbeck to make it for me. But I wonder if one can get yarn in Paris. I have everything else I need.

When you can, try to buy soap for yourself (Lux, Palmolive, Cadum) for later, as well as shaving soap, as it seems that it's getting scarce everywhere, and you can't get it with ration cards.

For you, my dear Jean, my most affectionate thoughts.
       Gaby

Gaby to Jean   Anduze, August 29, 1040

Mon bien cher Jean,

... Here is what we have decided: since Brother Meyer still has things to do and can't leave for about ten days, Lisette and I are going to leave Monday at 1pm for Alès where we will take the train at 0:18. It leaves Nîmes at 23:25, but Alès is nearer and we'll take it there. I'll send you a telegram this morning so you won't write me here anymore. ...

I'll write you again before I leave, and if you don't receive anything after that, you'll know I got through. ...

I'll stop now. Maybe this letter won't reach you until after I have left...

Affectionately,
       Gaby

There are still a few sheets of the letterhead from the Paris bookstore here in Anduze. Gaby writes on some of them.

Gaby to Jean LIBRAIRIE LES SIGNES DES TEMPS
130 Boulevard de l'Hôpital (13th)
Anduze, August 30, 1940

Bien cher Jean,

Yesterday I received your box of butter for which I thank you very much. You are so nice to think of me. When I opened it, I was afraid the butter smelled a little rancid, but it was just the surface. All the rest was good, and I mixed salt into it. That way it will keep for a while, and I'll have some for the trip, and anyway I love salted butter. ...

You never talk about Elisabeth. I hope you still hear from her and that all is well. I wrote to Sister Huguenin that if she was in Geneva for any amount of time, she could go to see Elisabeth to see how she is coming from the spiritual point of view. Maybe it would be good for her.

We decided not to send our baggage to the railroad station until we are sure we are going to get through. So we are getting everything ready and if by Thursday noon Mr. Daunis hasn't received a telegram from us, he will send our baggage the next day. If we haven't written, it will mean that we got through, and if we are sent back at least we won't be separated from all our things. In the suitcase that I'm sending, I put the rest of our provisions, the yarn and the blankets. I'm taking the office books and my dresses and underwear with me. The suitcase I bought is very handsome and large, just what I wanted and it only cost 105 francs. I was lucky to find it as it was the last one. There were only 3 small ones left.

I'll stop for today. Maybe I'll write again Sunday or Monday before leaving.

My most affectionate thoughts to you, my dear Jean.
     Gaby

... Sister Girou is very nice. She doesn't want me to help with the cooking anymore so that I have time for my preparations, and so that we have good memories of her. She is not bad at heart but she is an oriental and we will always have trouble understanding each other.

THE FLIGHT TO ANDUZE

Gaby writes again on the same day. Her travel passes may have to be signed by the A.O.K., the Armeeoberkommando, or the German high command.

Gaby to Jean

LIBRAIRIE LES SIGNES DES TEMPS
130 Bd. De l'Hôpital, 13th
Anduze, August 30, 1940, Friday afternoon

Mon cher Jean,

It's me again, here to bother you. I've been doing nothing but writing to you since yesterday.

Guess what, at noon I received a letter from Brother Meyer saying as follows:

"Here is the exact text of the information I was given at the railroad station and which is posted as very <u>important notice.</u>

'No traveler can be admitted traveling to the Occupied Zone without a special green or yellow pass carrying the heading "Demarcation Line" and numbered.

These special passes must be signed by the A.O.K. 12, the Armeeoberkommando [German High Command] in Besançon, Armistice Commission, Wiesbaden, Special Commission on Paris.'

I was told at the Prefecture that they don't know anything about this. It changes all the time, it seems. If you want to take your chances I give you carte blanche and wish you success."

Well, what a blow. But we are going to leave on Monday anyway with our certificate of repatriation. At the zone demarcation line we'll be told exactly what to do. …

I'm pretty discouraged but we are going to try our luck since the rules change constantly. Fortunately we won't have much baggage with us.

I leave you then for today, with many kisses.
    Gaby

On the morning of departure, plans must be changed again.

Gaby to Jean Anduze, September 2, 1940
Monday morning

Mon bien cher Jean,

To think we were supposed to leave this afternoon at 1 o'clock, and that we changed our minds again! Here is what happened: as I wrote you on Friday afternoon, we had decided to leave anyway in spite of Brother Meyer's letter. But then yesterday morning the Cabanises told us that there was an announcement on the radio that seemed related to what Brother Meyer wrote in his letter. Unfortunately the announcement wasn't repeated in the evening. It will doubtless be in the newspapers this morning. There we are in kind of a muddle because if we leave anyway, we risk being sent back, since whatever it was, it was officially announced on the radio. This morning Lisette went to the Town Hall to get our certificates of repatriation on which the secretary was to put today's date. But she is going to ask if we really shouldn't take the last train of refugees which leaves Wednesday from Nîmes. They'll doubtless tell us that foreigners still have no right to take it, but we can try. I'll let you know this afternoon the result of her inquiry. ...

Lisette just came back with our certificates. The secretary says that he made us the same papers as he does for the French and that we should try to take that last refugee train because it's the only way to get through. So we will leave tomorrow morning at 8 o'clock on the bus to Nîmes and we will register at the Reception Center. If they won't let us leave on that train, we'll try to take the ordinary train, and if that isn't possible, we'll do the collecting in Nîmes. If you only knew how much this all worries me. To go in this unorganized way. ... I will write you tomorrow before we leave, as the refugee train leaves Wednesday morning at 10 o'clock.

So, more news tomorrow. Je t'embrasse bien fort.
    Gaby

Now Gaby is in Nîmes, about 40 kilometers southwest of Anduze, ready to start her journey to Paris.

THE FLIGHT TO ANDUZE

Gaby to Jean Nîmes, September 3, 1940

Mon bien cher Jean,

... I was told that now foreign refugees can enter the Occupied Zone, and what's more, we can take the refugee trains. So we left Anduze this morning, Lisette and I, since we had to register today at the Reception Center, and that went very well. We have to be there tomorrow morning at 7 o'clock, the departure is at 10 o'clock. I have no idea what the itinerary is. We were registered by a German. He spoke French very well, but still, he had the accent and the type. ...

I had a little trouble with my bags, because if I had them sent through Brignon, nobody would have been there to sign for me. At the Post Office I was told they would just stay in the baggage room until the zone border opened up, or else they would be returned to the sender. So I told them there was butter in the package and the Post Office manager got into the discussion and said that the sender and the person to whom it was sent could be forced to pay a fine for sending perishable goods through the Post Office. So don't send me any more butter. ...

Yesterday, while cleaning the rooms in the wing, Lisette found a pair of your underpants behind the bed. If I had had it sooner, I would have been able to wash it, but it was too late. So I am sending it as is to you in Lyon. ...

So tomorrow I'll send you a note en route. Je t'embrasse bien affectueusement.

    Gaby

Gaby to Jean Nîmes, September 4, 1940
Wednesday morning, 7 o'clock

Mon cher Jean,

I am at the Reception center waiting to be called. ...

Take care of your health. Don't neglect yourself from the point of view of food. I will think of you especially on Friday evening when I used to have you to dinner. Maybe those times will come again. Also take care of your clothes and underwear. Wash them all regularly.

It is 10:30 and we are still at the Reception Center. The train is in the station, but we are waiting for a telephone call from the Kommandatur to allow us to leave. How much longer will we be here? A refugee train is not exactly ideal. True, it is free of charge.

They just brought us milk and hot chocolate, as much as we wanted. It was very good. ...

... It is 4:30. Still in Nîmes. The Kommandatur is supposed to send the train's number, otherwise we can't leave. We don't dare go too far from the Reception Center, as we have to be ready all the time. We will have the answer before 5 o'clock. But if we don't leave, we won't be able to leave for three days, because of the papers that would have to be made out again. And I was so happy that the trip would be over before the Sabbath, but now that we're registered, we can't go back. We have to leave with this train. Besides, it is more and more clear that this is the only way to be sure of getting through.

A man here told us that he had been turned back with an entire train load because a revolver had been found on the preceding train. I hope that doesn't happen to us. ...

Lisette is struggling with her hairnet whose elastic is broken. In Lyon we should tell the train to wait while we go and get a new one at Julien's! ...

... 6:30

At 5 o'clock we were told to come back tomorrow morning at 9:00 when we would probably leave. We'll see about that. We then went to Madame Sabatier's to see if she could put us up, as she is very nice. Now I am at the Post Office to finish this letter and then we'll go to eat at the Women's Home. It appears that it is like this nearly every time. The last one, a week ago, the one on which the Sommers, the Habérys and the Mardens left, was supposed to leave on Sunday and didn't leave until Tuesday at midnight. A little patience. ... Good thoughts to you. Gaby

Gaby's next two letters, one and three days later, still from Nîmes, are written on small (4 ¾" x 6 ½") sheets with perforated edges, which were then folded and addressed and stamped on the outside. They are addressed to: Mr. J. (or Jean) Weidner, Poste Restante (General Delivery), and Guéret (Creuse). Probably the addressee opened the letters by removing the perforated edges that were pasted together.

THE FLIGHT TO ANDUZE

Gaby to Jean Nîmes, September 5, 1940
Thursday evening

Mon cher Jean,

As you can see, we were made to wait at the Center all day, with a 2-hour break at noon, only to be told at 5 o'clock that they were still waiting for authorization from the Germans. It's better that they make us wait here rather than spending several days in some railroad garage in some tiny village. But it really seems like a long time. I'm sorry for the people traveling with children. Last night we stayed with Sister Sabatier who is very nice and we're going back there tonight. We were told that refugees could eat for free in a big new school. We're there tonight because several people told us it was very good, and it's less expensive than a restaurant.

... Kisses, Gaby

Gaby to Jean Nîmes, September 7, 1940, 3:30

Bien cher Jean,

As you can see, we're still here. Yesterday they had us come at 10 o'clock, and then again at 4:00. Nothing new. Today at 11 o'clock, and then at 2:00. The news is: we're leaving. I had desperately hoped that this would not happen today, the Sabbath. This morning we went to Holy Communion given by Brother Raspal. ... It's too bad we are leaving today, as it's very hot and I have a headache.

[The last three lines are in shaky writing, and the last few words were torn off when the recipient tore off those perforated edges.]

It's 4 o'clock. We're leaving the Reception Center for the station. I'll mail this letter and a post card en route.

The next letter from Gaby to Jean is from Paris.

4 Daily Life in Occupied Paris

Gaby is safely back in Paris, living at "130", where many of the personnel of the Adventist Church also live. To reach her room, four floors above the sanctuary, she climbs the spiral staircase from the lobby. She passes the second floor (the French call it the first floor, as the ground floor is the "rez de chaussée" or the street level) on which the office where she works is located at the end of a corridor. The two floors above the offices are each divided into two apartments where members of the church administration live with their families. Finally she reaches the top floor where the secretaries' kitchen is located to the right of the stair landing, and turns to the left to the sunny corridor at the front of the building with windows overlooking Boulevard de l'Hôpital. Hers is one of the six rooms along this hallway.

In Occupied Paris, far from her scattered family, Gaby is lonely for her parents and siblings. Her sister Annette is with the parents in The Hague in Holland, a country also now occupied by Germany. After the Anduze exile, older brother Jean had returned to Lyon in the Unoccupied Zone of France.

In this final quarter of 1940, mail from Holland is almost entirely disrupted, and no news has come from the family in The Hague since June.

Even within France, contact between the Occupied and Unoccupied Zones is severely limited, a situation which Gaby had anticipated with dread in her letters to Jean from Anduze. Business correspondence could be authorized, but private letters had to be sent via friends, or friends of friends who could most easily pass through the Demarcation Line. Despite restrictions, Gaby, undaunted, wrote at least seven long letters and sixteen postcards to Jean in Lyon between her return to Paris in September and the end of the year.

Gaby writes her first letter to Jean since her return to Paris. Her letters at this time are handwritten in pen and ink.

Gaby to Jean   Paris, September 14, 1940

Bien cher Jean,

Simone Rochat tells me she can get this letter through, and that's why I'm writing you a few words very fast. My return trip went well. We weren't even asked for our papers when crossing into the zone. We can buy anything we want in the markets, but there is nothing in the stores. The prices on clothes are crazy. Buy your suits as soon as possible. Here they cost at least 1200 francs. I ordered a coat at Larcher's for 500 francs. It's expensive, but at least there is still good material. Later it will be really awful. If you can buy me some rayon stockings for around 25 francs, large, shoe size 40 [US 9], buy several pairs. I have some but here we can't find any stockings for less than 75 francs. For food supplies, buy what you can, especially and if possible, powdered or condensed milk, Maïzena [corn starch], tapioca, salt, rice for the chickens, 2 or 3 jars of jam, milk chocolate or ordinary chocolate. Here we don't find any of these things. We have to stand in line to get milk, butter, etc. ... If you get some provisions, keep them as I don't know yet if the other packages will arrive. I heard that sometimes they are confiscated at the border. I'm putting all that in God's hands. If you can, buy me a pink slip in non-run knit size 44 [US 14 or L] and a pair of panties size 46 [US 16], as here they are prohibitively expensive. I have two, but you never can tell when there will be any more...

Tuesday morning

All our luggage arrived yesterday. Can you believe it? I'm so happy and so grateful to God because I'm not afraid of winter now with all that I have. Mr. Daunis was so nice. He opened my suitcase and put in the two boxes of butter that you sent before I left. The butter kept well, and I melted it down last night. Such riches! Here the [ration] cards are for 4 weeks, not for one month the way they are in the South where you get a few more days each time. ...

I was at Hauser's to ask if the salesgirl knew who wanted to exchange the cheese card for my meat card, and she said yes. If absolutely necessary I could begin to eat meat, but I would avoid it as long as possible. ...

We can't go out anymore after 11 pm.

Je t'embrasse bien fort.
Gaby

Gaby to Jean September 24, 1940

... Starting tomorrow we will have ration cards for bread (350 grams), sugar (550 grams), soap (125 grams), pasta (250 grams). As for rice, only the children get 100 grams. We also will have the meat card and the cheese card (200 grams a month), butter, oil and other vegetable fats (400 grams a month in all). But this is better than before when only those who had the time and the strength to stand in line ever got anything. Since I have been here I have gotten butter, but not even once did I get cheese. Cards for milk will start on October 1st. I have a doctor's certificate and I have to go to the Town Hall for it. I hope I will have the right to 1/2 a liter a day. For the moment I have only 1/4 liter per day. I hope we have potatoes this winter. We miss them right now.

Other former exiles from 130 are returning from the South of France.

Gaby to Jean September 28, 1940

Mon bien cher Jean,

Thursday morning the Desmets and Brother Meyer arrived. They had left Nîmes Tuesday evening. So I was really lucky because it took me one less night than it took them. Brother Meyer told me he had read and torn up your 2 letters, as you advised him to do, and then he gave me all your news. ...

It appears that there is now rationing in all of France. I'm sorry about that for your sake, because you don't have any provisions, and eating in the hotels all the time is really hard and very costly. You must have a lot of expenses. I also think that you won't be able to drink as much milk. But still, you must take care of your health, because as you know, when you're not eating well, you feel it right away.

As for me, I'm fine. Everyone tells me I look well. I'm just beginning to feel the results of my vacation. In the past 2 weeks I've gained 1kilo800 [approximately 4 pounds]. It's really marvelous! ...

Since we have the family cards, I'll send you one from time to time, but also letters whenever I have the opportunity.

  Je t'embrasse bien fort.

   Gaby

The "family cards" Gaby refers to are the only officially authorized means of communication between private individuals in the two zones. At first these government issued-cards were pre-printed with a choice of phrases, so that the sender could cross out the inapplicable ones, and add a word or two in the spaces provided. At the bottom of these cards two lines remained blank where the writer could express him or herself more expansively as long as he or she was transmitting family news only.

  The stern French instructions at the top of the card and the somewhat dire and unimaginative alternatives to be selected from can be translated as follows:

After having completed this card which is limited strictly to correspondence of a family nature, cross out the phrases that do not apply. Nothing is to be written outside of the lines.

  ATTENTION: Any card containing messages not strictly of a family nature will not be sent and will probably be destroyed.

_____. _____19___
_____ in good health _____tired.
_____ slightly, seriously ill, wounded.
_____ killed _____ prisoner.
_____ deceased _____ without news
from_____ The family _____is well.
_____ need provisions _____ money.
News, baggage _____ is back in _____
_____ works at _____ is going to enter the school of _____. _____ passed the exams
_____. _____ to go to _____ on_____
_____
_____

  Affectionate thoughts, Kisses.   Signature.

DAILY LIFE IN OCCUPIED PARIS

Gaby says she will send a card to Jean "from time to time" but sends 16 of the above cards to Jean before the end of 1940, and over two hundred of them during the war years. She mails her first "family card" to Jean the very next day after her letter above.

Gaby to Jean   Paris, September 29, 1940

<u>I am</u> in good health.
<u>I am still</u> without news from <u>our parents</u>.
The family <u>of Gérard returned and</u> is well.
Baggage <u>arrived</u>. <u>Pierre</u> is back in <u>Melun</u>.
<u>Since my return I have gained 1.8 kilos. Not much work. I am managing to get food supplies. How about you?</u>
                          Signature. Gaby

Gaby to Jean (in a letter)   October 6, 1940

... I have written you several letters, but I don't know if they reach you. I'm going to try again with a different routing, for the sake of greater security. ...

Gaby's pre-printed family card to Jean on October 10 reveals that she has heard from "Henri," who is Jean himself, as she explains in her next letter. ("Henri" is Jean's middle name.) She reminds her brother to pay his tithes, as every Adventist member must do. Tithes are 10% of the church member's income. The tithes pay for the upkeep of the church and support Adventist Missions. Offerings during church services are made in addition to tithes.

Gaby to Jean (a letter)   Paris, October 15, 1940

Mon bien cher Jean,

    A few days ago I sent you a family card in which I said I had received a letter from Henri dated September 26. I hope you understood that I was talking about yours. If I mention Henri, you'll know I mean you. Needless to say I was extremely happy to hear from you. I think of you so much also, and I pray for you. I am glad to see that God blesses you and that your business is going well. But when you return to Lyon and you do your accounts, don't forget to pay the tithes.

Before I forget, here is the name of the tablets you used to gargle with when you came to my house and you had a sore throat: Kynosol. You buy a big tube of them, because it's more economical, and you cut each tablet in fours. Do take care of your throat, because it's your sensitive spot.

Thank you also for the package which arrived on the Sabbath. Everybody tells me I am so lucky to have such a thoughtful brother, because all the products are rationed. I now really have enough provisions, because, after all, these things won't keep until next year. What a shame I can't send some to our parents, as they probably don't have the time or the means to make provisions. We have to hope that God will take care of them and won't let them want for any necessities. The silence is very painful, but maybe someday we'll hear something from them. ...

The weather is quite nice these days. The cold is much more bearable than when it rains all the time. I hope it continues to be sunny during the day, as we can't turn on the heat until November 15, and even then it will have to be turned very low. We have received 4 tons of coal and as we still had 3, that makes about a third of what we normally consume. Let's hope we don't have too severe a winter. Anyway, if I'm cold I'll turn on the electric radiator.

Charles Gerber is going to the Free Zone and will take this letter. He will leave Marseille on the 30th of this month. If you can write me before then, put your letter in a blank unaddressed envelope, and put that envelope in another one addressed to Ch. Gerber at our Marseille office. He will bring all the mail to Paris and we will see what there is for this one and that one.

Since your birthday is a week from today, I'm taking the opportunity to send you my best wishes and my sincere congratulations. May God keep you and may he give you the health you need in order to serve Him, especially among the youth. I can't send you a gift. If Ch. Gerber had come here I would have been able to ask him to take something, but we have to send this letter to Melun. So that will be for another time.

The Steinbach family came to lunch with me on Sunday and in the afternoon we went to see the botanical garden with the little boy. They are always so nice to me, and that was a nice change. Madame Steinbach is knitting me a sweater. ...

DAILY LIFE IN OCCUPIED PARIS 71

When the Brothers return from the Havre-Rouen-Lorient circuit, they say that things are terrible there. Le Havre is bombed every night and life there is nearly impossible. It appears that the English have good aim. London and Berlin must be getting it also. Now people are beginning to get enough of the Occupation. ...

Je t'embrasse affectueusement.

Gaby

Between October 17 and November 4, Gaby writes seven of the official pre-printed family cards to Jean. As probably everyone did, Gaby uses these cards as creatively as possible. For example, in French "to pass an exam" is to be "received" (reçu), and Gaby frequently uses the printed word "reçu" to convey that she has received something, not passed an exam.

In all seven October-November cards, she tells Jean that she is in good health. Within the printed section and the two lines of writing at the bottom, she manages to transmit a good deal of other news as well. Some examples:

Gaby to Jean (cards) October 17-November 11, 1940

October 17. received packages. Thank you. Best wishes for your birthday.

October 24. I hope the floods haven't affected you. Nice weather but cold.

October 28. [2 cards on this same day] I'll be in Mantes-la-Jolie 29th and 30th. Was able to write Aunt Hermine. It's cold. I wear my coat in the office. Is it cold in the south? Life is expensive here.

When I got back from the Post Office I received your two cards.

November 5. We're turning on the electric radiators in the office.

November 8. Still no news from parents. Went to Red Cross on the 7th of this month to get news. Was able to write 25 words but it could take 3 months for an answer. Got your card of the 27th.

November 11. Received news from Henri [Jean] dated October 25. Received your card of the 1st. Sent a long letter to the parents yesterday. We have bombing alerts again. Will write to Henri and Odette in a few days.

The letters traveling between the zones in France still have to be sent secretly and are not always sure to arrive.

Gaby to Jean   November 11, 1940

Mon bien cher Jean,

I think Ch. Gerber must have returned, because this morning a big envelope arrived at the office containing several letters and one of them was for me. I was so happy to have at last a few more details than just on cards.

Up to now, I was able to write you quite regularly, but on the Sabbath Simone brought a letter that I had written you two weeks earlier. The person who had taken charge of it doesn't go to the other zone any more. ... I'm going to summarize what I said in the letter that came back: ...

It seems soon we'll get ration cards for clothes. ...

Every time I hear from you I go and look at the map so I can follow your itinerary a little.

I am so happy that your business is going well, and I hope that you will soon be rid of your debts. ... Be careful, because I know your good heart and when you see friends worse off than you, don't go giving them money. When you no longer owe anything to anyone, you can do what you like, but for the time being, that's not yet the case. I hope you won't be angry with me for saying this. ... I just received my 50 kilos of potatoes. It's very lucky because generally they get confiscated when they arrive here, but they were hidden. ... The ones we buy now are really bad; it seems they are German. (Nice of the Germans to send us their potatoes just the same.) ...

Last week I was given the address of the Geneva Red Cross on rue de Vaugirard. I was able to write 25 words to the parents, as well as to the Overtons and my English friend. But I was told that it might take three months to get an answer, since it has to go through Geneva. Maybe you'll get an answer before I do. But would you believe that yesterday I was at Mme Steinbach's who still works at the Belgian Red Cross. Someone came who has a lot of influence in the Dutch Red Cross and she asked if he would take a letter. So on the spot I wrote a long letter, being careful of what I said in it, and she took it to him today. I hope our parents will hear from us that way, and maybe it will give them a way to write to me.

On Thursday night we had an alert which lasted an hour. Yesterday evening also. This morning at 7 also. But it's odd that we didn't get an alert during the night last night when they bombed Orly, and yet they alert us when there's nothing. It's really too bad that we can't say everything in our letters now. But it seems there were student demonstrations last evening, and it is feared there will be more tonight because of November 11 [anniversary of Armistice, World War I]. I just heard some unbelievable things, but I can't write about them to you. I'll tell you when you come to visit.

I really think you are going to remain a bachelor. So maybe you don't want to marry Elisabeth—which is your business, after all—but I hope that someday you are going to find someone you like. You're not a boy who is made to live without a wife. You need someone to take care of your clothes and make you good puddings. ... I pray every day for Elisabeth's conversion, for all hope is not lost. ...

Gaby to Jean   November 14, 1940

What a joy this morning when Sister Karpelès brought me 2 envelopes from the Red Cross. I immediately opened the one addressed to me in which Papa wrote me this: "Heard about you through Jenny. Then found out that you are in the Gard [department in which Anduze is located], but where? We are very well." Then I opened the one addressed to you in which Papa writes a little more news. I am glad to know that they are a little better off financially, and that Annette is still studying at the clinic. At least this way they have fewer expenses. I will write them in a few days as the answer is prepaid. But if it takes another four months they will have certainly heard more before then.

This afternoon I went to the Dutch Chamber of Commerce, as the Red Cross had advised me to go there. They don't take any mail, but I was able to write 25 words, as I did at the Red Cross. I didn't have to pay 6 francs as I did at the Red Cross, and it will go much faster, they'll probably get it in a week or 10 days. I asked if I could write by this route every two weeks, but they said once a month at the most. But it's better than nothing, and if I get an answer by the same route I'll at least have recent news.

I talked to a man who came back from Holland three days ago. He says they have good food supplies there, better than here; oil is scarce but they get 2 and a half times as much fat as we get. But clothes are rationed there and that's more of a problem. You can only get a new dress if you show the worn out old one. So if I ever get a chance to send them a package I'll know what they need the most. Stockings are also difficult to find. I wonder if it wouldn't be a good idea to buy a slip and panties for Annette, size 46 [US 16], but no undershirt. Maybe we could get it to her one of these days. It depends on your financial state, too. I think it won't be long before we have rationing cards for clothes too. I heard that there is not enough leather even now to get 2 pairs of shoes resoled per year per person. If I had some money I would buy another pair, but it's impossible. ... I'm afraid you aren't finding much in Lyon either. But do the best you can. Things are cheaper in Jewish stores than elsewhere. Now they all have little signs that say "Jewish Enterprise." ...

    Je t'embrasse mille fois [a thousand times], Gaby

If neither Gaby nor Jean has heard anything from the parents until now, it has not been for lack of trying on Papa's part. On November 18 he wrote from The Hague to his friends the Tissots in Berne, Switzerland, that his letters to his children have not been getting through.

Papa to the Tissots   November 18, 1940

    ... Several times we have had the great joy of receiving letters from our children: 2 letters from Jean and 1 from Gaby. But these letters show that, apart from the postcard in early June, they haven't received anything from us and don't know if we are still alive. It's a shame, as we have written several times, but we aren't giving up. Sooner or later our persistence will be rewarded. Dear Brother Tissot, would you do me the kindness of sending the enclosed letter to Jean if you know his address? I don't know how to reach him, Thank you in advance. But read the letter first, and then I won't have to write it all again for you. We are happy to be back in our native land. It's almost if we had never left. I have but one regret: and that is that I didn't refuse categorically in 1910 to work anywhere else but in the "promised land." I mean this literally, as I had been promised that I would work in my own country. But there it is, it's done and there is only one thing to do and that's to make the best of it. ...

DAILY LIFE IN OCCUPIED PARIS

The Tissots do find Jean's address, and forward Papa's letter, but it won't be until a month later, December 12, that Jean and Gaby will receive it.

Papa to Jean   13 Columbusstraat, The Hague, November 18, 1940

Our dearest son Jean,

You are really good to us; this makes 3 letters we have received from you. A thousand thanks. What a joy it is to know that you are well in every way. When this is all over, sooner or later—what a wonderful dream—, Mama, Annette and myself, we are already regaling ourselves with the idea. You are so good to think of Gaby the way you do. It is a great comfort to us to know she is so well taken care of. Give her our greetings and also to all our friends. Also Elisabeth. We are so sad that your last letter of October 31 shows that you haven't yet received any of our letters. But we are not giving up. Sooner or later word will reach you. Uncle Wibbens received the letter Gaby sent him. They sent it to us immediately. It took only a few days to get from Gaby to us. What a joy.

Let's hope you receive this letter. Now I'm going to tell you a little about how things are going here. But maybe you know everything I am writing about.

All is well here. Never before have we been so well situated. My health is good and the finances are in great shape. We really don't lack for anything. God has opened the ways for us marvelously.

On May 10 nearly all my lessons stopped. But God has provided what was missing in our small revenue to live the way we like. Here's how: I printed up a little vade mecum [handbook] for changing to the new currency. Several sales people took them to sell. They went very well. Then came the problem of the ration coupons for groceries. I had a white card made with 12 bands. In each band a slide can be operated so that the numbers and letters remain visible, the number of the coupon, the merchandise, tea, sugar or whatever, and then the last day of validity. This way the grocers had the possibility of seeing at a glance what they need to know and the customers also. Here in The Hague and in the surrounding towns we sold a good many. That gave me a nice little tip. We use the profit as credit for buying provisions like a case of dates. A few days after the purchase I would have had to pay a fourth more. We have enough vegetable oil so that we could remain vegetarian four times longer than Mama was in the sanatorium in Gland. Even longer. Then my lessons began again, and as the ultimate financial and personal satisfaction, from time to time I do the corrections for some of my publications. Just yesterday I submitted the corrections for a book that is going to be re-printed. We are in very good circumstances without a single exception. Every month I preach here and in the meantime in some of the churches in the area. I have more visits to make than I can do. But the services and the visits are non-paying.

Mama is very well. She is happy to be back in her own country. She has time to read and she borrows books from everyone. Of course, like me, we realize we aren't 15 years old anymore. But we could be feeling our age much more than we do. People tell us we are getting younger.

Annette is very happy in her work at the baby clinic. It is very near home, so she comes every day to say hello and also to do tooth gymnastics [Papa's joke; he means "to eat"]. There are always some leftovers. There is also a nice young man who goes to the academy and who is kind of interested in a certain blond [Annette]. We'll see what comes of it. ... She is on vacation right now. She returned from Utrecht from a visit to the boy's family which welcomed her with open arms. She is a lucky girl. Her vacation ends tomorrow. She isn't so overweight anymore. She is normal.

... We live so well. You wouldn't believe your eyes if you saw our living conditions and the milieu we live in. Yes, God has brought us so many satisfactions after the painful times which are now finished.

We are so happy to know that Gaby is in the care of our celestial father. Let's all remain faithful to Him until the end. Love and kisses from us three and greetings to Beaujolin and all our friends, and kiss Gaby for us when you see her.

Your affectionate father

... So you're selling silk scarves now, according to Gaby. Good luck.

In the meantime and well before she learns of the above letter from Papa, Gaby writes to Jean. This letter is typed, probably in the office. Gaby's typing and French are both impeccable, as she has been trained as a stenographer in France. However, her letters written in her neat, clear handwriting are easier to read than many of her typed ones. This one with its bright blue typewriter ribbon is on thin paper which allows the type on the reverse side to show with as much strength as the print on the first side.

Gaby to Jean   November 20, 1940

Mon bien cher Jean,

... Since you're back in Lyon, you should find out if it is possible to correspond with the other zone through business affairs. I've heard that it could be done.

Bernard's Mom telephoned me yesterday to tell me that I could bring her a letter for the parents as well as a little package (about the size of a shoebox). I prepared everything and I'm going to take it to where she works in just a little while. I hope it will reach them. I put in some rice, a cake of soap, shaving soap for Papa, some thread, darning cotton, two of your balls of yarn (I hope you weren't counting too much on them for socks), Maizena and 3 pairs of stockings for Annette. I would like to have put in a little oil; but it's too hard to transport and too dangerous. And since it is so precious, I don't want it to get lost.

Gérard heard from his family who saw a young man who saw Papa and Annette at a meeting six weeks ago when he was traveling. So we have to hope that they are well. ...

Can you believe that yesterday I had the following to lunch: the Doctor, Charles Gerber, Brother Meyer and Brother Wehrli. I had invited Brother Wehrli, and I wanted to invite Brother Meyer at the same time. But he had invited Charles Gerber to lunch. He asked me if I wanted to invite him, too. I hesitated a little and then I said yes. But then the next day the Doctor telephoned Brother Meyer to tell him he absolutely had to talk to him and asked him to come to lunch with him. But Brother Meyer said he couldn't. So, to make a long story short, the Doctor came here and they all ate here together. You should have seen me in the middle of these 4 men. Fortunately everything went well. The worst part was having to do the dishes, but since we start work in the office now at 9AM because we don't have the heat on, I did them this morning before going downstairs to work.

According to the newspapers and what they're saying at the Post Office, it appears that correspondence is possible again with the countries occupied by Germany. One has to write in French, German or Italian, on business size paper, use unlined envelopes, with no riddles, pictures or crossword puzzles, nor anything else that's controversial or evocative. I found this out yesterday. I haven't had the time to write yet, but I'll do it soon. I'll see if the letter gets through. I will be very happy if it does, as it is very hard to be without contact with one's loved ones. It also has to be in very legible handwriting. So I will type it.

I don't have much hope of this letter reaching you. ...

Maurice Guichard has begun peddling, as he is out of a job. He has worked for only one day but had a lot of success. I think he will be a good colporteur. [The colporteurs sell church books and brochures.] Another Brother of the church who has just been baptized, and who lost his job because of the Sabbath, is also going to do the peddling. ...

I'll stop for today. Many kisses.
    Gaby

Gaby types another letter with heavy print-through.

Gaby to Jean   November 26, 1940

Mon bien cher Jean,

I wrote you a letter several days ago, but it seems it has not left yet, and since I received yours of the 19th I still have time to answer it.

I was so happy to get such a good long letter and to see that you are happy with your business. It's really too bad you had to cut off orders because of not being able to fill them. Let's hope that everything you bought will be delivered as quickly as possible, while the money still has some value. Everybody is saying that we have to buy while the prices are still reasonable because we could have inflation later. That's why people are buying just about everything they can find. ...

A little while ago we had a visit from Brother Girou. He says that his wife has not yet had permission to return from Anduze. She really would have done better to come at the same time as we did. I wonder what Mémé is doing in Anduze at the moment. ...

I hope that it doesn't tire Annie Beaujolin [sister to Gilbert Beaujolin] too much to have you take your meals with her, as she has a lot of work already. But for you it's nicer than the restaurant. Fortunately you haven't had to eat meat yet. Nor will I eat any unless it becomes absolutely necessary. ...

Greetings from everybody.

I'll stop for today while sending you my most affectionate thoughts.
    Gaby

Gaby to Jean December 11, 1940

... I am really worried about not hearing from you. Usually you send me cards about twice a week, and since yours of November 11, absolute silence. I wonder what has happened to you. ...

According to Ch. Gerber the clue I gave you for writing to me doesn't work anymore. It's too bad. Besides I don't think I can write you very often. It's too dangerous for those who carry the letters. Fortunately we have the cards.

The heat is on since December 1st when the temperature is below 5 degrees [C]. Above five degrees, no more heat.

I hope you will get this letter. If I don't get anything from you this evening I'll write a card to Julien.

 Affectionately,
 Gaby

Not hearing from her brother, she does write a card to Julien Beaujolin in Lyon.

Gaby to Julien Beaujolin Paris, December 11, 1940

... I hope you and all the family are in good health. For two weeks I have heard nothing from Jean. Can you tell if you have any news or if anything has happened to him? I worry all the time as before he wrote more often.

 Gabrielle Weidner

At last Gaby receives a long letter from Jean. It brings the news that the parents have been heard from, too. The letter from Papa of November 18 was sent to Jean via Mr. Tissot.

In Jean's letter the carbon paper isn't wide enough to cover everything Jean writes all the way to the right hand side of the page, but usually logic can fill in the missing words.

Unlike Gaby, Jean makes many typographical errors and a few errors in French. His lack of paragraphing and the running of many diverse topics together could be an intentional deterrent to the censors, should his letter fall into other hands. Wading into his dense unbroken single-spaced pages is no chore for Gaby who is eager to read his letters, but for a bored and unwitting censor searching illegitimate correspondence for clues to wrongdoing, his pages might well be daunting. (They may also be daunting to the reader, so the translator will offer some editorial paragraphing in Jean's letters.)

In this letter, Jean tells of Elisabeth being invited to attend a lecture by Charles Maurras, a philosopher, prolific royalist and anti-Semitic writer. In 1899 he founded Action Française, which was later condemned by the Catholic Church for involving the Church politically. Maurras supported the Vichy regime and after the war was condemned to life in prison as a collaborator.

Jean to Gaby   December 12, 1940

Ma bien chère Gaby,

... This morning I received your card of the 7th on which you wrote me that you were worried about not having heard anything from me for two weeks. I'm really surprised that I haven't sent you anything because it seems to me I sent quite a few cards, but I have so much to do that I don't remember exactly what I have sent you, but I am certain that last week I sent you 2-3 cards saying that I had received news from Papa dated November 18th. But you have probably received all this by now. Also last week, I had the great joy to receive your long letters of November 11 and 12, for which I thank you very much.

As far as I am concerned, all is well. In business I am managing despite the hard knocks of not getting deliveries. When I got back to Lyon I found out that very few of my orders had been delivered. But fortunately deliveries are still being made and everything will be delivered before long. ... You know, you hardly need traveling salesmen anymore because you sell all kinds of things and then can't deliver them. ... But I am hopeful. And one thing is certain, I have made good money and have not run up any more debt. I have paid off some small debts, sent accounting for others, bought two suits, two new pairs of shoes, 6 very beautiful shirts, socks, clothes, underwear, etc. etc. I also bought a railroad pass, and I was able to reimburse you 500 francs. Probably next week, Monday I'll send you more. I have some other good news. You remember I was waiting to receive authorization for importing the organdy and sheer material. They arrived yesterday and Porgès wrote me that the first merchandise has been sent. If this could continue like this I will be able to make a profit. One of my friends, Mr. Lemay, is supposed to go to Paris in a few days. He will bring you 500 francs for sure, as he owes me for the silk scarves that got left in the Occupied Zone. You can absolutely count on it before the end of the year. ...

I hope you got the 500 francs I sent you last week from Vichy. I had my black suit cleaned and mended and now it looks like new. So that makes 3 suits, and I'm going to buy some nice material in the next few days on Beaujolin's account, and I'll keep it until next year. Beyond that I'm doing some other things which bring in enough to live on without too many daily restrictions. Next year you can count on my sending you 500 francs each month. ... My health is perfect. Julien is doing great business. I have my meals at their house, and pay for them, of course, and I sleep at the hotel. Meals in restaurants can be very reasonable in Lyon. So everything is fine right now, though in a few months, things will be harder. I think the war will last a long time and that Europe will go through a famine. So we have to be very careful and economize the food supplies and not reach into the reserves. ...

Imagine my joy last week when I received a long letter from Papa via Brother Tissot. And it was fresh news since it was from November 18. What a joy after 6 months to receive a good letter. I'm sending it to you herewith. I copied it so that if it gets lost, I can send it to you again by a different route. You'll see that all is well with them. I really think that right now Papa and Mama are maybe living the best moments of their lives because they have managed very nicely. Since I am going to make good profits with Mr. Porgès, I will be able to send them a little money from Switzerland, and then they'll have an even easier time of it.

I have even more excellent perspectives, and I have lined up a good clientele who write me to ask about such and such a product, so I can get the commissions and that will get better and better as they get to know me. As you see, the letter you sent them [the parents] via Arthur reached them, so they have the latest news, too. You see, we were right to have confidence and that everything comes out all right in the end. I am glad that Annette is doing well. As for you, what scares me is that you might put on too much weight. With what you have put on, you must look like Annette when she was in Paris! But I am really glad that you eat well and put on weight. I really think the time in Anduze did you some good. ...

... No, I don't think Elisabeth can write to you, why do you ask that? I'll ask her to. She writes me about once a week and I write her about once a month, if that. But what can you do, it's a never ending story. She asked if she could meet with me, and maybe I'll do it just to please her. Of course if I listened to my heart, I would act differently, but reason tells me that there is no sense in continuing since there is no hope based on any reality. Everybody at the Seminary is very grateful to her for the things she did for them. Mr. Beach invited her to dinner, and to go with him the other day to hear Charles Maurras, but she certainly deserves it as she devoted herself to the Seminary which didn't do anything to earn her gratitude.

Poor Arthur Vaucher, so he lost his job, he sent me a card on which he calls Gerber a bandit. But we mustn't forget that his father Vaucher certainly did nothing to help Papa stay at the Seminary or that Madame Vaucher said to Desmet (you can talk to him about it), "That Jean Weidner seems to be marking time, not getting ahead." You see, every job has its advantages and disadvantages. I remember that Mama also used to say that she would rather I get a position instead of going into business. But someday I will succeed in a big way and all the past worries will be forgotten. Already now my situation is profitable, I'm working and earning money, and you will see that you can count on me. You have been so good to me and you have always sacrificed yourself for me, and you will see how you will be paid back handsomely, my dear Gaby. I will soon send you a package containing the pairs of stockings and also the necklace. There is also an undershirt, but that is nothing, it was a bargain. I bought it a few weeks ago, and if I bought it now I would have had to pay double for it. I'm sending you a little chocolate etc., as you did when I was in Paris. It's a Christmas present. I'm not sending you a special gift, as I prefer to send you the money. I'll send you that gift after New Year's, so that way you know you can still buy yourself a few things this year. Now, tell me frankly if you have enough to live on. You mustn't restrict yourself and you have to have enough to eat. As far as I am concerned, I'm not lacking in anything. I am very well. But on the other hand I have completely forgotten the taste of those sweet desserts, puddings, rice puddings, etc. When will we have those good times again? I think it won't happen soon. But let's keep our courage up. Here and there we can see that winter is coming. The weather is cold, skies are gray and rainy. Moreover, Lyon doesn't have the best climate in the world, and it certainly wouldn't be good for you. The climate isn't right for Julien either, as he suffers a lot from rheumatism.

According to the letter from Papa, you'll see, he has managed very well. I think he is happy because he has a lot to do, in the Church as well as the translating. Papa needs to work and to be respected for his religious work, so he is happy. Mama seems to be living a tranquil little life and reading a lot. According to what they write they must have a nice place to live. He thinks you could try to get a round trip pass to go to The Hague. He thinks the Germans could authorize one as they are both here in France and over there. See what you can do. It would make you so happy and parents too. I don't have much hope of doing that because afterwards I wouldn't be able to get back here. According to the letter Papa sent to Tissot (which Tissot sent along with Papa's letter) as you will see he still has his little obsessions about what he was promised in the past, etc. but we have to let him talk, because there is no way to make him understand it any other way. He also thinks like a Dutchman, as Beaujolin would say. I am so glad that Papa got my letters. I wrote more than 3 but at least he got those and now they know a little about what we are doing. How hard it is to be so far from those dear parents and dear Annette, but that's life and we must keep up our courage, and one day all this will be forgotten, and we will all see each other again. We can be grateful to God for taking such good care of us thus far, and we are all in good health and free of immediate financial worries. ... I am so glad Annette is doing well. She is sowing her wild oats a bit. This time it's a young man who is studying at the academy. I think she'll end up being the first of us to get married. Papa has been very ingenious with his little arrangements for ration coupons, etc., and I am happy he has made a little money with it. Beyond that he has a good bunch of stamps, and right now those are selling awfully well. Money is losing its value and everybody wants to put it into stable values. ...

From Lyon, Jean sends a typed letter to Pa, Ma and Annette. The letter is in Dutch, though he prefers to write in French. He catches his family up on his news, including much of what he has also told Gaby in his letters to her. He is quite frank about his status with Elisabeth and takes pleasure in his business successes. The following are a few excerpts from his letter.

Jean to his parents and Annette   Lyon, December 20, 1940

My dearest Pa, Ma, and Annette,

    It was a great surprise, when ten days ago I received Pa's letter that he wrote on November 18. It was the first letter we have had in six months after Pa's card in June. Mies [Gaby] got a few sentences a month ago that

Pa wrote in July, through the Red Cross in Paris. So we were anxiously waiting to hear from you about how you are doing and worried that something may have happened, like an illness or something like that. I immediately notified Mies that I had received news from you. And I was thankful to God that He has spared you. I am very glad to hear that you have no financial worries and that Pa was so ingenious to come up with those good commercial ideas. Keep this up and Jopie [Jean himself] might someday join his father's big business. I am also glad that Mama and Annette are doing well. Sometimes it must be sad for you to be so far away from us. But we have faith in God and we hope that we will see each other again. Wouldn't it be possible for Pa to try to go to Geneva so I could meet him there? Financially it could be done because right now I am dealing in organdy for my shop in France. France and Switzerland have made a trade agreement, so I can sell there again, and I make a lot of money through my shop.

Beaujolin has a good business right now, and he lets me work with him. I sell all sorts of merchandise. I even sold cutlery for three months. In the last four months I have made 20 000 francs. ...

I am so glad Pa is so much appreciated in our Work in Holland. ... I know that the Brothers did not know how to use Pa's good qualities. But I believe they are beginning to see things in a different perspective. They will think of many things for him to do with all that is going on. ...

I can picture Ma from here, with her spectacles on her nose, reading all the books she can find. Yes, I think about my family every passing minute. Here Brother Meyer [Paul Meyer, brother to Oscar] is very nice to me. He invited me to dinner several times, and it is not easy to invite people to dinner, because food is scarce. He asked me to become President of the youth group. I declined, remembering what happened in Paris. But he insisted that I was the only one with experience. Then I reluctantly accepted. ...

Brother Beach wrote me a very nice letter, and he asked what I was doing, etc. He spoke of Elisabeth as my fiancée. I'll have to reply to him that he is a little mistaken. He invited Elisabeth to a lecture by Maurras in Geneva, and asked her out for dinner, etc. She does many services for the Seminary and the Brothers in Bern. She helps them with visas, etc. Everyone thinks she is so nice to do these services for us. I wrote to her only 3 times in 6 months, and then only to ask her to do something for you. She writes me all the time and she still loves me. I also love her, but I won't be able to marry her, so it will be better to end things with her. I'll probably find someone in Holland, or maybe I'll never get married. ...

Things are not going well with Francis Monnier and Edith Bedaut. She is living with her mother in Paris and he is living in Chaux-de-Fond [Switzerland]. She does not want to go back to her husband. He has a mistress in his town, and she also has someone in Paris (Dr. Nussbaum). What a mess. ...

Girou has returned from Spain, and is back in Paris. He will find work in Paris. His wife and son stayed in Anduze but will join him soon. However, when Mémé gets back to Paris, it won't be a good thing for the youth group. ...

I am writing this on Beaujolin's typewriter. Does Pa still have his? His last letter was handwritten, so I was wondering if Pa had perhaps sold it. I will give him my own as soon as I can. But perhaps Pa wrote it by hand so that it looks more personal. ...

Dear Pa, Ma and Annette, keep your spirits up. I pray for you every morning and night. Au revoir, kisses from your Joop who is very happy with your letter. Jesus will be coming to get us soon.

    Joop

Near the year's end, Gaby squeezes the following news to Jean on a pre-printed postcard:

Gaby to Jean   Paris, December 27, 1940

I am still in good health. My cold is over. Madame Bruchez died of cerebral congestion. From the trio I received a handbag for Christmas. Your much delayed cards are arriving little by little. I suppose you are in Collonges. I hope that Henri [Jean] has heard from me as I have written x times. Love and kisses, Gaby

5   The Hague Rejoins the Conversation

The correspondence cards continue to travel between Gabrielle and Jean. As before, the ones from Jean are not in his files because he can't make carbon copies of them. In hers, Gabrielle writes of "Henri" and "Mies" in the third person. These are the names for Jean and herself which she uses on the government authorized correspondence cards rather than her letters, which are sent via clandestine carriers and complicated routes. On the cards Gaby also addresses Jean directly as "you."

Gaby to Jean (card)   Paris, January 2, 1941

Hope you are in good health. The cards arrive little by little. Thank you so much for the package which brought me so much pleasure. I got the money order today. Thank you. Gaby

Gaby to Jean (card)   Paris, January 5, 1941

… Got your card of the 26th and Henri's of the 26th. … Happy to know all is well. I had a nice holiday. Still cold. Gaby

Gaby to Jean (card)   Paris, January 24, 1941

Ask Henri if he received my letters of the 10th and 19th of this month. Gaby

Gaby to Jean (card)   Paris, January 29, 1941

… Mies hasn't received your letter. … Wrote to parents on the 27th. Gaby

Gaby starts a letter on February 2nd, but as it often happens, it does not get sent on its way immediately. She continues the same letter on February 18th, on the 26th and on the 28th.

At last the parents and Annette in The Hague have been heard from. There has been no news of them since June, 1940, when the family separated and fled Paris, the parents and Annette to The Netherlands, and Gaby and Jean to Anduze and Lyon.

Gaby to Jean   February 2, 1941

Mon bien cher Jean,

    Last Monday I was able to write to our parents via the gentleman [Mr. Laatsmann] who goes there regularly. I gave him their address, so I hope to receive a letter from them soon when this person gets back. But then I received a letter from Mama written on December 28 through someone who had gone there. Everything is fine with them. I also had received a letter from the Red Cross, sent in November, telling me that the parents had received my letter. Now I'm very relieved about them. I tried to write them via the Post Office, but the letter came back with the message "postal relations suspended." Yet we were certainly told we could correspond with occupied countries. Letters from Belgium only take a week and I don't understand why we can't correspond with Holland also. I'm going to go to the post Office for more information. …

    Your package came and I was very happy because we just can't get green vegetables. It's better the last few days, because it's not as cold, but there still isn't a lot of choice and everything is so expensive. It's terrible how the cost of living has increased. I wanted to buy some handkerchiefs, but they're almost impossible to find. I found some for 6 francs 50 apiece, little tiny printed handkerchiefs which would have cost half that much last year. But we have to stock up because when we get ration cards, we won't be able to buy anything. Mr. Palanges was here last week and he said that in Belgium you can't buy anything, not even handkerchiefs, without a ration card, except neckties and hats. Maybe it will be like that here. But I have everything I need, especially if you can send me a little of the fabric

I asked you for earlier. ... [Gaby signs her name by hand but she has already typed: "G. Weidner," which she explains: "Forgive me, I thought I had written a letter from the office."]

On her correspondence card of February 25, Gaby puts to good use the lines surrounding the card's printed choices concerning health:

<u>In a few days I will be</u> in good health <u>as I am better</u>
<u>I was only</u> slightly ill ["gravely" and "wounded" are crossed out]

In the two lines at the bottom of this card she writes: "According to O. M. [Oscar Meyer], it seems you want to leave the field of business and that you are taking steps to go into something else. That would be really too bad. Gaby."

The letter Gaby began on February 2nd has not yet been sent on its way. She continued it on February 18 and on the 26th and on the 28th she adds to the same letter.

February 26

... On Sunday I wasn't very well. I spent a bad night and since I had a temperature on Monday, I stayed in bed. Yesterday I was much better and today I'm up and about again. I came down to the office for just a few minutes to send some orders and at the same time to add a few lines for you. Tomorrow I think I'll go back to work, maybe not in the morning but perhaps in the afternoon. I think I just had a little flu, but it wasn't much of anything, as I am fine now.

Yesterday I received your card of the 20th, and I wonder if your letter to me will eventually get sent. I don't want to count on it too much, so I won't be too disappointed if it doesn't arrive. I think these few days of rest have been good for my nerves. I've been sleeping well for several nights and I'm much more relaxed. Last Friday I went to the doctor again, and he didn't think my nerves were in very good shape. He asked me if I was worried about anything, and I told him I was really homesick for the family, and he told me that normally he would prescribe two weeks with the family immediately, but since we can't even think about doing that at his point, I would have to resign myself to it. He gave me something to perk me up. Fortunately on the Sabbath I received a long letter from the parents via the gentleman who took my letter. As you can imagine I was very happy to get so many details. I will send it with this letter, and it will certainly interest you. I am so happy that they have everything they need. I answered the letter and I think that the gentleman will go back in a few days. I will probably get another answer in a few weeks. It certainly helped to cheer me up and if I can hear from the parents regularly, I'll be less depressed.

... Now on to something else. On the two cards I sent you yesterday, I told you I was worried because Paul Meyer wrote his brother (a letter dated the 14th of this month) that the new ration cards were giving you a lot of trouble in your business, and that you were taking steps to get into the Dutch sanitary works. That really surprised me because Mr. Lemay, who talked to me later about this letter, didn't say a word about that. Or maybe you didn't want me to know? I think would be really too bad if you couldn't continue in business as I really think you are very qualified for it. Is it really impossible? ... When Brother Meyer told me that, I felt very sorry. I said to myself: Here Jean has more roadblocks just when everything was going so well. But then I thought that, after all, that letter was written the day after rationing was established and that it was nearly impossible for it to have affected you so soon. And maybe that was just an idea you spoke of. ...

If you are still dealing in hairnets, maybe you could send me a blue one; the holes are too big in the one I have. ...

If François had lived he would be 25 years old today. The years go by so fast. He was 16 and 1/2 when he died. Instead of sending the money to the parents who don't particularly need it, I wonder if you shouldn't write to someone in Gland to have the letters on his tombstone re-gilded. I remember that needed to be done when we went to the grave the year of the Youth Congress. That's just a suggestion, but maybe you can't do that either if business is so bad. ...

February 28

The postman came and since he didn't bring me a letter, I wonder if yours is lost this time, because it had time to arrive (if it left the day you told me on your card of the 20th). I'm beginning to think that it is not worth sending me letters as they never arrive. But write me postcards often because since your letter of December 27 I haven't heard very much from you.

I'll leave you now, sending my most affectionate thoughts. Gaby

THE HAGUE REJOINS THE CONVERSATION

It took the whole month of February to send the above letter on its way to Jean. Finding ways to send letters is a never-ending problem. In her letter of March 6, Gaby complains to Jean that a certain truck driver is charging too much for transporting the clandestine letters: one or two francs per letter. "It's too expensive," she says, "and you must not be the one that sends everybody's letters and then ends up paying for them all." And besides, she adds, "it could be dangerous if everybody sends mail to you, because if it ever gets opened, you could be in trouble."

Gaby appreciates the addresses Jean had given her of people who might carry mail, but for the moment she doesn't need them, because there is a "Sister" in Nevers who takes letters quite regularly. "If we don't write very often, it's because we don't want to abuse the privilege, as she does it for free and we don't want her to get into trouble… and we have another address which we almost never use, I don't know just why, but there must be some reason."

Gaby likes the fact that they are numbering their letters so that they will know if something has been lost. "We have received only Numbers 2-3-4. Number One must be lost."

In the same letter Gaby comments on the motivation of the people at the Collonges Seminary who seem to be nicer to Jean now that he is making money: "It's true that money does a lot of things. But after all, it's human nature to respect those who know how to get along in life."

Gaby also worries about a plan Jean may have had to visit England. Her code for a trip to England is "visiting Overton." It will be remembered that Mr. Overton was one of Gaby's possible suitors before the war, about whom Jean enjoyed teasing her (in his letter of January 31, 1936). Mr. Overton had returned to England with his mother.

Gaby to Jean   March 6, 1941

… I would really worry if you went to meet Overton, not from the financial angle, but because of the danger that would represent for you. We would worry about you all the time. And then when you came back—if you came back—you wouldn't have anything in hand and would have to begin all over again to set up a business. But, as you say, it will be a while before you are on your way, but anyway, give it a lot of thought. I wonder if it is really worthwhile right now.

Gaby has news of Mémé Girou.

Gaby to Jean March 7, 1941

... It seems Mémé wrote to the Koukoutches that he wasn't about to come back. The only way they can come back is in the car, and the car has the flu from the snow and the cold. Poor Brother Girou is all alone in Marolles. It's funny because when his wife was there he wasn't and now that he's there she isn't. You told me that Mémé is worse than before. ... Here, when anybody mentions Mémé, Lisette always says that he's not mean. She seems to be saying that she wouldn't mind if he came back. True, he isn't a mean boy, but with others he's unbearable. But if he came I wonder if Lisette would still talk that way. ...

In the month of March Gaby writes fifteen postcards to Jean, sometimes two on the same day. She wrote on March 4, 5, 6, 7, 8, 11, 12, 14, twice on the 20th, twice on the 23rd, and on the 26th, 27th and 28th.

Gaby's card of March 12 reminds Jean that "today is Annette's birthday (20 years old!)."

In Jean's letter of March 12, he expresses himself on the role of women and also notes that some people have crossed the Demarcation Line with few problems.

In February and March, the Italian forces (Jean calls them "macaronis") are losing their African territories to the British.

Jean to Gaby March 21, 1941

... It's nice that everybody helps you from time to time in all sorts of ways. I'm glad that you have gained weight, as it is a sign that you needed to. I'd love to see how you look now. ...

Yes, the ration cards are working and much faster. ...

Give my greetings to Oscar Meyer. If I were him I would have already crossed the line and made a little trip in this direction. A lot of people come and get through. When Lemay goes to Paris I will tell you what route he takes. If you use the addresses I gave you it can be done. If I had more affection for those dear Occupiers, I would have made the trip several times already. ...

In St. Julien and Annecy, the store windows are full of eggs, but here in Lyon there aren't very many. Merchandise cannot travel from one department to another.

More and more bad things are being said about Mémé Girou. Sauvagnat was telling me about it the other day. I think Mémé is much more dangerous than many others, because he works underhandedly and many don't see the danger right away. When you have to do with a bandit, you know it and you watch out, but with a Mémé one never knows what harmful effect his behavior can have on others. As for Lisette always defending him, if St. Paul had to deal with girls or women like her, I can understand that he said women should be silent in the church and I also understand why in our Work we don't give directors' jobs to women. Men have better judgment than women. There I go again with my little obsession. But just between us, I am very glad I have a sister like you who have always helped and encouraged me. ...

As for our parents and Annette, I don't think we have to worry, as I think they are now safe from problems. Papa probably remembers his experience during the last war and took precautions. And their material existence is just about assured, and Papa can use his time as he wants. ...

Here everybody is very hopeful, and they sing, "Ah, how wonderful macaronis are when cooked," but we don't see them very often, due to the increasing rarity of the merchandise.

My dear Gaby, I'll leave you now. I have a lot of work as usual, and I have chatted with you for a long time. I think of you day and night and I hope you will continue to be well. ...

Please give my best to all my friends, those at 130 and the members of the church. I kiss you affectionately and remain your brother who doesn't forget for a minute all you have done for him.

Your [Jean's signature does not appear on the carbon copies. He adds a note about Annette at the bottom of the page.]

Annette is some little number. She could write a book on her love life. But I am very happy that all is well for her.

On April 24, Papa writes a one-page letter to Gaby in Dutch from The Hague. When Papa speaks in this letter of acquiring supplies he writes of his own family as if it were another family, so the 20-year-old daughter is Annette, and Papa is trying to hide his stores of supplies from the censors. Papa refers to Jean as both "Joop" and "Jopie."

The letter reveals, too, that it is Mr. Laatsman who has been carrying letters between the parents in The Hague and Gaby in Paris. Mr. Laatsman is Dutch Consul in Paris at this time, but later he becomes involved in Jean's rescue work.

Papa to Gaby April 24, 1941

Ma bien chère Gaby [Papa's salutation is in French],

Yes, that was a surprise to receive such a long letter from you! Isn't it nice that there are still good people around who see to it that parents and daughter are still in touch with each other.

My congratulations that you have enough sense to buy whatever is still available, especially when it concerns food. Keep doing that, dear child, because once you have it, you have it. I know of someone who had accumulated quite a few provisions and it seems that he is always looking to buy more, because these people have a daughter, about 20 years old, so she needs to be fed well. I think they are absolutely right. It seems that when they recently counted the cans of condensed milk, they found 30 of them. If I had the money, I would do the same.

Mama and I talked about your letter for a long time. It is so nice to know that you are being cared for and that you have a brother who sends you money; naturally that is worth having in these hard times. Looking at it that way, Joop and I are even now, and he'll like that better. But just accept everything, dear child, because if you do so, it will please Joop the most. He is indeed an exemplary brother. Wouldn't you like to have 20 more of them? ... We felt so much better hearing all the good news about you and that you sleep much better nowadays. I also sleep soundly, even when the sirens go off, I just turn over and snore and snore.

We are looking forward to the day when you can come. But we are not going to be impatient, because most likely quite a few bullets will be fired before someone might say, "OK, I lost." You know that Jopie did not always say that very quickly in the past, and sometimes I had to cut him off. Do you still remember that?

Though I regret that I can't be there with you, it feels good to be back in my own country. An "Ollander" is always strongly attracted to his country. I feel at home here.

It was nice to meet Mr. Laatsman! And it was very kind of him to do that. If by any chance you see him again, give him my regards, even though he does not know me. Tell him that the saying "unknown, unloved" does not apply in this case, and that at some time I hope to thank him personally for his kindness. Sometime you should visit the Zendingskerk [mission church] in Ghent so you can see the portrait of your grandfather in the consistory room. That's where the portraits of all the previous pastors are hung.

I am glad to be able to give many lessons here. It is quite a mixture: Greek, French, Dutch and English, and today I am teaching a lesson in German to someone who is taking two lessons in succession. The first one is Dutch, and then a little later a lesson in French, and then the other two. So I'll be making 3 guilders today. Tonight I'll be doing some translating, so I am earning a little doing this as well. As you see, dear child, things are a little better than before. Recently I have been making visits to a family who is showing great interest. They almost do not know how to thank me. They are upper-class and employ a maid-servant. We'll see what the outcome will be!

The spirit among the [Adventist] Workers here is high. We all love each other and work together under God. In these times, one feels more than ever how insignificant our earthly expectations are and how splendid it is if one loves Jesus and prepares for a better world.

Well, dear Mies, you know you are always in our thoughts. Many kisses.

Your one and only, Papa

Gaby to Jean (on the same day Papa writes to her) April 24, 1941

... Our rooms are being done over. Mine will be done sometime next week. ... Marthe's is already finished. ... I would like to redo the furnishing of my room, which really needs it: the bedspread, the closet curtain (which Mama and I were already wanting to change when we were at Rue Thomire) and the covering for the screen which Brother Stauber is making for me. I would just love to have some upholstery material something like the sample herewith. The wall paper in my room is light green (sample herewith) and if you found something in rosewood or dark green or beige, it would go with it. I have some rose because the lamp in my room is pale pink. And we can't be too particular right now, so just do your best. Ask Annie Beaujolin if you're unsure, as she has taste and can advise you. It would really please me so much, because if I don't have that, my room won't be so pretty and as the others have beautiful rooms, I would like to fix up mine. I have asked Mr. Gaston Thomas, and Mr. Gadonnet, but they can't get anything for me, so you're the only one I can count on. So I would need 8 meters of upholstery material. I wonder if it's expensive. If you could find me something for around 30 francs a meter, you could get me 3 meters more, as I could make lined drapes. But if it's a lot more expensive, and I'm afraid it will be, then don't send any more than the 8 meters, as the lined curtains are not indispensable. You would be doing me a huge favor, especially if you can do it as soon as possible. Mon cher Jean, you're going to think I never stop pestering you, I ask for one thing after another, and I'm always making you spend money. But I hope after this I can leave you in peace. As for the money, since you won't have to send me any after that, maybe you can manage to do this. Anyway, I thank you so much, even if you can't send me anything. ...

Yesterday I talked to Brother Meyer about you. ... He asked about Elisabeth, and I told him what you had told me. He said, "Of course Jean could say to her 'since you are ready, you're going to leave your job now, and we are going to get married, and you can get baptized." But I told him that was just what you didn't want to do, and you wanted Elisabeth to make the decision herself, and that you didn't push her, but tried to influence her. So he said to me, "Of course with Jean's principles, that's understandable," so I think he approves. I do so wish that Elisabeth would take the decisive step, whatever it costs her in her job and in scenes with her mother, and that you could be happy together, because even if she doesn't have every quality, she gets along well with you, and as she is very docile, you could shape her. I pray for her every day so that she will give herself to God, and also for you so that God may guide you and give you wisdom for her and for the youth group in Lyon.

Pardon me for all my errors, but I am writing very fast. This isn't a typing test, and with you I don't have to worry. I have so little time.

At the beginning of this week, I heard that postal relations are on again with Holland. So I can write to the parents again, under the same conditions as with Belgium. But I suppose one can also write in Dutch. I'll write one of these days. I don't feel there's any hurry since they heard from us through André's father and I sent another letter a week later by someone else.

I feel better the last ten days or so. I'm terribly tired, I don't have a temperature, but I haven't much energy, and my appetite isn't very good. ... For a couple of days I have been drinking that absinthe tea, you know the one that is so bitter, maybe that will help. It's probably spring, so many people feel tired at this time. ...

THE HAGUE REJOINS THE CONVERSATION

Food is getting really expensive. ... The thing that is really going to be terrible is the scarcity of bread. Now we see people that are really hungry.

... I was so happy to read Papa's letter but there are still several things that I don't understand very well. Someday soon when I have the time, I'm going to re-read it carefully to try to understand everything. If it were in French, I would understand it much more easily. ...

Yes, it must seem to you like a big change from when you were in Paris and you were completely broke and you had to ask me for 10 francs a day, and in the evening I asked you what you used it for (because I thought you were buying too many newspapers)! But I am so happy for you, especially since you have always been so generous to others that you deserve a little more ease of circumstances now. ...

Is it because you are a foreigner that you can't be a businessman by yourself? I seem to remember that at the beginning of the war there were regulations like that. It's a shame. But you can't really complain. ...

I'm going to stop. I wish this letter could go as soon as possible, but Marilou is the only one who can take it, and at a very inconvenient time. ... So, mon cher Jean, I'll leave you for today... Greetings from everyone here, particularly Brother Meyer and Brother Wehrli who want to thank you for all the trouble you take with the mail, and many affectionate kisses from your sister.

Gaby

P.S. Should I take steps with the Chamber of Commerce to send you your typewriter?

Gaby writes Jean, another "journal-letter" written over a period of nine days. The letter includes a re-typing of parts of a letter from Annette in The Hague.

In her part of the nine-day letter, Gaby reports that one cannot send more than two sheets of paper at a time in letters to The Netherlands. For this reason she wrote two letters to Annette, trying to encourage her younger sister, who is depressed and "homesick" for France.

Gaby to Jean May 6-May 15, 1941

... I told her that right now it is better to be in one's own country. More and more bad things are said about foreigners, and if she can make a living in Holland, it would be better for her. I can partly understand her.

She loved France so much. If she could have come to spend a few weeks here last summer, or for the holidays at the end of the year, it might have helped her be less sad. I hope she can get some rest, too, as I think it may be due to her physical health. ...

Gaby hopes to be able to send a package to the family in The Hague, but only used clothing may be sent. So before putting it in the box for Annette, Gaby wears the pullover "for a few days, just enough so that it doesn't look entirely new."

[May 7]

... I want to continue my letter to thank you for the package that I received this morning. What a surprise, because I didn't expect it at all. Dear Jean you spoil me so much. I assure you I don't know how to thank you. I don't think there is a brother in all the world who spoils his sister the way you do. Thank you especially for the magnificent scarf. Everyone thinks it's really splendid. I guess it's natural silk. Thank you so much also for the slip. I was so happy with it, first because it is very pretty and secondly because I had just sent one to Annette. ... Thanks for the chocolate, too and the candied fruits. Everything is so wonderful that I am the envy of everybody around me. Sometimes I let people taste the things I receive, but not always, because if I give some to everybody, there won't be anything left. Today I didn't give any away because the truffles were so delicious that I thought it was too bad to give them to anyone else. ... And thank you so much for the oranges. Here they are absolutely unobtainable, and I haven't eaten any fruit for a long time, except for dates. ...

Gaby has just heard that one of the people who "takes letters through for us has been caught," and hopes that neither she nor Jean will get into trouble because of it.

And a lady has called her on the telephone to ask her to make a phone call to Lyon for her. This worries Gaby.

[Thursday, May 15]

... I would be surprised if we can telephone to the Free Zone. I'm going to find out if it's true. She was very nice on the phone, and told me she would like to get to know me. Maybe I'll go on Saturday afternoon, because she lives right near the Buttes Chaumont [a park in Paris's 19th arrondissement which has a varied landscape including ponds, waterfalls, cliffs, caves and a belvedere]. I would take a walk in the park afterward. And I could also tell her to be more careful on the phone, as she told me she received letters every day from Lyon, and asked me if I received any or wrote any, and it's very risky, as all conversations are monitored. So I talked about the family cards to change the subject. ...

I wonder where I'll go for vacation this year; it is time to begin thinking about it. I'll go to the Consulate to find out if there is really any hope of getting a visa to go to Holland, but I doubt it. If I could go to the Free Zone, I'd go to Collonges, but it is impossible. I have invitations from various people...but it bothers me to spend two weeks with people I don't know well enough to share life with them in their homes. Well, maybe between now and July, something will get settled. ...

Now see Annette's letter,

Annette's letter: I have been on vacation in Enschede for two weeks and yesterday I received a letter from Mama enclosing your two letters dated January 20 and February 23. I was so happy. It has been so long since I have heard anything from you. Yes, sometimes I am so sad and I would so love to see you. And the minute the war is over, I'll go back to Paris immediately. I just can't get used to Holland. I still feel like a foreigner. On the outside, I give the impression I have adapted, and I don't talk to the parents about it as I don't want to worry them, but I assure you that inside I am so homesick for France that sometimes I can't even be cheerful. I have a very different nature from the Dutch anyway, and I don't think you would recognize me. I have changed a lot. But I don't want to complain, I just want to tell you the truth. I had a very bad time at the clinic. The supervisor couldn't stand me; I think she was jealous. Every time I made a mistake in Dutch I got a scolding. And I think the other reason she couldn't stand me is that I am Adventist. What's more, her nerves are shot, and she should go to a clinic and get some treatment rather than being a supervisor and making life so hard for the students that they get sick. There were 3 students she liked and 3 she detested. Two of the latter couldn't take it and left. The third is moi. I stayed, but she made my life so miserable that my character completely changed. I never laughed anymore; I became all closed in, and I never said a word at the table, and I lost 10 kilos in 11 months. But last month I looked so bad that everybody said to Mama, "What's the matter with your daughter? She looks so awful it's frightening." I wasn't eating anything and I threw up every morning. I wasn't sleeping hardly at all and I cried all the time. At the end of March the doctor prescribed two weeks of obligatory rest, and that is why I'm on vacation at Enschede. On top of everything else, I have water on the knee, so I can hardly walk. It's really too bad, because otherwise I could have done some bicycling and walking in the area. And I love walking now that I am not so fat anymore. But in 3 weeks I gained more than 2 kilos. I weighed 59 kilos and now 61.5. I look better that way. I have round cheeks and better color. I got over it very quickly and I am my old self again. But I won't go back to the clinic. This summer I am going to study Dutch so I can write it without mistakes and go to the beach a lot. The sun will do me a lot of good and in September, if my medical exam is satisfactory I will be accepted in a maternity hospital. After a year and a half I'll have a diploma. It doesn't cost anything; I'll live at home but I won't earn anything. But I'll have my diploma, and it's a good job, because we are sent anywhere in Holland for six weeks in a family to take care of a mother and baby. There are several categories, and the least one can earn is 4 Florins a day. In the higher categories, it can be 10 Florins. It depends on where one is placed. In the working-class families, there is a lot to do and there is almost never a maid.

You'll probably laugh at me when I tell you that it's all over with Lenn. But there are several reasons for it. First, I don't think I love him enough to spend my whole life in Holland without pining for France. To do that I think one would have to love one's husband so much that one is happy to sacrifice everything, and I don't think that is the case with me. I thought a lot about it before making this decision, but I think it is better for both of us. He wouldn't be happy, and I wouldn't either, and you know, marriage is for life. Secondly, he isn't baptized yet. I've known him for more than a year and his mother always told me, 'Yes, he wants to be baptized. He knows all our principles.' But I don't see any progress in him, and I'm afraid it will never happen. Of course he doesn't drink, he's a vegetarian, and doesn't smoke, and comes to church every Sabbath, but I don't think he really understands the New Testament. He is willing to become an Adventist, but doesn't understand that one must be baptized. And only his mother is Adventist; his father doesn't believe in anything, while he leaves his wife free to do as she wants. I'm afraid he will have the same indifference and that inside he has never had what we would call a conversion.

THE HAGUE REJOINS THE CONVERSATION 101

And it's no small thing if later I couldn't talk to him about these things, and despite all my efforts, I can't get him to say anything about any service afterwards. My parents leave me free to decide for myself, but I think Papa is glad it is over, because he was worried that Lenn wasn't making spiritual progress, even though Papa was willing to give him Bible lessons. Lenn wanted us to get engaged in a few months, but I didn't want to before he was baptized and I didn't want him to do it just for me.

It was a difficult time (it has been a month since it was over). For my birthday it was still fine, and the whole family came to our house and spoiled me a lot: an umbrella from Lenn, a magnificent bouquet of lilacs and tulips from his father, a silver napkin ring with my initials from his mother and from Mama and Papa a little wicker chair that you can open to put things inside it. But now I'm glad it's over, because I see myself as too homesick for France, and I realize more and more that I will never be happy here. Just try to imagine never being able to hear French spoken—Lenn didn't know a word of French—and bringing up one's children in Dutch. Oh, no, you can be sure that the minute I can I'll return to Paris. I'll be so happy. ...

[Since Gaby has re-typed Annette's letter, there is no signature.]

The Government-issued post cards changed their format in mid-May. The new pink or beige cards, with instructions at the top and seven ruled lines below, gave the writer a good deal more freedom of expression. However, the instructions darkly threaten awful consequences if the writer does not follow them precisely:

ATTENTION

Card exclusively reserved for family correspondence

The sender is permitted to write below seven lines of correspondence of a family nature; but it is strictly forbidden to write between the lines, or to include news that is not of this type. It is necessary to write very legibly to facilitate monitoring by the German authorities.

Any card irregular in its form or content will not be sent; its purchase price will not be refunded.

Gaby makes use of these new cards right away, on May 17th and May 19th. Here is what she writes on hers to Jean on the 19th:

Gaby to Jean (new 7-line card)   May 19, 1941

Mies [Gaby] is very happy that she just got yours of the 16th of this month. She wrote to you Friday but will write you again tomorrow as today she is very busy. I think of you so much and particularly of Elisabeth. I pray for her to have the necessary courage. I would like so much for you to be happy. You really deserve it as you are so good to me. I understand that it is hard for her, especially because of her mother, if she risks losing her job.
    Signature:
        Gaby

On the same day Gaby writes a long letter to Jean. A few excerpts follow:

Gaby to Jean   May 19, 1941

Mon bien cher Jean,
    ... Friday afternoon, I went to the Consulate. The Consul was very nice and anytime I want to send a note to the parents, I can. But since we can now write directly, it's not necessary. He told me that he didn't think I could get a round trip visa. For one way, yes, but I couldn't come back. Only people with diplomatic and commercial reasons can get them. The last time the vice-consul asked for a visa, he was refused. But I'm going to try anyway, since you advise me to do so, but it's true that I don't have much hope of getting one. It might be easier to get a visa to go to the Free Zone, to do a cure at Vichy or elsewhere. But I'll see. The Consul told me that in Holland they were better off than we are for food. At least they are better off than in Belgium, which is considered to be still at war, maybe because of the attitude of the king, I don't know. As for Holland, in a way they have annexed it and appointed a Stadhouder.* It's almost as if it were a part of Germany. I asked if Dutch money was still being used; he said yes, because when people get marks they go to the bank immediately to

---

* According to Maarten Eliasar, a *Stadhouder* was a kind of steward. He writes: "the Netherlands was placed under civil rule (unlike Belgium and France that were placed under military rule). We had a Reichskommisar" appointed by Hitler representing the German civil regime. The Netherlands were annexed indeed. The Germans expected not much resistance and placed it under civil rule because they saw the Dutch as "Brudervolk" or fellow German people.

change them. I also asked a few questions of the gentleman who took my letter to the parents, and he told me that they don't have the right to listen to British radio, but that many do. Here it seems we can listen to it just in the family, but we can't have guests. Anyway, people don't hesitate to say what they have heard on it. Milk is also rationed, and they get one fourth of a liter a day. He told me that despite the events, people hope for liberation. ...

Tonight I have to leave the office early because I'm going to the opera with René. It begins at 7:45. "Le Roi d'Ys" is playing.* You are probably thinking that I go out with him a lot. But you know, there is nothing between us, at least nothing serious, maybe a little flirting now and then, but it doesn't mean anything on either side, and he isn't at all the right boy for me, and he doesn't want to get married. But for going out, it's very convenient, as he likes me and since he lives near here, he can always walk me home, which is safer in the evening. I never get to go out with the threesome, so I'm happy to have him to go out with sometimes. ...

Typewriter ribbons are scarce but we have a few in reserve in the office. For the bookstore I have about a dozen of them, so that should last a little while yet. ...

You say I should buy myself a radio. You couldn't have mentioned it at a better time, as I've been thinking about it for a long time. I've looked for one, but they are really expensive. You have to spend around 1600 francs for a little one. They have gone up a lot in price, and I think it's a shame to put so much into a device, especially since we don't know what is going to happen in the next few months. I have to think about it. ...

Yes, the package I received from the Consulate, was a gift from Holland to its citizens abroad. I asked the Consul if it was a gift from the Queen, and he smiled but didn't answer. On Friday he told me that the next packages hadn't arrived, otherwise I would have already received mine. The packages came from Holland and contained Dutch products.

I told people here what you said about Collonges. Someone asked me if you had said that Collonges was a real chicken coop. ... You know, Jeanne Revert does whatever she likes with unmarried men, but that doesn't bother me, as I think when one is free, it doesn't matter very much. We have to get a little fun out of life. But for me a married man is sacred,

---

* *Le Roi d'Ys* ("The King of Y's") was an 1888 opera by composer Edouard Lalo, libretto by Edouard Blau.

and I would never want to mess with one, and you can be sure that if I get married I will behave. But when one isn't married, I think one can have a little fun, that is, if one is careful, of course. ...

I am glad you can't go and see Arthur Raitt, as I am not crazy about your going in that direction, and I'll tell you frankly that I hope your attempts to do so are not going to work out. If it were to go to see the parents, that would be different. [Arthur Raitt is English and is the source of the Weidner family's code using the name "Arthur" for England when discussing the war in their later letters.]

It is getting warmer. On the Sabbath I was at last able to wear my summer coat. It's about time. Last year it was warmer by this time. ...

I'll leave you with many kisses. Greetings from everyone. Marilou never stops talking about your helpfulness, and says that you have a reputation for this in Collonges.

Your sister who loves you and would love to see you,
Gaby

Jean's letter to Gaby speaks of his refusal to do business with the German Occupiers. His name for the Germans is "Fischer," a code probably limited to the Weidner family as is "Arthur" for England, "Arthur's uncle" for the United States and "Charlotte" for Belgium.

Jean to Gaby   May 29, 1941

Ma bien chère Gaby,

I won't be able to write you much this time as I am very busy and must leave tonight for Annecy, and I will arrive in Collonges tomorrow morning, where I'm going to spend a few days, particularly for the ceremonies for the end of the school year. You'll probably tell me that I'm always in a hurry, and it's true that hasn't changed, but for the first time in my life, money is coming in, and I have to take advantage of the times when business is good. This month has been the best yet. You know that I sell a little of everything, silks, knives, socks, cleaning materials, everything I can find to sell. The things that are scarce are stockings and wool fabrics...

About our correspondence: first, from your cards, I know that <u>all</u> the letters have reached their destination. ... Let's thank God that they have all arrived. It's really miraculous that <u>none</u> have been lost. ...

So I'm leaving tonight for Collonges. I'll see Elisa on the Sabbath in the afternoon and the next day, and the party is Sunday. Sunday night this week I went to St. Amand-Montroud where I arrived on Monday morning after spending the night on the train. I left there on Monday night and arrived here Tuesday morning. I made a huge sale of cotton thread (300 kilos) to a shoe factory. ...

Last week I sent you a package containing some yardage for a skirt and a coat for you, and I paid about 200 francs a meter. Soon I'm going to send you a lot of white rayon fabric, in little lengths of 2 to 4 meters, for dresses and blouses. I'll have 4 meters of cotton to make you a work smock. But don't sell any of that because the price has gone up terribly. Here the merchandise is getting more and more rare and the prices are higher. I am receiving the Swiss organdy, and though it takes a lot of effort, it brings in a lot. I'm keeping my commissions in Swiss money because it is worth so much more, and as I don't particularly need it, I leave it over there, and if Papa comes or ever needs money, he can use it. I must have about 300 Swiss francs. So you see if you need money for a special expense, you can ask me without hesitation. All my debts at the Seminary and in Marseille are paid, so you see, you won't have to blush with shame about your brother. ...

I absolutely refuse to do business with Fischer and Co. I miss a lot of deals that way, but it is an absolute principle. I could also make a lot of money by going into your area and to that of our parents, but it is against my principles. As you can see, I am putting my convictions into practice. It costs me, but everyone should do what he can in this domain to hasten the failure of the house of Fischer, which has done us so much harm.

I spent a Sabbath afternoon with Paul M. [Meyer] at the church in Roanne. They have a new hall which is absolutely magnificent, very nicely arranged, with much taste, on the ground floor, very light, with the entrance in the middle. This church is really pretty, but it is the members who are especially admirable. There is a good atmosphere, and an intense spiritual life, it really does one good to see such active Christians with such zeal, and I can certainly understand why Paul likes it when he goes there. It's a change from the coldness of the Lyon people. Here the church is fine. ... The youth is doing well, except for Alexis Dejean...who is a little crazy, and who recently left for 48 hours and nobody knows where he went. He spent the night outside, and he had spent about 200 francs of the youth group's treasury. He was the secretary-treasurer of the youth group. ...

You told me to keep the chocolate and things like that for myself but you know, it's impossible for me. As soon as I have chocolate etc. in my room, I can't do anything else before eating it, and that's too bad. I prefer that it be in your room. ...

I love your long letters full of details. ... I am so glad you do not want for much and that you are so brave. For me too, it seems a long time since I have seen you, but I try not to think about it and plunge into my work from morning to night and the time passes quickly. And also I'm reassured about the parents and Annette, and that calms me. It is such a joy to know that the mail from Holland comes so rapidly and that you can write to them. I assure you, that lifts a great weight off my shoulders, because when the mail works, everything works, or almost. Poor Annette, I think she was depressed for a while because of her love story. But she must be glad to be safe from want, and if she dreams of coming to Paris there are at the same time plenty of people who would like to leave it, especially those who are being sent to camps. And we have to be reasonable and think of those who are without news of their loved ones, separated from them and without enough food. Sometimes I think of the Polish soldiers who are fighting in England and who have no news of their children, and that's really sad.

For your vacation, try again for Holland and if that doesn't work, come this way for a rest cure on the advice of your doctor. I would love it if you could come. ... Thanks for copying Annette's letter, I was so happy to read it. ... I would like you to buy a pretty little radio, get a good quality one and try to get America on it. ...

About Elisabeth, the situation is very hopeful. She has decided to get baptized this summer and we will probably go to arrange that definitively next Sunday. ...

I don't agree with you, as even when one is free, one should be careful, especially a woman, and conduct oneself correctly especially if one is in the Work. Between Mathy and Revert, the more guilty one is certainly Mathy, who isn't worth much, but Sister Revert should conduct herself correctly. Of course they are both free, and if the affair between them is serious, then that's different. I'm not absolutely opposed to flirting, although there is the risk of going further very quickly, especially since young girls easily create illusions for themselves and that leaves sadness afterwards...

If you could see me typing this letter you would be appalled. I began it at 8 o'clock in the morning and now it is 4 o'clock and I am back at it for the 20th time. ...

I am rather disgusted with Charlotte [Belgium] right now, but I am sure she is preparing to take charge of Fischer, although I don't approve of her tactics. What a joy it was yesterday to hear Arthur Raitt's uncle [the United States] spoken of; it gives me tremendous courage. Arthur [England] has a lot of courage, it will be a long struggle, but he will hold on and soon his uncle will help him totally. ...

Dearest Gaby, I'm going to leave you now... Be of good courage and God bless you and write to me. Make carbon copies just in case one gets lost.

A thousand kisses and friendly greetings to all. Affectionately I remain your grateful and devoted brother.

In June, after spending a few days at his alma mater, the Seminary at Collonges, Jean has some good news about Elisabeth, his fiancée, who works as a secretary to the French Consul in Geneva.

Jean to Gaby   Thursday morning, June 5, 1941

Ma bien chère Gaby,

Just a few lines in haste. I got here at noon. I left Thursday evening from Lyon and spent the night in Annecy. ... I spent Friday, Saturday and Sunday in Collonges. Friday evening was very nice, Olsen spoke, and he also spoke the next morning in church, and then at chapel on Sunday morning. On Sabbath afternoon Elisabeth came up and we talked together all afternoon. She had to work Sunday morning but came up Sunday afternoon but couldn't stay for the party which began at 8 o'clock, as the border has to be crossed by 8 and she had to go to work the next morning. But she had supper with us at the Seminary on Sunday. I was at the same table as the Charpiots, as his wife and son had also come. Elisabeth met them all and also Olson, who thought she was very nice and told me she would be a very nice wife for me. She had in fact written me a few days before that she wanted to be baptized soon and she told me that again on the Sabbath; so I am very happy as you can imagine.

Olson talked to me a long time especially about my trip to Arthur's He advised against it because, as he said, the Sabbath question poses a lot of problems, and that if I had been directly summoned, that would make it a necessity, but it would be better not to put oneself voluntarily in the middle of these problems. Especially if Elisabeth gets baptized, she will still be weak and fragile and would need to be cared for. So I am giving up this trip (I had just been advised last week that I could probably leave around June 15, and I had absolutely decided to do it). So that question is settled for the moment. ...

Elisa will have her vacation next week and she will spend a few days here in Lyon, maybe we'll take a little tour to Grenoble or Annecy, we'll see. Anyway she has made up her mind. I think she will lose her job if she brings up the question of not working on the Sabbath, but I think we can be married very soon once this question is settled.

... Now to the graduation ceremonies. Everything took place in the little chapel at the spring, you know the one, it was the first chapel at the beginning, and afterward it became the boys' living room. The Central building had been out of use since the beginning of the school year. There were 13 graduates sitting on one side of the stage. The teaching staff were sitting on the stage facing them.

On Friday evening, after Olson's speech in which, by the way, he said that his son Carl was supposed to go into the service soon, the young people gave testimonies, especially the graduating class. Odette Autin and her husband had come on Friday also, and they met Elisa, and I think they will get along well as they are very French.

On Sabbath morning Olson led a beautiful service on the qualities of a Christian and the young who come out of Collonges.

On Sunday morning everybody made a little speech, especially Walther made a long and very fine speech which made us laugh. Vaucher's was short and emotional. He said that he had burned his old papers that morning along with all his bad memories, and that he was keeping only the good ones. He had to move out yesterday and go to Gland. Olson thanked everyone very nicely.

In the evening the party began at 8 and ended at one o'clock in the morning. It was a great success and I will send you the program when I have the chance. There were some very successful skits about school life.

THE HAGUE REJOINS THE CONVERSATION

They gave a chronometer—which cost all of 500 French francs as they didn't find anything better in Annemasse—to Vaucher and a beautiful book on Switzerland to Walther. In my opinion these were kind of poor gifts, but the young don't have much money and there weren't very many of them. If the situation had been different they could have taken up a collection among the alumni for Vaucher and given him something very nice. Beaujolin and I had given 100 francs each and when they presented the gifts, they cited our names particularly as donors, which was a little embarrassing but flattering at the same time.

Mademoiselle Eppner invited Elisa, Julien and me to drink grape juice. Everybody was very nice to us and send their greetings to our whole family. ... Marcel Imbert is getting married probably in September, I saw his fiancée, very nice, a farmer's daughter, very gentle and reserved, kind of like Elisa, they have money and he's the one getting the good deal. ...

I'll leave you now, my dear Gaby. I think of you and love you very much. Write these bits of news to the parents.

Gaby to Jean Tuesday, June 10, 1941

Mon bien cher Jean,

... I am surprised not to have received anything from the parents. But it's possible that the mail is interrupted for a time as the soldiers are moving north to the coasts because they are preparing the offensive against England. ...

I suppose you are on the trip with Elisabeth now. I hope that you are having a good time. As you can imagine, I was happy to hear that she was so firmly determined to be baptized. I hope she won't change her mind at the last moment out of fear of her mother. I pray for her every day. I was also very glad that you talked to Brother Olson at Collonges and that he was able to advise you. I would have been sorry to see you leave. It would have been a great worry for the parents also to have you so far away, and right now, really, one man more or less [in the Dutch Army in England], what difference can that make? In the meantime I really wonder how everything is going to turn out. It's getting a little frightening. If there's ever any bombing, I'm going to put all the fabrics in a suitcase which I'll put in the print shop [the Adventist print shop in Dammarie, outside of Paris] where there would be less danger, don't you think? It would be too bad to lose everything. ...

The lady who sometimes sends me butter and cheese sent me some last week and she also sent me 70 eggs, but 26 of them were broken, but still usable, which I sold to some of the people in the house. I hope that they will keep for this winter. I'll try to put some more away if I can get them. In Paris there is no way to get them. I haven't been able to get even one at Houser's for two months. It's lucky we have other sources! ...

On Sunday I got the answer through the Red Cross to the message I had sent to Edouard [Overton] in November. He tells me they are well and that they live in a house near Coventry. They must be in the country. They would like me to come to see them, but I'd rather be here than there! Though they are probably safe where there is less danger. ...

I'll get some information about the possibility of coming to see you this summer, but I'm not counting on it. ...

After all my other expenses, I will buy a radio as it would give me a lot of pleasure. If I buy it in August, it can be your birthday gift. It's hard to believe that I will be 27 years old, it's terrible how old I'm getting! ...

It's too bad you aren't here as you could hire the young people. ... If you get married, Elisabeth can give you a hand at first, although it would be better if she stays at home some of the time, to get into the habit of taking care of the house. Many women who have worked outside neglect their housekeeping a little. ...

Indeed, Jean, I see your predictions have come true and that now you have succeeded in life. But I don't think you got the letter where I told you to be careful because you have a tendency toward pride and to say, "Moi, je" ["I myself"]. Of course you have so much talent for business and it's really your vocation, but you mustn't forget that it's still God who gives you success and it's He whom we must thank. Many have the required qualities, but don't succeed because the circumstances are against them.

I also asked you in another letter about my tithes. I'm wondering if I should give 10% of the money you send me. You have already paid your tithes on it, but for me it's income. I am a little confused about it, and I wanted to know what you think. Maybe I should ask Papa what he thinks.

I think I'll stop for today. As you're always in a hurry, I don't see how you'll get time to read my letter all the way through. I don't know when Marilou can take this letter, but if she isn't leaving tomorrow I might add something.

Again, a thousand thanks for all your kindness. I do so little for you in return. You see, it wouldn't have been worth my sacrificing myself by marrying Edouard Overton, since you have money without that! besides his mother might well have held onto the purse strings. Greetings to the Beaujolins and especially to Elisabeth. Tell her I wish her strength. As for you, je t'embrasse très fort.

Gaby

[Handwritten after Gaby's signature and up the side of the page] Wednesday morning, June 11. It's just a year ago that we left. What a trip that was! But I wouldn't be at all averse to spending another two months in the south to get a little sunshine. It rained all night and it's still raining.

... Do you want me to send you back your empty Post Office boxes? I have them all here, and I know that packaging is very expensive and hard to find. I could easily do it. ...

Gaby to Jean (correspondence card)   June 11, 1941

I just received a letter from Mama from the first of this month after a month of silence. You can imagine how happy it made me. They are very happy to have received my package which arrived safely and Mama was especially happy with the flowered dress which was from you. Everything is useful to them. I just wrote to Henri this morning, but next time I will send him the letter from Mama. He'll like that. Your package hasn't arrived yet. It's raining all the time. It doesn't do anything for my health. Gaby

Gaby types a letter on both sides of a half page before the mail leaves. Getting provisions is harder than ever.

Gaby to Jean   Wednesday, June 18, 1941

... Today I invited Brothers Wehrli and Meyer and Marilou and André for lunch. We were able to make a good meal. But the food supply is getting terrible. Those who work all day can hardly get anything. You have to stand in line for hours to get beans, peas or carrots. ... Yesterday I was very lucky. I went to a grocer to whom I go only rarely, and I don't know what got into him, but he offered to save me some vegetables for the evening. I got two cabbages, a kilo of tomatoes, a kilo of carrots without waiting in line. I'll go back to him to see if he doesn't want to do that again. That would be so nice. ...

Now the family cards have changed again. They are entirely blank on the writing side, and Jean has just sent one to Gaby. She writes a long letter to him.

Gaby to Jean June 25, 1941

Mon bien cher Jean,

... Yesterday I got your card of the 17th. It's strange because the last one was one with lines and they say they go faster than the ones without lines, but this proves that isn't true. Just sometimes cards go fast and other times they take longer.

I am glad you had some good times with Elisabeth. It's too bad the weather wasn't better. The heat wave came after that but that isn't very pleasant either because nobody wants to move. Right now while I'm writing you, there is a terrible storm. It has been raining buckets for a half hour and there is lightning every minute. For me who doesn't like storms, this is not what I need. True, I am less afraid in the city than in the country because it's less dangerous. I'll keep on praying for Elisabeth because until she follows through, there is the danger that she will fall back. But I hope God will give her the necessary strength. ... You told me I could probably get a pass to come to your wedding. But it seems that's just for French citizens; but since our country doesn't count anymore, I might be able to get one too. I would be so happy to see you. In that case I wouldn't take any vacation here this summer; I would reserve it for the other side, and I would go and spend a few days at Collonges. So I will wait to hear your plans before making any of mine about vacation. ...

Since the Sabbath I have spent some pretty terrible days. Can you imagine that on Sabbath afternoon I received a letter in German from the letter censorship service telling me to come to their office during the week about a letter addressed to Madame Landowski (a name something like that) in Holland. I didn't remember it, but by gathering together my recollections I remembered that I had in fact forwarded a letter with that name. I think it must have come from you. I was very worried because depending on the questions they might ask I could be in trouble. It seems they are very severe for letters going from one zone to the other. Some people told me I just had to lie; but I didn't want to do that. And I was afraid to get others into trouble if they asked me if I often received letters and from whom or if I wrote any and sent them through whom. When somebody interrogates you, there is no way to get out of it. I was sick about it. I asked advice from several people, but I had decided to tell the truth without saying any more than was necessary. I went yesterday afternoon with André who speaks German. The adjutant whom we saw was very nice as was his interpreter, and I wasn't expecting that as in general when we go to those offices, we get treated pretty badly. He showed me the envelope and asked if I was the one who sent it and how I sent it. I said I had mailed it. He said, "but do you know that it came from the other Zone?" I said I supposed it had as it came via the Post Office and it was probably someone who thought that I would mail it. I asked, "What was I supposed to do? Tear it up?" He said, "Yes, you are not a mailbox." He also told me, "In the letter it says that the answer should be sent to you. What would you have done if somebody had written to you?" I said I didn't know either the person who had written the letter nor the person to whom it was addressed, which was the truth, and that if I received a letter telling me to send news to such and such a person in the other Zone, I could always send a family card. At the beginning he told me to tell the truth and that he didn't want to do me any harm, and I said I was telling only the truth. They told me it was very dangerous and illegal to get mail from the other side and I said that anyway I wouldn't forward any more letters which might arrive without my knowing how they came. Well, at least it didn't last long. I think it helped that André speaks German, and we both must have looked pretty innocent. Of course spies don't behave that way. I don't know who could have written that letter and anyway the person who did wasn't very intelligent about telling where to send the answer. But anyway, I'm through, and I'm not going to get mixed up in things like that as I think they keep a file on me at the censorship office. It came out all right, but it could have been different. I am sure God was helping me, as they could have asked me a lot of other questions. I had prayed a lot and everybody here was doing that while I was over there. When you send me mail, it's usually for Dammarie. I would rather you sent it directly. Send me only the mail for Paris and then not every week, only once in a while. At the moment with the new family cards, there is really no need to write letters. Of course they are nicer, but once every two or three weeks would be often enough, at least for the time being as you never know if they are going to watch my mail. But I don't think they will. I could have kept this from you, but I'd rather tell you about it so that you will be careful and not accept more letters as you see what can happen. But I assure you, that yesterday I was almost sick. In the kitchen I had promised them all I would open a bottle of grape juice if this thing came out all right, and I did so. ...

I don't know if Papa has taken steps to come here. He didn't tell me about it. But if he does, I'll let you know immediately. ... Still it's risky. ...

Je t'embrasse bien fort and I thank you again for all the nice things you do for me. Brother Meyer wants to make sure I add greetings from him also.

  Gaby

6   The Encroaching War

Elisabeth will not have to work on the Sabbath, if she becomes a Seventh-day Adventist and keeps the same job at the French Consulate in Geneva.

Gaby to Jean   July 2, 1941

Mon bien cher Jean,

Your letter no. 22 of June 23 was a complete surprise, as I had already received one earlier in the week. But this kind of surprise is always happy...

On Saturday I received your card of the 22nd. I was especially glad to learn that Elisabeth had asked to have her Saturdays off and that her request had been granted. I think that is a big step, as it agrees with our principles, and because then she can be baptized soon. Later if she has to work on the Sabbath, she should of course leave her job, but as she is firmly resolved to do so if necessary, I think there is nothing in the way now. I can understand that you are very happy.

I do hope that Annie Beaujolin [sister to Gilbert Beaujolin, Jean's business partner and longtime friend] isn't going to have another baby. Her two others are still small and in these times and with the restrictions we have now, it's not a good time, as much for the mother's health as for that of the child. And so many children one right after the other is not good. Of course if she had the same idea as you, she would have a dozen! But seriously, I hope she will be better soon. Does she still have that same girl to help her as last year? Because if not, I don't think you should continue to take your meals there. I've never seen so many pregnant women as I do these days. It's probably because of the family subsidies [*allocations familiales*].

The Russians don't appear to be holding on very well. Of course, it will still give the British a little more time, but I wonder what will come of all this. I don't think about it too much.

I'm enclosing Mama's last two letters. Wouldn't it be great if Papa could come and spend two weeks here? I wrote him last night to tell him he could have meals with me and that if he came he could have a beautiful suit made with the cloth you sent me for a suit I was going to have made for me next year. I can always have one made from the gray flannel. But I don't want to get too excited so I won't be disappointed if Papa doesn't come.

Yesterday I wrote to Brussels to get a copy of your birth certificate. When I get it, I'll try to send it by the official means, so that if you are asked how you got it, it won't cause any trouble for you. Wouldn't that be better? Official papers can be sent, and I will find out how to do it. ...

On Monday evening I went to rue Thomire [where the Weidner family were living before the parents left Paris] to see if our jam jars were still there. The young lady said you gave them to someone when you cleaned out the cellar with Papa. I would like to have had them as I often need glass jars, either to keep butter in, or because I want to make some jam with our extra sugar ration, but there are none to be had. But I'll manage. Everybody tells me that I have gained weight and that I look very well. It's too bad the parents can't see me now, as it's really true. ...

I'll leave you now, as I must do some work. Besides, Marilou is going to leave with the mail pretty soon. Je t'embrasse très fort. Greetings to the Beaujolins and the Meyers.

      Gaby

Gaby begins a letter to Jean on July 13 and finishes it on July 15 when the mail is about to leave.

Gaby to Jean   July 13, 1941

Mon bien cher Jean,

The conference went very well. The meetings were interesting. But I really don't enjoy listening to Brother Badaut, first of all because I have a lot of trouble understanding what he says, and then I always get the giggles when he starts his tremolos. And I'm not the only one. This conference was a little tiring for me, as I had three people to lunch every day, and in this heat things couldn't be prepared in advance, so I had to go to bed late and get up early to have everything ready. But the colporteurs were happy, and that's the main thing. Everybody in the house had a lot of guests, and that got a little expensive for all of us, as I, at least, wanted to spoil them a little. The colporteurs are not rich and they work very hard. ...

On one of your recent cards, you told me that Elisabeth has problems with her mother. Is it because Elisabeth wants to get baptized or because she wants to get married? Does her mother still have the same ideas on that subject? And yet when her daughter goes off to Collonges or to Lyon, she must have some idea of the reason. Anyway, if she is making difficulties for her daughter, she certainly won't give her anything for her trousseau when she gets married. But you are doing the right thing in getting married as soon as possible. When I asked Charles if you were planning to get married soon, he said you had to take the financial possibilities into account. Of course that's true, but it seems to me that in some ways you wouldn't have too many more expenses if you got married. For the price you are paying for your room, you could certainly find a little apartment. And then, at least at first, maybe Elisabeth could give you a hand as a typist, which would save you some expenses. On the other hand, the cost of food and clothing is higher, and then there could be children, and as you are both not so young anymore, I suppose you don't want to wait too long. ...

I wrote to Brussels for a copy of your birth certificate, but then I received your card saying you wanted two copies. I'm going to wait and if necessary I can write to them again. Don't forget that these copies have to be recent. To be valid they can't be more than 3 months old. Moreover, you must get information about what papers you need to get married, as you may be required to have papers proving you are not Jewish. In any case you have to have them here to get an identity card. Probably Elisabeth will keep her French citizenship. That could make things easier for you if there are problems for foreigners. ...

While it's on my mind, Papa's birthday is August 10, and mine is August 17. If you can, write him a note. You can send it to me and I will forward it, but be careful how you write it, you understand why.

It's too bad Elisabeth can't be baptized in Lyon. But if you go to the conference in Collonges, it would be really nice if she could do it there. It's best not to delay too long, as she has definitely decided, and usually the more one puts it off, the more obstacles there will be. ...

Is what you told me about J. Mathy and Mme Depierrepont really true? Because people say so many things that I don't like to believe them if there is no real proof. If we had to believe everything people say, the reputations of half the Adventists would be ruined. ...

Today I'm invited to spend the whole afternoon at Mme Wyffels's, she's the one who lost her husband during the war and who has a little girl of about twelve. ... I'll leave at 11 o'clock; I am alone in the office, and as I always get my work done and I always arrive on time, I can arrange to leave a little early. That way I can get there for lunch and I'll have dinner there also. Tomorrow I will use my free day to do some mending as I haven't done anything in the last few days because of the heat. I'll also take out all the pieces of cloth and beat them because we have to be careful of moths. Not only do you have to keep them in camphor and moth balls, but you have to air them and beat them from time to time. ...

July 15

... This morning André telephoned the German Embassy for me. He got the answer that for the moment foreigners may not travel to the other zone. Supposedly it's the French Government that forbids it. On the other hand, I was told at the Prefecture, that if the Embassy issues a travel pass, the Prefecture would give me one automatically. Now just try and make sense out of that! Anyway, it's clear. But they said it could change and that I should call back in about a month, because that restriction is temporary. So there's still a little hope. All the same, I'm going to write to the parents to get papers proving that my parents and great-grandparents were not Jewish, in case I need them later. ...

On July 14 [French national day] a lot of people got fined because they were wearing red-white-and-blue rosettes. Mr. Desmet saw three people being arrested here on the Boulevard. In the Workers' house, the women hung red comforters from the window along with blue sheets and blankets. There were several of them. But a German officer came by and went to get the police who forced the women to take them in. It seems that that happened in several places. But as I didn't go out at all yesterday, I didn't see anything. ...

I'll leave you now. Greetings to Elisabeth and to you affectionate kisses from your sister.
    Gaby

Jean to Gaby   Monday, July 21, 1941

Ma bien chère Gaby,

... Yesterday, Sunday, the youth group went swimming at Trevoux, about 20 kilometers from here and it was very nice, although there was not much sun. The previous Sunday I was at Collonges, and on Monday at Annecy where I met Elisabeth and we went swimming and we had a nice day. I got back here on Monday evening. I got a long letter from Papa and Mama, and it was Papa who actually wrote. I'll send it to you soon. I'm enclosing a letter I wrote to them through Elisa. But you should send it to them also in case it got lost. Papa wrote me that my last letter arrived in the same envelope as your letter. He supposed that the censors received your letter and mine via Elisa at the same time and that the stamp on Elisa's letter interested them, and they kept the stamp and put both letters in the same envelope. But I think it was more likely that it was the letter I sent you and that you put it with a letter from you. Probably my letter sent via Elisa did not arrive. The main thing is to have one of them arrive. ...

I was so happy to get your letter. You did the right thing by inviting the colporteurs. Of course it made a lot of work for you and was tiring. But you made people happy and God will reward you for it. Things are fine with Elisabeth as far as our relationship is concerned, and we are making all kinds of plans for furnishings, etc. Right now I am looking for a three-room apartment in a new house that gets a lot of sun. It will be hard to find, but I have high hopes. Later we'll look for furniture, etc. Her mother is causing problems particularly about the marriage. As yet she doesn't know much about Elisa's conversion. I think it's definite that Elisa will be baptized in Lyon. She will have some free time during the month of August, and she will come here and get baptized. She's not too crazy about getting baptized at Collonges, but that would happen only if she didn't get any vacation. In that case she would prefer to go to Gland. ... For me, that would work out well, as I have about 1000 Swiss francs in

Switzerland which I can withdraw in two months, and therefore could afford good furnishings. I think that Madame Cartier will move to Annecy, as there is no reason to stay in Geneva. I think I will have to send her some money each month so that she can live on her small war widow's pension. Maybe Elisabeth can work a little at first, even though I would prefer that she just take care of the household, and that will depend on our financial situation. That won't stop me from continuing to help you financially as in the past and you have nothing to worry about on that score. I hope to send you 500 francs at the end of the month. You can count on it and for the month after that at least that same amount as a minimum. I can do it without any problem at all, and it won't cause me the least difficulty even if I get married. As I told you before, if you needed some special help for yourself, 2 or 3 thousand francs, I would send them to you immediately. Do not under any circumstances deprive yourself of anything, buy the good bargains, and always tell me frankly about your financial situation. Again, I am in very comfortable circumstances now. I would also like to know how it might be possible to send money to our parents via Paris. Can you find out how many francs to the florin? Maybe it would be better than sending it through Switzerland and I want to send them a nice little sum. ...

If possible I would like the copy of my birth certificate to be in French. My wedding is still three months away, so take your vacation now. If you can get a visa for the trip, ask Meyer for a few days of <u>unpaid</u> vacation, and I will reimburse The Work for the lost days. Thank you for the birthday dates. I will take care of it...

The story about Depierrepont-Mathy is really true. It's a pretty weird story. One day Mme Depierrepont is furious and wants Mathy to leave and the next day she begs that he be allowed to stay and that she will kill herself, etc. etc. She's crazy. ... Anyway the Church has censored them for 6 months. ... things have always been on a different plane for the unmarried as opposed to the marrieds. Back at the beginning, several of our good Brothers also had scandals, and almost all have been forgotten with time, but I know several of them. ...

I hope you can come to spend a few days here at the time of my wedding. I will probably get married in Anduze, because of the fact that my legal residence is there and I can't change. (Foreigners have a lot of trouble transferring legal residence, especially to a big city like Lyon.) Once I'm married I'll have Elisa live in Lyon and and will apply to join my wife in

Lyon, and they can't refuse as she is French. For the moment I have a travel pass for the whole zone and that way I am legal wherever I am. … Bravo to Parisians with their comforters and rosettes. I certainly hope Papa can come here or to you. …

At the Seminary in Collonges, they are going to host 50 poor children from Annecy, and they are going to house and feed them. It would have been better to send children from the cities. It seems that Paoli is aiming at being Mayor and is very zealous. He's the one getting the children to come to the Seminary. Ten days ago in Annecy, I ate as many fries as I wanted, you can imagine how happy I was. Annecy is very fortunate and the food is good. …

A thousand affectionate kisses and keep your courage up. I think next year will see the end of our troubles. Affectionately from your brother who loves you and doesn't forget you.

J

In her letter of July 22, Gaby copies some of Annette's letter for Jean and hopes he can read it. "It isn't very clear because of the thin paper, but I couldn't use thicker paper," Gaby writes.

Annette to Gaby   July 22, 1941

… I sunbathe in our neighbors' garden, that is, the neighbors who live below us, as we live on the second floor. They are very nice people who have daughters from ages 15 to 25. The oldest is married and has a two-month-old baby. I can use their garden as much I like. Everyone is very nice to me except, of course, the head nurse of my former clinic, but I never see her anymore, fortunately. That's a bad dream for me and I try not to think about it, but I know that if I had stayed there I would have died of sadness.

Fortunately my knee is better. The doctor says, "A lot of rest and sun." That's all I need. But a few weeks ago some friends recommended a herbalist who does miracles with herbs and plants. A month ago I began to drink the herbal teas and I'm better every day. Last week I came down the stairs normally instead of one step at a time. I still can't scooch down or ride a bicycle, but that will come. You can't imagine how happy it makes me. I think I'll be able to go back to my studies on August 1st if it continues to improve. My tan is the envy of my friends. But of course, the minute the sun comes out I take advantage of it. These will be good calories in reserve for this winter, as I'll have to work for a year with no vacation. But I am glad to be studying to be an assistant mid-wife, because I like doing that and I have a goal in life. When one gets the diploma the work pays very well. And when I'm a student there I can live at home, since I don't like living in a dormitory in Holland, as we are so restricted and with my independent spirit, it's unpleasant.

Next week, I will go with Papa to an Adventist youth camp in Mepel. On the same trip Papa will take me to Amsterdam, Hilversum, etc. I have to take advantage of being in Holland. We will leave a few days early. The camp lasts a week. I never go to the movies anymore. It no longer interests me. I would love to see a beautiful French film. I've gained a lot of weight.

Annette.

In a long letter in late July Gaby tells Jean how to preserve butter ("You have to melt it and put it in earthenware pots") and she discusses Jean's marriage and remembers their brother François, who died when he was only sixteen.

Gaby to Jean July 29, 1941

... You told me you have to be married in Anduze. But I imagine you will have only the civil ceremony there and after that you'll go to Lyon for the benediction. That would be much nicer than doing only the civil ceremony. I suppose you'll want to keep it very simple. I was talking with Etienne the other day about your possible wedding, and he said that it wasn't very nice of you to get married so far away, as it seems you promised them a nice little "spread" when you get married. Maybe that's for later when things are better. ...

Your suitcases are in the Youth Group library. I think they are safe there. I went to look again the other day, but everything is in order. I could tie a rope around them. Brother Grisier is probably going to get a travel pass in a few weeks (it helps to be French) and will travel to the other zone. I asked him to find out if he could take a used portable typewriter, and if so I will give him yours to take. Should I give him anything else? ...

Mama wrote on the 9th anniversary of François's funeral, and she says she still thinks of it so much; it's as if it happened yesterday. But she says she would rather know he is at peace than in this difficult life right now when so many young people are dying terrible deaths.

Copper is being requisitioned in Holland.

Annette is much better, She can now ride a bicycle without having pain. Papa is going to be 60 on August 10, but Mama says that he still thinks he's forty, he still wants to do so much; but he always has to have a little nap after lunch. ...

As to what you told Papa about Elisabeth, I think she will understand these points later on. Just think, I remember very well Brother Winandy saying to Papa once that at the beginning he couldn't understand why we had to observe [the Sabbath] one day any more than any other, and that he thought God was too great to bother with these details, and that part of Adventism had really bothered him. But I don't remember how he became convinced. At the beginning he couldn't believe in Sister White either, and now he does. Of course I think there is a special blessing attached to the celebration of the Sabbath Day rather than Sunday, since it is the day God rested, but for me, it's more like a sign that we don't want to obey the commandments of the Catholic Church which changed the day. Anyway, I hope that Papa can give you the arguments that convince Elisabeth. But for my part, on the other hand, I think you should marry her. Do you really think that all girls who are Adventists because their parents are believe all the points of the doctrine? If you married one of those girls, who wouldn't have had the same opportunities to prove what they believe or what they don't believe, do you think you would be better off? I think Elisabeth will definitely come to understand. Besides I know there are several among us who are certainly less good Adventists because they don't agree with several of our principles, and yet they hold important positions. It seems to me that the main thing is that Elisabeth is a good Christian and is always trying to be a better one.

Does Mme Cartier [Elisabeth's mother] still work? If so, it would be hard for her to leave Geneva to go and live in another city where she might not have a job. ...

It seems Mémé [Girou] is in a youth camp. His father is said to have been afraid the camp would be a bad influence on his son, but Marthe answered that he had nothing to fear on that score, and that it would be more likely that the others were at risk from him! Parents are so blind about their children. I even think ours are a little the same about us, but at least they don't have much to complain about in their children. Really, we are very lucky to have the parents we have. When I look at other people's parents, I think we have been very lucky...

This winter I took several photos with the camera you gave me two years ago for my birthday. I didn't have them developed until last week, and as they are very good, I'll send you several, I think you will like them.

In the Métro and in the street there are some huge red posters with this on them:

a huge   V

with a swastika under it

Victoria

the triumph of Germany who is fighting for the New Europe

It's because there were "V's" everywhere, people even made "V's" and "H's" and Crosses of Lorraine with their Métro tickets which they put everywhere and the Germans have used this letter to their own advantage. It's really funny ...

We hear that in Russia it's a terrible carnage. An Adventist Brother whose brother is there told us that there were piles of bodies as far as you could see on both sides. It is really sad that men kill each other like that.

    ... Gaby

Gaby to Jean (the Girou mother and son are still in the South)   August 4, 1941

Mon bien cher Jean,

... I saw Brother Girou today. He said that his wife is really worried about the car, and he wrote her to ask if you couldn't drive the car as far as the Demarcation Line. But he is wondering if you even have the right to drive the car, because only those who have applied (Mme Girou and Mémé) have the right to bring it north. If you go to Anduze, probably Madame Girou will mention it to you. ...

I am happy that you can see Elisabeth so often. It must really make you want to get married as soon as possible. I don't think long engagements are such a good idea. Poor Lizou with all those visas. I agree, really, that it's just too much. You are right to suggest that she tell them all off, and I hope she has done so. Let's hope that that will all be over soon. I'm thinking of you these days, and wondering if you have an appointment with Mme Cartier. I know she's unreasonable, but I still hope that everything will go well. Remember that she's a sad lady who hasn't had much happiness in life, and try to stay calm. Fortunately Mr. Porgès likes you and says good things about you. That can carry some weight. And if she knows that you are earning a good living, she won't worry so much about her daughter. Remember, too, that she only saw you in Collonges, and that then your business wasn't doing all that well. Anyway, if Elisabeth marries you, it certainly won't be because she was won over by your beautiful suits or the look of your car! Of course it's different now, and because she loved you then, you can be sure that it's true love. You couldn't say that about all girls. Anyway, although I'm not a gold digger, I don't think I could fall in love with a young man who had no money at all, unless, of course, he had great possibilities and had a real future. After all, that may be your situation! ...

In early August Gabrielle receives a long letter in Dutch from Papa written to both "Joop" and "Mies" [Jean and Gaby]. Gaby will forward the letter to Jean. Papa's letter is cheerful and spirited, though he is sorry to have been refused a visa to visit Gabrielle in Paris. His letter uses his code to discuss the progress of the war.

Papa to Gaby August, 1941

... We are also glad that Arthur is feeling better now. It is easy to see that his health is improving, because he is so full of life that he can be big trouble. But without the help of his uncle, he probably would not have made it. I don't worry about him anymore, but I do worry about Charlotte, as lately she has been spitting up blood. ...

Papa is glad that "Elisa" (Elisabeth, Jean's fiancée) wants to be baptized into the Adventist faith, and he sympathizes with her difficulties in understanding the celebration of the Sabbath on Saturday. Papa is also happy that Jean helps Mies so much and thinks that Gabrielle's support of her brother in former days is paying off.

Papa gives the latest news about Annette, who has begun her three stages of internship in preparation to becoming a maternity nurse. Each stage will last six months. In the first period she will be a resident student, in the second, older students will guide the incoming ones, and in the last one, the students become maternity nurses. "They go to the poor in the city, all of this without earning a penny." Hopefully Annette will not have a problem with some of her classes being on the Sabbath night, when she could not attend.

... Mama is doing well and so is Annette. Lots of kisses from both of them. I am going to make a bike tour through the country one of these days before the cold days arrive. And then it's back to work again.

Greetings to all and a bunch of kisses to you,

Your always-thinking-of-you Papa.

Gaby to Jean (card)   Paris, August 8, 1941

Bien cher Jean,

Brother Meyer returned a little while ago and voilà! my vacation plans change again. He saw the Daniels who insisted that I come to spend two weeks with them. You know she likes me a lot, and her husband liked me when I saw them at the Conference. So I accepted because this change of air will do me a lot more good than just going outside of Paris. Of course there will be travel expenses, around 500 francs. But you told me not to spare any expense, and so I am obeying. I'll leave August 17 and be away until the end of the month, unless Papa comes and that would change all my plans. I won't have to pay any board there, as they have the means. I hope the weather will improve. Kisses, Gaby

Gaby to Jean (card)   August 12, 1941

Bien cher Jean,

I just received your cards of the 4th and 5th of this month. I am glad to know you had a good trip and that all is well. ... About your wedding, we called the travel pass office, but there is nothing to be done. They don't want to give me a pass for unofficial travel. I'll ask again in September, but I think I should give up this trip. I am really sad about it, but I will think of you. Of course it isn't the same thing. ...

In Jean's usual style, all six pages of his letter are one closely typed paragraph. Comments about "Fischer" (the German occupier) hide among advice about food preservation and family news. His letter includes a detailed description of the red tape he encounters

when trying to establish Anduze as his place of residence. *He needs to do this, as he plans to get married there and a six-month residence is required. Some of the bureaucrats he deals with enjoy being helpful and others enjoy making things difficult for him. But he obtains his visa card in the end, and it is valid for three months. While he is in Anduze he pays a visit to Madame Girou.*

Jean to Gaby   Lyon, Friday, August 29, 1941

Ma bien chère Gaby,

    I did receive your cards from 15, 21, and 24 August. Thanks so much for them. I also received your letter of August 16 containing Papa's letter of June 10. Thanks so much for the news. I hope you got all my cards and my letter no. 27 of August 19. ... Yes, it's very sad that Papa couldn't get a travel pass. The other day I was reading in the German journal *Signal* that with the new European order that the Germans have established, there are no longer barriers between countries. ... But never have there been more problems doing business and traveling. ... I hope the upholstery fabric will work and if not I'll buy you something else and you can use this for other things. I think I can get some better material. So let me know. ...

    I'm glad you made tomato purée. Couldn't you make some Fischer purée? That would boost our supplies. ... Put away some good provisions for this winter. A lot of people make crates and put beans and tomatoes under salt by making a layer of salt on top of each layer. Anyway, do what you can. ...

    Yes, what Chinamen these Germans are, not letting the Chamber of Commerce go through. [In French the word "Chinese" in casual language indicates a lover of complication and red tape.] At the moment, all imports from Switzerland to France have to go through Bellegarde and not Annemasse as they did before. Since the train from Geneva to Bellegarde has to go through German territory...they can inspect everything and take whatever they want. It won't cause me much trouble if they confiscate something because since I get my commission from Porgès, even if the Germans take something the Swiss get reimbursed by the Germans, through their commercial agreements. ...

    Yes, if Grisier were willing to bring me my typewriter it would indeed be very useful. ...

Papa's letter was dated October 6, but October hasn't come yet. It was probably August 6. ... I'm returning Papa's letter to you, as I have the copy. His stories of Fischer and Charlotte, etc. are very amusing. I don't think he likes Fischer very much.

I'm leaving for Annecy this afternoon and tomorrow, the Sabbath, Elisa will come up from Geneva via the Annecy bus to meet me, and then she'll go back that evening as she has to work on Sunday morning. Maybe it's not very good to use the Sabbath for this meeting, but it's very important to our plans, and since I have precise information, and she doesn't very often get to the customs office in Collonges, she can cross the border more easily at St. Julien, and from there a bus goes directly to Annecy. I hope we will have a wonderful day and that it will be sunny.

What a guy Papa is to cycle for 180 kilometers against the wind. He hasn't changed, he is just the same. But I'm really happy about that, as the more active he is, the better life he will have. He seems to have gotten over the crisis of his departure from Collonges, and that's the main thing. There's no reason he can't live to a ripe old age or that he won't live until Christ's coming. ...

Your photo is very nice and everyone here thinks you look really well.

... Mme Girou had a bunch of endless little stories to tell, most of them of no interest. She thinks you're the nicest and the most interesting of the three girls [the secretaries in the Adventist Church office]. Mémé is in a youth camp in the Tarn (department) where he hopes to do some musical theater. In Anduze he worked with the owner of the cinema and in the intermission, he did some musical entertainment. He sang his songs. But despite people making fun of him and whistling at him, he is so proud that he just kept on. In Anduze nobody took him seriously, and he never understood when people snickered when he tried to be funny, that they were laughing at him not with him, and on all sides I heard people say that this doesn't do any good for poor Madame Girou's missionary work. From time to time he worked at the town hall. He was everybody's friend but nobody takes him seriously and he was considered a fake. I heard from a good source that he had once messed up everything on purpose concerning his mother's departure, because he was seeing a girl and didn't want to leave, so he told his mother that the papers weren't in order, etc. I was also told that the proprietor of the cinema said that Mémé had asked him several times to tell his mother that he had to go to Marseille to pick up films when it wasn't true, but he just wanted to do a little tour. Madame Girou

THE ENCROACHING WAR 129

believes everything Mémé tells her and he lies to her all the time. ... He gives her lots of problems but she doesn't seem to beat herself up over it much and she still gives him money. ...

Now I'm back at work in Lyon. I'll have a lot of work and everything looks good.

My dear Gaby, I'll leave you now. Send my news to the parents. I think of you all so much and I hope to see you all before too long. We have to keep up our courage. God is with us. ... I'm making progress spiritually and I'm very happy about it. I hope you will be able to continue the missionary work and share our beautiful truths, as the world really needs them.

... Your brother who loves you. ...

Gaby to Jean (card)   September 9, 1941

Marilou just got back so I can write to Henri soon. ... Grisier is leaving tomorrow. I gave him the 2 Bibles for you...maybe the less handsome one will do for Elisabeth, as she will probably use it less than you. ... I would have liked to make you a cake, but I didn't want to make a bigger load for Grisier and there are others who give him things to take. ...

After her return from vacation at the Daniels' home near La Rochelle, Gaby writes a long letter to Jean. She mentions the "assassinations in the Metro." These began in the summer of 1941 with the shooting of a German officer in the Paris subway, resulting in the taking of hundreds of French hostages.

Gaby to Jean   September 11, 1941

Mon bien cher Jean,

I wanted to start a letter this week, but I have been so busy that I couldn't. But last evening I heard that the mail was going to leave this morning, so I'll write you a few lines. ...

Brother Grisier left yesterday, and I hope he won't have any trouble with what I gave him to carry. I told him if he couldn't take the typewriter with him that he should leave it at the Demarcation Line. ... Be careful what you tell Grisier. He is a very good Brother, but he often gets things wrong and his information is not dependable. We have already had experience with that. But don't let him know that. ... I hope Grisier will have given you your birth certificate so you can publish the bans soon. As soon as that's done, you can send me a notice of it with the seal from the Town Hall saying that the bans have been published. That will allow me to get coupons from the Town Hall here for clothes and shoes. I don't particularly need the clothes, but I would like to have the coupons for the shoes. They certainly aren't going to ask me if I am going to attend the wedding. The whole Gal family got clothes coupons because of Hélène's wedding which wasn't even being held here. ...

These assassinations in the Métro are really scary, because now, if anything happens they can take hostages from those who just happen to be in the same subway car, and innocent people risk being arrested, and it doesn't help anyone. Of course so many people are at their wits' end. And when people don't have enough to eat, they'll do anything. ...

My vacation went very well, as you know from the cards I sent you. The Daniels were so nice to me and I was very touched by how nice Mr. Daniels was to me, as he is not an Adventist. He canned tomatoes for me. I picked blackberries for jelly, and he pressed them for me in his press. He fixed up a crate for me so that I wouldn't have too much baggage on the way, and he added some vegetables to fill it, so I checked that. As for food, I was really spoiled there. It's not always just the Adventists who are the most helpful. His wife is very happy with him. It was up to her to decide if she could marry someone of a different faith, but he leaves her entirely free and even shares some of our ideas. And I think it is a good thing for her, as her health was really poor and she really could not have continued as a colporteur. Now she doesn't have to worry. Of course, there's a big age difference, 27 years, but it isn't always those marriages that are the most unhappy. ...

I hope Elisabeth gets her vacation and that she will be able to be baptized. I always pray for her so that God will help her understand the things that aren't yet clear for her. But I am sure that will come with your influence. Tell her to be careful at work and not do anything that will come back to haunt her afterwards. I hope she won't be working at the Consulate much longer if you are getting married in October.

When you're married, couldn't you set up a business in your wife's name? Because you say that you earn less as a mere salesman. That would be good.

THE ENCROACHING WAR 131

The Embassy wouldn't grant me a visa because I wanted to go to the Free Zone for personal reasons. They are probably more lenient for commercial ventures. Of course, I would have been happy to come to your wedding, but I have to resign myself. ...

I thought of something. If you get married you really should get life insurance. Then if something happened to you Elisabeth would be free of immediate need. You know Samuel Badaut did that and it certainly served them well. You never know what can happen, and it is surely useful when one has children and no personal fortune. You may say I'm meddling in things that don't concern me, but it's always useful. And also, fill out some papers that leave everything to the surviving spouse, in case anything happened to one of you. If one does that immediately, it avoids problems at the time of the death of one of the couple, as the inheritance taxes are terrible otherwise. ...

About eggs, here's a way to keep them which works well. The eggs have to be as fresh as possible, of course, and you wrap them individually in newspaper, and then you put them in a tin box in a dry place. Eggs will keep for months that way. Unfortunately large tin boxes are scarce now. A cookie box is ideal for that but they are hard to find. Anyway, I'm giving you the directions in case Elisa doesn't know about it. ...

Why did Madame Girou stay there the whole winter? And Mémé must have destroyed a lot of things in the house, beginning with the piano. Maybe that's why the rent is so high. ...

Now I'll leave you. May God keep you and guide you. ...

 Gaby

Jean to Gaby   September 12, 1941

Ma bien chère Gaby,

... Yesterday I had the much-awaited visit from Brother Grisier and his son. They had a good trip. It was a joy to hear in his own voice that you are well, as he had left you just a few hours before. How can I thank you for buying me those beautiful Bibles? One will be for Elisa and one for me. And I was so glad to get the copies of the birth certificate. I was anxious to get them. Now I have everything I need to get married. Thanks again, a thousand times. ... Near the end of the month our offices will have changed their location. The new offices are very nice; the outside of the building is like all Lyon buildings, dirty and ugly, but it will be very nice inside; we'll each have our own office and we will be less on top of each other than here.

What luck that Grisier has a permanent travel pass for The Work, as that will be great help to us, and besides it gives me the feeling of being more in contact with you. I wish I could see you and the parents and Annette. Do tell them about everything I am doing. I'm putting in a lot of time at work, as right now it's very successful and I have to take advantage of it. But I will write them next week for sure. This month I will easily make 50 000 francs. That will be a big help when I get married. ...

On Sunday I will see Elisa with the Vice Consul in Annecy and we will have lunch together. Julien founded a Society of mutual aid for foreign refugees, and the members are Villiers, who is the Mayor of Lyon, Gerlier, Boegner,* who is President of the Protestant Federation, and a whole honorary committee of important people. I am on the executive committee. It's particularly to help the Jews. Beaujolin is supposed to see a lot of important people. Today he is in Vichy as he has an appointment with the Yugoslav Ambassador. I wonder what Oscar would say about all that, he who always said Julien and I were little ne'er-do-wells. Maybe we are, but less so than he is.

It's very hard to find an apartment. I found a small furnished room which I will probably sublet. There is a little furniture which I can buy for 4000 francs. I'll take it anyway, and then if I find something better, I can always change. At least we'll have a place to sleep. I'm not too worried about that. ... Thanks for your cards and letters. I hope Marilou will get back soon so you can send me something. Give her a chocolate bar or something to thank her. (I think you pay her 10 francs each time?) ... Thank you so much for my typewriter. It's going to be very useful, as we only had one, and couldn't find another at any price. I'm going to get a check-up for my typewriter so that its keyboard is aligned and so that it is in good working condition. ...

I still hope to get married next month, God willing. Elisabeth is going to be baptized very soon either in Grenoble or in Gland. Her health is good. On Monday I will get my complete pre-nuptial medical exam. As you can see, I'm doing things in the right order. ... Here everybody is

---

* Pastor Marc Boegner (1881-1970) was a pastor of the Reformed Church of France and a member of the French Resistance during the Occupation. He worked to improve the lot of the Jews and many other refugees.

talking about the thrashing Fischer is getting. Today I heard the speech by Arthur's uncle who is going to take measures for firing on the Fischers who might be navigating in the Atlantic. ... Food supplies are getting scarce, and I think February and March will be very hard times. ...

Papa writes to Gaby in French this time. French is easier for Gaby despite her Dutch nationality and is essential for Elisabeth if she is to read the letter. But after beginning in French, Papa forgets and writes a few thoughts in Dutch about Gaby's vacation and her dashed hopes for attending Jean's wedding.

When Papa discusses Germany he says the opposite of what he thinks and believes, because that will be acceptable to the censors. At the same time Gaby will understand his true thoughts.

Papa to Gaby   The Hague, September 15, 1941

Ma bien chère Gaby,

    ... Oops, forgive me, I see I'm writing in Dutch, and as my father taught me to always continue what I start, I'll follow that rule now. But as for Jean's wedding, the main thing is that Elisabeth be there; and the rest will work out according to circumstances. And when everything gets back to normal, a big bus will be seen to stop in front of 130, and out of it will come Father, Mother, Mother-in-law, Son, Daughter-in-law, kid no. 1, kid no. 2, etc. etc. And you'll be the one that has to cook for them, paying special attention to the fact that they all have different tastes. [Papa writes "Pelle Mère" for "Belle Mère" (mother-in-law) and Pelle Fille for "Belle Fille" (daughter-in-law), as he is imitating a Dutch accent for these words.]

    ... As for your advice that I shouldn't do too much cycling, I obey religiously. So I never ride between 10 in the evening, and 6 in the morning. What a joker your father is!

    I see that you don't have very much food. We are better off. Take care of your health: the minimum of effort and the maximum of nourishment. Go into winter with a good dose of health. Eat, eat, eat, anything at all if necessary. ... I'm so glad that Jean has helped you so much financially. By this we can see that he can do something else besides borrow money from his sister! ...

    I am glad that Jean can get married, as that would have been the last straw if circumstances had been on the side of the "pelle-mère". So I hope to hear soon that Miss Cartier has joined another name to her own. How is the mother behaving now? I'm going to write the last part of my exposé on the Sabbath, and I will send it to you as soon as it's done. I won't make it too long.

I am curious to see the stamps that Jean bought for me. I hope that he didn't pay too much for them, but it is the most practical gift he could give me, as the more the money decreases in value, the more the stamps' value increases. ...

Your news about Charlotte really made me happy. I was sort of expecting it, frankly speaking. I knew that she didn't care for Fischer at all, and that on the contrary she couldn't care less. I'm betting that she will return to her first fiancé. And I heard from a good source that she was seeing him secretly and so I said to myself, "I knew she would come back." Only don't say anything to her about it, all right? She doesn't need to know that I'm interested in her, but just between us we are going to see that she will come back to Arthur. And on that day I will buy a round of drinks for Mama and Annette!

I am so glad that you see the bright side of things. That way there is always something we can be happy about. I had a striking example of this recently. There was a girl in Lysin who was an invalid from age 9 to 15. When she came back here, she broke a leg and again she had to stay lying down for 6 months. She is still lame and has to listen to unpleasant remarks from boys in the street. Well, the day before yesterday she said to me, "When I can walk for two minutes, I'm so happy that I say to myself, 'I can walk!'" She is always full of joy. Yesterday I saw her before she left for Germany where she will continue her studies (painting) and we prayed together.

When will we see each other? When the war is over. And who knows if everything will be over soon? You can see how enormous the Russian losses are; all our newspapers are full of nothing else. And you understand how much the British ships are being torpedoed, and soon that country will ask for mercy. Besides you know how happy I'll be to see the British on their knees before Hitler. Do you remember when I told you at the very beginning when H. came to power that this was the solution, since all the so-called democracies are in the soup? Do you remember that unforgettable evening in 1936 when I had a fierce discussion with Mr. Dufour on the subject of politics, when he slapped me so hard, or rather he gave me a punch with his fist under the left eye, and my eye was swollen for a whole week? Well, now who was right, he or I, when I maintained that the only salvation for Europe and even for the whole world, was to allow a man like Hitler to govern? Everything comes to him who learns to wait. So, we may see each other sooner than we expected. If it still should turn out to be longer than this year, let's be patient, as that day will come.

But I see that I'll have to stop, and I have hardly said anything yet I will write more very soon. In the meantime, eat a lot, sleep a lot, walk a lot, work a little, that is, work no more than your health will permit, and say hello to everyone for me. Kiss Charlotte for me (when Fischer isn't around). And for you a big loud kiss from

>Your Papa who sees that you are happy,
>Papa

Don't worry about the tithes. Jean has given the part that belongs to The Work.

Gaby to Jean September 16, 1941

... About your furniture, if you are thinking about what you might want to buy, I advise you not to get modern bedroom furniture. Everybody who has any says it's terrible when one has children. Every little kick shows. I know several people who regret buying it and if they replace it, they always get beds of the classic style covered with flowered bedspreads, in the style of Louis? I don't know which one. I don't know if you know the kind I mean. For the dining room furniture it appears it's less important as long as one takes care of the table top. Anyway, if one is careful, one can always make do with anything. But I wanted to tell you about other people's experience.

In the same letter Gaby expresses herself about some indiscreet Seminary staff in Collonges.

... Collonges is really a weird place. I had heard something about the Delavaut girl...but I had understood that she had been utterly astonished about Brother Tièche's attitude, but according to you she was allowing it. It can happen that a man kisses you once in surprise, but one doesn't get taken in a second time. Well, it's their business. But all the same, I think that when one is married, and is in The Work, it shouldn't be allowed.

Gaby to Jean (card) September 15, 1941

... I got a card from Mama saying that Aunt Hermine complains that they have so little to eat. They have one liter of skim milk for 5 days. I wish I could do something for them, but it is impossible to send food to Belgium, the same as Holland. ...

Gaby passes along some advice from Mama to Jean about the date of his upcoming wedding.

Gaby to Jean (card) September 27, 1941

... This morning I got a letter from Mama that I'm going to send Henri this week. She said to tell you that if possible you should get married on October 13th, as that will be their 30th wedding anniversary. It's too bad we all can't be there. We were separated on their silver wedding anniversary, too. But Mama says we'll have the party when we're all together. ...

Writing to Gaby, Jean mentions the death of Walther Fischer, an acquaintance who may be the person whose name is being used for Germany in the family code.

Jean to Gaby September 22, 1941

Ma bien chère Gaby,
... Elisa will probably be baptized on October 4th by Paul Meyer, and I think we will get married at the end of October. Her mother is more and more difficult. ... Last Sunday I had lunch with Elisa and the Vice Consul in Annecy. It was very nice. The Vice Consul does a lot for Elisa and as he knows her mother very well, he will tell her things very firmly. ... I have to go to Anduze to publish the bans, as you have to do it three weeks in advance. Elisa had thought she would get some vacation at the beginning of October, and then we would have taken a little trip to Anduze to publish the bans, but then I think it would be too late to get married at the end of October. ... I had my prenuptial medical exam. Everything is fine. ... Walther Fischer died on the Russian front from a bullet to the heart. It's

sad because we knew him, but it's even sadder that the Dutch, the Belgians and others who have never done any harm to anyone also died. ... Thank you for the recipe for preserving eggs. I'm giving it to Elisa. ...

Gaby's letter to Jean, begun on September 22, on the same day Jean wrote his, becomes a serial letter awaiting the departure of the mail. She continues the letter on September 24, 25 and 29.

From Jean, Gaby has received the terrible news of the sudden death of Paul Meyer's daughter, Oscar Meyer's niece, after what should have been a routine appendectomy at the Adventist clinic in Gland, Switzerland. She also has news from Edouard Overton, one of the two suitors Gaby was hesitating between in 1935, and who left for England with his mother when the war started.

Gaby to Jean September 22, 1941

... The letter from Edouard which you sent me was dated November 27 and it arrived in Anduze on January 15, according to the envelope. You know, you could have taken it out of the envelope, there were no secrets in it! But that way I could see how long it took to come. Jeanne Revert says one can't write from the Free Zone [to England], but that one can from Switzerland. I'll get a letter ready which I'll send to you so you can send it from Berne. Edouard said that he is well, and his mother is too. He is working with Passive Defense [civilian support for the war effort] and has to take care of those who are wounded and remove the dead. I think he also has a paying job. His mother is more and more feeble but she is still living! I think it is really shameful of Mme Girou not to have forwarded the letters to Lyon, especially those from the parents. We hadn't heard anything from them for such a long time, not for months and months and I was so worried. Really, I think we are too good. It's not worth helping people, most of the time they don't deserve it.

Yesterday I had a nice afternoon. Michèle called me to see if I was free, as her husband was gone for two days. We met and went to a Chinese restaurant. It was very good, but the bill was a shock: 77 francs for the two of us, plus the tip. I was Michèle's guest, as I had invited her for meals two or three times. Then we went for a walk as the weather was splendid. We came home early and had a very ample dinner. We wanted to make crepes and we also invited Mr. Meyer to have some, as he had just gotten back.

Then we listened to music. Next week I'm going to buy "Dreams of Waltzes" which I have wanted for a long time. We played it a few times. But Michèle had to leave early as she had to be home by 9. In fact, because of all those attacks on Germans, we're grounded for 3 days, from Saturday to Monday and we have to be home by 9 o'clock. It's a real bother, but we have to submit, because those who are in the streets after hours will be taken as hostages. So we might as well go home. ...

Wednesday, September 24

Jeanne Revert leaves this evening. I hope you will like the pastries and that you will keep them for yourself, because if you give a slice to everybody it isn't worth it. On Sunday I said to Brother Meyer that I wanted to make you a cake and he brought me three eggs, saying they were for your cake. Isn't that nice? ...

Monday morning, September 29

... It was just by chance that I found your letter addressed to the bookstore Saturday evening. ... I went up to the small meeting room and hurriedly opened the letter. I cried out while reading it, I was so surprised. I told the other members of the committee after the meeting, and Dr. Albaric said he would go to the railroad station to meet Brother Meyer to tell him the news gently. ... Oscar Meyer was quite overcome and rightly so. ... The whole family is very touched by the way you wrote about it and they want to thank you for your condolences. ... It's terrible for the parents, especially since their marriage wasn't going so well, and Marthe was the only link between them. Paul wishes his brother could come, as it seems that it was always Oscar who helped in the difficult periods of his life. It isn't very good publicity for [the Adventist clinic in] Gland, but it's true that accidents can happen. I can't get this sudden death out of my mind. I think about our parents' grief when François died, and yet they still had three children and they had time to prepare for his departure. Whereas for the Meyers, it's so sudden. ...

Luckily it's not too cold yet. Let's hope it lasts. We have almost no coal for this winter, and we have been told that we can use only 60% of the electricity we used last year, so we thought we could make it up in heat. ... Oh well, if we are too cold we can stay in bed until noon! ...

I think that if Raymonde were married, she would be a very nice girl. In fact we would all be nicer if we were married. ...

I am so happy for you that you will soon be married. ... When you are married, should I address letters to both of you or should I continue to send them to you? I would be happy to address them to both of you and maybe Lizou [Elisabeth] would think that was nicer. ...

Je t'embrasse bien fort.

Gaby

Since this letter doesn't weigh 20 grams, Marilou is going to add something, so I won't have to pay the supplement, as it's 10 francs for each 20 grams.

When Jeanne Revert leaves for Lyon, Gaby writes to Jean that she was so sad watching that train leave when she couldn't be on it. But it doesn't do any good to complain. "I have to be brave. We'll see each other some day."

Papa writes in Dutch from The Hague to both Gaby and Jean, knowing they will share his letter. He again speaks of the war in terms of a German victory in order to mislead the censors. He is able to say the opposite of what he thinks and still convey his true thoughts on the war's outcome. At this time, the United States is sending naval escorts to reduce German U-boat damage to ships in the Atlantic, and these are the "toys" Papa mentions.

Papa to Jean and Gaby   The Hague, October 6, 1941

Dear Joop and Mies,

It's time to take about two hours to write to my French children, who could have already become a father and a mother, and one of whom is in line to become one now. However, it would be better for him to produce four children at once after the war is over than for his wife to have only one during the war, because if things there are anything like what happens here, some pregnant women are getting some very primitive help.

Annette has told us how earlier she had to treat everything very carefully with cotton swabs, and nowadays things are done more or less comme ci comme ça [Papa uses the phrase in French: "sort of half way" or "any old way"] because of the shortage of necessary materials. Well, those are personal matters for someone who is almost 30 years old and a woman who is close to putting on St. Catherine's cap, as they both know what is best. Anyway, this is a strange introduction to a letter when one is writing to one's kids.

When your letters arrive, they are opened at once, read, and later read again, and again, and soon after that friends get to hear quotes from them when they are visiting. And there is no lack of visitors here. Of course we only read them the things about Charlotte, etc. We keep the strictly personal items to ourselves.

Well, Mies, you are a dependable one. You keep us abreast of everything. You make us feel so good with that and we feel so close to you. And you, Joop, we don't hold it against you that you waited so long, because we know our busy Popie [Jean] is a first-class work horse. Furthermore, there is the preparation of a sensational event, the fact that our "little fellow" is getting married. But we were very happy to get your letters of September 17 and 23. So that was two letters, but they were so extensive that they almost counted for six. Thanks a lot, dear fellow, and you, too dear Mies, for always giving us news about Joop [Jean] so faithfully, and sending his letter together with yours. It pleases us very much to see how strong the relationship is between the two of you. One never knows what can happen, and it is so comforting to know that you take such good care of each other. It also pleases us to know that you gave Joop those two Bibles. And, you, dear fellow, you are a good brother to your Parisian sister, you hear? You show that friendliness and good-heartedness is not only in words. How we would love to send you all something from us, for example, after I picked up a tin full of dates this morning, I said to Mama, and she completely agreed with me: "They'll be good for another half year," and who knows, if the Germans take Moscow quickly—and there is no reason they couldn't—then we would have come a long way toward peace. I know they're not in London yet, but Churchill seems to have acknowledged that Germany is strong enough to carry out a war on two fronts. We must not forget that Germany has always been extremely clever to organize that, so no one knows what surprises may be in store for us, and Germany is winning faster than anyone would have thought. It is still just fantastic how much that nation has achieved so far, thanks to its power and its talents for organizing. However, we can't be too sure, as we are only laymen; we just have to wait and see. But let's make an agreement: we would like you to have some of these dates, because they are delicious. If

THE ENCROACHING WAR   141

Moscow is taken within two weeks, we won't eat any more of the dates because then everything will come to an end very quickly, and you will get your share when you come here. In that case, you'll be able to come and visit very soon. That would be so nice, wouldn't it? And Joop can scratch his father's head just like two years ago. Though you might have to rock a baby to sleep then...

Oh, yes, before I forget, I was so happy that little Arthur [England] recuperated so much. Yes, it doesn't surprise me all that much, because children can bear quite a lot; they don't die all that quickly. Nice that his uncle sent him those toys.

Yes, he has such a big heart that he would do anything for his little nephew. Nice of him that he promised to visit. And you can count on that, he is a man of his word. And so if you are drawing a pension and you don't have to worry about pennies even in this difficult time, then naturally you'll think of a sick little nephew. By the way, Joop, don't forget to send our heartfelt greetings to Arthur's uncle when he comes to visit you. Will you promise me that? Agreed, right? I especially ask you that, because you might forget those things in your new household. And I think the uncle is such a nice guy. I admire him greatly. He will definitely not rest until little Arthur is totally recuperated. ...

Speaking of C., like you, I believe that she has made a mistake to get together with F. Fortunately they have no kids yet. ... [Belgium's King Leopold surrendered to Germany in May, 1940, against the advice of his cabinet, and subsequently fled to London.]

Well, it's a good thing that you are reading good literature. You said before that you read Vinet, an excellent writer. I also have one of his books in my library. Do read a lot. It is food for the heart and brains. Make it a habit also with Elisa. To feed the spirit daily is healthy. You wrote that Elisa is not too keen on F. I can understand that completely. That comes naturally, and don't think that will disappear in her. You can tell her that I too despise that brute for what he has done to Charlotte. ...

That's nice of Elisa's employer to announce your wedding plans to her mother. Poor Elisa, she will probably spend some miserable days with her mother, but if it goes too far, she probably will find some other place to stay, right? But when you receive this letter, perhaps already she will be known as Mrs. Weidner. ...

And now to your wedding. When you receive this letter you might be married already! If so, you should know that we are very happy for you as well as for Elisa. We are so sorry that we cannot be present, but the main thing is that the two who marry each other are present. It is a totally different life, because from now on, love unites in such a way that the two people will finally become one. The marriage, if understood and carried out according to God's will, is already a heaven on earth. It is, however, also a training school, in which one puts himself steadily in the background and finds happiness through self-denial. If the husband seeks to make the wife happy and the wife the same, that would be a state of happiness that always gets better. May God help you both, dear fellow, to prepare each other for that true eternal happiness, of which the present is only a faint reflection.

Later on we'll celebrate. If you have any practical question, Mama and I are always willing to help out, providing we are able to. Never be so imprudent as to tell Elisa that your mother does things better than she does. Never put Elisa in your mother's shadow. Also, never say anything negative about her mother, even if Elisa says so herself, and you should still excuse her mother somewhat. It always works better that way... If there is ever a misunderstanding, you should be the first one to make up. That gives a surprising amount of satisfaction.

All three of us are doing well. ... Mama has some trouble with her varicose veins, but it is bearable. ... Slowly but surely old age is creeping up on us and things happen to people. ... Last week I bicycled to Utrecht via Hilversum, about 80 kilometers, but I took two days. A few days later I returned, but made it in one day because everything is flat. Then for the first time I returned to the village of Abbenes in the Haarlemmermeer and saw again the village where I was born. ... I had a shave at the barber's there and he told me all about everything.

I had to go to Hilversum, because there was an old man, 100 years old, who was going to be baptized. However, he got sick. I went to visit him in his home, and he cried because he was not able to be at the baptism... But we hope that it will happen. In the last several months I have preached in The Hague, Rotterdam, Utrecht, Hilversum, Baarn, Arnhem, Nijmegan and Leiden. ... the people were fascinated, for it is very interesting to delve into St. Peter's life and see how at last he miraculously understood the lesson that he did not comprehend before. I also plan to hand out brochures when the occasion arises. Also to counteract the Roman Church. ...

THE ENCROACHING WAR 143

And now I am going to leave you again, my dear Joop and Mies. We are really happy that you are such a courageous person, dear Mies. Keep going like that, and we'll meet again later, here, at your place, or elsewhere.

Many kisses to both of you, and Joop, if you are married when you receive this letter, then also kiss Elisa, but you'll have to give her one for Ma, one for Annette, and one for her father-in-law.

Bye, Papa

Gaby writes to Jean about the roundups of Jews and the searches in Paris's 13th arrondissement which is where the Adventist Church is located and where Gaby lives and works. She mentions Boulevard de la Gare, which is only steps from the Adventist Church's address, at 130 Boulevard de l'Hôpital. Gaby's occasional anti-Semitic remarks are curious and hard to explain. It is possible that this is her own code designed to misguide the censors should her letter fall into the wrong hands. It is also possible that she falls unthinkingly into the mode of expression of many of those around her in France at this time.

Gaby to Jean   Thursday, October 9, 1941

… You know that many Jews have been picked up and taken to the camp at Drancy. The Ichbiah brothers are there, too. They say the camp is abominable, they sleep on the floor, and those who are sick have absolutely no medicine. I don't like Jews very much, but I think this is going too far. …

Right now there are a lot of searches in the 13th arrondissement. They are looking for arms and Communist tracts. Last week it was in the Boulevard de la Gare. They went to the Bernérias's. When the German soldier asked if she had any weapons, she showed her Bible and said this was her only weapon. At the beginning of this week it was Boulevard de l'Hôpital, but not on our side of it, though that will come. Hundreds of police circle a house at 4 in the morning and the German soldiers begin the searches at 5. They say that in some houses they go through everything and in others they are less severe. I think there are people who are under suspicion. I don't know if it is being done throughout the city, but there are a lot of Communists in the 13th. I had already destroyed all your letters before I went on vacation, and I immediately burned all the ones you sent me since. I think it's safer, although I'm sure they don't read all the letters.

Ah, yes, the other day, while looking for something in the youth library, I saw a small cardboard box with 3 books in it; I don't remember the titles very well, but there was one about 32 ways to make love, and I didn't even open it. There were also some picture postcards of nude women. It is yours? If so I will put them in one of your suitcases, as I wouldn't want the young people to find it, unless they have already seen it or it belongs to one of them. ...

Gaby to Jean October 16, 1941

Mon bien cher Jean,

Your letter of the 2nd of this month arrived on the Sabbath and I was of course very happy to get it. The photos also delighted me, although, as I wrote you on a card, I was a little disappointed to see that Lizou had changed so much. She was so delicate and so slim a few years ago. But she is still pretty. And since you still love her that way, I think you will love her always. Anyway, it couldn't be said that she is marrying you for your money, because she loved you already when you were starting out in business and your car was running only on good will and patience! ...

You told me that Elisabeth has so much work; but how will they manage when she is married? They should have had her training somebody. You aren't thinking of letting her work in Geneva when you're married, are you? ...

O. Meyer didn't know that detail about the piece of music Marthe played on the day before she died. Maybe his brother will write to tell him that. He doesn't think that [the clinic in Gland] will make him pay the expenses of her illness, and he said "that would be the last straw." He is furious with Gland, especially since they didn't ask the parents for their permission. But the parents would probably have given it, since nobody would have thought that Marthe would run any serious risks. But we are wondering if they put her to sleep completely or if there was a local anesthetic. ...

Does Julien plan to come to Paris? It's too bad that you don't want to make the trip yourself. It seems to me that if you had a pass, you could come for a few days. Of course you would have a little trouble at first getting used to the atmosphere [of the Occupied Zone], but one gets used to it just as we have to. ...

THE ENCROACHING WAR

There is a young teacher who lives in Vitry le François and who is coming to spend his vacation in Paris. He is very nice and very well-mannered. Brother Mathy thinks he would be a good prospect for me, but he is much shorter than I am and you know that I would never marry a man who is much smaller than I am, even if he has all the qualities in the world. Anyway, this young man doesn't know me very well, and he only comes to the bookstore once in a while, and on the Sabbath. ...

Jean writes to Gaby that Elisa's baptism has taken place at last, but her mother is still a problem.

Jean to Gaby   October 21, 1941

Ma bien chère Gaby,

... Yes, on October 13th I thought of the parents for their wedding anniversary. But I have absolute confidence that we will see each other again and that we will have more happy days together. ... I think the war will continue for a while, and that Europe will be more and more famished. So you have to lay in supplies. ...

Wednesday morning I met Elisa in Annemasse. From there we took the train to Lyon where we stayed a few days, and then she returned to Geneva. We didn't have time to go south... Elisa had to be back on Sunday morning, so she had to leave Lyon Friday night. So we did the baptism Friday morning with P. Meyer. We were on the banks of the Saone in Collonges, the weather was nice and the water wasn't too cold. I set up a little cabin between two trees with two bedsheets I had just received. It was very nice. Paul Meyer was very good to take the time for us. There were only the three of us. I took photos and tonight I'll know if they came out well. I hope so. You can understand my joy as I have been waiting so long for this. God be praised.

You know, Elisa hasn't yet understood everything, but she told me she had confidence in me and that she would follow, and that little by little I would help her to understand everything. What is certain, is that she has decided to make Jesus her saviour and that she wants to follow and accept in her heart this force for good. She has had a decisive discussion with her mother. I had written a letter asking for Elisa's hand in marriage, a letter that she and her protector the Vice-Consul had created for me. So one evening the Vice-Consul and Elisa put Mme Cartier up against a wall. Because she had never spoken of that letter. So Mme Cartier said, "Oh, yes, that letter. He couldn't have done that all alone. Some idiot helped him." Of course she didn't have any idea it was the Vice-Consul. You can just imagine the look on the latter's face. It's lucky he is very friendly and close to Madame Cartier. Elisa told me she couldn't help laughing it was so comical.

The Vice-Consul is very favorably disposed toward me and does everything he can to help us. Finally, it seems, her mother said, "Well, if you wish it, you have my consent." You understand that Elisa wants her mother to accept it, so that there is no breaking off of relations, and I understand that. Now the Consulate has asked her to stay until the end of December as there is no one to replace her, and it's very hard. So I agreed to wait until then. Of course Elisa could leave right now, but that would cause great confusion. So I am going to exercise my patience until then, and it will be that much easier because now that Elisa has been baptized, I have much less apprehension and my great joy will help me swallow this slight delay. I've been waiting for 5 years, so a month or two more doesn't scare me. ...

Now Elisa is a member of the Lyon church; they voted unanimously for her admission on the Sabbath. ... We have bought a blanket, a comforter, and the mattress is finished. ... The money is going out like crazy. ... This week we will move into our new place which will be much better. Of course I have a lot to do, but my health and spirits are very good. ...

Tomorrow is my birthday, so it will be a good occasion to work double time. When we see each other, we will have a big party. I had bought some lemons for you, but since you found some I'll give them to Elisabeth, as she loves them. ... Now I'll leave you my dear Gaby, hoping to see you soon in good health and spirits.

Your brother who loves you and thanks you again for all you do for him.

Just two days later Jean writes again because he has now received her letter of October 16.

Jean to Gaby October 23, 1941

Ma bien chère Gaby,

The day before yesterday in the evening I received your letter of the 16th of this month containing Papa's of October 6. You can understand my joy at receiving these letters just in time for my birthday. And then yesterday morning the young woman whom you know brought me your two magnificent cakes. How can I ever thank you? Anyway, the rice one is already completely gone, consumed by myself alone, since it was your wish that I eat it all by myself, and I share your views absolutely. Don't worry about Elisabeth's beauty. She is already much better, and I think she will regain her figure. Of course in a few months I won't be able to absolutely guarantee that she will continue to get thinner!

Your cakes are delicious. Next time anyone goes to see you, I'll send a little flour and sugar that I have saved here for you. ... Yesterday on my birthday I received a card from Elisa with her good wishes. So I felt you all were here around me. ... This evening we have a special meeting where Paul Meyer will talk about nutrition, because it seems that several members of the church are in doubt on various subjects and several like to drink a little wine. For example, Bernichon (luckily there is an "H" in his name), who always drinks a little wine. [Without the "h" in Mr. Bernichon's name, the last syllable would be "con," a slang word for "idiot".]

... If that young teacher who got baptized is nice, you should accept him. What are you talking about on the subject of height, etc. In my opinion, that has no importance. Germaine Augsberger married Benezech who is much shorter than she is... Height doesn't matter, and you could stand on a little bench to kiss him, or rather vice-versa. Anyway you aren't so tall. And if you are inhibited by a detail like that, you are not worthy of the Weidner intelligence. ...

I am very glad to have Papa's consent, so now I can do whatever I need to do to make my marriage valid over there, too. It seems in Holland you have to have the parental authorization up to the age of 30. I guess the Dutch aren't very precocious. I wonder if you have to have the parents' permission to have children, too, but I didn't dare ask that question.

A few days later. Gaby is concerned about her mother's incautious use of the name "Jopie" for Jean in her letters. This name is reserved for writing to Jean on postcards only. The censors must not be allowed to connect all the names for Jean into one person.

Gaby to Jean October 28, 1941

Mon bien cher Jean,

Yesterday I received your card of the 22nd telling me a letter was coming, and I was excited at the thought of reading it. This morning I came down to the office early and Brother Meyer gave me your letter no. 5 as he came home much earlier, because nearly the whole coast is now the forbidden zone. I hope he can get a pass, because if he can't he won't be able to travel hardly at all. It's getting really terrible.

Right now I'm frozen and I'm having a lot of trouble writing. We don't dare use the electric heaters yet because of the great restrictions on electricity and since Thursday it is terribly cold. But if that continues, I will go work in Marthe's office, and from time to time we'll turn on the radiator. Even in bed it isn't warm enough. I think I'm going to ask for a coupon for a wool blanket. I think they would give me one as I can prove that I have only one wool blanket and then the one you bought before you left Paris, but that one is more cotton. I still have one from home, but it isn't enough. Or maybe I can buy a comforter, as that is not yet rationed, but I think they are very expensive. I'll look in the stores one day soon, because if the winter is as hard as last year, we'll have plenty of time to freeze. ... We won't turn on the heat until December; we have even less coal than last year. ...

The photos of the baptism aren't so bad as all that. Elisabeth does indeed look as if she had lost weight and I'm glad. ... I hope that at the Consulate they are in the process of getting someone ready to do her work, so that you can get married at the end of December. I can understand that Lizou doesn't want to leave them in difficulty as they have always been so good to her, but with two months to do it they could start working on it. I admire your acceptance; in your shoes I would be more impatient. I hope that nothing will happen between now and then to delay the marriage still further. ...

I'm glad you got your visa for Switzerland. I think the first thing you will do when you get to Geneva will be to make a visit to your future mother-in-law. Poor lady. But since she gives her consent, that's the main thing. It is better to keep contact and you mustn't forget that for Lizou, she is still her mother, and she can't be prevented from having affection for her mother, even if she isn't very nice. It is better to separate on good terms, but without Mme Cartier feeling obliged to come and see you from time to time. ...

Marilou is leaving in a few minutes, and I am sure you will want to have Papa's letter as soon as possible. So I'll leave you. Je t'embrasse affectueusement.

      Gaby (please turn over)

                                        Thursday, [October] 30

I'm continuing this letter begun the day before yesterday as I think it will leave today. ...

Last Thursday I received a letter from Mama and another Monday. I'm enclosing them, but I must find a way to make mother understand that she should be more careful. For example, in her letter, she tells me that she received a letter from you via Switzerland, and a copy of the same from me. Yet, I have already told them that I cannot communicate with Jopie except by postcards, but that I often get letters from Jean. One of these days I will have to find Mr. Laatsman, and maybe he could carry a letter in which I could explain it all to the parents. It would be better if you didn't send any letters that have your address on them, because if they are ever confiscated, it could make trouble for you. ...

I can understand why Lizou might have had the giggles when her mother talked that way about the person who wrote the letter [asking Elizabeth's hand in marriage]. For a woman Madame Cartier's language isn't very elegant. It really surprises me that she gets along so well with the Vice Consul.

As for the things that Lizou doesn't understand so well yet about our doctrines, she shouldn't worry about it. ... I assure you that I ask myself many questions sometimes, especially when I hear others talking about them. That doesn't take anything away from my faith, nor from my Adventist beliefs, but I regret that Papa isn't here. In a letter it is harder to discuss all these questions. But I've noticed one thing: in our group, either people are extremely narrow, or else they are way too lenient. ...

A letter from Annette in The Hague to Gaby in Paris. Annette's big bold handwriting is on three quarter size pages, and her final sentences are written up the side margin.

Annette to Gaby   The Hague, November 17, 1941

Ma bien chère petite Gaby [My dearest little Gaby],

    You must be wondering if I still exist, it has been such a long time since I sent you any news. But believe me, I haven't forgotten you. Just the opposite, as the longer our separation goes on, the more I long to see you. Luckily, my work takes nearly all my time as otherwise I would be depressed very often.

    My knee is fortunately completely cured. But at this time I am becoming very wise, my wisdom tooth is coming through. But the naughty thing is hurting me a lot. The dentist has already made incisions after anesthetizing it of course, but a few hours later I had a lot of pain, and have for a few days.

    I just did two weeks of night duty. Usually I don't like to work at night, but this time, I have had such a good time that the nights have gone by very, very quickly. There are seven students who get along very well, and one midwife. We have so many laughs. One night we carried the midwife (she is very small and slim and we call her the doll) in the baby bathtub which we put in the middle of the corridor. She couldn't get out and begged us to help her. But we were all bent double with laughter. In the end we picked her up, one other student and I, by her head and her legs and swung her until she cried for mercy.

    The first week I had kitchen duty, and every night I made them all so much to eat that they all gained at least 3 pounds. The second week I had the birthing room. I had 9 births in 8 days and I passed my exam on giving first care to the baby and its first bath. I am the first in my group to have the right to care for the newborn without a midwife or supervisor beside me. And I can do nearly everything in the sickroom, while many of my companions don't have the right to take care of the sick but they empty bedpans all day, scrub floors, etc. I love the work, and I can now assist at births. My first one was a beautiful experience. What I don't like is when the doctor stitches up the mothers when they are torn. They don't anesthetize the place, so you can imagine what these poor women suffer. Luckily it only lasts a few minutes.

    I loved your package. I had your coat made over for me and now it looks very good on me. You know it doesn't make me look fat even though it's belted. That's good, because it's just amazing how much weight I've gained, but that's better than being so thin. I also had my big brown coat turned inside out, and the fabric is so beautiful that one would think it's a new coat.

I am living at the clinic now; I like it here and we get a lot to eat. Actually we have more privileges than at home. I share a big room with 3 others and it is heated. I'm very lucky because it's the only nurses' room which has heat. All the other have gas heaters and with rationing, they are not allowed to turn them on. ... Thanks for the socks and gloves. What a magnificent scarf. Here they cost crazy prices. Many kisses from your little sister.

  Annette

Excerpts from a "serial letter," November 21 to November 26, from Gaby to Jean. She has not been able to obtain a travel pass to the Unoccupied Zone.

Gaby to Jean   November 21-26, 1941

... I went to the German Embassy with the same gentleman as before. I must say that we were not well treated, and I don't think this gentleman can do much about it. The officer spoke to him in German, but I understood that he was being asked why he always accompanied people, and he was told that they didn't want to see him there any more. Then he was sent out, and the officer told me that I couldn't get a pass for a personal reason. I said, "And what if I were French?" and he answered, "Maybe," and that was all. There is nothing I can do. I went to the Consulate again to see if they could do anything for me. I was sent to the Dutch Chamber of Commerce, but, even though they were very nice to me, they told me to apply directly to the Embassy, which I had already done that morning. So I have to give up, but not without a lot of sorrow. Yesterday I behaved well all day, but when I went to bed, I cried my heart out. But now it's over. I would have been so happy to see you, and I would have liked to spend the holidays at Collonges. But I have to resign myself. ...

I am glad your trip went well. I hope you aren't going to delay your wedding any longer. You have already waited long enough and there will always be a reason to put it off. Since the bans are published you have to do it. I hope you give all the details about the ceremony. Fortunately Mme Cartier is in agreement now. I can understand that it's a relief for Lizou, because when one is sensitive, one wants the parents' moral support. Anyway, that would be how I would feel if I were in her place. ...

The 18th arrondissement is under lock and key, because of an attack there. People can't go out after 7pm, I think. The first day there was a lot of confusion, because some didn't know about it and couldn't return home.

   Je t'embrasse bien fort and Lizou as well.
   Gaby

Jean writes to Gaby about the preparations for his wedding and his visit to Switzerland.

Jean to Gaby   November 28, 1941

Ma bien chère Gaby,

For the last week I tell myself every day that I am going to write to Gaby today, and each time there is something absolutely urgent to do, but I don't want the week to pass without writing you a little. ...

So, I went to publish the bans in A. [Anduze] I saw mother Girou who was very happy because, as she said, her son has gotten wiser (?) and that he was more of a "man" I asked her if her son was still singing his songs, and she answered yes. Things between her and Mr. Daunis have cooled a bit; it seems that she is so close with her money, that life with her is difficult. She had bought a goat and she accuses Daunis of taking its milk, etc. Anyway, they still get along, but I have the vague impression that Daunis just tolerates her. She was very nice to me and cooked me a meal, etc. I stayed a day and a night. ... I came back here for a day and then went to Collonges where I spent Friday and the Sabbath. ...

So, on Sunday morning I crossed the border [into Switzerland]. What wonders to behold. Most of all I was surprised to see the pastry shops full of such good things, and every day. On the first day I ate with Elisa and the Vice Consul at the Berges. With the hors d'oeuvres alone (and only the vegetable ones) I ate 3 times as much as I do here in normal times. And during my whole stay I drank a lot of milk and ate a lot of cheese and pastries. It's wonderful to see the stores full of so much fruit, and merchandise, there are a lot of watches, gold, suitcases, etc. in fact everything that's missing here, and which we have forgotten ever existed. There is a great choice of suits, woolens, shoes, etc. etc. I had thought I would see

Madame Cartier on Sunday, but Elisa told me her mother was in such a state of fury, and that she had even said that a head would fall that day. So we went to the Comédie, as Elisa had received free tickets. ...

On Saturday evening I went to see Elisabeth's mother, and I was hardly through the door (she was expecting me), and I hadn't sat down or taken off my coat, when she began to absolutely fry me every which way, saying that her daughter had an education and that if she had known she was going to get married, she wouldn't have bled herself white, etc. etc. The Vice Consul was with us. I let her shout as much as she wanted, and then she calmed down, and I said very nicely that our decision was to get married at the end of December. More shrieks, saying that was out of the question, and that we had to wait at least until April, etc. I told her that if there were valid reasons I would even wait ten years if I had to, but not one day more than useful or necessary. But she had already accepted the idea of marriage in a few months, and that was an important victory. Of course I complimented her a lot on her courage in bringing up Elisa, etc. She said it was for personal reasons that she wanted us to wait until March or April. I told her that these were not reasons as far as I was concerned etc. etc. All without getting worked up (though I was itching to answer her back), and finally our departure was a little cool.

The next evening Elisa told me her mother was taking me out to dinner, and we went with the Vice Consul. This time she was very nice (I had also told her that she could count on moral and material support from us once we were married). So she told me she was giving us the sewing machine which was worth 15000 French francs, etc. She seemed to be regretful that she had nothing to give Elisabeth. She also talked about Elisa's trousseau, and I told her we had all we needed, etc. In the end she was charming. I didn't mention a wedding date, etc. etc. In Gland I visited François's grave. I stayed there a long time remembering our dear little François, always so gentle and calm, he was an example for me. And during those moments of silence I thought of you and Annette and our dear parents, and I shed tears. I left instructions with Schw. to re-gild the letters on the gravestone. I invited Madame Cartier and Elisa and the Vice Consul to dinner and then I had to cross the border again before 9pm. I had the impression I was going from Paradise into Hell.

At dinner Elisa's mother was very nice and Elisa called me this morning to tell me that her mother isn't making scenes anymore, and that soothes Elisa's nerves. I just wrote a long letter to her mother saying we would like to get married after New Year's, and I was leaving Elisa with her so that she didn't spend the holidays alone, which was what she seemed to dread more than anything.

On the French side of the border I was completely searched (undressed) for an hour; they were hoping to find money, and I was laughing like crazy, because I didn't have any. ... Before I left Elisa and her mother gave me a magnificent gold watch, a real beauty. They even wanted to give me some trouble about it at customs. But it got through. I brought back a little chocolate which I will send to Mama. ... Several people have already given me beautiful gifts...a magnificent dessert service...and my friend in Anduze wrote to say that all the town would do for my trousseau was either a suit for me or a pair of sheets, unbelievable but true, so you can imagine that my conscience will be clear if I buy something on the Black Market. ...

In Gland they took a blood sample and did a complete analysis, and they told me it couldn't be better, so you see, I am quite ready for marriage. ... I am remorseful about taking Elisabeth away from her paradise country. ...

Your brother who loves you,

The Paris curfew has become even more restricting. Gaby also alludes to Papa's departure from Collonges, which had taken place somewhat under a cloud because of a dispute with Collonges Seminary administration about retirement and salary.

Gaby to Jean   December 8, 1941

Mon bien cher Jean,

... This morning we learned of the worsening political situation. And now we can't go out after 6 in the evening. It's really troublesome, and it stops all economic life and will cause a lot of disruptions. It's not very smart of the people who do the terrorist attacks, because it doesn't solve anything to punish us all. I can understand very well that people are angry and that some have had enough, but these attacks don't do anything to help. And it's really a problem that this comes during Prayer Week. All the meetings have to be cancelled. It's really too bad. ...

I think its' really terrible of Mme Depierrrepont to have turned in P. Rey. That shouldn't happen among us, even if we have resentments. We are nonetheless one big family and we should support each other unless someone does something really reprehensible. ...

I am very glad you had a good trip and that everyone welcomed you. Yes, now everyone is nice to us and asks for news of the parents. But before, they dropped us. Well, we have to learn to forgive. ... It must have done you good to eat so many good things. But I am sure that Lizou would rather eat dry bread with you than pastries in Geneva without you! But really they are amazing in Anduze to give you so little for your trousseau. I don't think they have the right to do that. The bride has a right to a pair of sheets and the groom does too. Ask if there isn't some misunderstanding. I'm also glad that Lizou's mother calmed down. It's not very nice for you to know that she is angry. Being Christians, we should try to be at peace with everyone. ...

Gaby to Jean (card)   December 8, 1941

We have to behave because the curfew is now at 6. Too bad we work in the same building where we live, otherwise we could leave work at 5.

The Japanese have bombed Pearl Harbor. On the same day, December 7, the United States declares war on Japan. On December 11 Germany declares war on the United States and hours later the United States declares war on Germany.

Jean to Gaby   December 13, 1941

Ma bien chère Gaby,

... I'm leaving this afternoon for Collonges as I'm meeting Elisa and her mother on Sunday (we are going to see the family in La Roche to announce our wedding). The mother is old fashioned and takes these things so seriously, and they are more important to her than the war with America. But, if that can please her, we don't see any harm in it. Elisa called to tell me that her mother still wants us to get married in March and moreover in the Catholic Church. So on Sunday I'm going to settle all that. I think things will work out, and if not, too bad, as Elisa is determined that we will do it in January, so I think that's when it will be, God willing. Every day I ask God to prepare the heart of the mother and also help me say what I should and not say disagreeable things. ... I'll go to Collonges for the holidays, and I hope to see Elisa once. I'll leave here on December 22. ...

The Meyers have asked us to eat with them, especially when Elisa will be here, if we would like to, and I accepted with pleasure so Annie won't always have to make us special meals as they are not vegetarians, and the Meyers are, so that works out well. ... She is a very good cook, so that will be wonderful. So if Elisa wants to work with me here, we can eat at their house at least at noon, and for the evening, we'll see. Anyway, I'll talk about it with Elisa when the time comes. Until we have children Elisa can be very useful helping me, and we won't have too many worries about food supplies, and Sister Meyer will do that for us. We will arrange to pay Sister Meyer very well. ... My suit for the wedding is nearly finished; it is like my black striped one but is navy blue and very handsome, and made to measure. ...

This American-Japanese war is really something. The prophecies are being fulfilled more and more and are going toward the same goal as the battle of Armageddon. ... I have an idea that Arthur's uncle wants to eliminate Fischer first so that Arthur will use all his strength to help him eliminate Japan. That way, the war could be over in 2 years, in 1943, because I think Arthur's uncle will come here and will help us. But it may last a lot longer in the Pacific. But all that should be an encouragement for us, because we know that the time is coming when Christ will return. I have hope and confidence for our country. I am certain that if we can wait until 1943, we will be reunited. ...

It is a great consolation to me that you are in good health without too many material worries. That's very good when there are so many in concentration camps separated from their families, with no news, suffering from hunger, and we can consider ourselves lucky. ...

Here's what you should do about your travel pass: write a letter to the Kommandatur that says, "I am Dutch, and as such you have taken me into your protection since you have replaced the Dutch consular authorities and since that country is under your administrative control. Now, my brother is going to be married and I would like to go to his wedding. I hope that you do not consider the fact that I am Dutch to be a disadvantage compared to those who are French in obtaining from you the authorization to go and see my brother. Consequently I would be very obliged if you would issue me a travel pass. Your government has always promised that Holland would be considered quite evolved and that you would give it certain advantages. I don't seek them, but I would wish that my nationality not be a reason for treatment inferior to that of other nationalities. Consequently I would be very obliged..." Well I'm only giving you sketchy ideas, so you can formulate them more precisely. Ask Gerard to help you with it. ... You have to try, even if there is little hope. ...

I spent a wonderful Sabbath reading and re-reading the letters from all of you, and I had the feeling I was living with you all. ...

Keep up your courage. ... Taking care of yourself is the main thing so that when we get together again we will look like little elephants nourished in Germany. ...

Jean to Gaby   Thursday morning, December 18, 1941

... So on Sunday I met my future mother-in-law and Elisa. We had a wonderful day and ate admirably. I ate at least a pound of cheese and brought back cheese and butter. Her family promised us that when we are married, they will send these things to us regularly. ... Everything went well with the mother. Sabbath afternoon with Elisa, we planned everything in order to have the maximum of success. And it went well. She agrees to the wedding being in early January. We decided to have it between the 20th and the 25th, and as Elisa's visa runs out on January 13, she can renew it and after we are married she can still go there for three months whenever she wants and she can buy whatever we need, and at the end of the three months, she will move all her things. Elisa's family was very nice to us. But Elisa's mother is a real tyrant. We don't interfere with her (she didn't leave us for a second all day). Elisa's mother will come to Anduze for the wedding. She will continue to work where she works now. There is a very good direct train that goes from Annemasse to Nîmes. Elisa's mother said she wanted the wedding to be in a Catholic church (because she doesn't yet know that Elisa is Adventist). So I asked the mother if she wanted a marriage blessed by my pastor, "yes. yes," she answered, "I particularly want a religious blessing." So everything is settled on that score, and we can do as we want. I had prayed so much for this conversation, and God answered our prayers. ...

On a card to Jean of December 12, Gaby wrote that she hoped Jean had worn his handsome suit to make a good impression on the family!

Gaby to Jean   December 23, 1941

Mon bien cher Jean,

... Madame Steinbach gave me a rather original Christmas present because she thought I would like it: 7 fresh eggs from her chickens. ...

Yes, it will be easier for Annie if you have your meals at the Meyers' as Annie is going to have her baby. ... And do you feel at ease at the Meyers', since they don't have a very good marriage? For them it will be a little company. But when you are married it seems to me you would rather eat at home, at least in the evening, if Elisabeth is working. ...

You told me to write to the Kommandatur. But, you know, I'm really not anxious to do it. When I went there the last time their answer was so categorical that I have no desire to try again. I'm sure it wouldn't do any good. I've heard that at the Demarcation Line they give passes much more freely, especially at Moulins. But to go there with all my baggage and then have to come back looking foolish, I wouldn't like that. And it's still rather expensive, and it would be too bad to spend money for nothing. What do you think? Should I risk it? Of course I am a foreigner, and that really complicates things. If I weren't, I'd get a pass in a few days or even a few hours. ...

Tell me, is the Geneva Vice Consul married? It seems to me he does a lot for Lizou, and it sounds a little suspicious! I wouldn't want to introduce the poison of jealousy into your heart, but it seems strange to me that he comes to see Mme Cartier so often. But then maybe it's the mother he's interested in. I just had the thought that maybe Elisa will read this letter and she would be angry. But I'm only kidding. ...

I have a lot of work just now, and it isn't fun, I assure you. When Desmet sees that I am writing to you he always has to make a remark so that I know that he knows. Again a little while ago he said, "So how is your correspondence going?" I just laugh. They do enough of their personal correspondence in the office, so I have no guilt feelings, and besides I do it very rarely. ...

If I had gotten my travel pass, I would have left this evening and we would have gone to Collonges tomorrow. That depresses me a little because I would have loved that. I had planned it that way because when I was applying, we thought the wedding would take place in the first few days of January. But even if I hadn't gone to the wedding, I would have spent a few days with you, and a little change of air and daily life would have done me good. But I must be patient. I can't complain from any point of view, and God willing we will see each other again.

Je t'embrasse bien bien fort, and I'm sending my most affectionate thoughts to you and Lizou.

  Gaby

7   A Party and a Wedding

Annette's spirited letter uses every available centimeter on the page. After filling the center of each page with her big, bold handwriting, she then writes up the side margins, upside down across the top and makes a box for "page 5" on page 4.

Annette to Gaby   The Hague, January 13, 1942

Ma chère petite Gaby,

This is the first time I have written you in 1942, but I hope to do it a lot more this year, as I neglected you a little last year. Please excuse the ink blot, but it isn't my fault. My pen makes them all by itself. It can't be repaired because the problem is in the pen point, and we can't buy a gold tip anymore, and to buy a new fountain pen you have to turn in the old one, and fountain pens cost crazy prices these days.

... I want to wish you a good and happy New Year. With all my heart I wish for your happiness, and what a joy it would be to see each other this year, I can barely imagine it. But we have to have faith and patience.

I see that you had a nice holiday and that you were really spoiled. So was I, and I had a wonderful holiday. First, we celebrated Saint Nicolas Day [December 6] at the clinic. In Holland on that holiday it's the custom to give gifts with poems. It lasted until 1 o'clock in the morning. We got tea and cookies and then a cup of hot chocolate, a real luxury right now. There were 60 students, and each one had to read her poem and show her gift, and then there were all the midwives and the directress, etc. I got a very pretty calendar with pictures illustrating legends. After the party we danced. The directress received a huge pair of double cuffs made of cardboard tied together with a string which she can hang around her neck because she never can find hers [another serious ink blot].

Maybe you'd like to see the poem I got: "A Poem for Annette, With a Christmas Gift of a Calendar"

> St. Nicholas, not long ago
> Heard Annette Weidner's tale, by chance,
> About her French descent, although
> She recently had moved from France
>
> To take up residence in The Hague
> Where she would have to speak in Dutch,
> Yet infant memories were vague,
> And talking left her out of touch.
>
> He learned how she would point it out
> To shop-girls when her language failed,
> But slowly she had mastered doubt
> And shown how effort had prevailed.
>
> So, when arriving at the clinic,
> Meanings never were confused,
> Though many friends, a little cynic,
> By her accent were amused.
>
> The Saint then saw her at her duties
> Standing sadly filled with pain;
> He hoped this girl with inner beauties
> Could be comfortable again.
> "I've never had a wisdom tooth,"
> She said, "that hurt so." With a look
> Of sympathy for words of youth,
> He wrote them in his golden book.
>
> And here the Saint now offers you
> A calendar to mark each day
> Of steady growth, advancing through
> Long hours of learning on the way.

A PARTY AND A WEDDING

I thought the poem was very well done. Of course I couldn't do one, and Papa did mine for me, the one I had to give someone else. I think everyone here is a poet!

For Christmas, I celebrated the first day of Christmas at the clinic and the second evening at home. On the first day, we had a Christmas dinner that was really terrific. Here is the menu:

Hors d'oeuvre: Russian salad [chopped mixed vegetables] with
    mayonnaise
Soup with meatballs
    potatoes, peas, buttered carrots,
Steak au jus, delicious
    cooked pears
Rum pudding and candied fruits, I think it's called a Diplomat
    grapes or apples.
Coffee, with artificial cream, of course.

We really had a feast, like nothing we have had in the last year. The dinner was only for those living at the hospital, so I got to participate. There were 35 of us in all. I had to help with the decorating as the tutor likes me, and always wants me to help her, and I'm really happy to do it, as I like that kind of work. The table was so pretty that everyone exclaimed "Oh" when they came in. We put the bowl of fruit in the middle of the table with fir branches and shiny balls around it. We put red ribbons across the table with holly. We sprinkled silver powder on the table and each plate had a little candle that made the silver powder sparkle even more. On the buffet there were candelabras and candlesticks, and the candles on the Christmas tree were lighted when everybody came in. Everybody was in the right spirit. There was an incident that I'll never forget. One of the candles on the tree was almost burned down, and we hadn't noticed it until a small branch began to burn. The girl sitting beside me jumped up and climbed up on a chair to put it out. She stood up on her toes to reach it and then the chair slid under her feet, and there she was falling into the tree. We were all paralyzed with fear. We pictured the tree falling and my friend burned. Luckily the tree didn't fall, because she had the presence of mind not to grab onto it. But it was like a movie. She looked as if she were diving into a pool. Only the best part of the story was that there was a large pail of water beside the tree in case it should catch fire. And just

imagine, she fell right into it with her derrière in it. Oh, when I picture her in that position with her legs kicking without being to get out of it, I still get the giggles! At last, I came to my senses and pulled her out of the pail by her feet, and she was soaked. She ran off to her room, followed a few minutes later by me who was practically wetting my pants from laughing. You can imagine the scene. At 8 o'clock, we did our tour of the wards and gave each patient and visitor a cup of coffee, and also, each student had made or knitted a child's garment and each mother received two or three things. You can just imagine how happy they were. On the second day of Christmas we received a gift. I got a leather case for a fountain pen. It's very pretty. Dark green with gold stars. in real leather. I went home and got stationery, two sets of undershirts and underpants, and an album with a key, very pretty, where I can write my memories or thoughts of this year. For St. Nicolas I received a magnificent bag for the back of my bicycle from Papa. They are very expensive, and I am so happy to have it. I also received a dark red shawl. I received a nice card. ... I'll stop now. Kisses,
    Annette

Gaby wrote to Jean on the same day Annette wrote to her. "A week from today," she writes, "will be the big day. I hope nothing will happen to hinder your wedding. When it's all done, send me a postcard so I can be sure. I'll let the parents know." In the same letter Gaby worries about Jean's frequent criticism of others:

Gaby to Jean   January 13, 1942

... Brother Desmet read us what you wrote about the Mathys. But I must tell you that it causes me a lot of pain when you talk that way. You who want to be a good Christian, I don't understand why you keep so much animosity against Brother Mathy. I can understand why you don't approve his methods, but between that and talking about it constantly, there is a big difference. We should learn to forgive, and I think it is really not good to talk that way. Especially since Elisabeth will certainly use you as an example. If you talk this way, she could say that you really don't put your Christian principles into practice. It seems to me that one should not criticize like that, even if it's true. Maybe you'll think I'm sticking my nose into things that don't concern me, but it really does bother me each time that Mr. Desmet tells me what you say about them.

A PARTY AND A WEDDING   165

In his letter, Jean outlines for Gaby his plans for the "big day".

Jean to Gaby   Friday, January 16, 1942

Ma bien chère Gaby,

    Forgive me for waiting so long to write you a letter, but I suppose you have now received my cards from Collonges and then from here. I am so busy. At last, I absolutely must write to the parents today, as it will be my last letter as an "old boy" [Jean uses the phrase "vieux garçon," the masculine equivalent of "old maid"]. This wedding seems to me like a dream, as for so long I have not been able to believe it's going to happen. But now I really believe it will happen. ...

    Elisa and her mother have a direct train from Annemasse to Nîmes. They have 2nd class couchettes. ... We'll take the bus from Nîmes to Anduze. Then on Tuesday [after the wedding] we'll leave again for Nîmes. Madame Cartier will leave at midnight and arrive home the next afternoon. Then Elisa and I will go to the coast for two days and will get back here around the 25th. Then at the end of the month Elisa will return to Geneva to extend her visa in order to have three more months of unrestricted travel. ...

    Everything is pretty much ready. I'll get married in the small church, the chapel of the Methodist Church. ... I have a beautiful new pair of black shoes, a good-looking suit, white shirt, etc. I'll send photos. I'm so sorry you won't be there.

    Madame Girou is really detested and the Daunises have just about had enough, as she is such a skinflint, and she is dirty and the house isn't well run. ... There is nothing to eat in Anduze, so I am taking everything with me. I already have some things there: potatoes, butter, eggs, cheese and I have been promised 2 liters of milk. I'll find pears and carrots, as I have been promised those, too. We'll eat in the Badaut's large room where the piano is. ...

On Jean's wedding day, January 20th, Gaby sends her thoughts: "My dear Elisabeth, my dear Jean...It's one o'clock. You are probably sitting down to dinner. This morning when I woke up, my first thought was of you. ..."

    In a 12-page letter Jean, who says he "hates to write," sends Gaby all the details of his wedding day. Even though it's already February, and well past the New Year, he gives the previous year's date. It is 1942, the year of his wedding, and perhaps he is preoccupied!

Jean to Gaby   Sunday, February 1, 1941 [Jean's error—it is 1942]

Ma bien chère Gaby,

Today I have some free time, no customers, and I hope to be able to write to you and the parents without too many interruptions...

Of course I too was very sad that neither you nor the parents could come to the wedding, but you know, my dear Gaby, we have to realize that there are more than a million prisoners who are separated from their families, parents, wives, or fiancées. And on top of everything else, they have no contact with them and they are without medical care and are undernourished. While we have relative freedom, and we can manage to get enough to eat, and we are sure that none of us are suffering too much deprivation, then I can get married. And on the whole we are relatively privileged, that's what I tell myself every day. Of course sometimes I'm also lonely for you and the parents, but I immediately think of the others who are much worse off, and yet they keep their spirits up. ... As hard it is for me, I don't think I should take any steps toward going to see our parents. I might even succeed, but my principle is to stay here until everything is free, and then we can see each other again. ... I can keep up my courage because I am convinced that won't last more than a year or 18 months. I'll be so happy to see our dear Papa and Mama, and I'm sure that I will find them in good health. I'm preparing pretty gifts for everyone for the beautiful day of our reunion, which will be a magnificent celebration for us and for others. ...

You know, Gaby, if I sometimes say things against people like Mathy and others, it's because I believe in my soul and conscience that these people are very harmful to our Work, because they are basically destroying what we have taken so much trouble to build. I believe with all my heart that the work Mathy does is comparable to that of Gamelin or Daladier.*

---

* General Maurice Gamelin (1872-1958) commanded Franco-British forces from September 1939 to May, 1940. Edouard Daladier (1884-1970), as Prime Minister of France, signed the Munich Pact in 1938, which permitted Germany to annex Czechoslovakia. In 1940, he escaped to Morocco, was arrested on orders of Pétain, and turned over to the Germans, of whom he was a prisoner until 1945.

A PARTY AND A WEDDING 167

They didn't do anything positive, and tolerated sloppiness and put in the least possible effort, and we have inherited the catastrophe, and from the religious point of view, we don't see it yet, but we will much later when Christ will return. So if I attack men like Mathy…it's not really them that I'm attacking, but their methods in the tasks they have the responsibility for. I agree with you that we should forgive them or try to make them better. Anyway, I believe that the principle of criticism should be permitted freely in a democracy. You know me well enough to know that I don't hold grudges against anybody. But if I see something that can do wrong to the spiritual life of other individuals, I will always rise up vigorously against it. … When I see someone develop in another the venom of spiritual dissolution, or when I see Mémé develop a spirit of anarchy around him or someone else a spirit of harshness and injustice, or Mathy shrinking from responsibility out of moral cowardice, then I will do anything to prevent these people from going on. Of course I can't use illegal methods, so I believe that one way is to try to make those who have the responsibility of directing our Work understand the harmful character of certain persons. Father Mathy did a poor job raising his children, and I don't see that he has any right to come in and tell people how to manage the youth when he didn't ever figure out how to manage his own. You are right to say that I shouldn't talk about it all the time, and I don't think I do. I write you often and I don't think I talk very much about the father or mother Mathy. … You are right to tell me what you are thinking, and I absolutely do not hold it against you. I'm just trying to explain what makes me act that way. I will think about it and try to decide if it's acting in a Christian manner, but so far I don't see any harm in it. I'll talk to Papa about it. It's too bad he isn't here as I would have so many questions for him.

I am happy that you thought of us on our wedding day and that the parents knew when it was. Elisa also read your letters and was very happy about them. From now on I will have her read all the letters also. …

People in Lyon are hopeless. They lack fire and enthusiasm, and the whole city is like that. No, it is no problem being with Paul [Meyer] and his wife, because they don't fight and are very correct, it's just that he acts as if she didn't exist. …

And now that I have answered your letters, I'll tell you a little about everything I have done since my last letter. So I left here on Sunday with a cargo of food and arrived in Nîmes about 5pm. I stayed there overnight and reserved a room for Elisa and her mother. They arrived at 5AM. I had reserved couchettes for them from Annemasse…but they were too nervous to sleep much. They had some time in their room, and then at 8AM we took the bus for Anduze. Elisa and her mother were very interested in this region as they hadn't been there before. We went to tell the mayor that all was ready for the next day.

Then we went to the notary to sign the act of séparation des biens [separation of wealth: in a French marriage the couple's holdings are all in the hands of the husband unless they sign such an agreement]. As you know, when I organize something it's done right. Then at the Town Hall Elisa had her food and clothing ration card made out, which was done very quickly. They even gave us the bread rationing card for the whole month's allowance of bread, (which permitted us to serve unlimited bread at the dinner). Then they went to the room I had reserved at the hotel. We went to the distributor of certificates for blanket coupons, etc. (I just got coupons for two sets of sheets, two blankets from Nîmes, pillowcases, etc.) The only thing that didn't arrive were the shoes, but I got a beautiful all-leather dress pair for 400 francs. Then we went up to Madame Girou's who served us dinner (I think it was her own dinner that she divided into three, as there was so little, so little). The weather was beautiful, not cold at all. …

In the afternoon we went to see the old part of Anduze. Elisa's mother came with us—until the day of her departure, she never left us alone for more than 3 minutes. I said to myself that it didn't matter, because after tomorrow I will have Elisa to myself for always. While visiting the old quarter through the cobblestone streets, she said, "But where are you taking me?" and I said that she was the one who wanted to come with us, and it wasn't my fault. …

We had dinner at Madame Girou's. I had also engaged a cook to do the work. When we had arrived in the morning, Madame Girou wasn't even dressed by noon. At 7 o'clock I went to meet Jockmanns who was supposed to arrive on the bus from Montpellier. By 7 he hadn't arrived and I telephoned to Montpellier where they told me the bus had had a breakdown (it was supposed to leave Montpellier at 4pm) and that the bus hadn't left and wouldn't leave until the next day or the day after that. But I had written to Jockmans that he could also leave Tuesday morning at 4AM and arrive in Nîmes at 5 and take the bus at 8AM from Nîmes to Anduze. So I didn't worry too much and told myself, "God will provide".

A PARTY AND A WEDDING   169

... Madame Girou was telling me that there was plenty of this and that, etc. I told her that I didn't want anyone to go hungry and that I wanted an abundance of everything, and that I wanted everything that I had brought to be used. The next morning at 5 AM she hadn't even begun to do anything. I had to shake things up. I had brought corn starch, sugar and candied fruit. With the eggs and milk I got there, I gave everything to Madame Daunis so that she could make the pudding. Mother Girou nonetheless managed to tell her, when I wasn't around, not to use everything and to bring back some of the candied fruits. Madame Girou asked me if it would be all right with me if she took the leftovers. So, after thinking about it for a minute and knowing her, I said to her, "When we have finished eating, you can show me what's left, and if there is a lot of anything, we will give it to a poor family that has children". ... So then she told me, "I put aside a few of the potatoes you brought, because there are enough." So I told her, "Show me what you put aside," and she showed them to me, and they were all the biggest ones, and at least half of what I had brought. So I said, "Come on, put all those in too, we have to eat well." I remembered that once at Christmas she had invited the youth group and the dish prepared for 15 would have barely served 3. But she still put aside 2 kilos. It was the same for everything. She had put aside at least a kilo of white beans all in the same way. She took some eggs to make a sauce which she never made, but she kept the eggs. ... I took care of the menu myself as I was scared to death she would make one of those awful soup mixtures for which she alone has the secret and which would instantly cause any mouse to drop dead if it even touched any of it. And then there was the question of the heat.

There was no fireplace in the room where we were going to eat. So we had agreed to put around those little heaters which work very well. But you have to have well prepared charcoal which doesn't put out any carbon gases. ... I told Madame Girou that I wanted the room to be heated, I was also remembering that unforgettable Christmas where we were all shivering with the cold. But at 10 o'clock nothing was ready. She said she had to have 50 francs for the charcoal. I gave it to her, saying I wouldn't spare expense as I wanted it to be warm. But she managed to put only one layer of charcoal in the heaters, so that it was nice and warm when we arrived to eat but it went out during the meal and she should have put in more, but she hadn't prepared any, probably in order to keep the rest. I told her it was getting cold, and you have to put on more charcoal, but she put in unprepared charcoal and by the end of the meal some people were sickened by the fumes. Others had headaches.

Apart from this everything went marvelously. I had my beautiful navy blue slightly striped suit, but I had trouble putting on the white shirt with the stiff shirt-front and collar was so stiff that I had trouble putting on my tie. And I had to watch Madame Girou all the time so she wouldn't make off with the eats. She wanted to keep an eye on the cook, probably so she wouldn't use too much butter and oil. ... When I came down in the morning, there were Jockmans, Beaujolin and Savignat waiting for me in the café with Elisa and her mother and who were all ready. Poor Jockmans had been on the road since the previous day and hadn't slept much. ...

Around 10:30 we started out for the Town Hall. We were waiting for Daunis, who was my best man (Beaujolin was Elisa's attendant). I had told them at the Town Hall that all was ready and that the attendants were registered. But no Daunis. ... We went into the room at quarter to eleven and still no Daunis. The mayor came in with his secretaries, still no Daunis. I said maybe we should use someone else as best man. I ran out on the road, and there at the second turn in the road was Daunis, seeming not the least in a hurry. I ran back to tell the others he was coming and then went back out to get Daunis and tell him it was nearly eleven o'clock and everyone was waiting for him. "But," he answered, "it's not even 10:30." Well, anyway he was there and that was the main thing. There were two chairs in front of the mayor's table and a lot of chairs behind them, and everyone sat down except Elisa and me. The mayor began to read (he is a good Protestant who worked in the Renault factories before he retired). He didn't read very well, and had trouble saying my names, Johan Hendrick Weidner, and when he came to Mama Linschoten's name he just couldn't get it out. I was looking at Elisa out of the corner of my eye, and she was smiling and I wanted to laugh. And then all of a sudden he said, "Oh we have to open the doors, otherwise it isn't legal." It seems you have to open the doors when you get married. There was a lot of noise in the corridor, and the mayor sent someone out to quiet them down. When he finished reading he asked me if I wanted to take Elisa as my wife and vice-versa, and we signed a lot of papers, and the attendants did too. ... When everyone had signed we got congratulations from the mayor and the secretaries, and we got our very pretty family register. Elisabeth was asked if she wished to keep her French nationality and he wrote that into the register... Elisabeth looked the register over carefully to see if there was

A PARTY AND A WEDDING

anything that might invalidate our marriage and didn't find anything much to her regret! ... I gave an envelope containing 500 francs to be distributed among the various charities and 350 francs to be divided among the Town Hall's employees.

Then we went to the Methodist Chapel which was heated. Elisabeth and I sat in front in the two armchairs and the others sat behind us. ... Brother Jockmans led a ceremony which took an hour. He was wonderful. He talked about goals in life, and rights and duties. Everybody was very pleased with it. Mother Cartier said afterwards that it would have been the same in a Catholic Church and that Jockmans had been wonderful. Daunis was very good, too. He praised the sacrifices of Madame Cartier in bringing up her daughter all by herself, and now she was making the greatest sacrifice but that she would be happy knowing that by letting her daughter marry she was contributing to her happiness. He recalled that Elisa's father had done his duty. He said that Papa would have liked to perform this marriage, and that my whole family was with me in thought on this day. But that being one of Papa's best friends that he had known and appreciated for thirty years, that Papa would have been happy that it could be Jockmans who was replacing him, etc. etc. He also remembered Mama who was always so good and who had tried to give me a good character, etc. etc. He began the ceremony by reading from the Bible and then gave his talk, and then he asked us to stand and then asked us, as the mayor had done, if we wanted to take each other as our spouse. He put the wedding ring on my finger and then did the same for Elisa. Then we both knelt and Jockmans blessed us with a prayer. Elisabeth had brought the gold wedding rings from Switzerland. Then we stood and he gave us, as from you and the family, the pretty Bible you sent and which I had brought for the occasion, and he asked us to read from it every day. Then we all stood and after Jockmans's prayer we all left. The organ was played several times during the ceremony by the wife of the pastor. We registered in the marriage book of the Methodist Church. I gave the pastor 300 francs for the church and Beaujolin gave him 100 francs, and I also gave him a big box of nougats for his children. So I think we gave the pastor a good impression of us, and he was very nice to let us use his church, and showed a generous spirit in doing so. The ceremony impressed us all and I was especially happy for Elisa's mother. ... All the people you will see on the photos were at the meal... The photo we like best is the one with the background of fir trees with Elisa and me. I had it enlarged and I will send it to you.

For the dinner, Mr. Daunis had set up planks to make a table across the room and we weren't squeezed together at all. Sauvagnat did the prayer. Of course I was beside Elisa at the table, but after a little while, Madame Cartier seemed to think it was a little cold (that was her pretext, as she was burning to sit by her daughter) and as the heater was on our side, I gave her my place.

We opened two jugs of grape juice, and I can assure you we drank a lot. The juice was excellent. Mr. Daunis had advised us to get the 1937 juice. I gave one jug to Jockmans to take with him to remember us by. But we did have enough as there was quite a lot left, and Madame Girou must have taken care of it after we left.

We began with a very good potato soup and then green salad, white bean salad, olives, then vegetables: leeks with white beans and carrots in a beautiful white sauce, it was all very good. Then sautéed potatoes. By then we had all eaten so much there wasn't much room left. We had the cornstarch pudding (I had brought 250-gram packets). Everybody had eaten so much that there was a whole pudding left and a lot of pieces. We had a fruit salad of prunes, apricots (Brother Petit had given me 5 kilos of apricot pulp for my wedding), apples, all with juice and sugar, it was delicious. At least half of it was left. Then there was a tangerine for each person and two big chocolates with fillings that I had bought in Annecy for 3 francs 50 each. I bought the tangerines just before leaving Lyon on the Quai de la Gare. Then there were still 3 king's cakes, with which we filled our pockets, but there was at least a whole one left for Madame Girou. She did give some away. Nobody touched the almonds. And there were still some Jordan almonds.

During the whole meal Madame Girou really stuffed herself, and you would have thought that she hadn't eaten for 3 weeks, and everybody laughed at her. I forgot to mention the beautiful piece of Swiss cheese of which there was a big piece left as nobody was hungry anymore. Anyway, it was a great success. …

At 4 o'clock those who had to leave got up as the bus left at 4:30. When we came out of the hotel the bus was arriving, and Madame Cartier had just arrived and had to go up to her room to pack her suitcase. I grabbed everything, bathrobe in one hand, shoes in the other, everybody had something in their hands and we dived into the bus and I gave

A PARTY AND A WEDDING

something to the driver for having waited for us. And that dear Madame Cartier still sitting next to her daughter, even in the bus. I told Elisa we would catch up later. The trip went well and we arrived in Nîmes. Having eaten so much we weren't hungry for dinner.

Beaujolin and we 3 had taken rooms. Elisa and her mother together and me all alone. But at one o'clock Madame Cartier was to take the direct train with couchette to Annemasse. We all slept and then at midnight I and the two Cartiers got up and went to the station where she took the train and then Elisa and I returned to the hotel and here I draw the curtain.

The next day at 11 Beaujolin and we took the Lyon train, but we got off at Avignon and Beaujolin went on. Elisa and I traveled in 2nd class (for a honeymoon it's allowed). On Wednesday afternoon we went from Avignon to Marseille…and Friday morning we went to St. Raphael almost at the border of the Var [department] as the Alpes Maritimes [department] is closed to foreigners. And an application for a permit takes two weeks. The weather was beautiful and we were in a hotel right on the shore. In Marseille Elisa had forgotten her hat in the armoire at the hotel, and we phoned and they said it wasn't there. What thieves. For once Elisa had a hat I liked.

On Sunday at my insistence Elisa went to Monaco all alone, as she had never been there and I had gone there several times. I took advantage of the time to write, etc. On Monday we took the direct train to Lyon… Along the whole coast and as far as Valence, the weather was beautiful, but the closer we got to Lyon the more we rediscovered the nasty climate. Sister Meyer had prepared us a lovely evening meal, and everything was perfect. On Thursday evening Elisa took the train to Annecy where she stayed overnight and on Friday morning she took the bus to St. Julien to go to Switzerland. The dentist still has to work on her bridge and she is going to bring back a lot of things and settle various other things and is there to make the separation from her mother a little less sudden. … Lizou was very sad to leave me. We get along very well and we love each other very much. Morning and evening we pray for you and the family, and it is so nice to hear her pray. She has a golden disposition. She is very sensitive, and the minute I say anything a little emphatically, she cries. The other day she cried, because, as she said, I have all the worries and she doesn't do anything. Poor little thing. I think I'm very happy, but will she be happy with me? She says she will, but I have my doubts.

On Tuesday evening I will leave for Annecy and on Wednesday morning I'll take the bus to Collonges and leave Collonges at 2pm and will see Elisa in Annemasse at 3 o'clock, and from there we will go to Morzine (between Thonon and Clusés) to do some skiing and at the end of the week I'll return to Lyon, and Lizou will go back to Geneva and then will come back to Lyon and won't budge from there again unless there is some unforeseen event. Elisa will look for an apartment and will go to Switzerland sometimes to see her mother…

Now my dear Gaby, I'll leave you. This is a long letter. Send some details to the parents and I will write them when I get back. So now you feel as if you had been at our wedding. I gave Brother Meyer a few wedding announcements that you can send to friends. … Send one to Uncle Wibbens and to our office in Brussels.

My moral and physical health is excellent. Business is going along, at least better than for Fischer [Germany]. I think we may have lost the Dutch Indies.*

Until later, my dear Gaby. May God help and protect you and let us see each other soon. Arthur's uncle, as Papa calls him, will pay us a visit soon. Here it's snowing hard, and there? There are a lot of avalanches in Switzerland. Affectionate kisses from Elisa and me. From now on Elisa will write to you sometimes in my place. What a boon for me who hates to write.

Your affectionate brother, …

Gaby to Jean (card)   Paris, February 1, 1942

Mon bien cher Jean,

I was so happy with everything Brother Meyer brought. I have looked at all the photos 20 times, and yesterday when I woke up the first thing I did was look at them again. I put the wedding announcement into a frame and put it downstairs. In the afternoon I passed around the photos at the youth group meeting. … Last night I dreamed that I saw the parents in Holland and that you were there too. I had a two-week pass and we went to get Annette at the clinic, and we were all crying with joy. Alas, it was only a dream, but it was a nice one. I kiss you both. Gaby

---

* Japan invaded the Dutch East Indies on January 11, 1942.

A PARTY AND A WEDDING

Gaby to Jean   Friday, February 6, 1942

Mon bien cher Jean,

    Just a week ago Meyer returned and brought me all you sent. How can I ever thank you? ... The material is splendid. I hardly dare sit on the divan. On Saturday evening I went right into cutting the curtains and on Sunday afternoon I cut the divan cover. I gave them to Sister Dethier to sew. On Monday evening, the curtains were already hung and I couldn't stop admiring them. This morning she brought me the divan cover and I'm going to press it right away this afternoon and put it on my bed. I didn't need that to remind me of you, but now I will think of you all the more. There are so many things in my room that came from you, my dearest Jean, that really I'm afraid Elisabeth will be a little jealous. ...

    People are saying these days that the Germans are going to evacuate Paris within a 50-kilometer circle. Others say the demarcation line is going to be moved farther north. But it is said so often that it probably won't happen, at least not for now. But still I need a few more details on the location of your eventual Paris apartment. If the line were to be moved northward, I would immediately rent you an apartment. But if they are only going to evacuate Paris up to 50 kilometers around, and there was only a corridor of Free Zone, should I still rent you one? And, yes, in what neighborhood do you prefer? Two rooms and a kitchen, bathroom, or three rooms. The rents have gone up now. Try to give me some guidelines when you can, and then I'll know. ...

    Oh yes, while I think of it, you should really be careful what you say to Brother Meyer because he doesn't always keep things to himself. Yesterday in the office, in front of Marthe and me, he said that you recognized that you have not always understood Elisabeth very well. and that sometimes you had been abrupt with her, and that since you have been married, you have understood how sensitive she is. I would understand if he said something like that to me, but I really think it's no business of Marthe's. Just don't tell him that I told you this, as he would be annoyed. But anyway I advise you to be careful.

    I'm glad Madame Mathy is in charge of the heat situation; she economizes on coal as much as possible, even while keeping us warm. She is really dedicated, and that compensates for her other faults. Sometimes she annoys me a little, but on the other hand she never misses an opportunity to do something for me. This winter she has often stood in line for us...

Wednesday, February 10

On Sabbath morning I came down at 10 minutes of 10, thinking there might be a letter from you, as the mail arrives at 9:30 or 9:45. And sure enough there was one. I ran up to the kitchen and I was so surprised, but happily surprised, by the length of the letter. You were so good to give me all the details. I'll recopy some parts of your letter on the typewriter, and I will send it to the parents. Papa can translate, and that way they will have the news without your having to write it all again, as you are so busy. ...

Of course I read some parts of your letter at noon and we all held our sides. You really had some adventures during your wedding. If you had made a film of it, people would have said that you accumulated all those things on purpose: Jockman not arriving, Jean not being able to put on his tie, Mr. Daunis being late, the doors not being open, the precipitous departure on the bus, and especially Madame Girou and her stinginess! It makes us a little sick to think that it was she who was going to get all those leftovers, because she certainly has more money than all the others who were there. But she did help out some. But that business about the charcoal really made me angry, because since you had given her more than enough to pay for wood charcoal, she shouldn't have held back on it. Well, it's all over now. ... You all look wonderful in the photos. Lizou's coat is really very pretty. And Jean was impeccable. Not like when Brother Meyer left Lyon and you had a torn pocket in your jacket and had a safety pin in it which showed on your collar! Of course, he would tell me that. So, I beg of you, Elisabeth, next time Mr. Meyer comes, make sure that Jean is decent. Mr. Meyer told me last time already that Jean was much better dressed than he was in Paris. But if you have the least little hole, some little defect or a spot, he will always notice, and of course he won't keep it to himself. It makes me laugh. I like people to be neat and clean, but I never see the little stuff as he does! ...

If I don't hear from Mr. Laatsman in a few weeks (because I hope he will have news of the parents when he gets back) I'll go and see if he is back. I'm planning to give him 100 francs for the poor, but maybe it would be better to give him a personal gift. I'll ask him if he has a little girl or if he is married (I'll find a way to ask it in a natural way) and maybe you can give them a length of organdy or lace, something not too expensive. That would be nicer than my giving him money for their charities. What do you think?

A PARTY AND A WEDDING

Yes, maybe he would be willing to take a gift for Papa. But he doesn't go very often. As Papa doesn't have a fountain pen, I bought one; we were able to get a few without any gold in them a while ago. But it isn't very big and I know that Papa prefers pens that have a big ink sac. Maybe you could buy him one; or else I can do it myself. Even with a bookstore ration coupon, I can't count on it, because they aren't making them anymore, and you have to supply your own gold. But sometimes they're available in the stores. In your things that are in the basement, are there any fountain pens? When you get your apartment, should I send you the things in your suitcases little by little? I'm afraid they will deteriorate because in the cellars, and in fact the whole house, it is very humid. And about the letters. Should I organize it somewhat? If they ever came to search the house, which often happens, though it has never happened here yet, but has in other houses, they would look at all the mail, and maybe it would be a good idea to destroy part of it, maybe not the commercial correspondence but the personal letters, maybe like the letters you wrote to the young people during the war. I won't touch it yet though, I'll await your orders. ...

We haven't a single piece of coal left. Yesterday was the last day of heating inside, and of course, wouldn't you know, it was freezing outside. Fortunately today the temperature is milder. We telephoned and begged them to bring us some more coal as we have the right to 4 more tons, but the merchants have so few trucks that they are making their clients wait. It's not much fun. We can't complain, though, because until now we have had enough to keep warm through the coldest times. Let's hope they will deliver some on Thursday as they have promised. Alas, people don't keep their promises as much as they did in the past. ...

I like working in the office, but as I said to Brother Meyer the other day, if there wasn't a war, I would ask to be placed in Marseille or Collonges. I've been in the bookstore for 7 years, and I'm getting tired of it. Of course, if there wasn't a war, I would also have been traveling a little this summer and at Christmas, and that would have made a nice change. So I have to be patient. I can be glad I have a job, and it is, after all, a fairly interesting one, with good bosses. ...

Because of my desire for change, and because I can't go anywhere else, I changed the arrangement of my room. I tossed out the horrible armoire made of imitation mahogany, which belonged to the house, as I couldn't stand it anymore, especially since everything is now so pretty with all the fabric you sent me. Now I only have the hanging space, but it isn't big enough for everything, and I put the red armoire in Zaza's room. I can go there when I need something. But since you told me in your letter that eventually you would send me the money to buy a studio, that was so nice that I just choked up (I didn't get to sleep until 4 in the morning), I'll try to buy a pretty armoire. That's expensive enough. But I really don't need anything else. My room is very nice and once I have an armoire, it will be perfect. ...

I really hesitate to have Zaza's room done over for me. It only makes a temperature difference of one or two more degrees at the most, and my radiator is bigger. It's when the sun is out, which doesn't happen very often, that there is a difference; one can open the door into the corridor and the sun comes in that way. But aside from that, the room is less well laid out; the washstand is in front of the window, which makes it hard to put up the screen to hide the washstand. Moreover, I go to bed rather early, and Lisette pretty often has company in her room, not every day, of course, but it does happen, and when you can hear people talking it's bothersome when you want to sleep. So I hesitate. ...

You did the right thing letting Lizou stay with her mother as long as possible. I would have stayed with my mother too until the last moment, especially if I had been the only daughter. I hope that she will not be too lonely. Fortunately they can write to each other.

If Lizou is sensitive, she will have many reasons to shed tears, as you shout pretty often! It's nothing if you're shouting to say you love her, but if you're angry for one reason or another, it's different. Do you remember once when you were in my room, you began to shout, "I love my sister and no one can stop me from loving her." And the more I told you to be quiet, the louder you shouted. We were talking about that with Marthe the other day and she wondered if you would do the same with Elisabeth. Well, I hope you won't make her cry too often. And I can understand her, because I am sensitive too; but I don't cry as easily as I did a few years ago.

I wonder if they will deliver the coal today as promised. Last night it was below freezing again. In the office it's bearable, but in the rooms it's awful. Yesterday (Wednesday) it was 4 degrees and this morning 3 degrees. And it's not as cold as it was last week. And I assure you I dress warmly. I have on two wool undershirts, a wool slip. ... If we have to go through another winter like this it will be terrible because it weakens us a little all the time. I also have on a wool sweater, and a very warm skirt with suspenders, a wool cardigan and my smock. I am also wearing wool stockings

A PARTY AND A WEDDING 179

and wool socks over those. ... You see, I am being careful. But it still doesn't replace central heating.

... I understand better now your attitude toward Brother Mathy. Of course he isn't very courageous and he behaved badly toward you. It wouldn't hurt the church any if there were another more energetic pastor, and I think that will happen soon, because he has been here such a long time. But on the other hand, he has other qualities; he is very conciliatory, and here you don't want a pastor who breaks everything up. ... There's no point in making a bad reputation for him as he will retire in a few years, and then that will be the end of it. That doesn't prevent some members from liking him; to each his own taste. And since you have said what you think of him, I don't think it is necessary to continue to do it. I can see you aren't holding anything against anyone personally, since you say you don't hold a grudge and that you would be ready to help all those who might be in need. That's good because that's the hardest thing to do when we don't like someone. But I don't think you could do anything to change Brother Mathy, as he is close to retirement. It's true that you don't talk to me about it very often. But the thing is, I am very embarrassed when Brother Desmet or Brother Meyer talk about it in front of Marthe and I know that your attitude surprised them a little. After he received your last letter, I told him that you didn't have anything against Brother Mathy personally, but that it was his methods that you disapproved. And you know how it is, when one says something, the others immediately exaggerate it, and make a whole big thing out of it. But I am glad you explained your point of view, because now I understand better. ...

I have written so much already that I don't know if I can still talk to you about my love life! which basically isn't a love life, but only an affair of the mind. I already talked to you about the young art teacher who was recently baptized. He came at Christmas and the Mathys invited him to lunch on the Sabbath as well as Sister Marie and myself. Other than that I hardly know him. He orders books from the bookstore from time to time, and so we correspond a little. He told Brother Mathy that he would like to get married, but that he wanted a girl with whom he could study the Bible. In his last letter he said to Brother Mathy that he was putting himself in God's hands for this. I am very embarrassed because Brother Mathy really has to answer him somehow. He doesn't know him very well but says that I would certainly be right for him (he doubtless thinks I am the most pious of the girls here! and yet I have such a long way to go). On the one hand he [Mathy] doesn't want to be a matchmaker, he regrets enough having had anything to do with Edith Badaut's marriage. On the other hand, he realizes that the young man wants him to suggest a girl to him. Brother Mathy doesn't want to talk to him about me without my consent and I don't want him to because I have no idea if I could love the young man. As I told you, he is shorter than I am, but I want to be reasonable and not take that into consideration. But I know nothing about his character. If he lived in Paris, we could see each other and get to know each other, but this way it's difficult. On one hand, I don't want to miss an opportunity for happiness, but, as I said to Brother Mathy, I have not waited until now and refused the possibilities I could have had, whom I didn't like anyway, just to make a mistake now. I told Brother Mathy that it would be better not to speak of me, and that if something were to happen, it should come about without help. But of course if I don't like the idea, Brother Mathy will try to put him in touch with another girl. I really don't know what to tell him. I've always told myself that when the time comes, and if He wishes, God will let me meet the person who is destined for me. But in that domain, I always have terrible doubts. Probably because I haven't really met anyone who is right for me. I think that when I really love someone I won't have any hesitation. Of course if this young man were tall and handsome, there would already be some physical attraction which would help prepare the way. But that is not the case, as there is nothing extraordinary about him. But really, I don't want to tell Brother Mathy to say something about me, at least for the time being. I pray every day that God show me the way, because if I were going to get married, I too would want someone who is pious, with whom I could make spiritual progress. I wouldn't want be alone for my whole life, but I wouldn't want to marry and be unhappy either.

I must be boring you with my problems, you who are in the middle of your honeymoon and you have so much to do. ...

And now I'll stop, as I have really wasted your time. I hope you won't be angry with me, but I had to answer your long letter. And anyway, I don't write you such long letters all the time; usually I am in a hurry when I write you.

Dear little Lizou, dear Jean, I'll leave you for now. Affectionate kisses.

The coal arrived. We will turn on the heat this afternoon.

Gaby

A PARTY AND A WEDDING

Wednesday February 13

... The concierges [Koukoutches] will have to find another situation. They are getting out of the hospital. ... She can go to the convalescent home. ... They are not so badly off. Lots of things were found in their cellar... there were two whole boxes of laundry soap [savon de Marseille] even though they complained to everyone that they didn't have any. They are Jews; what can I say. ...

It's so nice to have heat again. Madame Mathy went right away to turn it on again yesterday as soon as the coal arrived. The committee voted to give her several bottles of grape juice to compensate her for all this work; she deserved it. ...

Papa to Jean, Gaby, and Elisabeth   The Hague, March 4, 1942

Mes bien chers, Jean, Gaby et Elisabeth,

"Age before beauty," I said to myself when choosing the order of addressing you. [Papa quotes the first phrase in English.] I hope I won't be criticized for not saying "beauty before age," because then I would have to reverse the order of all three, and my son, whom I consider to be among the best, would have to come last.

But I hardly have the courage to begin, as I have before me 3 letters, one from Miss Beauty, another from Miss Conscience, and one from Mister Diligent. But I have to believe they're all really here, because otherwise, all three would come by plane one day to reproach me for my laziness. And I even would like to have them come here, and as soon as possible, but not with severe expressions. So, here we go. ...

It goes without saying, our dear Elisabeth, or Elisa, or Lisa, or Lizou (choose the name you like best for us to call you), it goes without saying that the two others will close their eyes and put their fingers in their ears, because this is for you alone. A big and very sincere thank-you for the kind letter which did us so much good and which you sent us on February 18, the first letter from Madame Weidner-Cartier. Of course you also wrote it for Jean, as his secretary, but still not only as his secretary; that was shown in the contents of the letter, because it is surely "from the heart's riches that the mouth speaks." Your delicious letter allowed us to follow you both "High up, high on the mountain" and I added "I see an old chalet,

Where Jean and his companion, Drink lots of milk each day." [Papa makes his rhyme fit the old French song.] Yes, it was really a piece of luck to find so much of that "white wine" [milk]. But what a drinker your husband turned out to be on your honeymoon already, to let himself be so overcome by drink! 1 to 3 liters a day!! His mother and I are ashamed of such a son and Annette of such a brother.

Say, Lizou, would you give a message to Jean for us? And that would be to scold him very hard because he took the risk of going into the mountains. And try to do it very harshly. Well, no, maybe that would be beyond your strength, and your good heart would suffer too much from doing that, as I don't see you as quick to anger. So I'll suggest another way: Look at him in a very feminine way with your heart showing in your eyes, and beg him to reflect upon the fact that his little wife suffers so much at the thought that her dear husband is exposed to danger [when skiing]. That rôle will suit you better and that method will have more effect on a young man who is a little like me. Because I too resist when I am scolded or even when I'm threatened, but I can't resist when someone enters my heart.

Dearest Elisabeth, do I need to tell you again how welcome you are in the heart of this family? I think these words would not do much to strengthen the conviction that you must have had when spending time with us, either in Collonges or in Paris. In any case I regret not having consulted a soothsayer during our stay in Collonges, because if I had known what I now know, I would not have missed even one opportunity to accompany you when you went down on the tram and my wife and I would have had the pleasure of your company more often, not to mention what Annette would have done. But there you are, the past is the past, and all three of us are so happy to have as daughter and sister the one whom we all three love so much. And we too, just as you suggest, we pray to our good Heavenly Father to grant us the privilege of seeing each other soon. And in the meantime we are happy to know that morning, noon and night you put us before the throne of grace and we are happy to do the same for you. We also pray for your dear mother so that she be consoled still more at the thought that by following nature's law which is a part of every human being, a daughter does not abandon filial love, but simply adds to it, just as she does also with another kind of love.

And now it's Miss Conscience that I address next, and of course the others will pretend they neither see nor hear anything.

A PARTY AND A WEDDING 183

Chronologically, I should answer you before Lizou, dearest Gaby, because you wrote your letter a day earlier, but I know you are patient and you are able to forgive your father a lot, especially since he isn't shaving anymore. Ah, if anybody should send you a photo of me, I would have to sign my name to it, otherwise you will think you are seeing one of the inmates of The Hague's zoo (I won't say which section, so as not to offend my progeny). I have admired you, Gaby darling, and your mother has also, for keeping us so well up-to-date. You took a lot of trouble to re-copy that whole letter. But you did us an inestimable favor in doing so.

You also were an angel to think of us through your friends. We received everything this time. If you only knew how happy we were! Poor Gaby, you have so little heat in the house! Be careful. Paper is very effective in the shoes and on the body. But everything has its limits. Here we are also suffering from the cold which is intense this year. On the radio I heard Hitler say that there hasn't been a winter like this for a hundred years. I didn't verify the statistics, but as he never lies, I'm willing to believe him. This year the cold is really terrible. A few weeks ago I could hardly stand it any longer, so Mama had the bright idea of making me a hot water bottle from time to time. It warms me enough to be able to stand the low temperature, as we have to be economical with the heat. ...

We just read in the newspapers, that Paris suffered damage during the enemy bombing. These British are pitiless. What do they deserve, when one thinks of all those victims? I can well understand that a day of mourning was observed. ...

Annette went back to work a little too soon after her recent illness. Because they don't have enough help, they put her on night duty for two weeks. As a result she never really got over her illness completely, So she had a relapse 3 days ago. I went to see her this morning in her room at the clinic. She has no appetite. But that will pass. They are taking pretty good care of her. And if necessary we will bring her back here. But we don't think it will be necessary.

Mama just refilled my hot water bottle. As you see, she treats me like a prince. The weather is still cold. This morning we found the streets turned to ice, because yesterday it rained for hours. Then last night it snowed and then it froze. A little while ago I saw a woman fall down, I was sorry to see that she wasn't wearing pants like a man. Many women are doing it here now. Annette wears them too. ...

And now it's Mr. Diligence's turn, and yet I don't dare just address him "Mon bien cher Jean". I want to address not just one half but to both, because, and here is another proverb, a married man is worth two. So I include Miss Beauty. True, Mama, to whom I have just read my prose of the last two pages, drew my attention to the word "Miss", but as I then drew her attention to the fact that pseudonyms don't take such obstacles into account, my other half is satisfied and so is Miss Beauty herself, I hope. But to complete my effort at appeasement, I will write:

Dearest young Couple,

You have now been united for six weeks, and are, I suppose, not ready for divorce. It's impossible to convey the great joy of all of us here, but especially Mama and me.

I still remember, Jean, the moment when you told us of the love that had been born in your heart, and you asked our advice. We were so happy that you had confidence in us. You know the answer we sent, after having asked for God's guidance. Certainly there was one obstacle at that time: that the conception of life and duty to God might not be the same for both. But we expressed to you our full confidence that this obstacle would not remain, and God has arranged everything in such a way that you didn't have to sacrifice your earthly happiness to your principles. ...

Dearest Elisabeth, through your union with Jean, you reestablish the number of children we used to have. Your gentle character reminds us so much of the one we lost. When we think of you Mama and I are a little consoled, and we are so happy to know that you will have great patience in directing this strong current of a lively, active and enterprising personality away from the mountainous and rocky regions toward the plains where calm and peace reign. I know that you love him, and not only with earthly love, but that you wish for his eternal well-being. You will become ever more a moral support by encouraging him with the tact that is yours to make his plans for eternal life. And if God gives you the blessed responsibility of raising lambs for the great Shepherd, may the guardian angels of these young rejoice constantly in the wisdom and unity which you both show in taking that direction. ...

Yes, Jean, your bachelor life is over now, that life where you can come and go as you wanted, come home whenever you liked, and do whatever you wanted. What a burden. But I am sure you wouldn't want to return to that life, even if it made you a millionaire, as you already possess millions.

A PARTY AND A WEDDING 185

... We loved reading about the preparations for your wedding, and we laughed so many times. Too bad nobody made a film! We could see you all, a hairbrush in the hand or some other thing, rushing to catch the bus. And what a relief for both of you when you could say, "Alone at last!" You deserve it. Nothing in the family register to render the marriage invalid, Lizou? And that poor mayor covered in sweat and with the doors closed! ... And what a meal! With the hideous shadow of the Miser hovering over. ...

Speaking of weddings, how is that of Charlotte [Belgium]? I don't think it's anything more than a marriage of convenience. Whatever happens I don't think she will ever love him, and even if you tell me that the marriage took place in all the proper form, I would maintain that it can't last. Isn't that true? ...

Congratulations, Lizou, on your beautiful coat for the wedding. Everything was very pretty: coat, hat and the person holding them together. ... Jean, your suit was terrific and also its owner. He looked very happy. And we are happy along with him.

[In French Papa's next four sentences end in rhymes:]

> I'll end my verbiage,
> As I wish to be sage,
> I cannot use another page,
> So this is the end of my persiflage.

For the first time I kiss, through my delegate Jean,
The One who has already been kissed by her new mother,
    Pa

On the night of March 3rd to 4th, 1942, the British Royal Air Force targeted the Renault factory at Boulogne-Billancourt on the West side of Paris. Renault had been forced to make trucks for the German war effort.

Gaby to Jean and Elisabeth (card)   Paris, March 4, 1942

Ma chère petite Lizou,
Mon bien cher Jean,

I think I will hear from you soon, but I must send you a card in case you worry about me. Our district was not harmed at all during the bombing last night, but at Billancourt everything is destroyed. Zaza phoned to tell us that all their windows were broken, and all the doors destroyed. It's terrible because there were hundreds killed. There was no alert. ... The Renault factories don't exist anymore. I heard a little of the beginning of it and then I went part way back to sleep. From time to time a heavier boom would wake me. ... Kisses from your

Gaby

Gaby to Jean and Elisabeth   March 9, 1942

Bien chers Elisabeth et Jean,

... Mme Sandberg brought me the radio. It was the same day as we had vaccinations, because as you have probably heard there are several cases of smallpox, and nearly everybody got vaccinated. Dr. Nussbaum came to the house and vaccinated everyone who wanted it, that is everybody who cared about staying alive! The Mathys, Brother Meyer and the Grisiers didn't want to be vaccinated. I'd rather take precautions myself. The reactions did not happen to everyone at the same time. I've only felt the effects, that is the itching, in the last 24 hours. Marthe's arm swelled a little, Brother Desmet's also, but it's not serious.

I am so happy to have the radio. ... It is not a new set, and there was a lot of dust inside, but since it has 5 tubes, I will hear the stations very well. Brother Sonntag told me it is good to have a used one, as the new ones aren't worth anything. ... He also said it is better not to have a small one because one can't get all the stations, and they get out of order very easily. It sits on the bookshelf and looks very nice. ... Another of my dreams come true. I am beginning to realize that little by little they are all coming true. ...

Last Wednesday I went to see Sister Droz in the evening. The last time I had been there, I happened to mention that I would love to be able to take a bath, as it had been a long time since I took one. [Gaby, like most French people at that time, would have taken her "baths" as sponge baths at her washstand.] I think she didn't have any hot water at the time, but she told me she had it once a week from Wednesday evening to Thursday

A PARTY AND A WEDDING

evening, and she invited me to come take one. So I went and had a bath and then we had dinner and a nice evening. ...

I don't have time to get bored on the weekends. Sometimes I have appointments two or three weeks in advance, because I am so busy. ...

I hope you weren't scared by the bombing raid. All our members were saved and a lot of them lived in that district. Some houses had been built between the factories. And they dropped torpedoes weighing 1000 kilos, which make huge fires. Moreover, the workers were inside and since they have sliding doors they couldn't get out. Some succeeded in getting out through the windows. But there were still many victims and all the windows and doors in the surrounding area were broken and torn off. Brother Souplet lived in a six-floor-building which was completely destroyed, but he was in a garden shelter with his wife, and they were all right. They were able to find a lot of their clothing and linens. It's probably going to continue as this afternoon they bombed Poissy and the Matford factories are completely destroyed. ... I don't know if they will come here up over our heads. Delahaye is near us, but they don't make war materiel. They just make ambulances and trucks. Anyway, if it gets a little hot around here, we'll go to the Métro station at Place d'Italie. I don't want to go to the shelters, as there were many people who drowned in the cellars or were killed by gas or who were buried alive and they couldn't get them out in spite of their cries for help. On Tuesday night it was a very beautiful spectacle because there were rockets lighting everything up all around Paris. They also dropped leaflets. One fell on our terrace and one in the garden. But of course we destroyed them. ...

Wednesday, March 11

... On Monday Brother Grisier got America [on the radio] and they gave the list of factories that would be bombed. Delahaye was one of them. But as there are other much more important factories, I don't think they will begin with that one. So don't worry about me as long as you don't hear that Delahaye has been bombed. As a precaution, I wrote Mme Steinbach to ask if I could leave one or two suitcases at her place in Pavillons. I think there is no danger there and I could put in all my fabrics and my sheets and other things I don't need immediately. That way I wouldn't lose everything if ever the house were to be bombed. There are so many people in Billancourt who managed to save only the clothes on their backs, and I know myself too well. If I wake up hearing bombing and they don't sound the alert, I know I'll lose my head…

Gaby to Jean (card)   Paris, March 12, 1942

My dear ones,

I wonder if Jean remembered that today is Annette's birthday. It's an important one for her as she comes of age today. So no longer is she the "little" sister whom he teased so often. …

Jean may have sent Gaby the carbon copy of this twelve-page letter (all one paragraph!) as this appears to be the original. The carbon copy is probably easier to read than the pages typed with an exhausted typewriter ribbon on thin paper. Selections from his letter.

Jean to Gaby   Friday, March 20, 1941 [but it's really 1942]

Ma bien chère Gaby,

At last, a moment to write to you. … After my wedding, I had a lot of trouble catching up, as I receive so many letters, that if I'm not careful I'll be seriously behind, and besides I have this importation business, which is mostly paperwork in six copies, etc. etc. …

So Elisabeth returned from her mother's with a fever which got worse during the evening at the Seminary. So I told her to stay in bed, and she did until Saturday morning. … On Sabbath morning she got up and went to church. In the afternoon she went to her mother's at 6pm, where she stayed until Monday morning. Then we met at Annemasse to go skiing. Everybody at Collonges was so nice to us. … In a way, Odette is a little disappointed in Collonges. She came there with the idea of really helping the girls to supplement their education, and it seems there was nothing to be done, and that the girls are given too much freedom in their relationships with boys. A few girls came there just to have a good time, and a few who went too far were expelled. … I think she has arrived at the same point I came to with the youth in Paris. I wanted to help them, but we didn't have enough authority or means of exercising it when things went too far. …

A PARTY AND A WEDDING

From Annemasse we went to La Roche where we saw Elisa's uncle and aunt and several cousins. Everyone was very nice. They call me their "nephew", so my family is growing. Elisa's uncle has a bus business. He gave me some cheese and promised to send food supplies. … We stayed overnight and left the next morning for Morzine, which is between Thonon and Cluses. We found a very good room with central heating and hot and cold water. That cost us 70 francs a person per day. We had a wonderful time there, and nothing was rationed. I drank 2 or 3 liters of milk a day. Elisa had a lot of good cheese too, as she likes cheese (and she needs it for proper nourishment). With me Elisa is completely vegetarian, and that pleases me and she isn't worse off for it, either.

In Morzine there was a ski lift (like the one in Salève) which takes you to the top of the mountain from which one can ski down on the trails. The day after we arrived, in the afternoon, Elisa and I went to the top, but Elisa hadn't learned to ski very well yet, and I was unfamiliar with the trail. We had a lot of trouble coming down on the trail on which good skiers can come down in 20 minutes, and it took us 2 hours. We had to go through woods, etc, and around 6 o'clock a fog came up and then it was dark and we were the only ones who were unfamiliar with the trail. Luckily there were signs here and there. Poor Elisa kept falling down all the time and couldn't get up, and I was scolding her (you can just imagine the scene when I start yelling), and that made her cry. But by 7 seven o'clock we got back, and by the next day we had forgotten all our troubles of the previous day. The main thing was that we got back. We took some skiing lessons, and had some wonderful days. It was sunny, and Elisa got a tan. We went twice to a chalet-hotel far up on the mountain. We had whipped cream, fries, butter, cheese, milk and chocolate. It was unbelievable. Elisa and three other women went on a horse-drawn sleigh ride for 5 kilometers. With the husbands of those ladies, I went up the mountain on skis and came back by the road on our skis, and pulled by the sleigh, it was great. Only one regret and that was that Annette and the parents and you weren't there.

While we were at the hotel, there were about ten people who had broken their legs. Fortunately neither I (and you know me, I was rather reckless) nor Elisa were among them. We stayed a week and would have liked to stay longer, but we had to return to work. Elisa went down to Geneva, and I returned to Lyon. We were both the picture of good health. It did me a lot of good to clear my head also, as I had been very preoccupied before. Now I feel ready to do some good work.

Elisa was so nice, and I assure you, I never thought I could be so happy. Elisa has a golden disposition. You know how I can get angry very quickly. (Elisa calls me Donald in honor of the duck in Mickey Mouse, because the duck screams all the time.) Well, she doesn't pout and she never holds a grudge, and that keeps us from staying angry with each other. If she were hard to get along with, I think I would spend half of my life being unhappy, because I would never want to take the first step when I was wrong. Of course a Christian must learn how to forgive, but it's a struggle. But with Lizou it's wonderful. And then she is very gentle and kind. Everyone told me I was really lucky and that I don't deserve it, and I agree with them.

We still haven't found an apartment, but Elisa is looking. We rented a hotel room which is very comfortable, but in Lyon there is so little space and so many people. ...

Elisa went to see her mother and came home. Then she went back because she broke her dental bridge and it is guaranteed by the Geneva dentist. She also had to settle her mother's war widow's pension. Last week it was announced that war widows who haven't remarried will get 4000 francs instead of 3000. ... I wouldn't want to limit how much Elisa goes to see her mother, so she won't think I'm an ogre. Of course later, she won't go to Geneva as much, but as she has a visa now, she might as well take advantage of it, especially since there are still things to settle there. ...

Paul Meyer is less and less happy with the Lyon church, and I can understand that, as Lyon people (not just the Adventists) are very, very cold and unsociable. It's a whole different atmosphere from Paris. Elisa doesn't like the city or its inhabitants. Fortunately she has me. In fact she wrote me yesterday that when she arrived in Switzerland she felt as if she were arriving on a different continent. Of course Geneva is so morally and materially clean that the difference is enormous. But, we hope one day to go to where you are and then we will be happy. ...

I still have a lot of work and everybody asks me to buy this or that for themselves or for someone else. Three months ago the Seminary students asked me to buy them a set of boules [bowling balls like Italian bocce]. Fortunately Elisa is here and can give me a hand for a lot of things. ... In fact that's the reason I have caught up my work. She takes my suits to be pressed, and irons my shirts. And since I've been married, I always find my socks darned, whereas before I always had to choose among those which had the smallest holes. ...

Elisabeth gets back at 8 o'clock this evening. She always brings me a thermos of that wonderful milk chocolate that her mother prepares for me. I don't think I'll have any problems with her mother now that the marriage has taken place. In fact she hasn't said anything about the wedding that wasn't nice and perfectly correct. She didn't tell me, "Take care of Elisabeth or you'll have to answer to me." So I think we'll get along all right and that we have nothing to fear. ... Elisabeth was able to buy the same hat as the one that got stolen in Marseille. ...

I'm glad that none of the members were hurt in the Paris bombing. ...

Friday, March 27, 1941 [but it's really 1942]

I'm taking up again the letter I started exactly a week ago. I interrupted it quite suddenly, but I will do everything I can to send it today. If you only knew how busy I am. ...

I strongly advise you to take Zaza's room. Have it all re-papered, and I will pay for it, but make sure that you have a good living space. Later I might not be able to do it, so we should take advantage of it now. ... For our Paris apartment, we would like 3 rooms, kitchen and bathroom. It should be in a quiet area, like Rue Bobillot, a new building, top floor if possible, so that we wouldn't have the neighbor above and we would have plenty of air. Sunny exposure, near the Métro. If possible a well-built house with soundproof partitions, so one doesn't hear everything from the neighbors. You should rent this apartment when Paris is about to be liberated or evacuated. If necessary you can sign a lease with your name, and when I come we can settle everything with the managers. Maybe it's best if you don't say it's for someone else, so rent it as if it were for you. When the time comes I'll send you some money which you can use for an eventual rent. The area around Place d'Italie would be quite nice, as I think the air is better there. ...

Next time I will watch what I say to Meyer. It's true that he always tells everything. I will do my best to be careful, as you know how I have a tendency to talk about my concerns without paying attention. ...

Maybe it would be a good idea to look at what's among my things in the cellar. Of course papers won't deteriorate, but if there are clothes or suits, anyway look and see. If there are any old suits or pants, send them to me so I can see if I can exchange some to buy new things. You can destroy any letters you think might be dangerous. You can certainly destroy those to the young people. Do just as you think best, and if there is anything among my things that you like, keep it and use it. ...

Here the Consulates have been closed and replaced by "Dutch Offices" which don't do much, and the Swedish Consulate represents our interests. So I asked if Elisabeth could be on my passport or have [a Dutch] one of her own without being made to renounce her French citizenship, and they told me it was impossible. So then I wrote to ask if my children would have Dutch nationality. They answered "it is out of the question that my children would have Dutch nationality." I was very surprised and and I wrote to say so. In all countries children whose father is of another nationality have that nationality. I was outraged. Maybe you can get more precise information on this, as I think they are not taking us seriously. Elisa is going to ask about it next week. Anyway, Elisa got a certificate from the Dutch Consulate in Geneva confirming her Dutch nationality. With that she should easily be able to get a Dutch passport, at least in Switzerland. I think that my children will have Dutch nationality anyway. ...

About your sentimental life. I think that the young man you told me about seems very nice. Of course you have to study him a little more to find out if he is faithful, nice, etc. But in my view, you shouldn't be too worried about the fact that it isn't love at first sight and that you would be crazy about him. Love can also come gently with time and without forcing it. You shouldn't discourage this young man if he makes a few advances toward you. You can always stop if you saw he wasn't really the one for you. Especially if he is a good Christian, you might be very happy with him. That's the main thing. Don't be too choosy, because otherwise you might end up with no one. Moreover, without becoming too promiscuous, you could have relationships with certain men even without the eventual goal of getting married. You mustn't be too timid or reserved, because many opportunities could escape you. You might very well correspond with him and then see him from time to time. ... I think Meyer is partly right to say that the boys shouldn't come so often to eat with the girls. ... If you entertained young men in your room, and they spent the night there, you couldn't fall back on the fact that you have the right to do what you want in your room. We are part of a great Work and those who participate directly, like you and Marthe, have to listen to the advice and recommendations of older, more experienced persons, even if it sometimes seems ridiculous. We are democratic and believe in individual rights, but we are not anarchists who repudiate authority. There should be an understanding on both sides based on respect for a certain amount of discipline and for individual liberty. ...

Now the mail is going to leave. Be of good courage. In a year Arthur's uncle will come to visit us, and we will see each other again. Heartfelt kisses from Elisabeth and me.

8   Bombs and Refugees

In Paris there are bombing alerts, and the roar of the anti-aircraft guns can be heard. It is good to have friends in the country.

Gaby to Jean   April 1, 1942

Ma chère Lizou et mon cher Jean,

… I'm leaving tomorrow morning, Thursday, at 7:50 am on the train to Caen-Cherbourg. I'll get off at Lison, and I'll be met there with either a truck or a horse-drawn wagon. That will be fun, if only the weather is good! It's about 12 kilometers to Cérisy-la-Forêt. Madame Steinbach is very happy that I am coming and has already ordered milk and cream in another form for when I am there. I am sure I will eat well. …

[same day] Wednesday, 8:30

I have packed everything, which didn't take long, as I'm only going to be away a few days. But I'm taking along quite a lot of packaging material so that I won't have to send more right away. That will save me some shipping costs, as the trip is quite expensive: 250 francs round trip. …

Thursday morning

Last night there was another bombing alert. The problem is that they have put D.C.A. [anti-aircraft] positions everywhere, and that makes more noise than the planes and more even that the bombing. But last night, it wasn't too loud, and I went back to sleep after a little while, but of course, then the all clear signal woke me up again. It's tiring when we don't get enough sleep; it's not so bad when it's only once in a while, but right now there are several bombing alerts a week. Well, c'est la guerre, and we can't complain too much, because it has been very peaceful for a long time, while other cities have been bombarded for months. ...

I'll stop as Mr. Meyer is calling me to do some letters. I'm going to be very busy at work while there is no one else in the office. But I'm not too worried about it. I'll do as much as I can.

I think of you all the time and hope you are happy together and that you'll find an apartment soon, where you will feel at home instead of in a hotel.

Je vous embrasse très affectueusement and send my best thoughts.

Greetings from Brother Meyer.

   Gaby

Gaby to Jean and Elisabeth (card)   Cérisy, Friday, April 3, 1942

Bien chers Elisbeth et Jean,

I arrived here at 2 o'clock yesterday; the truck was waiting for me at Lison. I had had a bad night as my alarm clock was set for 2 o'clock in the morning. At 4 o'clock I was about to get back to sleep when I heard the big guns and sirens beginning to operate. Fortunately the alert was over at 5:30, because since the Métro doesn't operate until an hour after an alert, I was afraid I wouldn't get to the train station on time. The train passed right beside the Ford factory which had just been bombed. The fireman were still there. I think it was on the Argenteuil side. If Lizou were here [in Cérisy], she would certainly have liver problems. Of course I'll only be here a few days. The weather is nice, though not very warm. I hope Henri gets the letter I just sent. Now that I am a long way from Paris, I forget about all the problems, and I don't give a thought to all the work that is waiting for me. ... Kisses and good thoughts, Gaby

BOMBS AND REFUGEES

Gaby to Jean and Elisabeth (card)   Paris, April 8, 1942

Bien chers Jean and Lizou,

I got back yesterday evening, very happy to be home, as home is always the best place to be. I'm glad I went to Cérisy because of the food, and the good air, but it's too quiet there, and there was really very little in the way of conveniences. For a few days it was fine, but I wouldn't want to live there. I found two letters from Mama, one of which said Papa had intestinal flu, and the other, written a week later, said he was well again. I'll send them to Henri as soon as I have time to write. ... Je vous embrasse bien fort. Best thoughts. Gaby

Gaby to Jean and Elisabeth   Thursday evening, April 8, 1942*

Bien chère Lizou et mon cher Jean,

... First, I'll tell you about my visit to Cérisy. It's a place far away from everything, but the food supply is excellent. I can assure you that people aren't going hungry there. ... While I was there, I ate as much butter and cream and eggs and milk as I could. The first three days I didn't feel too well, as the change of air is significant, as it is near the sea. And then the change in food probably had something to do with it. But starting Sunday, everything was fine. There wasn't much modern comfort in the house, and Mme Steinbach would much rather return to Pavillons. But because of the food, and because the little boy is very nervous because of the bombing alerts that we have so often now, she will stay there. I wouldn't want to spend a whole vacation there as it is deadly dull and one gets very bored. But for a few days, if only to eat well and breathe fresh air, it's doable. ... The countryside is rich and the farms are lush. Normandy is really not poor. ...

Oh yes, one more thing about my replacement [in the bookstore]. We still don't have anyone. ... We can't take anyone who was never at Collonges. Sister Raimbault from Angers, was there [at Collonges] for two or three years, but doesn't type or take shorthand. ... But nothing is settled.

---

* It is probably April 9th, as in 1942 April 8 was a Wednesday, and she returned from Normandy on April 8. She is now working for the main office at 130.

I would like it to be a nice girl whom we could count on so that I wouldn't have anything to do with the bookstore anymore. ...

Time is passing and I won't be able to write as much as I would like. So I'll tell a little about Marthe's case, as I haven't done so yet. ... About a month ago, Marthe talked about resigning. And a few days later, it was done. She said she no longer felt in the spirit of our Work and that she felt that she was doing this work no differently than she would any other, and that she wanted to work somewhere else. She had had enough of it and wanted to change. ... She has a lot of doubts on certain points and she hopes to be able to judge better when she is no longer in the Work. It is true that in the offices, one sees everything, and all the mail passes through our hands, and sometimes it puts one a little off balance. But with Marthe that isn't a temporary situation as it can be with any of us. She says she has always felt this way. Of course she could have realized much sooner that she wasn't in the right place. But better late than never. It saddens me, but I think she did the right thing. I hope that when she is somewhere else, she will see the good things that were here and that it will make her think. ... The committee voted to give her 3 months' salary, as she had been in the Work for 11 years. ... She loses all those years for retirement, so that is a compensation. ...

Marthe is looking for an apartment and Lisette wants to leave and live with her, as she has had enough of living in a house where everyone knows everything. ... Since they are both leaving, I will take Lisette's room. ...

I just heard that Velluire, where I spent my vacation last year, is now in the Restricted Zone. So another door closes. I was thinking of going back there this year. Maybe there'll be something else.

Oh yes, about the radio. After it was set up, it worked for about a half hour. Mr. Sonntag says a tube has blown out. But unfortunately they don't make that kind anymore. ... Michèle will try to get one for me. ...

Kisses, Gaby

Jean to Arthur Vaucher   April 14, 1942

... For the first time in my life, my work is bringing me something. Before, I would work really hard and get nothing but criticism. But finally the wheel turns, and there is often a just return here below.

BOMBS AND REFUGEES

Annette to Gaby　　　　　　　　　　The Hague, April 8, 1942

Ma bien chère petite Gaby,

　You wrote to me almost a month ago, and I haven't answered you yet. You're going to think I've forgotten you, but that's not the reason. It's spring, and the birds are building their nests, and people are too, and in the clinic, the same thing is happening. There is not one free bed, and it has been like that for weeks. Every day we put another bed in the wards. You can imagine how much work we have and on top of everything, a lot of nurses are sick, and so we each have to do the work of two. Fortunately I can work very fast, but as you know, I can't very well keep going just on my nerves, and that reduces my appetite. In the last 6 weeks, I could hardly eat anything, and of course I'm losing weight. Anyway I hope it will pass. I take drops from a homeopathic doctor to improve my appetite, as I am not at all well lately. I think I need a change of air. Anyway in two months I'll get a two week vacation. That will do me good. I am so glad you are well. That time in the south did you a lot of good, didn't it?

　Mama is unlucky. Poor dear, she fell coming back from church and sprained her wrist, and she is quite upset. And tomorrow is her birthday. Aunt Marie is helping her prepare her vegetables, etc. I hope she will be better soon.

　Thank you for your good wishes for my birthday. Yes, I can't believe either that I am 21. Time goes so fast.

　I was so happy to get a letter from Mr. Meyer and to see that he hasn't forgotten me. I would be so happy to see you all. Sometimes I get really depressed. Here it is more than two and a half years since I left Paris, without the least idea that I wouldn't be seeing you all soon. I hope this war will be over soon.

　Fortunately I was able to celebrate my birthday at home. I had just been out of bed for one day and the doctor let me go home. Of course I couldn't go out to eat at a restaurant as we had planned, but that didn't matter because I was so happy to be out of bed. I had visitors in the afternoon and was very spoiled. From Mama I got all the instruments for my work when I get my diploma and a big zippered bag to hold my instruments and bottles, etc. From Papa I received an instrument case and 50 francs. From a friend I got a book (costing 140 francs) for my studies: "Kraamverpleging" ["Childbirthnursing"]. From another friend a silk table runner with a long fringe which comes from India, a vase and a pretty bouquet of tulips and a pound cake. From my roommate, a purse. From Feen's mother, you remember my former friend, a beautiful bouquet of tulips. Nice isn't it? She didn't come personally, but she sent it. Hey, why are you teasing me about Mr. Meyer? It's true that I like him a lot. He's a real sweetheart. But I don't think it's dangerous either on his part or mine.

... You really shouldn't have any illusions about me, because I really don't know what you see in my looks. I have nothing to shout about. I have fat legs, and I have almost no color. No, you will be really disappointed when you see me. Now, Lizou, there's a pretty girl, and you, you have beautiful eyes. When I show your photo to my friends, I always tell them about your velvet eyes. And as for my character, I am much calmer than I used to be. Oh, I still have my moments when I am a little nutty and very energetic, but as a general rule, I have changed a lot, and as for turning the boys' heads, I can tell you that I am very serious and that no boy has kissed me for 6 months. On this point you can be proud of your little sister. I give myself entirely to my work, and I hardly go out anymore. But, I am always so tired during my free time I don't have the strength to go out. We have so much work at the clinic. It's really terrible. I enjoy doing my work, you know, and I like it here a lot, but at this time it's almost more than I can do. Right now I'm on night duty and while you are in your bed having sweet dreams, I am thinking of you and talking to you as if you were right here beside me.

A few nights ago, 5 future mothers came into the clinic, all in the same night. We didn't have a single free bed. The next morning at 6 o'clock I was all alone in the birthing room and they all five began to cry out and I really didn't know what to do next. I ran from one bed to another to see if it was time yet to call the midwife. And you know, I hadn't yet been present at a birth outside the clinic. I already had stomach pains just at the thought of it. But now, on night duty, it was my turn to go, and if the phone rang at night, my legs would begin to tremble. Well, just think, last night I had to go out. I had worked from 9 in the morning to 11:30 at night without stopping, and I was hungry, and I said to myself, "Now I'm going to rest a little in the kitchen and have a cup of coffee," and then the telephone rang. It was a mother giving birth, very far away, almost an hour by bicycle, outside The Hague. If you could only have seen me. I was trembling all over. But there was nothing to be done, I had to go. A policeman came to get me, and we went out into the black night. I couldn't see anything and I was going along by guess. I was so scared on my bike. I was afraid I would hit a tree or get my wheel caught in the tramway rails. And the policeman didn't know the way very well and took me to a completely different district. There we went to the police station and another policeman, who knew the way better, guided me. It was very hard to find, as it was pitch dark and it was a new street in the middle of the woods. The policeman was a handsome guy and tried to flirt with me, but, as you can imagine, I had other things on my mind. I kept thinking, "I hope I get there in time to prepare everything."

At last I got there at one in the morning. Luckily the doctor was already there scrubbing his arms in order to be sterile when the solemn moment arrives. Madame was quietly lying in bed, not even moaning at all. I said to myself, "Oh the doctor is getting ready much too early." The instruments were already sterilized. I quickly went to get a pail in the kitchen and some containers to put the placenta in and to mix some Lysol to make sterile swabs. Then I prepared the crib with a warm water bottle and put the baby clothes against it to warm, and two towels to catch the baby in. I hadn't been in the house for 15 minutes when Madame said quietly, "Doctor, I feel as if I had to push." I look, the doctor looks and we look at each other and say at the same time, "Well, we aren't too early." 5 minutes later the baby was born. I cleaned him up and bathed him, and then I straightened up, as everything was in a mess.

They had thought the baby would come in two weeks, so she didn't have everything ready. I had to hunt in the armoire and finally found everything. Then I scrubbed myself and I bathed the happy mother. She was hardly torn at all, so there was no need to sew her up. I even got a compliment from the doctor, that I had "changed the sheets very well." Then I rinsed the dirty linen and buried the placenta outside in the earth. The monsieur had dug a trench for me. The wind whistled around us. We could have been taken for murderers burying something. Finally at 4:30 I left all alone to return to the clinic and got there an hour later. But I'm not afraid anymore.

My dear, I'll leave you for today.
    Kisses, Annette

Letters from The Hague are limited to two pages, and Annette ran out of space before she ran out of things to say when she wrote the previous letter.

Annette to Gaby   The Hague, April 17, 1942

My dear little sister,

    I'll continue my letter of a few days ago. I had so much to tell you that I got to the end of my two pages before I knew it. Just think, a few days ago I had another call to a birth outside of the clinic. I left at 11 o'clock and return at 4 in the morning, but this time all alone, without a policeman. It was a fourth child for this family and it was a boy. They already had 3 girls. You can imagine how happy they were. But now I just learned that the baby died. The head nurse just called me into her office. She is cold as ice. I haven't had to deal with her yet because she is in charge of the nurses in their last 6 months, outside the clinic. Of course when I helped at the birth, these people get another nurse for three visits a day, and the head nurse goes from time to time to check and of course to ask if the nurse provided good assistance during the birth and if they are happy with her. So of course she asked about me. She is very critical and always finds something wrong. All she could find to criticize me for was this: that I shouldn't tell them that I would come back to see them. She absolutely doesn't want us to come back to see the people we helped during the birth. I think it's absolutely stupid, because it's so sad for us never to see the baby to whom we gave first care. So anyway, I said yes and Amen. We have to obey the rules of the house. Then she told me with an icy tone, "Moreover, the baby died this morning." You can just imagine what a blow that was. I was all broken up, as he was so cute and seemed to be in perfectly good health. Almost 8 kilos. I don't understand it. He had a bad case of jaundice right after the birth. Those poor people.

    You asked me why I need all those instruments. Well, it's because if the doctor arrives too late, we have to do everything ourselves. Otherwise, of course, we don't have the right, but it happens often, especially now that they no longer have cars. The doctors are really funny. They have so much confidence in us, and they tell us, "Call me when it's time." But it is so hard to tell. When we call them too soon, they are furious. And so if we have the instruments, we can sterilize them. The doctor at the last birth I attended was a real sweetheart. Very young and so nice to the mother. He was encouraging her, you should have heard him. He had studied several months in Paris, and we talked about Paname [a popular name for Paris]. When he left he said to me, "Ik dank u voor de buitengewoon fyne samen Werking." ["I thank you for the extraordinarily fine teamwork."] Just think, when he had just touched her inside with his sterile gloves, he told me, "It will be quite a while yet," and he went to the kitchen to take off the gloves and wash his hands, and then all of a sudden, the mother wants to push, and the head comes out. And there I was calling the doctor and having the mother breathe in sighs so she wouldn't push. The doctor didn't even have time to put his gloves back on.

Mama had a nice birthday. She received 3 magnificent bouquets of flowers from 2 friends and the aunts in Utrecht. Her wrist is fortunately much better. Tomorrow and Sunday I have two days free. I am so tired because I have been working for 3 weeks without a break. The weather is beautiful. Spring is arriving, but we can no longer go to the beach. Everything is barricaded. My dear, best kisses from your little Annette.

Gaby to Lizou and Jean (card)   Paris, April 20, 1942

Bien chers Lizou et Jean,

So yesterday afternoon, I moved into Lisette's room. I was a little sad to leave my room which I had had re-papered and painted the way I wanted it. But Lisette's room is not bad at all, and I will have a lot of sun. In the evening I went to the train station to meet the young Raimbault girl who is going to be in the bookstore. She began work this morning, but she'll have to study accounting and typing to do the work alone as soon as possible. She is very nice. At noon I'll have lunch at Madame Droz's. Maybe afterwards I'll go to see Laatsman. Was there some tea for him in the package Brother Ganty brought me? I was so surprised to get tea from Jean who is so against it. So am I, but in exceptional circumstances I sometimes do drink it. Love and best thoughts, Gaby

Jean has been working with Mr. Sevenster, the Dutch Consul in Toulouse before the Consulates were closed by the Vichy Government. They are helping Dutch refugees who are interned in refugee camps in southern France.

Jean to Gaby April 27, 1942

Ma bien chère Gaby,

It's been a month since I wrote you a letter, how time flies. I don't think I have written you many cards either, but thoughts of you never leave me, but I have so much to do. ...

We went to the Charpiot-Abot wedding in Collonges, which was very nice, and then went to Anduze. ... Madame Girou welcomed us very kindly and we had a meal at her home. We had bought a kilo of bread (in the evening she came to the bus to tell us that we had left the bread at her house, but she didn't bring us the bread). But we learned from Madame Girou herself what was going on with her son Mémé. It seems he had been in prison for two months in Albi. It seems he was stealing packages from his friends at the youth camp where he was, and also money from his leader, and he was trafficking the bread rationing cards which he stole in the office. etc. Since the youth camps aren't under military control but under civilian control, he was placed in preventative custody in Albi while waiting for trial. His mother told us that when he arrived at the camp, he said he was a theology student, and because of this a lot of things were left in his care; but after a while, it was observed that he was a good-for-nothing, and his leader couldn't stand him, and what's more, he was very undisciplined. ... Let's hope he comes out of it without too much damage. But you can see how this boy is ending up, and in my opinion his future is pretty bleak. His mother is beginning to be seriously worried about him. She asked me to write a letter as former president of the Paris youth group, saying that her son was not normal and had no sense of right or wrong. I wrote a very strong letter, but I wonder how it will all come out. ...

I'm planning to go to Collonges for the end-of-school year ceremonies, and Lisa was thinking of going to her mother's on May 13, because on May 14th her visa expires, and she has to take steps toward renewing it, but this morning her mother wrote to say she has to go as soon as possible, to arrange for getting a visitor's permit there. So I think she will leave tomorrow night and return two days later. ...

We are eating very well at Sister Meyer's, and she does so much for us. Every day or nearly every day, she makes crêpes or puddings, etc. Business is still going well, and I could be making a lot more, but then I would have to do nothing else, but I have so many favors to do for everyone.

We were firmly promised an apartment which was supposed to be ready in May, and now it is July, and it will probably be still later because the building isn't finished and some materials aren't available yet. Well, we aren't too worried about it. Of course if some day we were expecting a baby, we would worry more, but for the moment nothing is in sight.

I don't get any more merchandise from Switzerland, and the Ministry doesn't issue any more permits, but since I had already imported a lot, that gives me a larger quantity that I can sell little by little, as we sell only in small quantities. And besides I'm busy with a great many other things.

Elizabeth and I are very happy. We get along very well and the marriage is really wonderful. Before, I was always used to Mama or you taking care of my socks and now I always have a pair of socks ready and my suit is pressed, etc. ...

Thank you so much for all your cards. You are like Mama as you write me so regularly and so faithfully. Thanks a million, dear Gaby. ...

I don't advise you to go making a little jaunt to Belgium, as they could suddenly close the border and everybody would be caught in a mousetrap. For the men, it's no problem, but for you, with the certainty of your job at the office, it would be better to be careful. Of course if Papa or Mama were at Aunt Wibbens's house, I would tell you to go ahead, but not otherwise. ...

It's really wonderful that your identity card was renewed for two years. The Lord is good. We really have been privileged in many ways so far. ...

I hope the cloth I sent for Mama will arrive safely and that it is what she would like. It's a reversible satin, so she won't need a lining. I hope the handbag for Annette will get there, too, along with the 2 pairs of stockings for her, as she said there aren't any there. It's for her birthday present. ...

I'm glad you have Lisette's room. If possible, arrange it the way you want and get a different wallpaper if you want to. ...

About the tea, I sent it so you could distribute it as you wish. I paid about 50 francs per 25-gram packet. But maybe it can be a bargaining chip to do a favor or receive one. Tea is very much prized by some people, particularly Dutch people. So maybe it's for L. [Laatsman] or someone else, but they should appreciate for its true value. I can get a little more, but only drop by drop. Elisa is going to try to find Typhoo for you, but it is also rationed and there is very little. In my opinion you could drink ordinary tea from time to time, because it is no more harmful than Typhoo. Thank you for your cards of March 17, 23, 25, 30, and 31 and April 3, 8,

13, 14, 18, 20. And your two letters have been read and re-read. Lizou thinks you are very nice to her also, and I think she feels a part of the family...

I heard on British radio the other day that they are going to bomb more and more and they advise that people should demand shelters from the authorities. So we have to expect that the bombing raids will become heavier especially if the Americans begin bombing, too. ...

Would you like some poplin for pajamas, or some silk twill? If you want some organdy plain, printed or embroidered, or some ticking, I have all that too. Of course the best thing would be if you could come and choose here, but, alas, that isn't possible. Elisabeth is having a pretty red blouse made (a color that's in fashion right now). Do you want one? ...

I am sure the Arthur's Uncle will come next spring. Fischer is very ill, and the doctors are convinced that after he gets through another winter, he will die, as he cannot possibly hold on if a new attack occurs. Arthur is getting stronger and stronger, and everybody is happy about it. ...

This week I saw Sevenster. I'm doing what I can for the people in the camps, etc. Elisabeth and I are going to make several packages of food supplies, etc. as there are some people who have nothing. I also received an official communication that Elisa was automatically the same nationality as I am, even if Lizou keeps her former nationality, it won't change anything for us three. So everything is settled. They made an error in writing what they did, and the truth was exactly the opposite. So I'm relieved.

... At the office, they have at last received the gift they wanted to give us: a pretty set of silver-plated silverware which we are going to like very much. They haven't yet given it to us officially, as there will be a little ceremony. They are also going to give us a whole set of dessert and fruit plates. ...

Everyone who comes here says they are so happy with your work in the office. In Berne they are also happy that you remain so faithful at a time when they can't find anyone they can count on. I think appreciation of our family is very high now. I have become an important person, and your devotion and seriousness has been recognized, and Elisabeth is much loved by everyone, and the Division thinks that by their fruits shall the trees be known, so Papa gets back some prestige automatically, while Mémé Girou's father, for example... [suspension points are Jean's]

If you find a nice little apartment, rent it for you, and later Lizou and I can live in it. You can even rent it and not live in it, just to have it available later. I will pay all the expenses. ... You'll have a lot of work if you have to teach young Raimbault everything. Just don't get too tired, and get sick from it afterwards. I am like you, which is why I'm giving you this warning! I am so glad that you have moved up in rank and that you have this change. You will certainly have more responsibility in the Union, but if you remain faithful to our Work and to God, He could bless your efforts and your work much more than if you were doing some mercenary job. Don't ever forget that you are working for God, even if you are shocked by some things about the men; tell yourself that you are not responsible before God for the responsibilities of others, but only of your own. Of course if you can prevent evil or correct errors, you must do it, but never let that make you abandon your confidence in our movement which possesses simple and profound truth and that truth is your goal. Remain faithful to the teachings of our parents on all subjects, and don't be influenced by all these modern ideas of the Division. ... Read Sister White a lot and have confidence in what she writes, because I can assure you that when one compares what she wrote with the writings of others, one comes to realize the depth of sentiments which animated her, and of her consecration and her revelation. Poor Lizou has so much to do. She goes about doing my errands from morning till night, trying to find an apartment, etc. Now I always have darned socks and clean clothes, etc. I'm so glad she is good-humored. When I get angry, she always takes the first steps, and so I can't stay pouting or angry, as I did sometimes with Papa. ....

Gaby asks if Elisabeth can get her a "Bircher grater" in Switzerland. The tool is named after Dr. Maximillian Bircher-Benner (1867-1939), a Swiss physician and nutritional researcher, who advised a healthy diet of fruits, vegetables and nuts. His Birchermuesli (fruits, nuts, oatmeal and milk) became a popular dessert or breakfast food.

Gaby to Jean May 6, 1942

Ma bien chère petite Lizou et mon bien cher Jean,

How can I even tell you how happy I was to receive Jean's long letter on Sabbath morning. ...

They're sending mail this afternoon. I have been very busy for the last few days, and I wasn't able to write sooner. So I won't write very much today, unless the mail leaves a little late, and then I would have time to write at noon. If not, I'll write a longer letter next time. I've been helping the young girls, and I had to put things away and clean the kitchen a little, so that Sister Raimbault could come down to eat there. The "trio" ate here for the last time on Monday, and I was a little sad when Marthe and Lisette left with their last load of things. I've known Marthe for years and now I won't see much of her, but her life will certainly go in another direction, especially if she continues to work in the administrative offices. She has a good many qualities, and best of all, she is always cheerful. I hope that Lisette will not regret leaving the house also. I wouldn't want to take an apartment with a friend. ...

I hope Elisa got her visa, as it would be really too bad if she couldn't go to see her mother from time to time. If she's ever in Geneva, I would be really happy if she could find me one of those Bircher graters which grate in both directions. It's very handy and a while ago we could get them here, but now we don't know where to get them. ...

What Jean was telling me about Mémé Girou really made me sad. I didn't think he would go that far. ... It's particularly sad for Mme Girou, because even if she is Jewish, I think she is still honest. Of course Mémé never had a very good example in his father, who was always trying to cheat people. And then his parents raised him very badly, always giving him money, and it's quite understandable that this young man who always had piles of money, doesn't have enough now, and tried to get it by any means possible.

The young Raimbault girl is getting acquainted with the work. Since yesterday, she is writing the orders and I am trying to teach her a little accounting. This way, I'll have a lot less to do in a month or so...

Since yesterday I don't feel well at all; I caught cold and my throat is very sore. I would have stayed in bed this morning but I knew that Brother Meyer had some letters to dictate to me, and so I came down. Now I'm waiting for him to dictate, but he is talking with the others and so I'm writing you while I wait. I have two very nice bosses, and I really can't complain about them. If I'm not better this afternoon I will stay in bed, but still, I'm not really that sick, just a bad cold. Moreover, there was an alert last night and it woke us all up, but certainly not much could have happened because we didn't hear hardly anything from the anti-aircraft guns. ...

Jean told me I could rent an apartment which would be for you later. That is a very nice idea, but really, I think I would be bored if I had to live entirely alone. I'd still rather be at 130, even though there isn't much space. And I think it's a little early to rent one for you. Mme Droz was telling me Saturday that her brother (who got married 6 months ago) lives near the Bois de Boulogne. They are very pretty little apartments which cost 8000 francs. I think there are 3 or 4 rooms with bathroom and kitchen of course. It's a very nice area, but is it what you would like? ...

The other day I went into a store which has dehydrated vegetables. I wonder if they would still be good next winter, because if so, maybe I should buy some. It costs about 14 francs per 100 grams. What do you think? ...

I'll stop for now. My cold seems to be getting a little worse, that is, I'm beginning to cough. But I'm taking care of myself, and if it isn't better, I'll stay in bed. Affectionate thoughts and kisses, Gaby

There will be changes in the administration at 130.

Gaby to Jean (card)   Paris, May 13, 1942

Mon bien cher Jean,

As you have been at Collonges, you know of all the changes. The committee meeting was yesterday afternoon, and I am still completely overcome. ... The thing that bothers me most is that Brother Meyer is leaving, and I like him so much and he is very fond of our family. I could always ask his advice when I needed to and I'm going to feel very lonely. ... Now Brother Habéry is President (but people don't want that very much, and I'm not crazy about it either). Kisses, Gaby

Gaby to Jean   Thursday, May 14, 1942

Mon bien cher Jean,

This time I'm writing just to you, because when you receive this letter, Lizou will certainly be with her mother. Besides, I wouldn't want her to read this letter, and you will see why when I tell you more about the decisions made by our strange Committee.

It's 3 o'clock and I'm alone at the office. ... Brother Meyer will arrive shortly to dictate some letters. ... This morning he said to me, "It is understood that I will write letters to inform the people in the Northern Conference of the changes. So I'll ask you if you would be so kind as to take dictation for the letters, even though I can no longer give you orders, as I am no longer President." It made me feel terrible. I think Brother Meyer has taken it very well; he is very philosophical, and seems actually kind of happy. I would have thought that with his temperament he would have been more sarcastic, but no, he seems resigned to everything. ... The Division absolutely wanted Habéry to take his place. Maybe he's a good man, but I'm not crazy about him at all, and I much prefer Brother Meyer. ... I've heard that Habéry is ecstatic. On this so-called Committee, most of the Brothers didn't want him. ... The Doctor is basically the only one who wanted him, as he will be able to do as he likes. So we can already see that the Doctor [Nussbaum] will be in charge. ... The Doctor is always talking about Mrs. White [Adventism's founder], but I think he doesn't always follow what she says. He thinks it's very wrong to go to the theater, because she forbids it, but then he goes to the movies, because she doesn't write about that. I think that is not all how one should apply the spirit of Mrs. White. ... He criticizes those who don't believe in Mrs. White the way he does, that is word for word. I wrote to the parents about this yesterday, and told them I like Mrs. White well enough, but when I hear the Doctor talk and act, I'm almost disgusted with her. Once Gerber did a very good sermon, but the Doctor criticized it afterward during the Church Council meeting because it didn't mention Mrs. White. Soon we'll be saying more about her than about the Bible. I'm sure that Sister White herself wouldn't agree with that. We have to take her as a whole but not take apart every word she said. But I think they want to appoint narrow-minded men as our leaders because they are afraid of the broader ideas that some may have. ... The general opinion here is that the Division wasn't inspired when they did all that. Of course Brother Habéry went to the meeting and told all the little gossipy things in his own way, and they thought, "There's the man we need to set everything straight." ... I'm telling you all this so you'll have an idea how to interpret it. One is quick to form an opinion when one hears the sound of only one bell, and I think in our organization, before making such far-reaching decisions, one should ask around for information among those concerned. ... Papa saw so much of this kind of thing in the Work, that I'm really glad you're not in it. You know, Jean, I tell you all this because we are old Adventists and I know it will not diminish your faith. But I wouldn't want Elisa to read this, as it would certainly not do her any good, and yet what I'm telling you is all true. I'd also rather you not talk to others about it, so nobody can say all the stories come from me. ... I always got along with Brother Meyer, and now I'll only have Brother Desmet to laugh a little with, because with Brother Habéry, we'll have to be serious all the time. ... I already felt so lonely for my family but now I won't be able to talk about them anymore, so more than ever I can't wait for the Demarcation Line to be abolished.

... I went to see L. [Laatsman] last week and gave him the money. They didn't want to take the photos, as inspections are very severe now, and you can't even take a book through. But they took the cloth. When L. next goes by himself, he will take the photos, but he doesn't want to cause the others to be caught, and the photos aren't important as they are copies of your wedding photos with a few new ones. ...

The little package of tea, pleased him enormously. I think I'll bring him the other package another time. But you shouldn't buy any more at those prices. ... But I was glad to be able to do that for Mr. L. who has done so much for us.

Now I'll stop and maybe I'll add a few words tomorrow because the letter won't leave before then.

Friday morning,

I have so much work that I don't have time to continue. I'm really sorry, but I'll write you more later. Write me soon and tell me what you think of all this. ...

Bien affectueusement,
Gaby

Gaby to Jean and Elisabeth   Tuesday, May 19, 1942

Bien chère Lizou et bien cher Jean,

My last cards must have seemed a little sad, but I must say that all these abrupt changes really did disturb me. My spirits improved during the following few days, and so I said to myself, "I have to write to them, so they don't worry too much," and then today things are going badly again. Brother Habéry came to the office, and really, for me who never did think he was very nice, it really got on my nerves. He wants to poke into everything, and wants to know everything. He was already like that before, but then we could say what we wanted. But now that he is President of the Conference, we have to obey him. I have a pretty independent nature, and can't stand having someone always behind my back, watching what I do; I don't think I'm going to be very happy. But on the other hand, it's only the first day, and maybe it will be better tomorrow. There are people who improve with better acquaintance and maybe when I know him better, things will go more smoothly for me. ... Seeing that there were so many objections to his nomination, Habérey should have refused it. But then he doesn't have a lot of sensitivity. ... Most of the members are especially sorry about the two departures. ... Meyer was very much liked by all the members, especially the youth. Those in the know say that now it will be the Doctor who will run everything as Habérey will never be able to make a decision on his own, and will always run to the Doctor who already has a very marked tendency to impose his own will. ...

Another thing I don't understand: how can they offer Marthe a position in one of our other offices when she no longer agrees with a good many of our principles; in fact she isn't really an Adventist anymore. ... I suspect that when she resigned, she said mean things about Brother Meyer, even though he always defended her when others said she wasn't always truthful. I think Marthe isn't very honest. She has said before, that one can lie about unimportant things. But what is unimportant for her is perhaps important for others. I have often heard her tell incidents during which I was present and it didn't correspond at all with reality. And when a woman wants to hurt someone she can tell a lot of things that are perhaps true but which can be exaggerated. I don't have a lot of confidence in Marthe and for a long time I have been careful about what I tell her for fear that she will use something or other against me. ... She does have some good qualities. She is intelligent and cheerful, and that is why I got along well with her. ...

About the available positions, I'm not going to ask for anything. Of course if the war were to last one or two more years, it would be a hundred times nicer to be in the other zone, on the condition, of course, that I would get a permit to be there; then I would see both of you more often. But would the climate agree with me, especially at Collonges? And if the war ended and you came here, it would be much nicer for me to be here. I couldn't keep changing all the time. Anyway, I don't want to ask for anything. I will leave it all in God's hands. If it is His will that I stay here, then I'll stay here. And if I should go somewhere else, he will arrange everything so that someone thinks of me and offers a change of position. What a shame that you don't live in Paris. It would be super to have you close by. ...

When discussing the war, Jean can pretend to support the Germans and still get his point across, but he uses the usual code names when showing his real hope for an Allied victory.

Jean to Gaby   Thursday afternoon, May 21

Ma bien chère Gaby,

I hope you received my note of May 11. ... I'm leaving in two hours for Collonges, so I'm writing you in haste. Tell the parents I will write them next week, as I will be returning here with Lizou on Tuesday evening. I'm going to attend the ceremonies for the end of the school year. Lizou is still with her mother. A Seminary girl, young Cuiset, is going to return home via the illegal route. I hope all will go well. She will come to see you. I'll look into the radio tube for you.

Still a lot of work. There were some demonstrations here against the Germans last Monday night because of the concert of the Berlin Philharmonic. The young Cuiset girl will tell you about it.

I was so sure the Americans wouldn't undertake their offensive until next year, but now I'm beginning to think that they will do it this year. They have to hurry because of the Japs. The Swiss and the press seem to say the same. Needless to say that when they start their offensive, the Germans will sweep them out with their invincible force and that will be the end of England and America and the Germans will be the victors, and next year we will all see each other again. I am almost certain that it will even be this year, but I'm really counting on next year, and I think the hardest part is over.

Tell the parents that the reason I haven't written them is that I have been so busy, and that I know that you write them all my news, and that way I can use my time to earn money, set myself up financially, and help you all, which is my greatest goal. You understand that I am taking advantage of it now, as later it may not be so easy, and whatever I have taken in is taken in. But I think about them all the time and live for the idea of helping them and seeing them again and paying for a lot of things for them. For Papa I am collecting a lot of stamps, and Mama will have all the fabric she wants, and I'm reserving a whole bunch of things for Annette, as well as a little money so she can buy the things I can't give her at this distance. As for you, my dear Gaby, who devoted yourself to helping me and gave me all your pennies, you know I will never forget that, and you can count on me for everything. ...

Tell the parents that Arthur and his uncle will come soon. Fischer is very ill and has lost a lot of blood. I don't think he can live much longer. His fiancée doesn't love him anymore, and hopes to leave him soon and return to Arthur. Of course, if they could see each other more often, and talk to each other, many points of friction would disappear, but we mustn't pay attention to what mean people say about her. After all, she is a woman with much feeling and little common sense.

About all the changes, don't beat yourself up over them, my dear Gaby. Of course the departures are sad, but fortunately, you still have Gérard [Desmet]. He is really good and will protect you. About our Work, I believe the Division really didn't know about Marthe's situation, and if they had, they wouldn't have offered her the position they did. You know Beach has a good heart (he was ready to rescue Papa from that mess back then, as you recall) and he had a great deal of esteem for Marthe, who is certainly very intelligent and energetic, and knows how to pat people on the back. ...

I think that as long as our Work remains democratic and we can express our opinions in the assemblies, we can stay in the movement and work for it with all our strength, the important thing is that we ourselves remain faithful and that we cooperate with all our strength so that many people will hear our message and participate in it. That's not to say that we shouldn't see the wrongs and try to remedy them with solutions that we deem just. But all of this must be in a democratic context, leaving the majority of the Church to decide, in the final analysis. The Doctor can issue orders here below, but he won't be able to in Heaven. Have faith and don't worry about all these changes. I know how devoted you are to our cause, and don't ever let yourself waver. I am glad to have the parents we had, and especially glad that Papa explained Adventism to me from a realistic point of view and so I'm never surprised that these things happen. I believe in Ms. White and read her writings a lot, and I find much spiritual nourishment there, but we don't have to rely on her alone. There is also the Bible, so let's allow each person to nourish himself with Sister White however he sees fit and not by forcing her on someone and causing indigestion. The Doctor is doing more harm than good to Sister White's cause. Sister White herself would be the first to condemn that, as all her writings show. ... I'll talk more about this in another letter, and yes, I will not let Lizou see the letter. ...

Gaby to Jean and Elisabeth Friday, 1:30 pm, June 5, 1942

Bien chère petite Lizou et mon cher Jean,

... On Sunday there will be an outing for the youth group; there is one every two weeks now, and if the weather is good, maybe I'll go too. I do have less work here than at the bookstore, and fewer problems. Now that I'm up to date in my new job, and more familiar with it, I will be able to help the Raimbault girl. I left her on her own a little too much and I noticed she is a little scatterbrained. She made a lot of errors in the bills and she was even a little discouraged by all the claims she received. It is true that everything is new for her, and it's a new job, and she doesn't type very well yet or use the adding machine, and I think it has been a good lesson, and she will be more careful. Aside from that, she is a very nice girl and I get along with her very well, also in the kitchen. We have similar natures.

I am so sorry Lizou is anemic, and unwell. I hope the doctor gave her something to give her strength. If she could find some Hepatrol it would do her good. Veal liver is good for fighting anemia, and when one takes a dose of Hepatrol, it's the same as a lot of veal liver. Every time I have taken it, it has done me a lot of good. ...

In my last few letters I have forgotten to mention the young art teacher, because for me it was something that was over. When he came at Easter, I told Lisette that if she wanted him, I would be happy to let her have him, as he is really too short for me. I saw him standing beside Raymonde, and she is shorter than I am, and she looked like a giant. I think I'm quite tall and I would always feel ridiculous. Lisette told me she thought he was very nice and that she might like him. Brother Mathy wanted to recommend me to this young man, but I didn't want him to, and he told me that in that case, he would recommend Lisette. That's what he did and when this young man came at Pentecôte, they went out together several times. This young man likes Lisette, too, but she isn't sure yet whether she would marry him; she doesn't know him well enough yet. ... Brother Mathy is biting his nails over having recommended her to this young man. Brother and Sister Mathy are both furious with me for having let such a good opportunity pass me by, but I tell myself that if it were really the right thing for me and was God's will, this young man would not have been influenced by any advice from Brother Mathy. I hope it works out for Lisette, as it might mean her salvation if she married this young man. She deserves to be happy. ...

I'll stop because I'm at the end of the page. I think a lot about the time when you will come to live in Paris where we will see each other often.

My most affectionate thoughts to both of you.

  Gaby

Mama writes weekly and her letters are always in Dutch because she does not write French very well.

Mama to the children   The Hague, June 7, 1942

Dear Children,

This morning Pa and Annette left, all packed to go on vacation. Pa will go along with her for a couple of days, first to Nijmegen, where his cousin lives and then by bicycle to Arnhem; nature is beautiful there. Afterwards, Pa will put Annette on the train to Enschede. Pa will return to The Hague by bike, so I don't know when that will be yet. I think as soon as he is out of money he'll come home, probably at the end of the week. Annette will stay in Enschede until the end of her vacation, though she will spend a couple of hours in Utrecht on the return trip to say hello to the family there. How quiet things are this morning since they left. The first thing I did was to clean up. Around three o'clock I had visitors, who just left, and now it is nine o'clock in the evening. Normally I write you on Sunday afternoon, but that was not possible today. Now, I'll take a quiet hour to write to you just before I go to bed. We got your letter of May 23 this week on June 3rd. As always we were very happy to have it. We always feel so good when we hear from you, and this time you wrote about Joop and Lizou, so it was a true pleasure to read that letter. I'm glad you also got Pa's letter, as he wrote one to all of you. Pa has spoken a few times here in The Hague, and he still does a great job. But he has an entirely different expression on his face when he does that, and you will have to get used to that when you come home. Yes, every day we talk about seeing the children again. As long as we stay healthy, God willing, it won't be too long. We don't know what the future will bring, but we keep up our courage and have faith. At some time the war will be over. Everyone longs for that time, I think. I think that Aunt and Uncle Wibbens will stay in Antwerp until after the war, because they are afraid they won't find a place to live here. Uncle could not live in Aunt Marie's little house without any books. ...

Tomorrow I will go to the tailor who made Pa's suit to see if he can make my coat out of the material this kind Joop sent to his mother. ...

Are you getting used to the changes? Brother Meyer's departure? Yes, it will be a while before you know if those changes are for the better. Dear Mies, it is too much to have sent us a package with used clothes. We were very happy and grateful for it, but you had to put in the effort and the cost. We can never do anything for you. I would have given you a tin of apple syrup, even if I had to go without butter on my bread for a week, but that isn't possible. But I hope to make up for it later!

Yes, Mies, it is true, many of us have had sorrows. Pa was not the only who was not treated right, and everyone will be judged. However we should not judge people. We are all sinners, and that's why the Lord still wants us sinners to finish His work, even though it does not always go the way the Lord wants. Papa said as much in his sermon yesterday in church. What you wrote about Marthe does not surprise me. Since the day I came to Paris, I noticed that she was devious, and you remember that I warned you. She has a good many qualities, but she is not straightforward. ...

It is full summer here, and we hope that Annette will get a lot of sunshine. Annette was on night duty the whole week from nine in the evening to eight in the morning. As you can imagine, she was dead-tired when she came home in the morning. However, she goes to bed at nine until five or six in the evening, and that way she gets some rest. But night duty is hard work.

Now then, dear children, I'll say goodbye, as it is getting dark and it's bedtime. Let us keep up our courage and pray for each other. Our most heartfelt greetings and many, many kisses. Greetings to all the friends, especially to Brother Meyer.

Your loving parents and Annette

Gaby tells Jean and Elisabeth of a disturbing instance of misinformation.

Gaby to Jean and Elisabeth   Thursday, June 18, 1942

... Can you imagine that Brother Ducret came two weeks ago and said he had a letter from Belgium saying that Papa had died. He thought they hadn't dared to tell me since I didn't appear to know. Of course he didn't tell me about it either, and everyone was asking me if I had good news from the parents. But I didn't find anything strange about that. Finally, Saturday evening I got a card from Papa and on Monday a letter from Mama, and it was only after that Mme Mathy told me everybody here had been really scared. ... Once again I learned that one shouldn't believe everything anyone tells you about anybody. This time it was easy to verify, but if they had said that Papa had killed somebody or stolen something, how would we prove it wasn't true? Well, it ended well. Besides something like that couldn't happen without my knowing as Mama writes me every week.

Mama to the children   June 14, 1942

... The Jews here have been walking around with a star for quite some time now, perhaps for more than a month. ...

This morning Annette will be on her way to Enschede and Papa will be biking home. Annette seems to have enjoyed herself a lot. This "Jaap" that she writes about is the same boy Pa wrote you about a little while ago. I don't know if anything will come of it. He is such a nice boy, studying medicine, but a few years younger than Annette. I am glad you didn't write about him, as then she thinks that we, or at any rate Pa, come to conclusions too quickly. She says "Jaap" is a friend and nothing more. ...

Jean is becoming busier with his international contacts and his work with refugees.

Jean to Gaby   Tuesday, June 23, 1942

Ma bien chère Gaby,

Forgive me for not writing for so long, but you know the usual refrain: "too much work." I finally managed to finish the letter to the parents and now it's your turn. Thank you for all your letters and the letters from the parents. ... We had a good time at the closing ceremonies in Collonges. ... The final gathering wasn't terrific, but Brother Charpiot ended it in a very Christian manner and a nice prayer. ... Madame Cartier came up from Geneva that day so we had a real family day. We returned to Lyon that evening. Lizou then left on Wednesday evening to arrange her mother's widow's pension and to do some errands for me. ... She'll be back Thursday evening. Then Sunday we will go to Toulon for two days for some preliminary negotiations about a little fabric store in Annecy which I want to buy for Lizou's mother, as she works too hard in Geneva (right now she works from 6:30 in the morning to 6:30 in the evening) and for not much compensation, and besides she doesn't have much in her life. So if we could find her a little commercial enterprise, she could earn a living and I would make some profit. ...

On July 9 we'll leave for the Scout camp in Lasalle. The leaders meet from the 8th to the 18th and the young people from the 18th to the 30th. Since I want to take the leaders' course, I'll go on the 10th. I particularly want to go so that Lizou gets some fresh air. The doctor said she is anemic and needs sun and fresh air. While we're at the camp, I'll come back on weekdays from time to time for my business, and leave Lizou there. Then on August 1st, Lizou and her mother will go to Agay (near St. Raphael) and on August 8th Lizou's mother will leave, and I will go to there to be with Lizou until the 15th. Then we'll come back to Lyon. From August 1 to 8 I will be in Lyon for my business. There's our program. It's too bad we all couldn't spend our vacation together. What are your plans for your vacation this year? My business is going well, nothing to complain about. I keep busy with Lizou helping the Dutch. If you see L. [Laatsman] please tell him that. We are making up packages for the refugees in the camps, etc. The other day we took care of a young Dutch man, 23 years old, who is a baron and the son of an Army General in the army of our country. This could be a good contact for later, if God gives me life, as he wants to visit Arthur [England] and would probably leave on July 31 with a convoy. We became good friends and he is a really nice young man.

Our apartment is promised for around August (it was supposed to be ready in May), but we're keeping our hopes up. ... The Meyers are always extremely nice to us. Sister Meyer is going to leave us her keys so we can use the kitchen at her house while she is in Switzerland in August and September. ... It will be much nicer for Lizou when we get our apartment.

Lizou and I love each other very much, and she is a terrific girl, very sweet, and she never gets angry. ... As soon as someone goes to see you, I will give him the vegetable grater that Lizou brought back. ... I am glad you have conquered your worries; we have to keep our spirits up and have courage. ...

Please thank L. [Laatsman] for me for all he has done for us. If I can do anything for him, I would do it with pleasure. I can give him some silk or something like that. By the way, if you need some silk-like rayon or natural silk, let me know. ...

Fischer is lucky not to have died this year, and he will try to convince us he is healthy, but things will go better next year. I am sure that Fischer is much sicker than is generally thought and you know that Arthur's uncle is extremely well, and that he will astonish us with his vitality. On the subject of politics, this summer will bring a lot of great business, and I think the Germans will go to Egypt, and I think they will get as far as the Caucasians, and that Turkey will join the Germans. ...

The 8000 franc apartment would interest us very much. I wonder if you couldn't rent it already and live in it or put someone else there. Of course I would pay the rent. Do as you see fit. Maybe it would be better to wait a while. The day you think it [the war] may be over, there will be a rush on Parisian apartments. So at that time, try, or get someone to try to get us an apartment in a quiet area, thanks a million.

Do you by any chance know Dr. Dreyfus? Does he have any money? It seems he wants to go to visit Arthur. We are taking care of him here. Also, ask L. if it would be possible for him to carry a few verbal messages to the parents, along with addresses so that Papa could go and see these people and give them messages. For example the above young baron has his mother there and it would be good if Papa could go and see them and get in contact with them. ...

Remain faithful at your post, my dear little Gaby, and don't forget for an instant that you are doing God's work and that if others do wrong or if there are little problems, that you are responsible only for your own acts before God and not the acts of others. Remember that God is directing this work and that men can do nothing more than God will let them do... Pray for all those who lead us and have such a heavy task. ... Be of good courage and don't ever lose your faith. Je t'embrasse très fort. Your brother who doesn't forget you even for an instant.

Gaby, unlike Papa and Jean, seldom uses the device of showing pro-German sentiments to satisfy the censors. So perhaps we are obliged to take her at her word when she expresses a routine and uncritical anti-Semitism in this letter in regard to her doctor, whom she trusts and appreciates.

A curious incident of a strange man making a large "donation" suggests a connection to Jean's clandestine work.

Gaby to Jean June 29, 1942

Ma bien chère Elisabeth, mon bien cher Jean,

What a joy it was on the Sabbath to receive your letter of the 23rd of this month. I was beginning to worry. ...

This afternoon I learned that mail would leave tomorrow. So I'm hurrying to write a little this evening. Tomorrow I won't have time as I am going to get my permanent. I worked on Sunday afternoon to compensate for the time.

I'm enclosing Annette's last letter which I received Saturday evening. I answered it yesterday, but it is very difficult to advise her not knowing any of the people in question. I told her that the young man, 21 years old, was a little young, because if she has to wait 5 or 6 years before getting married, it is likely to break up before then. I pray for her a lot because I want so much for her to be happy. I can understand why she has so much success with young men, as she has a really happy nature and she is very pretty. ...

When I see L., I will ask him if he would like to take the messages Jean spoke of. But why are Dutch people in camps? Are they in concentration camps or are they demobilized soldiers? Anyway, I see you are making some good contacts. That could be useful. ...

I'm glad to know that you are able to put aside a nice round little sum for the future. That will help you in your business later on. I think Jean will always succeed now that he is well launched, because if he can succeed during a war, he will always find something after the war, when, according to what they say, commerce will be much better. I think the worst is over, and it is always good to have a little capital. ...

Last week a man came into the office and asked for me. Brother Desmet was absent just then and the man said he wanted to make an anonymous donation for our work. When I saw that he was taking out 15000 francs I was a little worried and I asked him his name so Brother Desmet could at least send him a receipt, but he said it wasn't necessary and he said it must be marked anonymous. I had thought it must be a donation and I asked how he knew my name. I thought I recognized his voice as the friend who telephoned me on your behalf during the week. But now Brother Desmet tells me he knows what it's about. It's too bad it's not a real donation!

On Friday I went to see my doctor. I wanted him to make me a certificate for my diet, because it is always Dr. N. [Nussbaum] who does it for me every three months, and it bothers me to ask him to as I am not his patient, especially now that the authorities are very severe about it. But I couldn't go in; the maid said that the doctor hadn't been seeing patients since Tuesday. I asked for more information, and she said he was Jewish. That gave me a real shock because I wasn't expecting it at all. I telephoned him that evening to ask if he could see friends, because I would have gone to say hello to him. But he told me he preferred to wait a few weeks as that could look suspicious. And he told me that he had appealed and that things might still work out. But I am a little doubtful as they are treated so severely. I was terribly sad about his having to wear the star, as you know how nice and generous he has been to me and also to others. He charged a lot for those who had money, but for the others, he charged almost nothing. Brother Desmet and I were talking about him just the other day. I know that there are many Jews who deserve what is happening to them, but still, there are some who are exceptions to the rule, and I think my doctor is one of those. He was already so devastated by his brother's death—he died because of these events—and this will just bring him down completely.

Dr. Dreyfus is also Jewish. He must have told you that. His wife is Catholic. We knew he had disappeared, but his wife didn't want to say where he had gone. I have talked about it only with Brother Mathy, and I won't tell anyone else. He is a close friend of Ganty, and I think it was he who led him to the Truth. He was baptized maybe a year ago. Brother Mathy can't say if he is really an Adventist, but he has been very helpful and made diet certificates for the members who wanted them. I don't think he charged the members for office visits. I don't know if he has money, but he had a good clientele, very near where my doctor lives, and it's a fashionable neighborhood where doctors must do well.

I'm going to stop, as it is getting late and I don't want to be too late going to bed. I want to wish you all a good vacation, get a good rest and store up lots of sunshine. It will be so wonderful when we are all together again. Thank you for all you do for me. Yes, Jean it's a good idea to try to be more economical. Without being miserly or egotistical, I think you have a long way to go in this area. If Lizou is more reasonable in this domain, she can provide a balance. Yet she is generous too… I am very happy that Jean has a little wife who doesn't prevent him from being generous with his family. Our family has always been very close and I see that hasn't changed. Now Annette and I have only to find husbands of the same sort, and we will all be perfectly happy. But maybe it won't be the case; we'll see.

I'll leave you now, dear ones, and I'm sending you my best thoughts and my affectionate kisses.

Gaby

The Weidners before the war. From left to right: François, who died of pleurisy and pneumonia when he was 16 years old; "Mama" Weidner; Jean; Annette (holding cat); "Papa" Weidner; Gabrielle.

Adventist Seminary in Collonges where Papa Weidner taught and where Jean and Gabrielle were students before the war. In the background are the dangerous cliffs of the Salève which Jean loved to explore and learned to negotiate, though this activity was strictly forbidden by his father.

Johan Heinrich Weidner, Sr. ("Papa"); Jeanne Gertrude Linschoten Weidner ("Mama").

Early family correspondence cards, at first the only form of family correspondence authorized by German occupiers.

Jean and Elisabeth.

Gabrielle's visit to her parents and Annette in The Hague, The Netherlands, in 1943. It is the first time they have been reunited since they all left Paris in June 1940, ahead of the anticipated German invasion. From left to right: Mama, Annette, Papa, Gabrielle.

By 1943, Jean's clandestine rescue work is becoming increasingly dangerous. He is a hunted man and travels in Nazi-occupied territory using a variety of aliases and false identity papers such as this one listing him as "Jacques Vernet."

Gabrielle Weidner, 1942.

"130," the Seventh-day Adventist Church at 130, Bd. de l'Hôpital, Paris, where Gaby lived and worked and where she was arrested in the entrance lobby by the Gestapo in 1944 (photos by Janet Carper).

Suzy Kraay, whose arrest and threatened torture by the Nazis led to the capture of at least 70 members of the Dutch-Paris escape line, including Gaby.

La Haye, ce 9-4-1944

Nos chers Tous Trois,

Votre aimable lettre du 21-3 nous a trouvé tous deux en bonne santé. Ma femme souffre encore de ses varices, et parfois même fortement, mais elle est heureuse de pouvoir penser à tant de bienfaits dont elle jouit encore. Alors, vs avez eu la visite d'Henri et il a fêté l'anniversaire de d'A. avec vous trois. C'est exquis. Ns étions heureux d'apprendre que sa sœur, malgré sa maladie, est pleine de courage dans la clinique. Espérons qu'elle soit bientôt guérie, grâce aux bons traitements et la bonne nourriture qu'on peut lui ajouter à ce qu'elle reçoit.

C'est charmant de l'oncle d'A. de vouloir rendre une petite visite. Vs verrez que c'est un bon copin. Quand il sera venu vs ns donnerez de vos nouvelles, n'est-ce pas? Car j'aime savoir ce que vs pensez de lui. Alors Ly loge chez A? Ça ns fait plaisir d'apprendre qu'on lui a donné une bonne chambre et qu'il mange bien. Les jeunes doivent bien manger s'ils peuvent le faire. Nous, vieux, ns pouvons ns contenter de moins.

Vs vs rappelez l'artiste peintre Bekking et son neveu de 15 ans? Eh bien j'y ai été l'autre jour. Lui était alité (grippe). Je l'ai vu quand même ainsi que le neveu qui est chez son oncle depuis q.q. semaines. Il avait vu la sœur d'H. pour la dernière fois, je crois le 26 février. Alors elle se portait bien. Il m'a fait rire, le garçon, quand il m'a raconté ce qu'ils ont fait pour se chauffer, tout ce qu'ils avaient brûlé. La question du chauffage donne du fil à retordre.

Papa's second letter from The Hague since hearing the terrible news of Gabrielle's arrest by the Gestapo. He must use the family code to disguise his discussion of the arrest for fear the censors will determine Jean's whereabouts. The blue streak across the page is the censor's mark confirming that the censor has indeed read the letter.

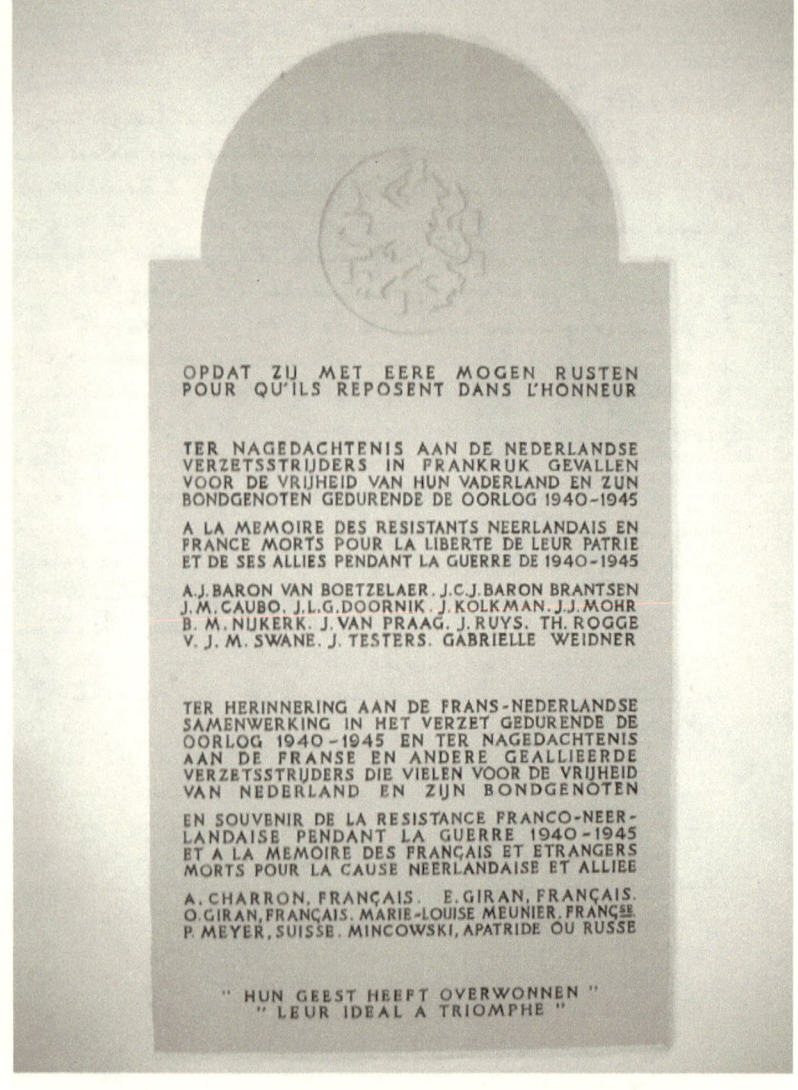

The memorial stone in the Dutch Cemetery at Orry-la-Ville containing Gabrielle Weidner's name along with others. The inscription, first in Dutch and then in French, reads in part: "In memory of the Dutch Resistance members in France who died for the liberty of their country and its Allies during the war of 1940-1945. ... Their ideal triumphed" (photo by Janet Carper).

9   The New Store

Jean gives the latest news to Gaby about the new store in Annecy. La Maison du Coupon will be not only a fabric store, but much more importantly a place to hide refugees whom Jean and his fellow rescuers will guide over the mountains to safety in Switzerland. In this same letter Jean describes the internment camps explaining why the Dutch refugees are there. With his usual style of pages crowded with unrelated subjects all run into one paragraph, Jean probably discourages any censor from reading between the lines in search of forbidden communication.

Jean to Gaby   Tuesday, July 7, 1942

Ma bien chère Gaby,
   It was a great joy to receive your letter of June 29. …
We succeeded in our negotiations for the store, and the closing will be on August 2. I am sure that it will go well now and also later, because I can supply it now and in normal times things sell well in Annecy. The store is in the new buildings opposite the Town Hall. I'll write you more when it is definitely settled. I'm really lucky to have found it, because it's nearly impossible to find anything of this kind.
   We got back on Monday evening. Lizou was able to attend the bi-millennial celebration in Geneva, which was not bad, and there was a parade which represented the two thousand-year history of Geneva, from the time of prehistoric man living in houses on stilts on the edge of the lake to the modern day army. We're leaving Thursday at noon for the camp in Lasalle. … I had a visit from Ganty and was very happy to see him. I gave him 2000 francs for your vacation. … Tell me how much I still owe

you, as I don't remember exactly. ... If you need any silks, let me know. Also I don't remember how much flannelette you wanted. I can't find your card. We are good friends with Dr. Dreyfus, and we do what we can to be useful to him. ...

We have heard that the Germans made a raid on the Dutch Consulate in Paris. Here all the offices have been closed as of last Thursday. Before that, Sweden defended Dutch interests and America defended those of Belgium. Now all that is changed to offices which are under the French and attached to the Ministry of the Interior, and all this was done under pressure from the Germans. ...

No, these Dutch refugees are in camps because they don't have any papers or because they are destitute Jews, or else they are foreigners in work camps where they must work very hard, often without much to eat. Moreover, the Dutch people who arrive without visas (and how would they be able to get visas anyway) are supposed to go to prison for a month. But now that has been stopped because the prefectures have received orders not to do it anymore, and to free them immediately if they have money, and to put them in a work group if they are penniless. All of them have hopes of going to see Arthur. They ask for visas for Surinam via Portugal. More and more of them come, many of them Jews and the latter aren't too keen on going to Arthur's to fight. As of last Thursday we don't know exactly how it is going to work out with all those Dutch Offices, but we suppose that the French will be in charge. Here in Lyon there is a very nice [French person], and I work with him a lot to help our compatriots. Switzerland wants to take as few as possible. Now they are setting up camps for those who don't have any money. If they come from Free France, they are sent back, and if they come from Occupied France, they are put in camps. ...

What would please Mr. L? He is really nice and I'd like to do something for him. Try to find out what would please him, something we could bring back from Geneva or from here. As for the apartment, do the best you can and if you rent it you can take it for yourself and I will pay everything. ... Near the forest would be marvelous. You shouldn't worry too much about the price if it's a big apartment because that way life is better. Yes, it's the same man who telephoned and brought the 15 [the 15000 francs]. Too bad it wasn't the real thing. ... I still believe Arthur will be successful next year. The English are not doing well, but the Americans haven't done anything yet, but when they start, they will not be

THE NEW STORE

insignificant. They will astonish us by their power. I'm really sorry to hear about your doctor. I hope you can see him again. Of course, you could put 4-franc Massenet stamps on the letters to our parents if there aren't any other special ones.* ...

Just the same it's really terrible to think that Ducret wrote that Papa had died. It just shows how things get really out of control. Yes, rumors travel fast. Good-by my dear Gaby. ...

The people in Berne are very happy that you are so faithful even when everything is falling apart. They are glad you didn't get influenced by Marthe and Lisette. Of course, it's sad to lose your friends like Oscar [Meyer], but hold onto your good humor and take life at its best. You'll see that all will be well. Trust in God and remain a true, faithful and enthusiastic Christian. We both send many kisses.

Jean asks his parents to visit the mother of a refugee he is helping. Jean writes in Dutch, a language he struggles with and hates to write in.

Jean to his parents   July 8, 1942

My dear Pa, Ma and Annette,

Just a few lines in haste. I have little time to spare, but I don't want to wait as long as I have in the past to write you. ... Business is good. I have bought a shop for Elisabeth's mother that sells silks and fabrics in the capital of the county where the Seminary is. The closing will be on August 3rd. I was so lucky to get it. Let's hope everything will go according to plan. I am lucky to be able to buy fabric because I have access everywhere, and so the shop will always have something to sell, and one can sell anything nowadays.

Arthur is not doing well lately, but his uncle will send him supplies and his uncle is rich and can help a lot. ... Mies sends me your letters. ... I'm glad to report that I heard from Schwartz yesterday, and he said that he finished re-gilding the letters on our little François's gravestone. The cost was 38 francs, and it just so happens that I had that amount of credit with him. ...

---

* Jules Massenet (1842-1912) was a French composer. A stamp honoring him was issued on June 22, 1942, just a few weeks before Jean's letter. Jean and his father are both serious stamp collectors and would want this recent stamp.

In my last letter I forgot to mention the street where my friend is: Benoordenhout. I would like you to visit her sometime and tell her I have a friend here who wants to give her his heartfelt greetings. This is her son. He is still here with us and is doing well. I make sure he has everything he needs, because of course he doesn't have many relations here, but he has a lot of courage.

That kind Mr. Schwartz [he of the tombstone lettering] wrote me a note: "I must tell you that I remember with deep emotion that I often visited your brother when he was so sick, and he liked me to play the mandolin. I thank God that He used me in these sad circumstances to soften a little the last days of his life. I must tell you also that the inscription struck me; it is so important and consoling at the same time; it is a prayer for those who don't understand the truth that the dead remain with the Lord."
... Yes, Pa, Ma, and Annette, someday we'll go and visit the grave of our little François. Have good courage. I think the Germans are very strong and the war will be over next year, and then we'll see each other again.

There is not much food to be had here, but so far I haven't gone without; many customers bring me eggs, butter, etc. I am able to give some to the needy. My dear Annette, don't worry, after the war I will give you a beautiful trousseau, but be careful, don't marry 3 or 4 men, because I can't give you more than one trousseau. It seems you have a lot of success with your blue eyes, so marry someone who looks a lot like me and then you will be happy. Fortunately Lizou can't read this or she might protest. Now, good bye everybody, and thanks to all especially to Ma for all her news. I am glad Annette had a good vacation and that Pa is so active. Continue like that, and let's all have patience. I still read Papa's exposé about the Sabbath and the Baptism. If Pa could write me one about the Church, I would be very happy. See you soon, my beloved parents, and Lizou and I greet you with all our heart. We pray for you morning and night and we are sure we'll see you soon. However, perhaps Pa should shave off his beard or I won't be able to recognize him. In case you need to sell the stamps to buy food, you must do that. The French stamps are being sold for high prices. I think it should be the same there. I'm keeping my stamps for Pa, so he'll have many beautiful ones.

Many, many kisses and have good courage and faith in God. Your Popie who will never forget you.

Gaby writes a "letter" which covers two postcards in order to tell Jean about her accident.

THE NEW STORE 229

Gaby to Jean   Paris, July 8, 1942

Bien chers Lizou et Jean,

 Yesterday at noon I came home from several days' vacation in—the hospital, Hotel Dieu Hospital. Yes, on Saturday afternoon, I went to walk in the Tuilleries with a few of the young people. We were sitting on a bench, and we were playing a sort of game. We were daring each other to do things, and for one of mine I had to stand on a chair. But the chair tipped and I fell backwards onto my back. When I tried to get up I saw that my left wrist had a very strange shape. It was broken. We walked a little and a policeman called a police ambulance which took me to the hospital. They set my arm right away but they kept me there in order to do a verification X-ray on Monday, as they don't do them on Sunday. So I was able to leave on Tuesday morning.

 [second card]

 Fortunately it was the left arm. I don't feel very well yet because of the fall, and the shots they gave me and the pills I took. But next week I'll go back to work. I have been in pain of course, especially because of the cast which was too tight, and my fingers were turning blue. So they cut it down a little on Monday and again yesterday before I left. Now it's better. I only have to have it for 3 weeks, so it isn't too bad. I will appreciate having two hands all the more afterward. Moreover, my fall could have been much more serious. I could have damaged the spinal column. I am in very good spirits, so don't worry about me. I have a nurse, a cleaning lady, a hairdresser, etc. Everybody helps me, and there are a lot of things I can do by myself. I hope you will have a good vacation. I'll take mine later on because of the accident. I have lost quite a bit of weight in 3 days. Kisses. Gaby

Gaby to Jean (card)   Friday, July 10, 1942

Ma chère Lizou et mon cher Jean,

 Yesterday evening Mr. Ganty brought me your package for which I thank you most sincerely. ... The nightgown is going to be very useful because I can't put on pyjamas with long sleeves because of my cast. ... I wasn't able to see Mr. Ganty because someone was helping me undress, but I will see him today and he will tell me all the news. I am better and have been back at work since yesterday. ... Thanks to Lizou for the grater. Best thoughts.

        Gaby

Gaby writes by hand on July 15th. With her broken arm she is unable to use a typewriter. She tells Jean that Dutch officials who have been helping Jews have been arrested. She also writes about the roundup of Jews in Paris.

Gaby to Jean   July 15, 1942

... Mr. L. is thinking of going to see our parents at the beginning of August and will be happy to take certain messages. ... The Dutch Chamber of Commerce has been seized as has the office of aid to refugees. They are all in prison, guarded by the Gestapo.

                                              Thursday morning, July 16

... This morning, they're picking up Jews everywhere, it seems. The police are taking them away with their bundles. It's getting to be really terrible for them. ...

On July 16 and 17, 1942, thousands of Paris Jews, more than half of them children, were arrested by the French police and taken to the "Vélodrome d'Hiver," the winter cycling sports arena. The cycling track around the huge arena was steeply slanted, and only the relatively small center had a flat floor. For seven days more than 7000 people were held here with little food or medicine, and no space for most to lie down. The sanitary facilities, which consisted of two toilets, were immediately overwhelmed and out of order. Only a handful made their way out of the arena before the rest of the families were herded into trains destined for Auschwitz.

    In her letter of July 20 to Jean, Gaby mentions the roundup again.

Gaby to Jean and Elisabeth   July 20, 1942

... The other day, when they were arresting Jews, it was only the Czechs, Russians and Poles. Not the French ones. There were 22 000.

They even took those that were ill in hospitals, on stretchers. That's a little too much, it seems to me. Even though I don't like them very much, there are limits.

    I'll stop now and wish you a nice vacation. Best thoughts and kisses, affectionately your,

        Gaby

    P.S. Greetings to those who know me in Collonges, Anduze, etc.

In the meantime, Jean has received the news of Gaby's broken arm.

Jean to Gaby   Friday morning, July 17, 1942

Ma bien chère Gaby,

    Just a couple of lines in haste. I was just terribly sorry to hear you had broken your arm, poor little Gaby, but I am so glad you kept your spirits up and that you are grateful to God that it wasn't worse, because, as you say, a fall onto one's back could have much more serious consequences. So, be of good courage, my dear little Gaby, I think of you all the time and pray for you every morning and evening. ... I received your 2 cards here, and you can write me whenever you want at my address here. ... If you have to pay the expenses for your arm yourself, let me know and I will cover everything. ... Lizou will be very upset about your accident. So we went to the Girl Guide camp, but it was a little disorganized because Maurice Mathy talked a lot without saying anything. ... Lizou and I camped in our little tent (lent us by Annie) and it was a little hard on Lizou, who really isn't very much the outdoorsy type. We went there on bicycles, and from there we went to Anduze on bicycles, and visited the Desert Museum where I found our names from June 1940, on the registry.* Then we went to Mme Girou's where I left Lizou and on Wednesday morning I came here and will leave here again at noon today to return to Anduze this evening and Lizou and I will leave there for Lasalle where the Sabbath service will be held tomorrow near the river. Mémé Girou has been definitively sentenced to 6 months in prison for trafficking in rationing cards (he was doing it on a grand scale, as he stole a large quantity of cards at the Town

---

* The Musée du Désert in Anduze is a museum of Protestantism. "Désert" refers to the period after the *Edict of Nantes (1685)* which took away all rights from Protestants. Jean and Gaby must have visited this museum when they came to Anduze as refugees in June, 1940.

Hall). As he has already done 5 months in preventive custody, he will be released at the end of the month, but he must return to the youth camp for 3 months, and then he will be free and will return to be near his father, and then I think Mme Girou will return to Marolles also. Your idea of coming here with your broken arm is excellent, as long as you can get a legal travel permit. Don't do anything risky. In Lyon, Marseille, and Grenoble, there have been huge demonstrations against the Germans. Discontent is increasing, as there is nothing to eat and the prisoners aren't returning. ...

My business is going well. Just now when I returned, I found some good news that will allow me to earn around 20 000 francs.

Be of good courage, my little Gaby, keep marching forward, while faithfully serving the Lord, we remain very close to you in our thoughts. Affectionate kisses from your brother who thinks of you all the time especially now that you have your broken arm, but it will get better. Dr. Dreyfus said that the place where you broke it is much more reparable and less serious than if you had broken your wrist. ...

Your brother who loves you,

On July 14th, Gaby had also written a card to Jean about her attempt to get a travel permit to "bring her broken arm" to Jean and Lizou.

Gaby to Jean and Elisabeth (card)   Paris, July 14, 1942

Bien chers Lizou et Jean,

On Friday I went to see Mr. L. who would be glad to take the messages, but it would have to be in the first few days in August. This morning I went to the German Embassy to try to get a travel permit. The officer told me that before I broke my arm I was certainly able to manage by myself and consequently I could just do so now. On top of that, he advised me to insist that the hospital take me back since I had no family to take care of me. A really delightful perspective. So there is nothing to be done. I am really sorry about it, as it is unpleasant to have to ask strangers for everything. Fortunately it's only for a few weeks, and everybody is very nice to me here. My health is good and I'm eating well. ... Kisses, Gaby

THE NEW STORE 233

When Gaby writes a postcard to Jean and Lizou on July 21, she confesses that she doesn't really envy them for their camping experience.

Gaby to Jean and Elisabeth (card)   July 21, 1942

... The youth group is going to go camping in August for 10 days or so, but I prefer to go on vacation at the Daniels'. Besides I can't sleep unless I'm in a bed. ... Do you both have bicycles, or did someone lend you one for the vacation? The only thing that will be a little expensive for my arm is the massaging, but the money for vacation will partly cover that, as I'll spend less. Affectionate thoughts. Gaby

When Jean writes to Gaby on July 24, he adds a page of messages for Mr. Laatsman to take to his father in The Hague. The instructions are on a separate page and have typed lines between them. The letter itself covers the same news as his letter of July 17 except for a few choice bits:

Jean to Gaby   July 24, 1942

... I'm so glad you didn't break your right arm, as otherwise you couldn't write to me. ...

Mémé Girou stole dozens of ration cards from the Town Hall when he was working there. He has only two weeks more to serve. ... Right now, in prison, he is writing a "Life of Jesus"!!! But he asked his mother for 3000 francs to pay his lawyer, or so he said. But his mother paid the lawyer directly, and it came to 500 francs for everything. ... Despite that, Mme Girou always regards her little Mémé as a poor victim at heart, and Mémé is a little angel. ...

We celebrated our six months' anniversary by going out to dinner at the hotel.

Things aren't going well for the Russians. ... The English have a lot of courage, but they don't seem to want to make the necessary sacrifices of men, and they haven't the strength to prevail, but the Americans are a different story, and their strength will surprise us and after the war they will rule over everyone. ...

Lizou and I each have a bicycle of our own. Bought new last year for 2500 francs. Lizou isn't the most dedicated cyclist, but still, she was very happy. Do you want one also? As for the massages, I'm the one that's going to pay for them. Just let me know what they cost, as well as <u>all the expenses</u>. The 2000 francs was for your vacation and not for your broken arm.

Tell Mme Van Voorst tot Voorst, wife of the general in the Dutch army...that Ernest is near Perpignan at present and is trying to get the papers needed to go to Portugal. The Spanish have refused the transit visa, but we hope he will obtain it anyway. I am taking care of him in every way and he lacks nothing. Very optimistic. A very well-brought up young man. Note: he is 23, is a baron, Catholic, his brother is a Jesuit, and Papa might be interested in seeing him. Very nice. He is much like our little François. Have become good friends.

Go and see 1) Jhr J.C.C. Sandberg, 32 Sweelinckplan in The Hague to tell him that his son Henri is in England and is a speaker on Dutch radio in London since June. He is well. He can write to him by sending letters to Elisabeth who will forward them. Be careful: the father is an officer and pro-German. So be careful to present Henri's departure for England with all possible tact. Henri was a correspondent of the newspaper Het Volk in Paris, and of course did not agree with his father about politics, but the family relationships were very good.

2) also see Jhr. H.H. Sandberg van Boelens in Arnhem and give him the same information as above. Henri insisted that we see him also and that he be asked to help his wife Jeanne in Paris. Henri is a great friend of mine and attended our wedding. He is Henri's cousin and is opposed to the Germans.

See Mme Bruno Hendrick Isings, Sloterwg 175, Badenhoevedorp (near Amsterdam), a person who is poor and has several children, to tell her that her husband is still in a camp at Vernet, France. That we are doing all we can to get him out of the camp and into a Dutch Welcome Center, and we also are trying to arrange for him to return home. It would be worth trying to arrange it also from there in Holland. He is a good Christian and we gave him a Dutch Bible. He is a good man and we are helping him all we can. Lately his health has improved. They must be of good courage and soon they will see each other. According to what he has heard here, Mme Isings was taken to the hospital.

I would very much like Papa to see these people himself, to have contact with them and to encourage them.

Gaby to Jean and Elisabeth (card)   Tuesday, July 28, 1942

Mes bien chers,

So this morning I went to the hospital, accompanied by Mr. Walther who wanted to see the X-ray. They took my cast off, but my arm is still very sensitive, and I can't use it yet. But I hope that with massaging it will get better very quickly. He does them very well, in warm water, which keeps them from being painful. It was the wrist that was broken, but only the radius. Henri writes me often and I'm so grateful. On Friday I will see Mr. L. … Best thoughts.

Annette to Gaby   The Hague, July 29, 1942

Ma chère petite Gaby,

I've been wanting to write to you for a week already, and I can't find the time. My poor dear, if you only knew how often I think of you, especially now after your accident. And to think that you were in so much pain, and that it was because of the doctor. I think it is a scandal that a doctor doesn't do his work better than that. I myself had a broken arm last year, so I know how much one can suffer in the first few days, and on top of that your cast was much too tight. Well, I hope that now you are not in too much pain. What a shame you can't go to Jean and Elisabeth. But let's hope the war will be over soon, and that we can all see each other. What a great party we'll have, isn't that right my dearest?

For the moment I am on night duty. I hope it's the last time. I'm finding the night shift really terrible. In the morning I feel so ill. At least there's only a week left. This was the 4th night that there was no midwife on the night shift. That's because one is on vacation and the other is sick. So the one that's left has to do both day and night shifts, and so I have to go and wake her if there's something happening at night. But it isn't fun at all because during all the last few days I'm the one responsible and that is just terrible. Can you imagine it? In the morning I am a nervous wreck. If it's a first baby, it's easy to see when I have to call the midwife, but if it's the 3rd or the 4th, it's very difficult. Like yesterday, for example. At 6 in the evening arrives a woman who is expecting her 5th baby. Her water had broken, and that's why she came, but she hadn't yet had any contractions. Her husband wanted to stay near her, and that's why she stayed in the high-class birthing room. Every hour I gave her some quinine to start the contractions. At 1 o'clock she began to have some pain, and at 3 o'clock the pain was regular. Of course you don't know very much about this subject, but you can understand that it's very hard for us to tell when to call the midwife. We aren't authorized to touch inside the mother, so it's very hard to see if the head has already come down. But luckily I called her just at the right time, neither too early nor too late. When I called the midwife, I couldn't see the head yet, but 5 minutes later I could see it, and 5 minutes after that the baby was born. I got a compliment from the midwife for having called her just right and not too early, which many nurses do, but you can understand how hard it is on the nerves and this morning I was at my wits' end. Fortunately, right now there is no one in the birthing room, knock on wood, as it is only 2 o'clock and between now and 8 o'clock a lot of women could come. I have two cute little babies that I must take upstairs to their mothers, as they feed at night, and then I have to bring them back down to the nursery.

Next week I'm going to be working "in the field". I don't know how to say "in der Wyk" in French. All day I'll be going on my bicycle to take care of a mother and baby. That will be hard to get used to at first, because it is a very different type of work from work in the clinic. We work almost entirely with very poor and quite isolated people, so as you can imagine, we have to check our hair every evening—! How ghastly. It wouldn't be the right job for you!

I took my practical and theory exams in the clinic. I passed them all on the first try. You can imagine how happy I was. So many have to take them 2 or 3 times. There were some very difficult ones such as "Thrombosis" and "Incubator". With the Thrombosis, they ask about the entire system of circulation of the blood, how illness begins, symptoms, etc. The head nurse questioned me for an hour about that subject alone. And we have 23 exams. You can imagine how happy I was to have all that behind me.

Papa left yesterday for 2 weeks traveling all around Holland. You know how he likes a little adventure. He'll also go to Arnhem and will see Jaap. Yes, you know, I chose Jaap after all. I am very happy now, as I think I have followed my heart. Likèle came for a goodbye visit. I had written him a goodbye letter to tell him that I love him as a friend, but nothing more. It made him very sad, but it didn't prevent us from parting as good friends. Since then Jaap came to The Hague for a few days. He is a really nice boy, still a little young, but we have to wait so long before we can get married, that it won't matter. A boy changes so much between his 21st and 25th year. He loves me very much, and we write to each other often. Mama likes him a lot, too, and he has already come here to eat. I hope that I have at last found the man of my life and that I won't change again! I can see you shaking your head!! And you, my dearest, I would love to see you get married. I am sure that it will happen. You are much too nice, and your eyes are too beautiful for a man to be indifferent. It's really too bad you are so tall. ...

Greetings to everyone. ... A big kiss for Mr. Meyer and one on each cheek for you. Send one to Jean and Elisabeth from their little sister, Annette

Gaby sends a postcard to Jean on August 15, Assumption Day, a holiday in France. Lisette, who took Gaby's advice and got acquainted with the young man Gaby found wanting (because he was too short), is going to be married to him.

Gaby to Jean   Saturday afternoon, August 15, 1942

... Paris is practically deserted on this August 15th. Practically all the Parisians are on vacation or away for the weekend. ... I'll leave tomorrow from Austerlitz Station and will arrive at 6:45. My vacation is beginning just as yours is ending. ... I'll probably return on Sunday, August 30. Lisette gets married on September 15. I hope Jean can send me the gift for her before then. ... Kisses, Gaby

Gaby to Jean and Elisabeth   Sunday morning, August 16, 1942

Bien chère Lizou et bien cher Jean,

My bags are packed and I'm leaving in half an hour. I had decided that if I had any time left, I would devote it to you, which is why I'm here to have a little chat with you.

I'll begin with the necessary things. A Mr. Saint-Denis from Orbe wrote to Jean to ask if he could supply him with merchandise. He is a former salesman. I sent him a note giving him Jean's new address. Another time I will simply put the address on the envelope and return it to the sender who can write an inter-zone card. But I didn't think of it.

Mr. L. was supposed to leave on the 9th and was going to see the parents. I gave him Jean's page of messages, and he will take note of it and then destroy it, as he obviously isn't going to take that with him. That was the right thing to do, wasn't it? If he had read it only once, he couldn't have remembered it all. But we can trust him completely. …

Was the vacation good for Lizou, and did she gain some weight? I pray for her health to improve. I am a little worried about her, especially since Paul Meyer wrote to his brother saying that Elisabeth had lost a lot of weight since her marriage. I hope, Lizou, that you get examined by a doctor from time to time. [Gaby uses the formal "vous," even though she is speaking directly to Lizou only.]

As for my arm, it is really doing well. My fingers are very agile, but it is hard to turn my wrist. The rotation movement is what I will have the most difficulty with. I don't have the courage to force it when I am alone. So I probably won't make much progress during vacation. I will do a lot of exercises with my arm, however. …

Annette is amusing with all the details she gives about mothers having babies. At least we get a free course in childbirth! You don't have to return the letter as it would be too heavy. You'll probably be happy to hear from her.

When I get back, I think I'll be able to write you on the typewriter again. I'll leave you for today, and I'm sending a thousand affectionate kisses. Gaby

On August 28, Jean writes to Dr. Van Tricht in Monte Carlo, a member of the committee on aid to refugees.

THE NEW STORE

Jean to Van Tricht   August 28, 1942

… Here more and more Dutch people are arriving, especially Jews, and the Offices are literally overwhelmed. … If I can be useful to you in any way, I will always be happy to do so. My wife goes to Switzerland regularly, and if she can do anything for you, she would do so with great pleasure.

As in the previous year, Gaby spends her vacation with the Daniels near La Rochelle, "eating well, (quantity and quality)," canning tomatoes and making blackberry jelly. Like most vacations, "it all went by too quickly." In September she writes to Jean and Elisabeth.

Gaby to Jean and Elisabeth   Sunday, September 6, 1942

Ma bien chère Elisabeth et mon bien cher Jean,

As the mail arrived yesterday, I think that one of these days there will be an answer and I always prepare my letters so as not to be caught by surprise. I have several letters from the parents to forward this time, so you will have enough to read. That is why I won't write a very long letter.

It was really nice of you, Jean, to write your little note on the 29th and your letter of the 30th when you are so busy. I understand very well that you cannot always write long letters and if sometimes you have mail to forward, don't wait until you have time to write a long letter. Just add a short note so that I know the date and can let you know I received it. …

It's now illegal to send butter through the Post office. If you get caught you get a fine of up to 3300 francs. Of course, there is no real risk of getting caught right away; you could do it 10 times and then the 11th package might be checked. The postmistress told Mme Steinbach that there is less danger if the package is sent as a letter-package sealed with wax, but in the end it could still be opened. In this case, I think it would be wiser not to have more of it sent to me, don't you think so? It will be a little hard as I am used to eating as much of it as I want, but I would be sorry if I ever got fined. Better to do without. …

… As you can see, I'm writing on the typewriter again, since I got back from vacation. My wrist hurts a little, but it's good exercise, and I had to get back to doing the mail. Sister Milès did it while I had my broken arm.

I got a nice tan during my vacation and everybody tells me how well I look. It did me a lot of good, as I was really tired, and I would even have been glad to have a few days more. ...

It surprises me that so many people want to buy stores now that there is nothing to sell in them. It appears that yours was a very good deal, as people are offering them to you. But I wonder if you can really make anything since everything requires ration coupons now. It's true, though, that a lot of people have the coupons but can't find the merchandise to buy. So if you have some, you may be able to sell it. The sad thing is that Lizou is going to be the one that has to run the store. You're going to be separated again for half the time. I wonder when you will get a real family life. And what about your apartment in Lyon. Is it going to be ready this month as you were promised?

If you can find me a tube for my radio, I would be so grateful. You can't imagine how many times I look at my radio and wonder if it will be working before the end of the war. Especially with winter coming, it would be so nice to have a little music in the evening. But I doubt that you will be able to find the right tube, as Michèle hasn't been able to get anything, even though she is well placed for finding one.

Yesterday I heard that Brother Meyer would be going to Neuchatel. He'll begin getting his papers tomorrow, and I think it will be all set for the first few days in October, because when it's a repatriation, the visa is hardly ever refused. He will leave a big empty spot, and it will be hard to get used to not seeing him. The house is so empty now. Before I could go and chat with the Mathys. But the Desmets are less, how shall I say, not very sociable. They invite people from time to time, but it's rare, and never would we dare to go have a chat with them. Don't ever let them feel that, Jean, when you write to them. ... They like to be with family members. Maybe when the Henriots are living in the house things will be more fun. And they have a baby, which always makes things livelier...

I'll stop for this evening. I'll certainly be able to add something before the letter goes.

Tuesday, September 8

I heard the mail would leave tomorrow. So I'll add a few lines as there were a few things I forgot to mention on Sunday. ...

THE NEW STORE

About the accounts. I didn't want to talk about the last deposit on a post card, as it is possible that the cards are read in the office. Jean told me that this money (5000 francs) was for the parents and for my birthday. I was really very touched by this kindness, and I want to thank both of you so much. But this time I really can't accept it as it's too much. You were already very generous for my vacation, and you are going to pay the expenses for my arm, so I arranged things in another way:

	Jean owes	I owe
end of July		250
deposit of Aug. 7/8		5000
4th sending to parents	2650	
arm	1300	
Aug. Larcher bill	300	
birthday	1000	
	5250	5250

In the amount for my arm, I included the few massages that Brother Walther is still going to give me. As for my birthday, I think that 1000 francs is enormous, but I'm willing to accept it because I know you sent it because you wanted me to have it. So, our accounts for the end of August come out even. Do you agree? If the Work reimburses me something for my arm (that wouldn't be more than 500 francs maximum, because they deduct a week's salary from the total expenses) I will let you know and I will put that sum on your credit. ...

This time I really am going to stop. I think of you all the time and rejoice in anticipation of the time when we will all be reunited here. In the area I told you about, near the Porte d'Auteuil, it seems there are only a few apartments free. 3 or 4 months ago there were more, but many people who live on the coast have come here. After a while I'll go and see the apartments to see what they're like and that way I can ask your opinion if there are problems, because when the moment comes, I don't want to hesitate. ...

    Gaby

In late July or early August Jean has taken his first Jewish refugees across the Salève mountain in order for them to reach Switzerland and safety. "We were the guinea pigs," says Regina "Re" Koster in her interviews with Alberto Sbacchi on May 12, 1994.

"We were the first." Re Koster's husband, also a *"textile man,"* had asked Jean to help them. *"John remembered from his days in the Seminary a lot of ways up the Salève and down again. It took eleven hours to get down from the chalet into Geneva. We were both exhausted. We did not have the right shoes and we were town people and not country people. We had a very dangerous and difficult trip there. John behaved beautifully, always trying to give us courage and strength. ... There were these iron things in the rocks to help climb, and it was pitch dark. John was absolutely marvelous."*

Upon reaching Geneva, Re and her husband contacted Elisabeth's mother, as they were instructed to do, and then were in Berne for six weeks. Re Koster's letter to Elisabeth (*"Lizou"*) is probably from Berne.

Re Koster to Elisabeth   September 7, 1942

Très chère Maddame Weidner,

We want to thank you again for all the kindness and friendship which you have shown us in these recent days.

We will never forget it and we fervently hope to see you again soon. I hope your husband [Jean Weidner] has gotten some rest after all the past fatigue and weariness.

I have taken the liberty of asking my friends to send you the rest of my clothes <u>before</u> September 16 in Annecy.

I thank you with all my heart if you can take care of them, but if it's too much to ask or if it's too much trouble, have them sent by a shipping company. There are <u>only used</u> items in the package. Among the stationery there are 90 francs that it might be best to remove. You can throw away or give away the four books in the yellow bag. If the old pink Japanese dressing gown is <u>not</u> in the suitcase, I must have left it in the hotel, could you ask there for it? There isn't much light to write by here, so chère Madame, my husband joins me in sending you our most affectionate thoughts and a big kiss.

      Our best to you,
          Regina

THE NEW STORE

Mama to the children The Hague, September 13, 1942

My dear children,

Oh Miesje [diminutive for "Mies," the name her family calls Gaby], I have so much to tell you and to answer your letters. Last week all I sent you was a postcard from Enschede, as I did not have time to write you a letter. ... Pa will answer Lizou's letter because it was written in French. We were glad to hear from Lizou again. We hope that her mother is better now. It is not very pleasant that Mother Cartier had an accident, as at her age one does not heal so quickly anymore.

Fortunately Lizou can still visit her mother and that is a big comfort. Pa will answer Lizou's questions concerning the shop. Pa also has to write Joop, because he has visited all the people Joop had asked him to.

I returned Thursday and Pa came home on Friday. He had been to Hilversum and Amsterdam and had a good trip. He was not as tired as sometimes. He met Joop's friends near Amsterdam, but Pa will write all the news about that.

I had a fine trip, too. Everyone was very happy to see me, my old uncle whom I had not seen in 40 years and so many cousins whom I hardly recognized. Everybody was very welcoming and they gave me an egg to eat. Things are better there than in The Hague. They say that the worst circumstances in Holland are in Amsterdam and The Hague.

There are two cousins of mine living there, sons of my uncle (Grandma's brother). These cousins own big furniture stores and even a factory where they make the furniture. They just bought a parcel of land so they can expand their business after the war and would like to have a section where they sell material to cover the furniture and tapestries, and would like to set up business with Joop, because these materials would have to come out of France. I told them that Joop would like that and would come to Holland after the war. These cousins are good businessmen. They pay their employees about 400 Guilders a week, so it may be good for Joop to do business with them later. Now there is not much to do in Enschede. Most textile factories are closed because there are no raw materials. However, later on things will get back on track, and Joop can keep this in mind.

Annette is very glad that I am home again. She was very busy because so many babies were being born. This morning she left at 8 o'clock and it is 3 o'clock now, and she is not back yet. I am still waiting with dinner and she'll be back at nine tonight. Fortunately she could eat at Aunt Marie's while I was gone. No, Miesje, it was not for financial reasons that Annette gave up living in the dorm at the clinic. But she did not get enough food when she was a dorm student working in that part of the city. She would come home at irregular times and the food was gone if she didn't get back to the clinic in time. So, I did not want to pay 25 Guilders for her board and then give her meals at home also. Now I have her food coupons and she might as well eat at home. I always hold her meals if she can't get home in time. But they can't do that at the clinic, and that was why it was better for her to come home.

I put up some rice, pears, beans and peas that I brought home from Enschede. I was very glad to have gone there. It was expensive, because one always had to bring something if one was invited to dinner. I had to spend at least 30 Guilders. That can be done only once in a while. It was only because Joop helped so much financially that I was able to make the trip. I am very grateful to Joop for that. I was very glad to hear, Mies, that you had a good vacation and had good weather. I also had good weather every day. Annette has taken the material she got from Mr. L. to the tailor, and there was just enough for a dress...

Annette said that it will take some time before you can use your arm again as you used to. It has been two years for her already, and she still feels it at times, but that's why it is not always necessary to get massages. It will heal slowly with exercise. Wet weather will tell you that things are not right yet. ...

This week Pa has begun his lessons again. A nurse just made an appointment. Fortunately Pa's good spirits have returned. He gets tired and he is not young anymore, but he is still in good health. People are dreading the winter. We are only allowed 350 kilos of coal and we don't know whether we'll get any more. In any case not before the New Year. Hopefully we won't get a winter as severe as the last one. ... Joop and Lizou if you read this letter, we think of you always with hope that the store is doing well. Pa is glad that Lizou asks for advice. He will answer soon. Much love to the three of you and kisses from the three of us who are always looking forward to peace so that we will hopefully see our children again soon. We go forward with our spirits high, and don't worry about us. Bye, dear children, your always loving parents and Annette.

THE NEW STORE

Mama nearly always writes on Sunday. In her letter of the following week, she has a good news/bad news story.

Mama to the children   The Hague, September 20, 1942

... Months ago I turned in the coupons for the 350 kilos of coal, but it never got here. Last Thursday, I was working very hard, as Thursday is my usual work day. I had cleaned my kitchen, hallway and stairs, and then, here comes the coal man. I was so mad. The stairway and hallway runners had to be rolled up and I had to start all over. So instead of being finished at four, it was six o'clock before I had finished and I was dead-tired. Afterwards, I was glad that everything was done and that the coal had been delivered. Because what is in the house is in the house. ... We have coupons for milk now. ... Getting food is a lot harder for Aunt Hermine in Antwerp, because she can never get out and things are worse there than they are in Holland. People sometimes stand in line for hours for vegetables. The last time we saw Aunt Marie she said she had to wait 1 1/2 hours in line and got only some lettuce. However, we have a vegetable man who comes to our door in a horse-drawn wagon. I pay a little more, but I still get vegetables and up to now we have always had enough. ... This week it will be three years since we left Paris, and we have not seen you since. ... Many kisses for you, Lizou and Joop from your loving parents and Annette

Gaby's letter to Elisabeth and Jean includes an account of Lisette's wedding (to the young art teacher who was too short for Gaby). Gaby is probably aware of Jean's undercover activities. At the beginning of her letter she expresses more than the usual worry about not hearing from him for 3 weeks.

Gaby to Jean   Sunday, September 20, 1942

... I really wonder if I should write to you because I'm a little worried about you. The last letter from Jean was dated August 30 which was three weeks ago and since then I have received absolutely nothing, not even a few words on a card. And since Jean was going to Anduze for his papers, I wonder if he had problems there or in Lyon. Nowadays one can be arrested for the least little thing and you just never know. Maybe it would be better not to send this letter to your address. Mr. Meyer could keep it or give it to you depending on circumstances.

... Lisette's wedding took place Tuesday. She went to the Town Hall in the morning, and then they went to lunch at the home of the young man's parents. Then in the afternoon they had the church ceremony, at 3:30, and then after that some refreshments where there were only 15 people. It was very good. I think that the young man is very much in love with Lisette, and that she is less so. I think for her it is a marriage of convenience, even though she says she is happy and that she hasn't regretted her decision even for a minute. ... We thought she was a little cold toward her fiancé, and even her husband on her wedding day. Now these are personal opinions, because one never knows what is in another's heart. Maybe she even loves him a lot already. In any case, I wish her happiness because Lisette is a good girl and has always devoted herself to others. ... Lisette had a little white linen suit that she made herself. It was very simple, but she was right not to go to too much expense. There should have been more flowers. There were very few and those were just bouquets that people had given. She wasn't carrying any when she arrived at the church. Of course that's all right in a small church but in a big temple like this one, you need a few flowers. I think it's so pretty. Mathy gave the blessing, but he didn't say very much. There were some songs and some organ music. They left the next day for Vitry-le-François. ...

As Mama promised he would, Papa writes to Elisabeth to address her concerns about minding the store in Annecy. But on the same day, September 22, he writes a long letter to each of his "French children": Elisabeth, Gaby, and Jean. All the letters are in French and all bear the blue-gray streak diagonally across the page, the mark of the censor.

Papa to Elisabeth   September 22, 1942

Our dear Elisabeth,

What a good idea to write us a delightful letter while visiting your Mama. But the news that she had fallen was far from delightful, and we hope with all our hearts that her recovery will be rapid and complete. I can't seem to find your address at your Mama's, or I would write to you there. But this will reach you nevertheless, thanks to a very helpful Parisian lady.

You have indeed done a lot of kilometers. If you weren't of Aryan blood (in one word, please) you could well be taken for the daughter of the Wandering Jew. [Papa adds the phrase "in one word please" because of the joke the French circulated during the war: "Un bon Aryen" (a good Aryan) sounds the same as "un bon à rien" ("a good-for-nothing.")] But anyway, what a privilege to be able to travel so often and so far. That would be really something for me. But I understand that the absence of comfort doesn't please those of the opposite sex so very much. A man doesn't pay much attention to that. Camping attracts some and others have a horror of it. You seem to be able to get along with both the cabbage and the goat. [Same proverb as explained earlier: "Il faut ménager le chou et le chèvre. You have to take care of both the cabbage and the goat."] One thing I regret very much when thinking of all your cycling and your swimming lessons taught by our Jean: that you couldn't load onto your bicycle for each trip and for each exit from the water, several kilos of good fresh bread, some Dutch cheese and some good ripe fruit. Do you agree? Poor Lizou to have been forced to fast as you did. But you took it in the right way and that helps to bear up under difficulties. That is the real wisdom of a happy life: to take things as they come and to try to make something of them, even in adversity, appreciating at the same time the sunny side. That reminds me of a few lines in English; I don't know if I can reproduce them exactly. If I don't succeed, you'll forgive me; you won't flunk me, I'm sure:

> The inner half of every cloud
> Is bright and shining
> I therefore turn the clouds about
> And always turn the inside out
> To show the lining.

Voilà. There must be at least one error in it, but maybe you won't notice. (Anyway, I hope not.)

With much satisfaction, we can see that you are a lot like the wife described by Lemuel's mother (Proverbs 31:10-31), the virtuous wife, more precious than pearls, because she is not a burden to her husband, but, on the contrary, she takes to heart the interests of her partner and she lightens the weight of his yoke. You have both decided not to give a stranger the task of launching your store in Annecy. What an excellent and luminous idea. In any case, I don't blame Jean not to have wanted this solution at first, as I can understand that he appreciates the agreeable and so comforting presence of his one and only Lizou. But, alas! sometimes reality forces us to deal with many things and to choose the lesser of two evils. God gives both of you the necessary wisdom to keep this from being in any way a trap, but proves to be an advantage in every way. In my thoughts I already see in Annecy a place where one does business in conformity with divine laws, where no one ever lies, and where one really SERVES the client. And if a business based on principles like these is more difficult to set up than one without Christ's values, it is also true that there will be just compensation of some sort sooner or later.

You ask, my dear Lizou, what we think of the decision of both of you to separate for a time for the sake of the success of the enterprise. Well, I can only speak from my own personal opinion, but I will answer frankly, just as if I had to respond to people that I hardly know, and by turning the question around to look at it from all sides. Don't be angry with me for this, OK? And Jean mustn't be either. My goal, of course, is not to offend anyone, but to say to those younger than me what my personal experience tells me, as well as the confidences made to me by many men and women in the past in my capacity of a shepherd of souls. Here is what I conclude, while thinking of all this information:

As a general rule, it is not advisable for a young couple to separate, especially when the two or one of the two could suffer undesirable consequences. There are, in fact, several disadvantages: The wife who is alone will take less care of herself than when she also prepares a meal for her husband. On his side, the husband may not get the food which is best for him or on the best schedule. Nothing is better than a wife's care.

Both need to confide in each other their pain and their worries because they share them. Communications by letter are not the same thing. At an age when physical tendencies push one quite naturally and legitimately toward bodily attraction, the constant presence of one another protects not only against infidelity, but also avoids temptation as well as illegitimate thoughts.

On this subject, a parenthetical thought: A husband and a wife will not willingly admit to each other such temptations, for fear that later the other party will have less confidence and respect. But my occupation has

THE NEW STORE

brought me intimate information which urges me to say to EVERY HUSBAND and EVERY WIFE, without wishing to offend anyone: Reduce the necessary separation to a strict minimum, because, in spite of the good disposition of the human mind, the flesh is weak.

For young married couples, the first years provide constant opportunities to learn to adapt to one another. Later that will happen better and more completely, and the unity of the couple will be more quickly established in view of later responsibilities, especially in view of the upbringing of (eventual) children.

Once the children are there, the presence of the mother and the father influences the young ones for the good and in turn the parents receive daily the benefit of contact with them. So, if they are absent they deprive the children and themselves of this privilege.

But separation may become necessary, for one reason or another, in case of illness or care for the sick, or military imprisonment or anything else (or perhaps conscience). Then one must remedy it as much as possible. And here the Christian has a special privilege: he can pray for himself and for the other party. And prayer is not a vain word, it is an absolute reality.

The advantages in the case which concerns us? In my opinion there are one or two important ones:

1) No one can take the new enterprise more to heart than Madame Weidner-Cartier, it seems to me.

2) A change of milieu, and a lighter work load may produce more physical benefit than all the other remedies put together.

Do these advantages counterbalance the shadowy side, especially in view of the fact that the overactive (and spendthrift) Monsieur Jean will no longer be under the guidance of his guardian angel? That is the question. [Papa writes this last sentence in Shakespeare's English.] But since the decision to separate temporarily is already made and executed, there is only one thing to do: face reality, watch developments carefully while devoting to people and things the attention due to them, and act in consequence, while praying to our good and heavenly Father to guide you both in the way which pleases Him best.

How terrible! I see I am at the end of the second page. Well, I'm also going to write something to our great enemy [Jean]; so please exchange the letters, yes? without too many arguments! And especially without fisticuffs. This time I will make an exception and write him in French, and that way you can read everything with your own eyes. But in the letters after that, I will continue, as a former teacher of Dutch, to maintain in my former student the knowledge of his native language which most likely could still be of some commercial use to him.

So, our dear Lizou, show that you are the wife of a businessman, right? One day I hope to hear you say: "Here is the store in which I was the first saleslady and the manager at the same time."

Many kisses from us three, ...

Papa writes to Jean and gives a disguised account of his visits to some of the people Jean asked him to see (in Jean's letter to Gaby of July 24). Papa also describes a British bombing raid in his own brand of code.

Papa to Jean   The Hague, September 22, 1942

Mon bien cher Jean,

At last a sign of life from me. Time goes by so fast. Of course a man like you, who doesn't know what to do with his time (!) can't possibly understand that the days aren't long enough. ...

Mother was so happy to find someone who wants to do business with you after the war. ... And the other day I was in Hilversum and I talked with a family who used to live in Brussels, during the last war. Madame ran a movie theater and they had a mushroom growing business. Beyond that, Madame directed a fashion studio. (She even had a client at court.) They are Adventists. I told her about you and she said if you need information after the war, she would be glad to help (subject: how to present fabrics). So you see, we haven't forgotten that our son is a businessman.

About your "protégé" [the third one of the people Jean asked Papa to visit in his letter of July 24]. It is safer not to mention his name here. He no longer lives in the village but in Amsterdam. Madame and the children are all well. I saw each of them, and I even wrestled with the children who love to have someone play with them. But you know, there is often rivalry between the men. So, in order to prevent Fischer from being in conflict with him it is better that the situation remain as it is at present. No need to give you a better description, you who know enough about Charlotte's husband [Germany] to know that it is better that way. Don't you think so? [Papa thinks it best that Jean should not help the father to return home, as

THE NEW STORE

Jean said in his letter that he would try to do.] The real husband claims a loss of memory as a reason he left! I can hardly believe it, but it's to his advantage to tell it like that. And that makes it easier to forgive a lot of things.

Do you remember your young friend Arthur Reith [England]? How he was so frail and weak? Well, you should see him now! In spite of poor food, he has become quite vigorous. Now, it must be said that when he has an uncle like his, that is real support. He is getting so amusing. He makes us laugh until we can't laugh anymore. The other day, at the bowling game, he made everybody laugh: at one moment he began to run around in a weird way, knocking over the bowling pins. Everybody had a good laugh, but I think that those who had been winning, didn't laugh so heartily, because they had to begin all over again. But nevertheless it is obvious that his strength is coming back and for a convalescent we can close our eyes to a lot of things.

We just received from Gaby the news about your store. [Papa appears to understand the real reasons for Jean's purchase of the store.] What a lucky guy you are for a lot of reasons: 1) to have the money needed to buy a business like that. Gaby says you could already have sold it for three times as much. So, it's entirely different from the earlier one in Collonges, right? And then Papa said "no" to that one. So you must have had your own reasons for not making an extra 100 000 francs [by selling it.] 2) My congratulations for having such a courageous and enterprising little wife, you really are lucky. She loves being active: doing business and doing her housework. Jean, I really think you have reasons to thank God. Imagine if you had a lazy companion who loves going out and spending money. What a cross that would be to bear! I am absolutely sure she will be a powerful support at least in the things of this earth. ...

Say, Jean, you don't know how lucky we are to have suppliers. Some of them come to the house to deliver their merchandise. But since a good many of them are forced to leave for Germany, those who remain must serve a growing number of clients. So that makes problems: the new suppliers make errors, etc. But still, Mama has always been served satisfactorily. The other day the coal merchant brought us our share. So, we are all set until January 1st. ...

Say, about your friend Henri or Ernest [another person on Jean's list of people for Papa to see], if I should transmit your greetings to him, just let me know. You can count on me. Or to see anyone, I am at your disposal. ...

I forgot to ask an urgent question of your little wife. Would you ask her for me? Here it is: Say, Lizou, I knew a certain Jean W., son of a certain Jean W; I hear you sometimes come across this young ex-bachelor and that he "sometimes" listens to what you have to say. So, would you try not to let him get overtired, as he strongly resembles his father who never takes a minute's rest. Yet, Jean no. 2 needs it so much, as after the war he will need a great deal of intellectual strength to succeed in life's struggle. I would be very grateful, as would my wife, to hear regularly about any results you obtain. Tell him that he must treat his little Lizou with much care and attention, devoting much time to her, and that will have a calming influence on him in return. Thank you in advance, and good luck.

So, my dear Jean, it's time to stop once more. The time will come when I can kiss you in person, but in the meantime it is so good to be able to do it in thought. Mama and Annette also. If you only knew how often you, Lizou and Gaby are the objects of our thoughts and our conversations. So, goodbye, "krabbekop" [head-scratcher—Papa used to like Jean to scratch his head].

Papa

Papa's third letter of September 22, the one he writes to Gaby, addresses Gaby's concerns about the value of her work, and the disappointment she feels about some of the leaders of the church.

Papa to Gaby September 22, 1942

... I have an account to settle with you, dear Gaby, about your remark that anyone could do the work you do and that you try to be nice to everyone, but that it HAS NO REAL VALUE. It's true that even a monkey can be taught to handle a violin and its bow, but, and there is a "but". For a deaf person, it may be amusing to watch a monkey perform. It's the same for work that is done any old way. He who is blind to real values doesn't see the importance of certain acts, but those who do see them can never undervalue them. ...

If I gave the impression that our early ideas had no value, I went beyond my real thinking. On the contrary, I admire those men and women

THE NEW STORE

who launched the Adventist movement, all the while knowing how little education they had on any subject, even the Bible, I am amazed to realize how just was their comprehension of many Biblical things...

Mama to the children   The Hague, September 27, 1942

My dear children,

    ... Papa has written you a long letter this week and answered your letters. It probably took you quite some time to read all that, and more so because everything was written on the typewriter and so it takes more time, but I have no doubt that all three of you enjoyed reading those letters and have drawn benefits from them. As you know, I just write about homey things and leave it to Pa to answer your questions as best he can. And I go over your letters and answer them in my own way. We understand that you are busy, Joop, and even very busy. That will probably be true all your life because you are following in your father's footsteps. Pa was born 5 minutes too late and all his life he was doing his best to catch up on those 5 minutes, but he has failed and never will succeed. Is that the same with you too, Joop? Or do you have ten minutes to catch up? However, we know that you are busy with your new store. ... I can understand that Lizou is very glad to have her own living-room and kitchen. ... I would love to see that store. I can remember the city [Annecy] very well. I used to go there often, and also to the lake. I always thought it was a nice city and hope to be able to visit it once again. Papa is busy with his lessons and writing things for people. ... and his days go by so fast that he is surprised to see that it is Friday already when he thought it was only Tuesday. But this is better than having nothing to do. ...

    You'll say, "Mother always asks questions." True, because whatever happens in Paris is of interest to us. It is nice that we have lived there and know quite a bit and can experience things with you. When I come back to Paris I would like to go to the Rue Thomire. I wonder if the old lady still lives on the top floor. Next month our Joop will be 30 years old. I can hardly comprehend that we have such a big son already. Yes, the parents are getting old. Here one might say we had "a son with three crosses." Yes, Joop, you have become a grown man, but to us you remain "Jopie." We will of course think of you often on that day. If we were in normal times, I think Pa would surprise you and come to see you in person to congratulate you as it is a crowning year. This year it may not happen, but we hope for next year. Annette would ask, "Are we getting cake and soda?" and Joop would say, "As much as you want." We hope that you have a fine day and have some festivities. ... It is getting colder here, but we'll wait as long as possible before lighting the stove. It usually gets much colder after New Year's, and we must be very frugal with coal. And now, dear children, the talking hour is over and we have to part again. Our love to all three of you and many kisses from your loving Dutch parents and little sister.

Gaby has just returned to Paris from Chartres where she has been "Ingathering" (an Adventist practice of collecting money door-to-door to support overseas missionary work).

Gaby to Jean (card)   Paris, September 27, 1942

... There were a lot of stores that were closed, as some are open only 3 days a week, as business is not going well at all. ...

Gaby to Lizou and Jean (card)   Paris, September 30, 1942

Bien chers Lizou et Jean,

    In a few minutes we will leave for Dreux, as we're doing that city this year. I don't look forward to staying in a hotel, as it is very cold and it's pouring rain. But the more we put it off, the less courage we'll have. I'm glad we'll be back tomorrow night. Yesterday I got Jean's card of the 24th of this month. I can hardly believe you found me a radio tube. I can't wait for someone to bring it. I have a lot of expenses right now and it would help if you could send me a money order when you can. I just ordered another 40 kilos of almonds. I am getting as many provisions as I can as the winter will be a hard one. Kisses, Gaby

10   Resistance and Daily Life

Jean writes to Gaby in early October, giving a glimpse of his activities, which are more and more devoted to helping Dutch refugees.

Jean to Gaby   Friday, 5 o'clock, October 2, 1942

Ma bien chère Gaby,

As always, my old song of "too much work" which occupies me and keeps me from writing as much as I would like. But since you are the good little sister who always forgives when it's that enfant terrible Jean, I feel safe. I won't write very much, but there is mail to go so I'll take the opportunity to write a few lines. Before I forget, tell Oscar that I strongly advise him to come here in the ways he must know of or with Frédéric when he comes the next time.

I have had an enormous workload recently, and it even happens that during the last 3 weeks I haven't slept much or eaten hardly anything. You know that the Dutch refugees here were rounded up; there were raids in hotels, etc. and they were placed in camps and from there they were sent to Germany. This happened to some Dutch people (by mistake, we were told) but now there are those in the camps, and no one knows what will happen to them. So there was a rush to Switzerland which does take them in. So we have had a lot of work in the Office (which replaced the Consulate), and I have done everything I could to bring comfort to these unfortunate people. One of my friends, Joop, who knew the border area very well, has been helping many of his compatriots to pass through. [Jean is telling Gaby here that he is doing this work of a passeur since Joop is Jean himself.] How he is doing it I am not at liberty to tell you, but I know that he has done some good work for his country's cause. Fortunately, now the job is nearly finished. Many are in Switzerland where they are living like princes, and right now it is practically impossible to cross the border, as there are, it seems, check-points almost every 2 or 3 kilometers on all the roads going out of Annecy. I wonder what these poor people have done to be hunted like this. Well, anyway, only the future will tell if we are doing the right thing. I can't really say that the Jews (most of them are Jews) are of any great interest, because when one has to deal with all those nut cases, one gets anti-Semitic. But they are human beings, and they shouldn't be treated like animals.

Beyond that there is Lizou's store which needs a lot of care while it's starting out. Fortunately all is going well, and I have succeeded in sending her a lot of merchandise etc. And now it's shaping up. She opens it only 3-4 days a week, but we sell an enormous amount. During its first month, that is, the month of August, we sold 30 000 francs worth of goods, which makes us a profit of 10 000, so you see, it's really worth it, and even then we have to slow down sales because if we didn't everything would be sold immediately. We sell the most popular things in minute quantities, such as the muslins and chiffons etc. Lizou's mother hasn't dared to come in yet, but now that she sees that it's going well, I think she will decide to come into it in the spring. Lizou likes Annecy a lot, and her health is really better; she has gained a kilo. She is getting attached to "her" store. She works very hard there all day. There is also a kitchen where she cooks up goodies, and she is very good at it, and she makes me good puddings, and sautéed potatoes etc.

Lizou has been to Berne for various business reasons [perhaps to respond to Re Koster's requests in her letter of September 7] and she met the Dr. [Dr. Nussbaum] at the Olsen's, and he modestly held the floor during the whole meal. ... Lizou's mother has recuperated very well from her accident. She came for two days this week. Lizou has been here only once in 3 months, I think. But I go to see her every 2-3 days, and from now on we will organize our lives so that she will come here 2-3 days a week, and that way we will not be separated too much. It's only temporary anyway. Thanks for all your good news. I'll answer your letter the next time. I was also very glad to get all the news from the parents, and I am so happy that things are going well for them. ...

The war will be over next year. Arthur's uncle will come here in the spring. Your affectionate brother.

Gaby to Elisabeth and Jean   October 5, 1942

Bien chère Elisabeth et bien cher Jean,

It's Monday evening. We did the dishes and I brought the typewriter up to the kitchen so I could write you. At this time of night we can't turn the lights on in the office because of passive defense [the blackouts]; but there are curtains in the kitchen, and I want to write to you this evening as mail will go tomorrow. ...

I'm sorry about this torn page. I don't know why it's happening; it has never happened to me before. Anyway, since it's for you, I won't do this letter over as I know you will forgive me.

Today I heard that we are getting a bonus of 1000 francs for the unmarried people, 2000 francs for couples, to buy provisions for winter. I am really glad, not just for me who am quite well supplied, thanks to you, but for so many others who have trouble making ends meet. That's going to put a little butter in our spinach. I'm especially glad for Armande Raimbault, who has a lot of trouble getting by. She is a really nice girl, and I am glad I work with her. Last Friday she gave a little party for my birthday. This had been planned for a long time. [Gaby's birthday is August 17, "last Friday" was October 2!] There were 7 of us, and we had a good time from 3pm to 10pm. She had prepared wonderful refreshments for us. She had brought back some things from vacation (butter, eggs, etc.). But I am sure all that cost her a lot. I hope to be able to return the favor in part, as I plan to give her some organdy yardage for a smock if Jean can send me some, as I asked. But of course there's no hurry. ...

I have a few letters from the parents to send you. Papa really took a lot of trouble to write us such a long letter. I'm also sending you the one he wrote to me, but please send it back to me as I would like to keep it. ...

Autumn is here but it's not too cold yet. But the humidity is unpleasant, and between now and December it will get worse. There is thick fog in the morning, but it lifts by noon. ...

This is the third Monday in a row that I got a card from Jean. This evening I got the one dated the 2nd of this month. It's really nice of you to write me so often, and yet I know how busy you both are. I assure you that if you were here, I would much rather help you in your work. You could really count on your secretary, and you can imagine how devoted to you I would be and would try to defend your interests. I realize more and more that in the Work one isn't really appreciated, even when we go to a lot of trouble, and if I worked for you, I would have the impression I was taking some of the load off your shoulders. But not much chance of that right now. Anyway, I'm coming to realize one thing: that those who do the least demand the most from others, and have the biggest egos. ...

I feel as if all that traveling is going to be tiring for Jean. Be careful Jean, and spare yourself as much as you can, because if you get sick, that won't help. I'm glad to hear Lizou has put on a little weight. Keep it up, Elisabeth, and please take care of yourself. Fortunately supplies are good in Annecy.

Did you get the pain d'épices [a bit like gingerbread] which a friend of Brother Meyer brought once, or were you not in Lyon that day? I hope someone put some aside for you.

Now I'll stop, as I must go to bed. I got back late last night and didn't get to bed until 11:30. Tomorrow it will be late again, as I have to go get the apples after dinner. ...

Je vous embrasse très fort, both of you, and I repeat: I think of you all the time, and I love thinking about getting together again perhaps next year.

October 13 is the parents' wedding anniversary (31 years). We will probably all think about them a lot.

Affectionately,
Gaby

Annette's handwritten letter bears the half-inch wide, transparent blue lines of the censors. On the first two pages the line travels down the left-hand margin, perhaps to make it easier for the recipient to read the text? But on the two last pages, the blue line is drawn diagonally across the page.

Annette to Jean and Elisabeth   The Hague, October 11, 1942

Bien chers Lizou et Jean,

I'm scared that you may think I have completely forgotten you. It is true that since we have been separated I've never written you. When I think about it, I'm really ashamed. But I'm going to use the same excuse as Jean. I have so much work that I hardly have a minute to myself. But I assure you that I haven't forgotten you and that I would give anything in the world to see you again. But, let's keep up our courage and hope that the time will come soon when we are together again.

My dear "Jopie," on the occasion of your birthday, I bring you my best wishes. Luckily I don't have to wish you happiness, with a little wife like Lizou who spoils you and cooks wonderful meals for you as you were saying in your last letter. I can hardly believe I have a brother who is going to be 30 years old. It's really a big historical event, and even though you aren't a millionaire yet (and consequently haven't bought a car yet nor a trip to America for Papa), I think you have a good start in life, and I am very proud of you! You have helped poor Gaby so much. Thanks to you, she has been able to eat fairly well in this time of war etc. which means my parents don't have to worry about her in the least. You spoil us too, Jean. Yesterday the seamstress brought me a striped dress and a pretty white blouse that she had just finished, the material for which I had received from a certain gentleman who spoils me rotten. ... I hope that sooner or later I too can do something for you; who knows, maybe I can take care of you, Lizou, when you will take on the role of a mother, and take care of little Jean when big Jean becomes a happy papa.

I also received a beautiful brown leather handbag, so here in Holland, I am really spoiled.

I have loads of work these days. In three months I hope to sit for my final exams to become an assistant birth attendant. The exam is really difficult for me because Dutch is not really my mother tongue. A few weeks ago, I had some trouble about the Sabbath. We just got a new head nurse in the clinic. The former one had exempted me from the Sabbath afternoon, but the new one didn't want to give me that, especially since there was a gynecology class which was the most important for the exam, and which was going to be held on Friday evening, when I couldn't be there. I was faced with two possibilities: either come to the classes on Friday evening and Saturday afternoon or be expelled. I prayed about it and refused to come to the classes. Papa wrote a beautiful letter to the committee which worked (Papa is so terrific, he takes care of me and always helps me through the difficult times) and the answer which the head nurse gave me was as follows: We have no jurisdiction in cases of conscience. (We have decided to leave you free on Friday evening and Saturday afternoon, and you can even present yourself for the examination, of course at your own risk.) As you can imagine, I jumped for joy, as, according to law, I do not have the right to take the exam if I haven't attended the courses. But, as you can imagine, my dear Jean and Lizou, I am now studying a lot to learn the written material of the courses. Of course if they ask me something on the exam that a Doctor talked about in his course and which isn't in the books, I will fail, but I trust in God who has helped me so much thus far.

So now I have worked for a year in the clinic. The course lasts a year and a half: a year in the clinic and six months "in der Wyjk." [The "Wyjk" is the district or area of the city to which the health worker is assigned.] And all without earning a cent, not even the meals. But once we have the diploma, we earn a good salary, you know.

So I have been "in the field" for two months. I go all over the city on my bicycle to take care of mothers and babies. I leave at 8 in the morning after telephoning the clinic to see if I have any new patients. Sometimes I don't get home until 3 o'clock in the afternoon. I leave again at 5 o'clock and don't get home until 9 or ten. When it is very dark in the evening, you can't see anything in the streets when you're on a bicycle, but you get used to it. We have two days off a month. So I'm free for two Sabbaths a month. I go to families both rich and poor. At the moment I am taking care of a woman who just had her 13th child. The oldest one isn't quite 16. You can just picture the lineup when I send them all out of the room where the mother is in bed. I see some terrible things which are really sickening. Such poor and dirty people. The mother lying on a dirty mattress where the fleas are jumping all around. Terrible odor. No, I could never have believed that in our city there was so much misery and filth. I don't bring any money home, but sometimes I bring other things—fleas! To Mama's great despair, naturally! And how are you both? I am always so happy to hear your news. Oh what a joy it will be to see you again. It is my greatest wish. Jean says that after the war I can ask him for whatever I want and I will receive it. Well, nothing would bring me greater pleasure than a trip: The Hague to Paris to Annecy, and maybe I won't be alone (but that's a secret). But maybe we will have saved enough to pay for that trip ourselves, and we would only ask for your hospitality for both of us! How happy I would be to kiss my little sister-in-law, as up to now I have only kissed her as Jean's fiancée. Dear Jean and Lizou, I think of you all the time and kiss you with all my heart. Annette

A birthday wish for Jean and some interesting arithmetic from Papa:

Papa to Jean   The Hague, October 11, 1942

My dear birthday boy Joop,

What a surprise, and how time flies! It is Tuesday morning in Nothom Street, in Etterbeek [Belgium], on the second floor at no. 7, a little monkey came into the world, and even though he had just barely appeared, you could still hear his little voice! His parents were so happy! His father felt overjoyed. Today he became a father!

What? Did that happen already 30 years ago today? It is as if it were yesterday. Yes, time flies, flies, flies!

Well, dear little birthday boy "Jopie", our heartfelt congratulations, because it is a fact that you are now 30 years old! Quite an age! Thirty years! I got married when I was just thirty and you are married already! So you are quicker than your father.

Who would have thought that I would be sending you congratulations from The Hague to France, and you are almost, with the difference of half a year, half as old as your father! Yes, and what is also strange is the following: When you were 1 year old, you were about 1/30 of your father's age. Now you are half my age.

So, 30 years ago I was 30 times as old as my one-year-old son. Now, after 30 years I am twice as old as he. So my conclusion: it won't be that long before you are as old as I am, and after a while, as time passes, you will become older than I am. Joop, you are a miracle person!

Yes, dear fellow, how grateful we can be that God has kept you all those years. We are especially happy that you have found such a good little wife, who will be more and more a real support to you. ... May God also in this new year of your life guide your way, so that "many will rejoice in your birth" just as they said of John the Baptist.

And Lizou, you cannot read Dutch, but someone will be there to translate this for you; I congratulate you also and hope you both have a delightful birthday.

Dear boy, if you know how often we think of you and Lizou and Mies. How glad we would be to see you and hug each other. However, that will come! Keep the spirit!

You might hear of people changing addresses here in The Hague, but don't worry about us because that most likely won't happen to us. Annette's clinic also informed her that younger students might have to leave soon, but this does not affect the more advanced, such as Annette. She would be able to go through her exam. Now, dear fellow, many kisses, more than if it were not your birthday, and heartfelt greetings to Lizou and also Mies. When Lizou visits her mother and writes me, then please have her write the address again, OK? Bye, 30-year-old son.

Papa

From Mama's weekly letter:

Mama to the children   The Hague, October 19, 1942

... Fortunately you were still able to buy some apples, Miesje. Hopefully they will keep. Apples usually ferment without adding sugar, so check them after a few weeks. You thought it was too much work to dry them as we used to. Mashing the apples is more work. I cored the apples with a knife, peeled them and cut them in slices. Pa put a cord through the holes and hung them from wall to wall like a clothesline. We let them hang there for over six weeks because it did not interfere with anyone and we didn't have to do anything to them afterwards. This winter, cook them and add some sugar to make applesauce. That was not more than an hour's work for three or four kilos of apples. So it was not as much work as you thought it was. I also canned some endives or lettuce. I had no pots but used a bucket. We cut the lettuce into little pieces, one layer of lettuce, one layer of salt, then another layer with salt. Put a dinner plate on top with a cloth and something heavy on top. This winter when it is freezing and no vegetables are available, one always has this lettuce. ...

Gaby is worried about Jean's clandestine activity.

Gaby to Jean and Elisabeth   Tuesday, October 20, 1942

Mes bien chers Lizou et Jean,

    How good of Jean to write me that letter last Friday when he is so busy. I really think it's wonderful, but you have to take care of your health, Jean. If you don't sleep or eat hardly anything, you'll suffer from it. I know that certain things can't be postponed, but I hope that now all that is over and that you can rest a little. But I was really glad to know that Lizou had gained some weight. Maybe having a home, however modest, raises her spirits. It is nicer than having a hotel room, after all. But I hope you will soon have an apartment in Lyon, although maybe that won't be worth it if you are going to move to Paris next year!

    I'll tell the parents what they are getting, but if you agree, I'll modify it slightly. I am certain that Annette would be extremely happy to have a little pocket money, as she has to ask for everything from the parents. So I'm going to tell them that there are 1000 Florins for them and 150 for Annette. I hope you will agree, as I don't think you had thought of giving something to Annette personally. This way, when the holidays come, she can buy presents for the parents, which she loves to do. ...

    Jean, tell your friend, the one Jean told me about in his last letter, that he should still be very careful, as he risks getting into trouble. I know we have to help people, but all the same. Personally I don't think I would have the courage. It's to be seen whether those he pulled out of difficulty will even be grateful. But it is very wonderful of him to do it. ...

    I have to stop as it's 7 o'clock. I still have to eat and do the dishes, and there is a prayer meeting at 8:30. These are livelier than they were with Mr. Mathy, I have to admit, and more people come. But on the other hand, Brother Mathy had qualities that Brother Winandy didn't. That's why it's good to change from time to time.

    I'll leave you then. Oh, yes, let's pray for Annette that she passes her exams, despite the classes she couldn't take. I also think that since God allowed her to be exempt from the classes, He will give her success on her exams.

    Je vous embrasse bien fort, my dear ones, while telling you how much I think of you all the time. I also rejoice at the prospect of seeing each other again, and that gives me courage that this situation will not last forever. Affectionately, Gaby

Gaby has her radio tube at last.

Gaby to Jean and Elisabeth (card)　　　　　　　　　　Paris, October 26, 1942

Mes bien chers,

　　What a joy this morning to hear by telephone that Mr. Lhermite had brought me my radio tube! I asked him if I could go and get it this evening, as I couldn't leave the office, and he said he would leave everything with the concierge. ... The weather is nice. We haven't suffered much from the cold. Yesterday I received 2 bags of potatoes from Collonges. Does that come from you? I won't get into it yet until I get some information. Best thoughts, Gaby.

On October 24, 1942, Jean writes to Mr. Sevenster about a recent "adventure." Jean works with Mr. Sevenster, who is Dutch Consul in Toulouse, to bring aid to the Dutch refugees who find themselves interned in camps in Southern France.

Jean to Mr. Sevenster　　　　　　　　　　　　　　　　October 24, 1942

　　... I returned to Lyon two or three days ago after some adventures which I hope I will one day have the "pleasure" of telling you about. Let me just tell you that I spent a day and a half in prison and that I was in handcuffs. Fortunately all ended well. So after the war I will be able to answer question 18 on the Dutch questionnaire, 'Have you ever been in prison?', and won't need to answer question 19, unless I answer, 'Why not?'

Indeed, Jean Weidner had been imprisoned a few days before. On October 14, 1942, he was arrested by the French police near the Swiss border because he was suspected of helping refugees to escape to Switzerland.* Despite Jean's attempt to make light of his imprisonment, this was no minor event. He was kept in chains and severely beaten for two days. His captors then gave up trying to get a confession from him and released him for lack of evidence.

---

* See Megan Koreman, *The Escape Line* (Oxford: Oxford University Press, 2018), p.50.

Less than two months later, Mr. Sevenster was himself a political prisoner at Evaux-les-Bains where he remained for eighteen months.

Mama to the children The Hague, October 25, 1942

… Annette is doing very well. She is happy with her work and her patients have no complaints. This is the work she likes, going from one patient to another. Only if it rains, it is not so nice on the bicycle. I have bought some leggings for her, and they are not made of leather, because that is not available, but are made of black canvas. She puts them on over her shoes and they reach over her knees. Water does not get through and she stays dry on the bike. With a waterproof hat on her head she is ready to go. …

We thought of you all day on the 22nd. When Annette came home in the afternoon that day, and saw that I had bought brown beans for supper, she was so glad, and I said it was Jopie's birthday. So you see, Jopie, we live with you in spirit and hope you had a very nice day. But perhaps you were so busy that you didn't even think about your birthday. It could have been just like your father who was almost never home for his birthday. All the birthdays in our family are over until March. Annette starts out the year with the birthdays [Annette's is March 12] since our François is not here anymore. [François was born on February 26.] I often think of that quiet grave in Gland. In my thoughts I can see the grave, the quiet neighborhood and the mountains. Later on there will be snow on the stone. Will I ever see it again? …

Gaby sends a postcard to Jean which says the radio is working. "My radio works so well with the new tube, and I am so grateful to you for getting it for me! It is so nice to have a little music."

Annette to Gaby The Hague, October 31, 1942

Ma bien chère petite Gaby,

Yesterday I was so pleased to receive your letter and at the same time one from Brother Meyer. It is so good to receive news personally from my friends in France, and from my dear Parisian sister. I think it's time I answered you, since, if I'm not mistaken, it has been several months since I wrote you. Can you believe that it seems strange to write in French now, since I'm so used to thinking in Dutch? Do you know what is really terrible? It's that I'm forgetting a lot of French words. A few days ago, the head nurse was asking the French words for diapers and those naval bandages. I could only give the word for the first, "langes" [today it would be "couches"], but for that band that babies wear around their tummy for the first few weeks, I really don't know the word for that. Could you tell me in your next letter please?

In your previous letter, you asked if all my exams were behind me. Oh, no. The hardest ones are yet to come. No, the exams I took before were to be able to work outside the clinic and we still had a lot of courses to take. Monday evening from 8 to 9, Thursday afternoon, Friday afternoon, and Saturday afternoon. Beyond that were practice sessions. Today I didn't get home until 3 o'clock, and I hadn't eaten anything since 7 o'clock in the morning. My patients all live very far from each other. I do all the traveling by bicycle, but it rains a lot and pedaling takes time. I'm hungry all day and eat like a horse when I get home. But I use a lot of energy pedaling. The first 4 days we do 3 visits a day, and then until the 10th day, twice a day, and then until the 14th day, once a day, and that's only to bathe the baby. So as you can see, I have 5 or 6 mummies and babies a day, and I'm busy from 8 in the morning to 3 in the afternoon, and then I begin again at 5 for the evening visit, and I don't get home until 9 o'clock, and on the days we have classes, not before 10 o'clock. We have two days off a month (at least up to now I have had two days off), and then somehow we have to find time to study, because in two and a half months we have the final exam, and the doctors ask very hard questions, I've heard. Well, let's hope it all goes well. Yes, you can study to be a midwife in Holland, but the studies are very hard, and you have to have the baccalauréat diploma to get in, so you have to be much more qualified than I am. But tell me, in France when women have babies at home, who takes care of them for the next two weeks? A nurse? Here many women stay at home and have an assistant birth attendant three times a day or, if they have the means, they have one for the birth and then have one day and night for two weeks. That is what I want to do when I get my diploma. I haven't the least idea how that is done in France. Not all women have their babies in a hospital, do they?

About Michèle, I'm really so sad that she isn't happy. Yes, actually there are not very many happy marriages. Now that I go into the intimacy of many households, I see a lot of things which make me stop and think. I have a lot of very young mothers who are already so disillusioned. Last week I had an 18-year-old mother who was already having her second child. Her husband was 22 and often left her alone at night. The second day after she had her baby, he didn't come home all night. A woman who had given birth two days before, all alone with a little baby and an 18-month-old kid. If you could have heard the scolding I gave the father the next day. He was trembling and didn't dare even open his mouth. He couldn't guess that I was only 21! Today I had a new patient. The mother is 25 and this was already her sixth baby. It's frightful. A few weeks ago I had a family of 13 children. A child every year. I can assure you that one gets to know something about men this way. And do you know that Holland, so known for its cleanliness, well it's a myth. Almost all my patients are so unclean and disgusting. I should scrub them to get them clean. Legs that are really black. They are lying on mattresses without sheets. Dirty blankets over them. I can assure you that I am sometimes fed up with all this filth. Last week I telephoned (I have to telephone 3 times a day to find out if I have any new patients) and I was given the address of a street in a very poor neighborhood. Well I can tell you I wanted to turn and run. There were no diapers, no towels, no blankets for the baby. The baby was almost frozen to death. His temperature wasn't even 35 degrees [C]. And in the kitchen, there was a huge pile of dirty laundry. Diapers, sheets, everything. And just try to imagine the smell, and the worms crawling around in it. The woman hadn't done the wash for several months, and just threw everything in the corner. Isn't that shameful? With a baby on the way?

I'm so sleepy. I'll continue my letter tomorrow, if I have a little time. Good night, my darling, my treasure, my cream puff!!!

Sunday evening.

Here I am again. Tomorrow morning I can sleep an hour longer because the time is going to change. That's why I can allow myself the luxury of writing to you late again this evening.

I was so happy to get your photo. I think that hairdo is very becoming to you. You are so pretty. You know, I think Brother Meyer likes you a lot. He writes me that you are a very good and precious person that everyone appreciates. He would like it so much if a good husband appreciated you also. I think I'm going to be jealous!! Tell Brother Meyer that I will write to him, I promise, last week. [Annette probably meant to write: "next week."] And in the meantime you can kiss him for me. I authorize you to do so! Yesterday we received your letter to the parents. You know, it's fantastic how much Jean spoils me. I got 150 Florins. This is a real capital! If you only knew how grateful I am. It's more than I would have dreamed of having. I put them aside right away. Jean helps so many people, but I am sure that it's also because God helps him so much and brings him success in his work. I am so glad Elisabeth can do her own cooking now. After all, it is much nicer when one is married, to be able to do one's own cooking.

Yes, now I have to talk about affairs of the heart. My dearest, don't think badly of me because I change all the time, but I can assure you that I have my reasons. I broke up with Jacques. He disappointed me enormously in a lot of ways. From the spiritual point of view, there was nothing there (a little lie never hurt anybody, etc.) no determination or initiative. No, I am just glad that I saw it in time. But now I have made my choice, and I assure you it's a good choice, because I have never before felt so happy. No, now I am sure of him and of myself. Those feelings can't be explained, but I know I would go through fire for him. It's Lykele, the young man from Amsterdam, the handsome one I told you about. And he is so happy, too. He has had a lot of little puppy loves, but he has never felt this way before. He has been faithful to me for over a year and loved me even when I gave him no reason to hope. But he claims that he knew he would have me sooner or later and that I would love him too. His patience has been rewarded. I love him so much, if you only knew. He is also so nice to me, and his character is rather more French. He loves to travel, and when the war is over, we have already made plans to go to France and Switzerland. But we won't be able to get married very soon, because we won't have enough money. He works for the Post Office, and earns 25 Florins a week. But he is doing his best to save money. Maybe in two years we can have a wedding! I put aside the money from Jean for my trousseau. If you also send this letter to Jean and Lizou, I kiss them with all my heart, and I hope to be able to see them to thank them. Greetings to all my friends and an affectionate kiss from your little sister. Annette

Mama and Papa write on the same day about Jean's gift of money:

Mama to the children The Hague, November 1, 1942

My dear children,

Pa wants to write you tonight. Annette is writing you now. ... This week we were so happily surprised by Joop's money gift. I had to laugh and cry at the same time when I received it. Did Joop gave us the right present? If I had not seen it in my own hands, I would not have believed it. ... I would not even have dreamed about having that much. And Annette is so happy, she has never had 150 guilders, and she can barely believe it. Pa and Annette do not want me to work so hard anymore and would like me to have a cleaning lady. I also do not want to do the entire laundry by myself anymore, as it is too tiring. This winter will be more comfortable for us financially if the Lord spares us. Pa won't have to exert himself so much with teaching. In any case we have enough to last us until Annette's studies are over. I never thought my son could give me so much joy, and the nice thing is that the Lord has put him in a position to help us, while we are still alive. If he had done this later after we were dead, he would always have thought, "I wish I had given my mother something when she was still alive." ... When I go to bed I will think of how sweet my son has been and when I wake up I'll think of it again. May the Lord abundantly bless my son and give him all the prosperity that is good for him, as he does not use these blessings for himself but also makes others happy. And now I will not write about it anymore as Pa is doing it and we would write the same thing...

There is a rumor that The Hague will be evacuated, but I just cannot imagine that. Where would all the people go? However, if necessary, we are more reassured with the thought that we now have some money to be able to move...

A quick kiss for Mies for the nice snapshot. You look good in it, Mies...

Papa to Jean, Elisabeth, and Gaby The Hague, November 1, 1942

Dear Mies, Also to Elisabeth and her husband the millionaire.

Yesterday evening after the Sabbath we received your letter dated Oct 21. Ma and Annette had read it already before they went to bed and also your Pa had read it three times. It is always a delight to hear from you.

However, now I am angry with you dear child. Why? Is it because you had waited too long before you wrote? Not at all. But we are angry because you might think that we might be. However, we will never be angry, because we know very well that you have no lack of good will. We know our Miesje too well for that. So remember this, dear child: if you are too busy and you need to help someone, you must do that first, and if there is no opportunity to write without having to change things, then wait. Really we do not mind at all, because when your letter does arrive, then we will know you have had the time to do it. So do we have a deal? If too busy, no letter to us.

Well, Mies, here's something you would like to know. You always wonder if we are poor. Don't be worried, we will make it. Would you believe that we got something from Joop's friend? [from Jean himself] Yes, and guess how much? 1153 guilders. Very nice of Joop, right? There were also 150 guilders for Annette. That child was so happy with it. She never felt so rich in her life. ...

Arthur has many reasons to be satisfied now. His illness that he had two years ago is much better now. He is convinced that he will be cured completely. We also heard that Charlotte is getting better. Fischer, on the contrary, seems to have had a setback. That does not seem to sadden Charlotte too much. Well, we can't blame her for that.

Well, Mies, how nice of you to send the identification photo. Yes, you still look very good. Nice of your brother to take such good care of you. You do have a faithful brother. ...

You asked whether we will have to move. ... No, child, we did not get the news that we have to leave, so we will stay where we are. We hope to be able to stay there until Annette has her exam in February. Nevertheless Mama wrote her family in Enschede, for it is a good thing to be prepared. Do not worry. Now, bye, bye, my dearly loved Mies, many kisses from Ma and your Papa.

Gaby knows what would please Mr. Laatsman as a gift.

Gaby to Jean (card)   Paris, November 12, 1942

Mon cher Jean,

Earlier today I saw Mr. L. to whom I gave the black material for Mama. He told me he had a ration coupon for a suit but can't find the wool material, even at his tailor's. He would need 3 and a half meters. Could you get it for him? If so, I will send you the coupon at the first opportunity, as it is only valid until December 20 and we shouldn't let it run out. If you can't, tell me as soon as possible. Even if you can supply it a little later on, as long as we know it, that's the main thing, so that you get the coupon in time. I would very much like to do this favor for him. Kisses, Gaby

Gaby to Elisabeth and Jean   November 16, 1942

Ma chère Elisabeth et mon cher Jean,

First of all, I want to thank you so much for the financial help that you give me. ... I didn't want to write about it on the cards, because they can be read by a third party, and I think Jean prefers that it not be too well known in the office.

I have to tell Jean, though, to be a bit careful, because I have heard on all sides that he is too generous. ... They say he has too good a heart and that it could get him into trouble. Jeanne Revert was telling me the other day that if anything happened to him, most of those he had helped would just simply abandon him. Of course some express their gratitude, but they are in the minority. Odette also told me that people think you have a fortune and so they don't hesitate to ask for things and accept them without a second's thought. So, Jean, though I don't like to intrude on your affairs, and I know you don't like that, but do be careful. You wrote us that you are now a little more reasonable, and that you don't give away more than half of what you would first decide to give, and that you consult Elisabeth. But I don't know if you do that all the time, because if those who love you have noticed that your generosity is sometimes a little misplaced, it would be a bad thing if others took you for a soft touch. God has blessed you abundantly and has given you an ease of circumstance. One mustn't be egotistical and think only of oneself, but you also have to think of the future. Harder days could come. When you get your apartment you will have to buy furniture, and you might have children (I certainly hope so) and for that you have to have a little money saved. ...

I am so happy to have a radio that works. The tube arrived at just the right moment, because with all these events, it's interesting to listen to the news. But I think I need an outside antenna or an anti-static device. ...

I wonder if Annette will at last stay faithful to her present love. Marriage is a serious thing and I think that sometimes she is a little hesitant. But this time she seems completely sure of herself. I'll send you her letter as I think it will interest you. Mr. L. had mentioned to me that parts of Holland were being evacuated and that the parents live just at the edge of the area which hasn't been evacuated yet. It may happen in two or three months. Let's hope it won't happen because they won't be able to take their furniture, and that would really be terrible. Well, God has taken care of us until now. so we have no reason not to have confidence.

I'll leave you for today. More soon.

On November 11 German troops crossed the Demarcation Line and invaded the "Free Zone" in the South of France. Jean hides his reaction to this momentous event among bits of family news in the center of one of his densely typed pages to hide it from the censors.

Jean to Gaby   Sunday, November 22, 1942

Bien chère Gaby,

It has been a long time since I wrote you, and I'm really sorry. But as Mama says so rightly, I must be like Papa being born 5 minutes too late and ever since my birth I've been trying to catch up. But through my postcards, through other people you have had news of me. At least you write to me faithfully and Lizou and I are very grateful. You know with my business and the store in Annecy, there is enough to keep me busy I can assure you...

I was so glad to hear that you are in good spirits and that the parents got their money. Thank you for all the good wishes for my birthday. As for Mr. L.'s ration coupon, I will do what I can, but I think it may be difficult to find him something; there is no longer any good combed wool like what we had before the war. I'll try to find him something decent anyway. One can find combed wool on the black market but that costs

5000 francs for 3 meters. So I suppose that would be too expensive even if we took some of the cost on ourselves, as is my intention, to show him our gratitude. I don't think the ration coupon is very important, but in any case we could always use it for the store, because we can bring our coupons to the bank later, and I can always advance the tokens.

I am happy for our poor Annette that she can at last begin to think about her trousseau. You were absolutely right to give her those 150 florins so that she has a little something for herself. As soon as we can be together again, I will give her everything she needs. As for her love life, we mustn't beat ourselves up over it or laugh the way Papa does. ...

In Annecy we have everything we need. The farmers' wives come to bring us butter, cheese, vegetables, and they even bring meat, but now they know that it's vegetarian at our house. The store is going very well. The telephone has just been installed. The central heating is about to be turned on, and Elisabeth is going to have an electric heater, that is, we are going to change from gas to electricity, we have enough power in the store, but the electricity is theoretically for cooking, but we can use it for heat as well. On the days when the store is closed we economize on the electricity that way and we can use it on the other days. We have had the kitchen entirely done over. It will be finished this week, and also we are going to set up a pretty little studio, as there is another small room above it.

The store is in a new building, and so it is very clean, and it is well located, and does very well. Generally we open it on Tuesdays, Wednesdays and Thursdays, and sometimes for a little while on Monday and Friday, and that depends on whether Lizou or I go to Lyon or to her mother's. Actually, we aren't too anxious to sell much, as the store would immediately be emptied. If you or Annette or Maman need anything in silk-like fabrics, let me know. We don't have any wool for sale as it is impossible to find, unless we go to the black market, which we can't do for the store. We can only get rayon. ...

I think we will all be able to return to our countries in 5-6 months, in fact I am firmly convinced of it. ... Forgive my disorganized chatting, but I am taking up your cards and letters and answering as things come to mind. I am glad that your radio is working. It seems that Phillips tubes break very easily, so it could happen again, so don't hesitate to let me know and I will find you one more quickly as now I know whom to ask. ...

I think the Dr. is totally wrong to hold the floor all the time, because he talks nonsense and he doesn't place the dietary reform in the right context. We should be Adventists first and vegetarians second. I prefer a non-vegetarian Christian with an exemplary family life and a good dose of humility, to a vegetarian Christian who has only that quality. I have the right to say so, as no one can accuse me of being a carnivore. The health reform should be placed in its true framework and not held up as a supreme goal, which the Dr. always tends to do, and by talking every which way about Sister White and putting her in every sauce, he will succeed only in turning off some people and discrediting Sister White among the intellectuals who don't know enough about her writings. ...

I'm glad the parents received their money and can live a little less frugally, and Papa can travel and Mama can buy some things on the Black Market. If only they were here I could help them much more easily and find them what they need. ...

I'll leave for Annecy tomorrow night (a friend minds the store when we aren't there), I'll return here Wednesday evening, then Sunday I'll go to Anduze to get my identity card which has arrived (it had to be renewed), and I have to renew my travel pass which will take 3-4 days so that I think I'll be returning to Lyon toward the end of next week, that is around December 5. ...

Mme Girou is still in Anduze. Mémé was sent back to the camp for three weeks after his months in prison, but while he was there he managed to get out and go to Anduze without permission and from there to Marseille where he again must have been doing a lot of stupid things, and now he is again consigned to the camp, and I wonder if he'll ever get out. Everybody thinks he is a totally a lost cause and that he had become a real creep. ... Tell Annette that I was happy to get her letter and that I will answer next time (one more promise that may take a while to fulfill, but she now has the money and that's the main thing). ... Yes, Papa went to a lot of trouble to write all those letters, and it's wonderful. His ideas are marvelous and I don't think there is anyone who has such an accurate conception of religious questions as he does. ...

You said in your letter of October 5 that one is not always appreciated in the Work, even if one does one's work very conscientiously. Well, get that idea out of your head, my little Gaby. People pay attention, but don't say anything good or bad, but one day all the truth comes out, the good and the bad, or else they criticise behind people's backs. To arrive at the point where no one says anything bad about you is magnificent and extremely rare, and that is the case with you and furthermore people say a

RESISTANCE AND DAILY LIFE

great many good things about you, which is also very rare. Elisabeth also had the same impression when she was working at the Consulate, that her efforts and loyalty were not noticed, but when she left after three years, her Consul said she had been his best secretary and the most loyal. For 3 years he had said nothing, and yet his judgment had been formed. Believe me, Gaby, you must not believe that just because no one says anything that they aren't thinking it, and one day it will come out to your advantage. Moreover, you know you are working for God and that you are cooperating directly in this magnificent Work. ... Always remain the good Gaby that we all know and you will fill us all with pride and joy. You know that I always say that you are the honor of the Weidner children. ...

According to Sister Revert, you are disappointed that we have not had children yet, but don't worry, it will happen some day. Right now it would be a miracle if we had one because we are almost never together, just from time to time during the day and never at night, so that gives you a vague idea. When one is in Lyon, the other is in Annecy, and when one is in Annecy, the other is at her mother's, and so forth.

I am in good spirits and good health. Now I am a little calmer as most of the work is done. Don't worry about me, Gaby, I do take care of my health. But sometimes one has to do one's duty without fear of endangering one's health; there are so many unfortunate people who need help, and everyone should do what he can, it's a social and national duty. Usually on the Sabbath I am in Lyon and Lizou is either in Lyon or at her mother's, so we are always in a church. I think we were in Annecy only once on the Sabbath. ...

Brother Petit distributed a kilo of sugar to everyone and a big can of apricot pulp, and since Lizou and I have enough sugar, I am going to send you these 2 kilos when I can. ... At Beau-Site [near the Collonges Seminary] there were about 50 members from the Occupation Army. The next day 3 Seminary students (German Swiss) went to invite them to church and to talk with them very nicely. ...

The whole border is now guarded by the Germans. It gives one a funny feeling. In Annecy we didn't see any, but we hear there are Italians in Chambéry. We see a lot of them in Lyon. On Monday morning I heard that all the diplomats as well as citizens of countries which are at war with the Axis [Germany, Italy and Japan are the Axis], even those carrying a French visa were not permitted to cross the border, by order of the Prefecture, so no Belgians, Dutch, etc. etc., could go through, only the French,

Swiss and neutrals, and those from the Axis. Then we learned that only those living on the border could go through, and that anyone with a Swiss or French visa could not go through. That's where things stand now.

On November 11 at 7 o'clock when I heard on Radio Paris that the Germans had crossed the line, I phoned the Division and told them that this was probably the last time I could phone them. I got Hazel Beach on the phone. I told them that I thought I could do it again in 5-6 months. In fact I wanted to begin my application for a visa to go to Switzerland since my identity card was renewed, but now I have to give that up.

On November 11th I also telephoned Lizou and told her to go to her mother's right away, as I think that way she could still straighten out her affairs and mine, and then if the border was closed, she could still ask to return to her home and her husband, whereas from this side it would probably be impossible to ask to go and see her mother. So she went down, with some regret (she was in Annecy) and now I'm waiting for her to come back up, but I can't be in a hurry, as her mother has a bad leg, and that way she can take care of her while waiting patiently for the border to open again, as there will certainly be a regulation for returning to one's home. Fortunately correspondence is still going through and so I hear from her.

... Lizou told me about one Sabbath in Geneva when a young girl who was not wearing a hat was reading the report, and a Sister stood up and proposed that a vote be taken immediately that girls without hats may not read the report. Then two girls, who were there for the first time, left the room. The following time when they were discussing respect in the church, they began to talk about the length of skirts, and one Sister said that Sister White had said that skirts should be 20 centimeters above the ground, to which another Sister responded, and rightly so, that Sister White wanted to give a minimum in a time when dresses reached the floor, and another said these days the young men look only at legs and marry for a girl's beautiful legs. Edifying. At least in Lyon there is a good atmosphere with no disputes or narrow-mindedness. ...

Henri says that between now and the end of the year Italy will be occupied, but you know what kind of opinions he has. I myself think that the Americans will never manage to make a serious attack on the continent and that we don't have to worry about that. Germany is unconquerable and will be able to organize all of Europe very well, and then we can see each other again. [Here Jean is again pretending he is pro-German, and Gaby will understand that he is saying the opposite of his true opinion.]

For many, it seems as if it's very dark and it's like someone who searches for the electric light switch in a dark corridor without knowing where the switch is. But I know very well where we are going. Arthur is in excellent health, and his convalescence is entirely complete, and he is taking long walks. We are happy to see him in such good health after he was so near death, but good food and good care have brought him back to his feet. Charlotte's children would really like to have him back with them, but since Charlotte is still officially married to Fischer, they fear there will be problems, but I am certain that Charlotte will come back to her first love, as she doesn't love her husband who actually brutalizes her. Arthur's uncle, it appears, is very nice and we hope to make his acquaintance soon. He wrote me that he was counting on visiting you in April or May and will bring you a whole bunch of souvenirs, and maybe I'll come with him, unless he goes directly to Paris to say hello to you, actually I think that's more likely, and I'll come with Arthur and Lizou and visit you around that time.

We have to be patient when it comes to politics, and now look, those idiot Anglo Saxons have taken Turkey away from us, so we won't have hardly anything to eat, so fortunately in a short time the Ukraine will be well organized and in new Europe we will have a new abundance, but Germany can't do everything all at once, and once they're finished with Russia we can all turn against Africa and retake what we momentarily lost. But we are only poor little guys and all we have to do is have confidence in those in our countries who will reorganize Europe on a new foundation.

Now my dear little Gaby, I'll stop. Please don't worry about us in any way, everything is fine, our thoughts go out to you constantly, and to our dear parents. We kiss you and ask you to be of good courage, and we'll see you soon. Greetings to all the friends, the youth group and the church. ...

Your affectionate brother, ...

Papa clarifies the evacuation orders in The Hague. Since he is writing on a postcard, he must make it sound as if he thinks the orders are just fine.

Last Wednesday was a celebration day for us as we had just received the news that we don't have to leave here because Annette works. Otherwise we would have to have left today, Monday. As you can see, one isn't given much time when one has to leave.

Papa to Gaby The Hague, November 23, 1942

Notre bien chère Gaby,

Mama begs your pardon; she will write in a few days as she has a lot of urgent things to do. Got your letter of the 13th of this month. The censors are right to say that letters should not be more than 4 pages.

No, it is not true that everybody has to leave The Hague. All those who work can stay. Nor is it true that they put all those who are forced to leave into barracks somewhere in Holland. All those who can find a shelter elsewhere in Holland can go there. There are those who claim that it is very hard for the tens of thousands who have to leave to find a shelter elsewhere, but we shouldn't be pessimistic, you'll see, we'll certainly find a place, and then in winter, it's not so bad to have several living in a single room, as they can keep each other warm. In the summer they have only to open the windows.

The day before yesterday I read the poster on the side nearest the sea saying that all B category people have to leave before December 10, so several of our members have to change homes. What a misfortune...

I was delighted to learn that Arthur is completely cured; no traces of tuberculosis. And the visit from his uncle, who is so generous, also did me a lot of good. I was also happy to learn that Charlotte is expecting. It already shows, apparently. Really, after so many years of marriage. And it appears that the divorce is well on its way to being granted.

Last week we were like Brother Meyer [who doesn't know where he'll go], but now we feel better, since we are going to stay. Aunt Marie is bringing furniture here as she might have to leave soon. Good-by, my dear, kisses from all 3 of us. Papa.

Mama also writes about the evacuations.

Mama to Gaby The Hague, November 25, 1942

As you saw from Pa's card, we almost had to move, but Annette was the guardian angel, because she was working and that's why we were allowed to stay. It is winter, and I'm not that young anymore, and we would have to go all the way to Enschede. It would not have been so bad for the two of us, but we hated to leave Annette all by herself in The Hague. She

RESISTANCE AND DAILY LIFE

has to take exams at the end of January. It would have been a pity if she were not able to do that. She would have to find a boarding house, and right now that is very expensive. And Pa helps her so much with her studies. All these things made me somewhat nervous, and it also affected Pa. But thanks to the Lord we were allowed to stay. Many of the people from the church have gone already and also many of our friends. Working people are allowed to stay. Because the whole of Scheveningen and part of The Hague are being evacuated, the working people are being placed in houses belonging to retired people. So it has become one big moving city. ... Annette's clinic has to be relocated to another part of the city. However, Annette and the other nurses will still be able to take their exams. ...

There probably won't be much of a Christmas. There is nothing to be found in the stores here. One can buy luxury items, but they are so expensive that I would not even think of buying them. ...

In November, 1942, in France, the "Unoccupied Zone" is no longer unoccupied. Jean's letter to Gaby mixes family news with war news.

Jean to Gaby   Friday, November 27, 1942

Ma bien chère Gaby,

The mail didn't leave when I hoped it would, but I think it will happen today, even though things are pretty complicated and there may be delays. Lyon is totally occupied today and we are waiting to see how things develop in order to be sure how things will be organized. Lizou is still at her mother's, and I don't know how she will be able to come back, but she was hoping it would be next Monday. Anyway, with things changing all the time, she may have to stay a little longer, but I am not worried at all as she is safe when she is with her mother. When I came back from Annecy, I was so happy to find your good letter of November 16, and all the news from the parents. Nonetheless I must write to them, and I have so much to do all the time. Well, we'll see. ... Tell Papa that I thank him very much for the poetry, and what is really surprising is that I remembered it perfectly, and I remember Papa doing it as if it were yesterday, it's really interesting what children's memories will register. Give them my kisses. I haven't forgotten them. ... You are right to call me back into line about my over-generous spending. I will do everything I can to keep it in mind.

Elisabeth also reminds me of it constantly. But chase out the natural instincts, and they come back at a gallop. But I am starting to be more reasonable, and I am less exploited than you think. ...

Fischer is getting mixed up in all our business and we can't say anything in our house, but as he is very ill, I think we will soon be rid of him. I'm not afraid of him, but he is really mean. ...

Thank you for the photo, which is very pretty. We will soon send some of us. ...

At the Seminary they wanted to occupy Central [building], and that was to happen Tuesday, but then it appears that there was a decree that says that schools should remain free and not be requisitioned, so we hope everything will be all right. ...

I'm thinking of going down to Anduze on Sunday and I think I will see the ineffable Madame Girou and maybe her no less ineffable son, who must be out of the camp by now, as it appears that they have been dissolved. See you soon, my dearest Gaby, be of courage. I remain your affectionate brother.

Mama faithfully sends her Sunday letters. She is right to suppose that her letter may be censored, as the long blue streaks appear on all the pages.

Mama to the children   November 29, 1942

... Soon it will be Christmas. Will we come together next year? We hope so, because the desire to see you grows ever stronger. Sometimes I just can't believe we haven't seen each other in more than 3 years. ...

The little harmonium from Grandmother has been brought to us by Aunt Marie. She may have to move out of her house and go to an even smaller place, and then she could not have that much furniture. I would never have imagined that I would have that little harmonium, that is already so old, in my house. ...

There is not much news to tell here, and I am hesitant to write more than 2 pages [4 sides] because of the censor, so I'll stop now... Your loving parents and Annette.

Papa's letter in French also bears the censor's blue diagonal mark.

RESISTANCE AND DAILY LIFE

Papa to Elisabeth   The Hague, December 1, 1942

Bien chère Lizou,

... We are wondering if you have been able to return home safely. ...

You know that the evacuation problem here or anywhere else doesn't get resolved without problems. Once the order to depart is received, there is so little time to prepare, that one can't count on it at all. That is why, as soon as we were summoned, we proceeded as if we were going to leave. But that was a preparation so intense with so many difficult arrangements that I wouldn't want to do it again for 10 thousand francs. And all that just finished me. Luckily, about ten days ago, we learned that we can definitely stay where we are—at least for the moment—because we have a daughter who works. If I tell you that the work certificate was given to Annette only the day before, you will understand how great was the tension we were under, as our case could have been considered doubtful. Once the danger was past—we would have had to leave within 5 days, and we didn't yet know where to go—the reaction was overwhelming. No way could I concentrate on anything. But let us not lament; the thing is past, and it was good practice for when it may actually happen. Because nothing is certain when the situation is as it is now.

You did the right thing by going to see your Mama. The reasoning behind this decision is worthy of both of you. And you have now seen Fischer. I wonder what he looks like. I am sure that Charlotte doesn't love him anymore, or rather she never did, as I am convinced it was a marriage of convenience. So the divorce is in the works. I'm glad of that because I have such good memories of her, when I was getting to know her from nearby [Papa's first pastorate was in Brussels] and I wish her well, as she is so kind, generous and spontaneous. I won't go on listing her qualities, as your second mother could get jealous, and she could interrupt me and say, "And what about me?" But it's a fact ... I know that Arthur is holding out his arms to her and he will not fail to cover the costs of the wedding. I also hope that we won't have to wait until the end of the war to witness this disunion and the new union, even if I can't get the permit to go to it. Please congratulate them for me, will you?

What sensational events in France, right? Politics is not my strong point, but I follow the developments with an intense desire to understand them. But, would you believe, Lizou, that I'm getting confused? I wonder if it is my great ignorance on the subject, but I try to organize my impressions in a logical order by reading the newspapers, from the earlier ones to the latest ones. Fortunately everything will take its course even if I don't understand it. But these Russians are a real enigma, as my readings in the past have given me a completely different impression of them; I thought they were nearing their final defeat. It's a good thing that Germany is solid and will provide a bulwark for a long time against the danger of bolshevism.

But let me hasten to the subject which interests you so greatly: the expenses incurred by the husband and wife and the manner in which they should be prepared for. I am very flattered, dearest Lizou, that you are asking my advice. So I am going to answer as well as I can, but I feel very inadequate to producing a solution which will fit every situation. ...

When my wife and I were married, we agreed to make each other as happy as possible. We knew that we could achieve this only by feeling as one. We knew that our different tendencies, which were sometimes even antagonistic to each other, should be used in such a way that would produce maximum happiness. We had to act in perfect unity of spirit, take advantage of the ideas of each, and to undertake nothing which would endanger the happiness of both. The fact that from that time forward we were the property of each other, meant that not only our own bodies no longer belonged to us, but that also included everything we possessed, and that only our conscience remained our private property. So my wife watched over my health and I over hers; my wife knew how much I earned, and I knew how she spent this money. I didn't consider that I had the right to keep any of it nor did she. My wife had the right to know where I was going and I knew about her activities. ... Some functions were more appropriate to the one or the other. ... The wife seems to have received from God the care of the interior of the home and the man, on the other hand seems to be in charge of the exterior protection of the interests of the household. ... I asked my wife to write down what she spent for a certain length of time. After a month I carefully checked this account, and I found that I could not have done better to budget everything. Since then, I give her my money monthly...and she consults me for the big expenses where there could be a difference of opinion. And my household has worked in such a way that I am often astonished at how my wife can manage with so little money.

There is only one thing I regret. It goes without saying that it is also useful for the husband and wife to have a little money of their own, in order to give little surprises to the other. ... So what I regret is that my wife has always thought I should have pocket money, but that she has always been so modest for herself.

In my opinion, in an ideal household from the financial point of view, the husband considers the value of the wife's work in the home as equal to his own, even if she doesn't bring in a penny. The law considers that a divorced woman has a right to half of the earnings of her husband. So this coincides with the above idea, I feel. ...

Horrors! I see that I have chattered on so much that I have no room left. [Papa uses the left-hand margin to write 3 more lines by hand.] We think of you all the time. We are sure that good will on both your parts during the period of adjustment which is sometimes painful, will prepare you for a delicious future! ... A kiss on each cheek from each of us. You'll write often, won't you? Adieu. Papa

Gaby to Jean (a half page handwritten note)   Tuesday, December 2, 1942

Bien cher Jean,

Is it true what I got from a reliable source that the mail is being checked in the Post Office every two days and that files are being kept on people whose addresses they know? I wonder if it's true.

Maybe it would be wiser for Henri [Jean, when he writes letters sent clandestinely] and me to stop all correspondence. But maybe he still wants me to give him news of the parents.

I'm anxious to have a note from you telling me if Lizou got back safely...

In her Sunday letter Mama writes about Annette's new suitor.

Mama to the children   The Hague, December 6, 1942

... Annette is going to Amsterdam for a day. Her day off is Sunday. She is visiting the parents of her friend. His name is Lijkele Faber. He sent us a beautiful package of nice apples this week. We think he is a nice boy and that Annette could be happy with him, but he is still studying in order to get a better job. Annette has had his picture taken, and we would like to send it to you, but we don't know how, because they only allow passport pictures to cross the border. ...

It is December 6 today, but there is nothing to be seen in the way of St. Nicolas celebrations. The people here are totally involved with the evacuation. More and more people have to go and the people that live near Scheveningen and are still working are being placed in the empty houses.

... Well, Miesje, when shall we go to the stores again on the Saturday night before Christmas? That was so nice the last year we lived in Paris, and also that party you had there. We have fond memories of that and think about it often, especially now that those days are coming up. Joop couldn't give us a lot that year, as he was not earning much money. Yet he had something for everyone, and we did what we could for everyone. They are all nice memories. Joop would be able to do a lot more now, if we could get together at Christmas time...

Gaby to Jean (card) December 5, 1942

... Your two cards of the 28th and 29th of this month arrived this morning, and I was very happy. So, Lizou isn't back yet; let's hope that she can return soon. In any case, her mother won't be able to complain about having been too separated from her daughter since your marriage. I think you have a huge amount of work and now you probably have to take care of the store as well. ... The apples were not very damaged except for a few and I made those into applesauce. I put them on a plank and I check them regularly. The last ones were absolutely beautiful and delicious. ...

This typed letter from Gaby to Jean, as well as some others, has two tabs of gummed paper which would have made the seal for the letter, which was folded and had no envelope. Gaby has written "Jean Weidner" beside this seal.

Gaby to Jean December, 13, 1942

Mon bien cher Jean,

I don't know if I should write this letter to Lizou too; she might have come home, and I hope so with all my heart. If so, this letter is also for her. ... I was happy to get your letters, as I know you are so busy. I don't think I am as busy as you are, but I'm busy enough. Life is not all the same as before the war. Before, I could go to the market and bring back everything I needed for two or three days. I would quickly go and get milk in the morning and that was it. Now, since we leave the office at 6:30, we have to go to one store one day and another the next. Then once we have eaten and done the dishes, it is often 8:30 and sometimes even 9 o'clock, by the time we are ready for the next day. Life was pleasanter before. Moreover, since the cleaning lady left, we have more problems. I haven't found another one yet. There is one of the Sisters who did the laundry last week, but she took 6 hours to do the work that the other one did in 2 hours. Moreover, she can't wash the sheets and yet thinks she should be paid as much as Mme Marguerite, that is 7 francs an hour. But I only gave her 5 francs and the midday meal. But she will do it to help us out until we find someone, and I hope we can make arrangements with someone who can wash everything. Mme Marguerite cleaned the rooms thoroughly once a month and Mme Marliac doesn't want to do it.

Don't bother to buy fabric for Mr. L. I went to his office on Friday. There was only one of his former employees. He told me that they all had to go back to their own country and that they were all at the train station except Mr. L., and they didn't know what had become of him. In the early afternoon I went to his own home as I had the address, but the concierge told me that they were no longer in Paris and told me that she didn't know where they were and couldn't forward mail. That really made me sad because he was, after all, a link to our parents and I always knew I could ask him for advice if I needed to. So there are a lot of reasons I'm depressed. And being so close to the holidays and knowing we can't spend them with our family again this year, that seems vary hard. It is, after all, the fourth year. At least I hope that you and Lizou will not be separated for the holidays, and that you will be together for the anniversary of your marriage.

… No, Mme Droz isn't married yet. Mr. Tettelin's divorce still hasn't been finalized, and it is taking a long time. I heard that Brother Winandy wanted to put an end to that, but it's a little delicate. Brother Tettelin doesn't sleep there and says (not to me, of course!) that he lives completely correctly with Mme Droz, and that they never have relations, and I think he is telling the truth. Of course Mme Droz is a little like a kept woman, but since they are going to get married as soon as they can, they could be considered a little like fiancés, at least I think so. …

I am glad to know you have heat in the store. In the house here, what is really hard is that they heat only when it's less than 5 degrees. But when it's 5 degrees [41 degrees F.] outside and 8 or 9 in the apartments, I can assure you that we're not warm, and we can get sick that way, especially when we stay all day in the office without moving around. They don't want us to use the electric radiators as we did last year, because there will be more restrictions. ...

About the suitcase, here is what happened. I think I told you that after the big bombing raid, I had put all the best fabrics I had, wool, non-run knits, etc. in a suitcase at Mlle Marie's. I didn't think to ask her for a receipt. Then she died suddenly. They put seals on all the doors, and those are still there. Mlle Marie had put her house on viager with a friend. [The proprietor wills property to another party who then pays rent for the lifetime of the proprietor, but the proprietor retains lifetime use of the property.] The latter claims that the inside of the house (furniture, etc.) belongs to him also, which is something that the inheritors contest. This gentleman had promised to return my suitcase. But I don't know what the inheritors will do. They are not here. I wrote and the notary told me it could take a long time. He doesn't think the inheritors will want to keep the suitcase, but that nothing could be done for the moment. I didn't want to tell you about it so as not to worry you, especially since absolutely nothing could be done. ... I have hopes of getting it back, but of course I will be very unhappy not to have its contents which would come in handy this winter. It's a good lesson for me. ...

Last night I heard that Annecy had been bombed. I hope neither of you was there. Nowhere is safe these days. You won't dare to be separated any more. Fortunately you have the telephone. That's good at least. ...

Raymonde Molet introduced her fiancé to us last Sabbath. He is a young man the same age as she, not an Adventist, but he is against Catholicism, which has disillusioned him, and he will leave her free. He is an engineer, I think. Denise Guerin is also engaged to a young man from the World. [The World is all that is outside of the Adventists' own world.] I wonder if that will make a good marriage. I can somewhat understand girls from here marrying young men from the World, because there are so few boys here. But personally, I would prefer not to do it, as I would be really apprehensive about the future. ...

Thinking of you and Elisabeth,
Gaby

In her Sunday letter, Mama is still worried about the evacuations and Annette's chances of completing her studies.

Mama to the children   The Hague, December 13, 1942

... More and more people are moving out. I don't know what will become of the city of The Hague; rows of houses are already empty. We are glad we can stay here, but for how long? Sooner or later we will have to leave also, but hopefully after Annette's exams. She is studying hard, and Pa helps her often. ... For her it is harder because she has trouble with many Dutch words. If she does not make it she will have to try again after six months, but she would find that terrible. The practical part will not be a problem, but the theoretical work is much more difficult. ...

Annette had a nice day in Amsterdam last week. Her friend gave her a pair of gloves, or rather mittens, you know the kind without fingers except for the thumb. Very nice white mittens made out of sheepskin and wool. Annette also brought home a small sack of flour, good flour. I would like to make "johnny in the pocket" with it on Christmas Day. We can't make "oil balls" [sort of doughnuts traditional for New Year's] because of lack of oil. ...

Gaby has many spiritual concerns which she shares with Papa. She summarizes some of the discussions that took place at the most recent Workers' Conference at 130, and she tells him how her broken arm was cited from the pulpit as an example of God's punishment.

Gaby to Papa   December 15, 1942

Mon bien cher Papa,

A month ago already I typed the first 3 pages of this letter, and I can't seem to find the time to do the rest. But tonight I'm ahead. I've had supper and I don't have anything to prepare for tomorrow. It's 7:30 so I have about an hour to chat with you, as the prayer meeting doesn't begin until 8:30. I hope you won't torment yourself answering all my questions. We have to hope that we will be able to do this face to face. Still, I'm going to ask you a few little questions which are going through my mind, so that you'll know what I'm thinking about and we'll talk about it when we can.

Since there are people who will be saved in all religions, why must we try so hard to spread the Adventist message? People aren't saved just because they know our message. I even think that there are sincere people who will be troubled by the truths we teach, but who will not follow them and therefore will be lost. Then wouldn't it be better if they had never heard our message? We also say that some people will be lost because we won't have done our duty or because we won't have been generous enough in the offerings (as in last Sabbath's lesson). But then it is unjust that these people are lost through our fault. It seems to me that they will have the opportunity anyway to convert eventually, even if we don't personally do our duty. On the other hand, how is it that pagans who have acted according to their conscience will be saved, while the Bible says that we have to believe in the Lord Jesus and believe that He died for us so that we might be saved? I think you can understand what I mean. There must be others who have asked this question, and you must be used to answering it.

Can one really place the Testimonies and the Bible on the same level? Mme White's supporters seem to say that. I have seen that at the workers' meetings. When there are questions that are a little bit thorny, for example about the dead or the ceremonial laws, we take many more passages from the Testimonies than from the Bible. Can one say that Mme White was inspired as importantly as the writers of the Bible? And about the inspiration of the Bible? If something is said in the Bible, do we have to apply it literally? It seems to me that the writers of the Bible put themselves into it sometimes. For example, God says it is not good for man to be alone, but the apostle Paul says it is best not to marry. All of these words are inspired. These are all things I wonder about but can't express very well. ... But Papa, don't think I am doubting the word of God. Not at all.

Conference of the Workers of Northern France. October 1942

<u>Meats:</u> Some claim that the law about pure and impure meats has been abolished. Of course some meats are much less healthy than others, but one can't prove by the New Testament that this law still exists. There were many who disagree with each other. ... The Doctor claims that when God has said something, he can't change His mind later. I wanted to say, "But God said 'thou shalt not kill' in the 10 Commandments, and yet He also told the Israelites to kill certain people." But since I was one of the youngest, I preferred to keep silent. I also learned that fat is forbidden and yet

some use beef fat. Personally I would have scruples about eating pork, for example, but I have eaten fries made with beef fat, since the war began, without thinking that it was bad. Of course I didn't do it in my home but in other homes. I would like Papa to tell me what he thinks about this. Someone asked the Doctor what he would do if he had only impure meat to eat. He answered that he didn't have any idea and that he would ask God for guidance. But I think he is being illogical, because a little before he had said that the law on meat had the same level of importance as the Ten Commandments. But I thought that under no circumstances should one break one of the Ten Commandments. Of course, one never knows in advance what one would do, but one does know that one should obey. So I wouldn't have even said I would see. I would say that, with God's help, I would not eat forbidden meat under any circumstances. ...

Exchanges: ... Some feel that we shouldn't exchange wine, tobacco, etc., to get butter. ... But most were for it. But they said that the Workers should abstain from doing it in order to give a good example to the members. But nearly all of them do it. ...

Youth: The question of youth is a big problem. Everyone thinks that children receive their greatest religious influence at home. The Doctor always talks about his childhood! But he forgets to say that there were four children, and of those four only he is Adventist. It's true that one of them died, I think. But still, what they said is very true, and I think that a Christian family has a great deal of influence. But we should do more for our young people to try to keep them, because nearly all of them go into the World. Yet we can't be too strict, according to the opinions of several. The observance of the Sabbath by young people was discussed also, and on that subject the Doctor couldn't restrain himself from talking about the young people who weren't respecting the Sabbath and were playing games. He told the story of several young people who went for a walk and were daring each other to do things, and one person had to touch a statue and that she broke her arm. He pointed out that this was a punishment and Mr. Mathy stood up to defend me (unfortunately I wasn't there). He said that the person in question, me, was pretty well known as a pious girl, and that there were other young people in the group who were also very pious, and that the incident should not be viewed in this way. I think the Doctor really stepped over the line. If I had been there, I would have said that if God was supposed to punish him for every time he sinned, then He should cause him to break his arms and legs every time he leads the service, because although he knows in advance when it will be since it's the 3rd Sabbath of the month, his secretary is forced to copy the texts or the testimonies on Friday evening or on Sabbath morning. It seems to me that that is much worse than what we did, as we played quietly for about a quarter of an hour. I am the first to say that we have to observe the Sabbath, but between that and keeping the young people immobile all day, there is a difference. When the members spend their afternoon in the garden badmouthing others, no one says anything, but they always jump on the youth. Well, I don't hold it against him, but I told him afterward, because someone told me about it of course, that it wasn't very nice of him and that my own conscience is perfectly clear.

Death: ... Personally, it seems to me that if nothing remains, that it is not I who comes back to life, but a new person who may resemble me, but it isn't me. In that case the first death is a not a sleep, but an annihilation. ...

These meetings were for the workers only, and not the members; and that is why we were asked not to tell the members too much about what was discussed, because some could think that we lack unity. The Doctor was nostalgic for the early times of the Adventist movement when everyone believed the same things, there was only one teaching. But to me it's a sign that we are thinking and not everyone has the same ideas about all subjects. One person will study one thing and another something else, and we have to submit the points of view, as we can't all know everything. ...

Anyway, I'm telling Papa a bit about this, and when he answers, Jean can also benefit from the answers. That's why I have made a copy of it.

I would also like Papa to tell me what he thinks of buying milk on the Sabbath. Right now it is practically impossible to get the day's milk the next day, and nearly all those who have a right to buy milk buy it on Saturday. That's all right for those who have children, or seriously ill people, but for the others? I personally don't feel free to buy it that day. I know there is very little of it now, and it's too bad to lose any, but on the day on which we can neither buy nor sell, we have to get along without it. I personally arrange to bring my milk can on Friday and pick it up on Sunday, and in summer the milk is then curdled, but I make white cheese with it. In the winter I go after sundown. Of course, when we absolutely need it, we can buy it. But I don't think we should say, since we can't do otherwise, we can buy it.

Papa and Mama both wrote letters in Dutch for the New Year. Mama wrote on December 20 to "My dear children" and Papa on December 22 wrote separate letters to "Mies" (Gaby) and Jean.

Mama to the children   December 20, 1942

... This letter is meant for all three of you, because this is what is known as a "New Year's letter." I wish all three of you the Lord's aid and blessings and much prosperity from the bottom of my heart, now that the New Year will soon begin, and probably will already have begun when you receive this letter. May this be the last Christmas that we are separated and may our fervent wishes and prayers be granted in 1943, and may the war end and we will see each other again at Christmas and New Year's Eve of 1943. Dear children, I wish so much that I could have been with you this Christmas. My thoughts always keep going back to the last Christmas we spent together. At that time we did not think that it would take this long before we would be back together again to celebrate Christmas. How well we were doing then and how well we were able to prepare for the festivities. We even had a Christmas tree on loan. And that night the gramophone was going all night long. ...

Papa to Gaby   December 22, 1942

... Dear Child, the old year is almost over and now we are thinking of those 365 days of difficulty and struggle. However, we are full of gratitude when we look back and see how God protected us. Yes, we are definitely blessed. Ma and I often talk about how we could live without certain things if we really had to. Even though we did not have to buy clandestinely, we were never short of the necessary food. And even now we still have some provisions although it seems to dwindle fast. If I look above me I see dried apples hanging. On top of the stove is a big can (the round can you sent some time ago, remember?). There are nuts in it ready to roast. In the kitchen we still have pots of marmalade, apple syrup, 2 bottles of syrup to make soft drinks. In the back room there are still several cans of condensed milk, herring, peas, applesauce. We even have a packet of speculaas [spice cookies]. We have 2 cans of vegetable oil left and a bottle of salad oil. So we can still go on for a while. I also bought a few kilos of beech nuts, picked out the biggest ones and shelled them. The little ones are not worth the trouble to peel, but we hold onto them anyway. If it is really necessary we can still do that, otherwise they are a good fire starter in the stove. We won't have a shortage of coal, because the people who had to leave gave us some. We are very glad to have it, because last year we were very cold at times. ...

Yes, now we are getting to the New Year. Best wishes from the heart, dear child. May this year be the one in which we see each other again. Yes, that would be so nice. And it could very well be possible. Why not? The time will come when there will be an end to the mowing down of human lives, don't you think? What kind of agreement shall we make: Are you coming to us first or are we coming to you first? We should say: whatever is easiest and where the most food will be. Don't you agree? ...

Of course we don't know what we will encounter in the future, for there will be a lot of trouble in many different places and it will not be very peaceful here, either. However, we are in God's hands. Whatever happens, we know if God allows it to happen, it will be best for us. And that will also console us. We do, however, dear Mies, want to wish you all earthly benefits, a year of spiritual prosperity, a year in which your character will be shaped more like our Savior, full of patient meekness and humility. May it often happen that you can lift up the despondent and console the grieving, help the needy and strengthen the wavering. That is the fullest form of happiness. And you can obtain this happiness, also in Paris. Dear child, you have been useful to many in the last year. May it be a crescendo in the year of 1943. ...

Papa to Jean   December 22, 1942

... My last letter this year to my only son. Yes, the year 1942 will soon be over, with another year closer to the ending of the war and also a year closer to the Redemption when Jesus will come again. ...

What can I wish for you, dear boy? Good health and the strength to make an honest living. Be tactful with others to give them what God has given you, but first of all, to your dear wife. Much patience to bear others' shortcomings, as God did to you. And most of all, the joy to be the one in God's hands to support her in everything she does, so that both of your hearts will be united more and more in the search of the highest good on earth: to be happy together. ...

You have been married for a year now. You are busy, and yet you take the time, I think, to take a good look at the past year, to count all God's blessings, material as well as on the spiritual level. The largest trap that Satan can set is self-satisfaction. ...

There is a way that helps understand the appreciation of others, and that is self-examination... God gave everyone gifts and talents. Those gifts at birth, however, are not in balance with each other...a person's spirit is the same as a person's body, for example the muscles. They always run in pairs, two by two. Every muscle has an opposing muscle. One muscle pulls the eye to the left and the other to the right. Both are necessary and complement each other. If one muscle, which pulls the eye to the left is stronger than the one that pulls to the right, how is someone then? Cross-eyed! That is not good. To make it right, one must make the one muscle somewhat stronger or the other a bit weaker. Only when they are equal in strength will the eye become normal again. ...

There are those who never learn to adapt to each other. And then the marriage will become hell on earth, and divorce is sometimes the only remedy. Uncle Harry and Aunt Dora did not understand this very well and consequently did not adapt to each other very well. They did not go through a divorce because they had a child that both of them loved. However, they had a miserable life together. Yet both had certain qualities that could have provided happiness for each other. Each time I visited them, Henry complained about Dora and Dora about Henry. I have often pitied them, because there was no shortage of money, and they could have been happy if they had adapted to each other. ...

There is something your mother and I are happy about. Lizou does not seem to be very dependent. That is worth a lot; look at your mother. Where would we be if she did not have a better idea of the value of money than I have? You know that I have the same nature as your grandfather. He gave everything away, and sometimes did not have anything to live on. He gave his best shoes away to someone who came to the door and was barefoot. That guy took them and crossed the street and tossed them into the canal because he wanted money for a drink. ... Your mother has saved us from giving everything away. ...

Lizou has returned at last.

Gaby to Elisabeth and Jean (card)   Paris, December 29, 1942

Ma chère Lizou et mon cher Jean,

... Needless to say, I was very happy to hear that you were together again (in principle at least!). It must have been hard for Mme Cartier to see her daughter leave, but we have to hope that soon you will be able to see each other more easily. ... Best thoughts, Gaby

Jean writes to his parents and Annette, in Dutch, the day before the New Year begins.

Jean to Papa, Mama, and Annette   Wednesday, December 30, 1942

My dear Pa, Ma, and Annette,

I do not want to end this year of 1942 without sending a few words to you. I am very busy, but I have to take time for myself also and not always work for everybody else. Last night I returned from my store, and tonight I am going back again. I will get there at 11 o'clock. Tomorrow evening I will return here with Lizou, and we'll stay here until Tuesday. When we are together we are very happy. Lizou is busy with her kitchen, which she likes so much and we are together. Lizou is gentle and affectionate and that makes me happy. I have learned from her that I have to be gentler and more patient, I am no angel yet, but I am well on my way, I think. We both read the Bible and pray in the morning and at night. ... We pray at all times that God will protect you and help you in this troubled time. I have a lot of work, and business is good, and I make a good profit. I am making good business contacts which will help me later. ... I have a lot of merchandise in the store that is all paid for. So you should not worry about us. I am in good health. Lizou's store will be heated and we still have the electric radiator, so we are not cold. In my office here, it is always nice and warm.

Now I must thank Pa and Ma for the letters and the news they send so regularly. I read all the letters you send to Mies, and you cannot imagine how much pleasure this gives me. When I receive a letter from you, I drop everything and read your letter over and over. I just received your last letters of December 6 and the previous letters of the November 25 and 29 and the one Pa sent on the 12th. I have to answer many others, but that will be next year. This year I will send you only the heartfelt wishes for the

New Year and don't eat too many oil balls that Ma used to make in the past. But I can't think about that, or I will get homesick. But keep up your spirits. You know I was always optimistic in my business and I used to say, "I will get there one day." It has happened and it will also happen that peace will come, and I am sure that it will be this year. Thanks so much, dear Pa, for the long and fine letters you sent me. When I see Lizou tonight, I will give her your letter of December 1, and she will be very happy to have it. You know she has a lot of respect for you. Thanks for writing her like that. She is going to be 28 on the 3rd of January, and yet she could be taken for 20! and she is still like a child. One can tell she missed her father. You must be careful not to work too hard. I want to see my parents and my sisters in good health upon my return. ...

Fischer has left Beau-Site with his children, as it was too cold there. They have all gone to the Riviera where it is warmer. ... Since yesterday we have had a lot of snow. Lizou and I will most likely do some skiing. ... She did have some trouble coming back, but she is here at last. However, she won't be able to see her mother very often, but we will keep our courage up. ... Greetings to all. ...

On the last night of the year Gaby sends birthday greetings to Elisabeth on a postcard.

Gaby to Elisabeth   Paris, December 31, 1942

Ma bien chère Elisabeth,

Since your birthday is in a few days, I want to congratulate you and send you my best wishes. [Gaby again uses the polite form of "you" to address Elisabeth.] I am happy to think that you have been able to spend the holidays with Jean. I was beginning to think that you might still be separated for your first wedding anniversary. I hope you won't lose the weight you gained in Geneva, as one could think it's Jean who gives you a hard life! Today it is snowing. It is very pretty when everything is white, but when it melts, it's not very nice. This evening I'm having a few friends in and we're going to celebrate New Year's and play games. My dear Lizou, je vous embrasse affectueusement. Gabrielle.

11   An Engagement in The Hague

January, 1943, brings no changes of location for the Weidners. The parents and Annette are in The Hague, Gaby is in Paris, and Jean and Elisabeth are as migrant as ever among Lyon, Annecy and Geneva.

Jean's first letter to Gaby tells of happy holidays and hope for the future, but he hints at the dangers in his clandestine aid to refugees. Jean gets the day wrong, as January 7 was a Thursday, but Gaby gets it right in her answering letter.

Jean to Gaby   Wednesday evening, January 7, 1943

Ma bien chère Gaby,

The last time I wrote a letter, I think it was December 30 or 31, I didn't have time to write you, only the parents, and I absolutely wanted to do that. Here, nothing new. We had a very quiet holiday, with Christmas with Lizou's family in Annecy and New Year's with Annie [Beaujolin Langlois] and with the Meyers. Anyway, I wish you had been in Annecy, as you would have eaten some good pastries. The stores were full of them, and real ones, and I took advantage of them as never before in my life. Lizou kept saying I would get sick, to which I would reply that this had never happened to me before, not for that reason. I received a nice card from the youth group, on which I was very touched to find your name as well as several others whom I haven't forgotten in spite of my silence. Do tell them that. Also please thank Oscar for his note which we were so happy to receive and to which I will reply later. I still have a lot of work as always, but I am in good health and very happy to still be free and to have Lizou with me. She was finally able to return. Her friends were very helpful to her and thanks to them she was able to come home, as otherwise it would have been impossible. ...

Thanks for the letters from the parents. Lizou was also very happy with the letter from Papa. I think that when Papa and Lizou finally get together, they will have a ball tearing into me for my liberalities with those in need, but of course they would do the same thing in my place. Your letter indeed sounded as if you were depressed, but I can understand it so well, my dear Gaby, as we need a lot of courage to bear up during these times, especially for you who are all alone without any family, but you know, we think of you a lot and I am absolutely certain that we will be together next Christmas, and I live with that conviction. Be sure to eat well and keep your spirits up. ...

Thank you for your good letter of the 13th which pleased us both, and Lizou read it too. She sends kisses. What a problem you're having to find someone to do the laundry and the cleaning. Do as I did when I lived alone, that is just let it all go. I hope your cold is all over now. As far as Mr. L. is concerned, don't worry, he is on vacation in the country at the moment. I saw a girl who was with them at their home and who came to see if I could help them and we are expecting a visit from them which I am looking forward to. I hope that they can visit Lizou's mother [i.e. go to Switzerland. Laatsman will become the Paris head of Jean Weidner's Resistance organization after visiting the escape venues with Jean near the Swiss border]. ... It's awful about your suitcase. Let's ask God who is all-powerful to make it so that you can get this suitcase back. You might want to consult a lawyer, and Brother Thibaut could give you information about that. There must be some laws that protect you even if you don't have a receipt.

No, the bombs fell in a very different area of Annecy, and there was no damage near us, but when you see the damage that a little 100 kilo bomb was able to do, you really wonder what would be left of a big plate of macaroni [Italians] if a thousand kilo bomb fell on it. ...

Your questions about the Workers' Conference were very interesting. The Doctor is an idiot who should be locked up. I can assure you that if I were there, he would have a bad quarter of an hour from time to time, as I would put in front of him a few pages of Sister White which would considerably confound him. I don't think God punished you because you played a game of dares on the Sabbath, though of course there could be better ways to spend that day, but there are also worse ways, and Brother

Nuss [Nussbaum, the "Dr."] would do well to re-read Jesus's question, "Do you believe that those who were killed by the Tower of Siloam were more guilty than any of the others?" [Luke 13:4-5: "... those eighteen upon whom the tower in Saloam fell and slew them, think ye that they were Sinners above all men that dwelt in Jerusalem? I tell you Nay."] I think the Dr. is a real Philistine and that has been my opinion for a long time, as you know. ...

As for the political situation, one never knows what will happen next. So many are being forced to leave for Germany and we don't know when that will stop. The Russians are advancing, and I personally believe that someday the military chiefs will take over the power and make a treaty with Arthur who is getting better and better. I believe that this year will see the end of it all. But the rationing may not end right away, and will probably increase in the future. The mail from Switzerland hasn't come for the last two weeks. I've heard that it has all gone to Paris to be censored, and today I received the first letters dated the 22nd and 23rd and the rest will probably come soon. What a mess. I think that Elisabeth can see her mother at the border on Saturday or Sunday, but I think it will be the last time she will be able to do it that easily.

Now, my dear Gaby I'll leave you with many kisses. Keep up your courage. Lizou sends her best thoughts also. Let me know if you need anything at all. ... Every day I ask God to protect you and to let us see each other again, and then Lizou and I will be in Paris and we will have wonderful times together. Affectionately from your brother who doesn't forget you for one single minute.

Gaby to Elisabeth and Jean   Wednesday, January 13, 1943

Bien chère Elisabeth et bien cher Jean,

It has been a long time since you got a letter from me, but I haven't had the opportunity. I should have more letters from the parents to forward to you, but I haven't yet received the one that should have come last week. The mail seems to be very slow, as I didn't receive Papa's letter of December 22nd until Monday. ... I'm really glad Jean wrote them a little note for New Year's because Papa seemed a little down and I think he feels we have been separated too long. You know, Jean, how much he cares about his son and how happy he is when he hears from you. Of course I regularly give him news of you, but it's not the same. Try to send them a little note from time to time, even if it's a short one. I know it would help Papa's morale until we see each other again.

I hope that will happen at the end of the year. Some say that it will be longer and others say the war will be over. Everything will depend on the events in Tunisia. It appears that the season isn't right and that we'll have to wait. So, a little patience.

I don't know if I told you that Brother Fuchs (Jean must know him), the one who was always talking about his "dear little wife" and who has been working at Pur Aliment for some time… Friday he had an accident. He was knocked down in the street by a cyclist who was going too fast. He was taken to the hospital. He has a slight skull fracture, and two broken legs, but the worst thing is that he feels absolutely nothing and all 4 limbs are paralyzed. They're afraid something is wrong in the spinal column. He is under observation at the moment. He is completely conscious but can't move. It would be terrible if he were paralyzed his whole life. He was a very nice boy who was esteemed by everyone in the church. He went out to do collecting often and came to prayer meetings regularly. I wonder why this kind of thing always happens to the best people. We prayed a lot for him in the meeting last night, but we have to leave it to God's will, and sometimes His plans are very mysterious.

I know Jean doesn't like my writing about money on postcards, and that is why I haven't properly thanked you for your great generosity. Here is what I bought with what you sent me for Christmas: first, a very beautiful linen tablecloth with 12 dinner napkins and six tea napkins. Lisette gave me a ration coupon she got for her wedding and that she hadn't used, and just then the sewing supply store had some tablecloths and I was able to choose one. It is really beautiful and is a wonderful reminder of you. And then I bought an umbrella, a "Chamberlain" as they are called. I think Jean is going to make fun of me, but I really wanted one because all women of style have one. And besides my old one was wearing out. …

Brother Koukoutch is making me a pair of shoes. I was able to buy a coupon for 100 francs a while ago, and that way at least I'll have a pair of all leather shoes, and not ones with wooden soles. With those I will be in good shape for a long time and I have nothing to complain about on that score. It will be expensive, but I think it will be worth it. …

Soon it will be your first wedding anniversary. For the occasion, Simone and I have decided to celebrate together and we will go out to a restaurant in the evening. Maybe we'll go to a Chinese restaurant. I'll also invite Armande. The poor girl has a lot of trouble making ends meet with her small salary. Besides, her father has been ill for several months (he has a painful case of shingles) and her mother who had a small job doesn't have one now. So they are broke and she worries about them. Fortunately the salaries are going to increase next month. From time to time I take her out somewhere, and she enjoys that a lot. She is a really nice girl. She is not extraordinarily intelligent, but she tries hard and is of good character.

Raymonde is getting married on the 21st. The ceremony will be at her home. Brother Winandy doesn't want to do it in the little room downstairs as is usually done for marriages with non-Adventists, because Simone Marliac's wedding was there two weeks ago, and since there are several non-Adventist weddings coming up, it makes it look as if [a mixed marriage] doesn't matter. ...

We heard on the radio that mail from Switzerland was stopped. It will be hard for Mme Cartier to be without news of her daughter. I wonder if it will start up again, but it may be a long time.

Since I have had my radio, life is so much pleasanter. Very often, when I have mending to do and when I can listen to music at the same time, it doesn't seem as if I've been working at all. I am so glad to have it. ...

I don't have much news, as I send you postcards whenever there is anything special. So I'll stop for today. We hear they're going to eliminate the line [between the two zones]. If they do, should I look for your apartment right away, or will you surprise me and come to choose it yourselves? That would be so wonderful. Well, let's wait a little longer and let's look forward to the happy day when we will see each other again. Je vous embrasse très affectueusement.

Your sister who loves you very much.
Gaby

Gaby to Jean and Elisabeth (card)   January 16, 1943

... I'm sending you all my congratulations on the occasion of your first anniversary. I think you will have a happy day on Wednesday. Since you have spent your first year together (I've always heard the first year was the hardest), I think you will continue to get along well. I will think of you that day and will go out to eat at a restaurant in the evening. I just received

Jean's card of the 13th of this month. I am always happy to hear from you. I hope Henri will get mine soon. I am glad Lizou was able to see her mother. When will I be able to see mine? This separation is so long. Well, we have to be brave. Best kisses and have a nice celebration.

        Gaby

On the anniversary day itself, Gaby and her friends send a greeting.

Gaby and friends to Jean and Elisabeth   Wednesday evening, January 20, 1943

While you are probably out partying, we on our side are risking indigestion. The first part of the celebration took place in a restaurant, and now we're having dessert in my room, while talking about you. Affectionately, Gaby

We ate at a Chinese restaurant and it reminds me of Geneva, do you remember, Elisabeth? I am happy for you today, dear friends. Bien affectueusement, Simone.

Good thoughts from Armande

Jean dates his letter to Gaby "1942", but it's actually 1943.

Jean to Gaby   February 1, 1942 [1943]

Ma bien chère Gaby,

In a terrible hurry as always, so I'm running. ... Everything is fine with Lizou and me. We celebrated her birthday and our first wedding anniversary at the same time which everybody thought was marvelous. I arrived here with Lizou on Friday afternoon, and she left again last night and this morning she has already telephoned me twice, so I get the impression she is thinking of me. We wanted to arrive on Thursday evening but there was that darn curfew at 8 o'clock, so we preferred to leave in the morning and not have to sleep at the train station here when we arrived.

Business is good and so is our health. We get along very well, except that Lizou reproaches me for not paying enough attention to her and giving too much help to the needy. Fortunately I am a Cornelian and I place

AN ENGAGEMENT IN THE HAGUE

my duty before my love, and Lizou is a Racinian,* so we have to find common ground, and we are still searching, but we'll find it eventually, when the war is over. What do you think of the events; I have the distinct impression that Henri [Jean himself] was right when he said that everything would be over in 1943, and that he would see you before the end of the year. That boy isn't stupid and will still be proved right, for once. Thank you for all your good wishes for our first wedding anniversary; the next one will be celebrated by all of us together, and what a joy for everyone.

I hope the parents received my letter of December 30. Here the weather is very mild, and that's good because what would all those poor people have done without coal this winter. There hasn't really been any snow to speak of here, and it's like the first days of spring.

I pray to God that He helps Annette with her exams so that she may pass them; poor girl, she is disadvantaged with the language, but she mustn't worry.

Lizou saw her mother at the border 10 days ago and she hopes to be able to visit her soon. She has powerful contacts, and therefore has many advantages. Everyone at the Consulate is very good to her so she has privileges that others wouldn't have. The mail from Switzerland was stopped for a while, which was a great handicap for me in my business affairs of course. Then yesterday and today I got a pile of mail dated January 23-25, so it's starting up again, but for how long? We never know which foot to dance on.

Identity checks were announced for last Wednesday in Lyon and Marseille, but they seem to have been postponed until this week, as the police from here had to go to Marseille to help with the verifications. The craziest rumors are going around; in Annecy they are saying that the city is going to be in the Red Zone, either annexed to Italy or in the forbidden zone because it is a border zone. Our friend Berthelot has moved to Annecy and he is hard to get along with. [Gestapo headquarters in Lyon was on Avenue Berthelot.] He thinks he can do anything he wants, and we used to have good relations with him, but now he is very sensitive and if Lizou just looks at him in the wrong way he gets angry. He argues with Charlotte, who also gives him all kinds of hard time. Fischer, whom you know, I think, has become very mean; he accosts people in the street for no reason

---

* Pierre Corneille, a believer in rules, and Jean Racine, more interested in the human spirit, were both 17th century French playwrights.

and screams at them, I think he is a little crazy. He is having setbacks and that muddles his brain. ...

I hope to spend a few days next week with Lizou in Morzine, for a change of ideas and to have some fresh air, I am exhausted, even though I am in good spirits, but I never stop working and Lizou has a lot of work, too. On Tuesday, market day, it's wild how many people there are and the store is too small to receive them all. [Many of Jean's refugees going through the escape line hid in his Annecy store before being guided across the Swiss border.] I worry about Mr. L. [Laatsman] who was supposed to come and visit me about now, and he hasn't come. With all the present events one always wonders what may be happening to people when they don't come. ...

It's lucky I'm not with you right now, because I would tease you unmercifully about your Chamberlain umbrella. ... What you told me about young Armande's financial situation is very sad. Do what you can to help her morally and materially when you can. I'm adding 500 francs to the 15000 for the parents. You can give the 500 to Armande, or if you think it's better, give her some food, do as you think best. ...

I think you could begin to see about a pretty apartment for us. If you find one, you can rent it in our name and when we arrive we can make the change. We would like to be in a clean neighborhood, in an apartment in a building with an elevator, on the top floor if possible, very sunny, with a bathroom, near the Métro, a new building, in short, the rare and unfindable pearl. ... Paul [Meyer] is waiting for the end of the war to go to Africa with his brother [Oscar Meyer]. Herewith is a little note for the parents and Annette. Goodbye, my dear Gaby, all our affectionate thoughts and kisses from your brother who hasn't forgotten you.

Gaby to Jean (card)　　　　　　　　　　　Monday, February 8, 1943

Mon bien cher Jean,

What a wonderful surprise when Brother Charpiot gave me your package. I couldn't believe my eyes when I saw this beautiful box of chocolates. It is magnificent. It is the very first time in my life I have received one like it, and so original. You are really extravagant for me. ... I hope you will receive more reassuring news as to Mr. L.'s health. ...

　　　Gaby

AN ENGAGEMENT IN THE HAGUE

Since the official postcards are still the only legal means of personal correspondence, Gaby has become a mail drop for letters. Probably she receives them in batches and redirects them.

An acquaintance is in the Drancy camp north of Paris. Conditions in this camp were unspeakably inhumane. For most of the detainees this was the last stop before Auschwitz. Abandoned children wandered through the hallways and stairways, cared for haphazardly by older children who had also been left alone when their parents were deported without them.

Gaby to Jean and Elisabath   February 17, 1943

Ma bien chère Elisabeth et mon bien cher Jean,

If I hadn't thought you were in Switzerland for a few weeks, I would have written sooner. But I thought there was no hurry. Since I know that you aren't there, unless you're going right about now, I'm sending you the parents' letters. … I'll write everything just as it comes to mind, so forgive me if it's a little disjointed.

On the Sabbath, during the service, several deaths were announced. Brother Fuchs died [the victim of the bicycle accident in Gaby's letter of January 13]. Still, it was better for him than being paralyzed all his life. That will be very sad for his wife, as they had been married only a few days; then there was the death of an 11-day old baby…it appears the baby died of lack of hygiene, they allowed him to get an infection; and then there was Hélène Jac. This last death is very sad also, especially for the baby she left behind, and who will have to be raised either by her grandmother or a stepmother. What consoles me is that Hélène Jac had a bad temper, according to what I have always heard, and maybe her husband will be more easily consoled because of that.

Madame Girou arrived this morning. She looks thinner and older. I can hardly believe that we left her two and half years ago already. …

I began the research for your apartment. But I think it will be very difficult; almost nothing is available. You have to plan on 9000 francs (including utilities) for 3 rooms (plus kitchen and bathroom, of course), and of course more for 4 rooms. The concierges everywhere say there is nothing, but that after the war it will be easier to find something, because people will go back to the provinces. But these people may not be able to return so easily, as it is possible that their houses will have been destroyed by the bombing. On the other hand, as Jean said, many people will return here after the war. ... Anyway, here is what I can do for the moment: I'll go to different neighborhoods and ask for the prices in different buildings, even if there is nothing available. Then I will tell you the prices in the different areas, and then you can tell me where you would most like me to search, as I obviously can't run around everywhere. ... The Dumesnil area and the Porte Dorée, near the Vincennes woods, is really nice. That could be better than the Porte d'Auteuil, where the food supply isn't terrific. Even in peacetime everything is more expensive there, and there is little competition. Well, you'll see for yourselves. I'm planning to go and look in a few neighborhoods on Sunday unless something comes up, and I'll send you a postcard next week with the results. ... I don't think it's too urgent, and yet I'm beginning to believe that Henri was right when he said we would see each other in 6 months, which at first seemed absolutely impossible.

Mme Girou said I looked well, much better than when I was in the south, and she was sorry Jean couldn't see me. And yet I haven't felt very well for a while. I don't know what is wrong with me. I got pretty tired during January, but last week it was very quiet at work and my head is better now, as I must have written you that I was losing my memory. But with rest everything came back. I think I'll go and see a doctor just the same; I'm not sleeping well at all, and maybe that's why I feel tired. Maybe the weather has something to do with it; the winter was very mild and maybe the spring is already beginning. Anyway, everybody I talk to feels tired and doesn't sleep well. So I'm not the only one. All the same I can't complain too much, as it must not be serious.

About the beautiful box of chocolates you sent me via Brother Charpiot. He gave it to me on Monday of last week, and yesterday, Monday, I was eating the last ones. I'm really ashamed to have been such a glutton, I didn't recognize myself. I had first decided to make the pleasure last and eat just one a day. But I couldn't resist temptation, and when I had eaten one, I had to eat a second one and then a third. You see, Jean, I am not at all the reasonable person you always seem to think I am. It was a real extravagance on your part, as this box was much too nice for me, not only on the inside but also on the outside, it was so prettily decorated. ... You can't imagine how happy I was. Mama always said that when a son marries, you lose a child, but when a daughter marries you get another child. Of course the wife is often the cause of her husband's becoming detached

AN ENGAGEMENT IN THE HAGUE

from his own family. But I can see that Lizou has never done anything to cause that to happen, and that she agrees with Jean when he spoils me. I am really glad, and I assure you I wouldn't want to change sisters-in-law.

Now I have to talk to Jean about the last few mails. In your letter before the last one, there were two for H. The one that was in an envelope I put in the mailbox without changing the envelope. The other one, signed "Jean Cornulis"? I wanted to put it in an envelope, as it was loose, and I saw that it had the name of the above at the top. That bothered me and so I had the idea of looking to see if one could tell where it came from. I then saw that it was impossible to forward it. It is a 5-page letter, written on both sides. If I have to send it back, I'll do it when the opportunity arises, but if I can just tear it up, please just tell me. I hope the other one didn't contain anything compromising. These people don't seem to think about the fact that these letters are read by the censor.

In the last mail there were 2 letters for H. containing photos. I took them out, having learned from the last experience, and I read them. On one of them (which contained 3 sheets addressed to 3 different people) I simply cut off the top of the page, so that the name of the town couldn't be read. But it was equally impossible to send the other letter, which was the more important one. Moreover, your name is mentioned in it. You have to require of people who give you letters that these letters be written as if they might be read by the censors, and that they not say that they don't know how these letters will be sent. These last letters were signed Nic. Should I send them back or send back the photos?

I wonder if you have had any news of Mr. L. I would be very sad if anything happened to him, as he is so nice. ...

Slovik is in a Jewish camp at Drancy. He wrote us a few times sending coupons. We sent him two packages, but since he sent a large quantity of coupons, we wrote to him that we couldn't send him more than one package a month. He isn't realistic. He asks for: butter, melba toasts, cookies, lemons, oil, potatoes, honey, sugar, etc. all the scarcest products of which we ourselves are deprived, except for the potatoes. He asked me to write to Jean to ask him to send him a package of vegetarian products. I answered him that you were already doing all that is humanly possible for the needy people in your area, and that I didn't think you could do more. These Jews are all the same. The more you give them the more they need. I realize that they must be very destitute and that they have very little to eat, but just the same, where are we going to get all those products? He told us he has money and can reimburse us, but in the meantime he asks us to send him 50 francs a month, which we will certainly not do as he is not a member of the church itself. If he has money, how is it that he has never offered to repay the money that Jean lent him at the beginning of the war?

Thank you so much also for the 500 francs sent for Armande. I won't tell her about it yet. Their financial situation has gotten a little better. The father is better, the mother found a temporary job in the tailoring company where she had been working, and Armande's salary has increased quite a lot. She now earns almost as much as Mlle Milès who has been in the Work much longer than she has. But if I see that their financial situation is getting worse, for example if the father's illness continues for a long time, or that the mother is out of work, which is very possible as long as the war continues, I will arrange to give her something. In the meantime I prefer to do some nice little things for her which don't really seem like aid, because it's always a little painful to feel one is getting charity. Anyway, it is really nice of you to think of those who are less privileged.

This week I haven't received the parents' letter yet. But I'm waiting impatiently for it because I want to know how Annette's exams went. I'm so afraid she might not have been able to take them. Of course if it wasn't wartime we would have more patience; but with all these evacuations, the authorities must have other things on their minds. But really for Annette it would be terrible if she couldn't take the exams and had to wait 6 months more. Unless I receive something before this letter goes, which will probably be tomorrow, I'll write you a postcard immediately to let you know.

It's awful about all these young men who have to leave. I wonder if they also take foreigners, and I don't know why they haven't done so before now. It's not that I particularly want Jean to leave; he would make such a face! but it could happen. Maybe the women will soon be taken, too. I wouldn't be so afraid of leaving, because that would be an opportunity to learn German, but I would be most afraid of the bombing. Well, let's hope it doesn't happen. …

And now, my dear ones, I'll leave you. It is getting late and I'm going to bed. I hope to hear from you soon that you came home safely, as one never knows, there are so many skiing accidents.

Je vous embrasse très fort, and send you a thousand affectionate thoughts.

        Gaby

AN ENGAGEMENT IN THE HAGUE

On February 16, 1943, the day before Gaby wrote the above letter, the STO, or Service de Travail Obligatoire was created to furnish workers for the German war effort. This "Service" replaced a supposedly voluntary one which had been in place since 1940. The "STO's" were young men in their twenties who were deported to Germany. Many escaped when they were "called up" and went instead into hiding or joined the maquis.

A postcard from Gaby to Jean on February 19 brings the news that Annette's exam was postponed because one of the doctors was sick.

Gaby needs Papa's advice, as she continues to be troubled by doctrinal questions. She sent a carbon copy of these questions to Jean as she did the last time so that she can eventually share Papa's answers with her brother.

Gaby to Papa   February 23, 1943

Mon bien cher Papa,

I want to ask you for some more advice on a few points that are troubling me.

First the question of mixed marriages. The question came up because of Raymonde Molet's wedding. She married a young man who is Catholic, but who doesn't like that religion at all, and he has come to our meetings from time to time, and he was very favorable and wanted to study the Adventist religion more in depth. Before, when there was a mixed marriage, it would take place, not in the temple, but in the little room just in front of the temple, where the afternoon meetings were held. Mme Molet had asked Brother Winandy to please bless her daughter's marriage, but Brother Winandy explained to her that he didn't feel free to do it, and then she asked him to come and give a religious benediction at home. Brother Winandy hesitated. He was even more in doubt because there were probably going to be two or three other marriages of this kind, and if he did it for one, he would have to do it for others also. ... He depended on the church manual which says this: "The church's customs and principles oppose a pastor's blessing of a marriage between a believer and a non-believer. This rule applies also to mixed marriages, that is, between members of our church and those of other denominations. A pastor who takes his power from the church cannot in good conscience allow himself to act in opposition to its customs and practices." ...

Brother Winandy talked with the Church Council, and I must say that several people disagreed with him, especially Brother Walther.

(Incidentally, I wonder what he would have said if someone refused to bless his marriage in the temple because he married a person of color. I think Sister White said that shouldn't be done, but I couldn't find where she said it.) The youth group had decided to give Raymonde a gift on Saturday afternoon after the youth group meeting, and no one knew if that could be allowed, since they had refused to bless her marriage. I said that if the Committee didn't want that to happen in the room where we have all our youth group meetings officially and which is used for all sorts of things, the room on the third floor, then we could just come up to my room, and that way it wouldn't have an official atmosphere. But they finally allowed us to do it after the meeting in the small room.

Raymonde and her fiancé were rather offended by Brother Winandy's refusal. That completely repulsed the young man because, because, as he said, he wasn't after all a pagan or an infidel, as they were suggesting he was, because he was a believer. Raymonde very much wanted a religious ceremony, especially because of her family and the young man's family, because, as you know, that is very important to Catholics, so she said she would go to her former Protestant church where the pastor would not refuse to bless her marriage, but her mother asked her not to do it for fear that the pastor would be surprised that someone would refuse to give a benediction in a home. So the young couple had to do without a religious ceremony, and the family was very surprised. Before they went to the town hall, Raymonde's father simply read a few passages and prayed with the couple.

I would like to know what you think of this, Papa. I can understand that a ceremony might not be allowed in the small room, and even a real benediction in a home, but can a pastor really refuse when he is asked to come and say a few words on that occasion? It seems to me that it would be an opportunity to draw attention to the fact that they weren't of the same faith and that they should strive to educate themselves to arrive at a single ideal. If the family wanted a religious ceremony, they either had to go the Catholic church or a Protestant church. I understand that we should be warned about the dangers of such marriages. But we mustn't forget that for Adventist girls, the choice of husbands is very limited. Already in the World there are plenty of girls who don't get married, so all the more so in our more limited circles. One doesn't always find one's ideal spouse among the Adventist young men whom we know. And if we don't get married, we are also exposed to dangers. So should we condemn so severely those who find their ideal in a young man of a different religion? I know that personally I couldn't be happy with someone who didn't share the same religious ideas as I have, but for the most part that is because I was raised in that religion. In our circles I see many girls who, already being partly in the World, would adapt very well to a life with someone who hasn't the same religious convictions that we have. In Raymonde's case, he is a very serious young man, who doesn't like the World and I think they should make an exception in this case. ...

Now I would like to ask several questions on the subject of donations. When we did our budgets in accounting class at Collonges, we put 5% of our salary aside for our donations. Of course that doesn't include gifts. I put so much aside each month in order to be sure that I'm not giving too little, because I think one has more of a tendency to give too little than too much, and I do dip into it. But that's about my salary. It's about the money that Jean sends me that worries me. In a way, it's income for me. I don't tithe from it, because I figure that J. had already given from it and that I don't have to. Maybe it would be better for Jean not to give from what he sends me and that I pay it myself. ... But tithing aside, I should really give 5% of that as donations. I use some of this money to help people less fortunate than I, and sometimes I give meals to people passing through, but that certainly doesn't come up to the sum I should give. Papa, I don't want you to think that I want to be a Jew and to be stingy, when God has blessed me so much, through Jean, of course, but I do take full advantage of it. ...

In our last lesson...we talked about the Flood. Sometimes you have said, Papa, that the Flood could well have been partial, and that only the inhabited part was covered with water, which would explain a lot, because "earth" can also mean inhabited regions, it seems to me. Yet in our lesson, it was said that it is indisputable that the entire earth was submerged, and they quote verse 19 of Chapter 7, "All the high mountains under the skies were entirely covered." How can that be explained? ...

Forgive my typographical errors, but I'm writing very fast, because I have so little time. ...

From Gaby, two postcards in two days with good news. The Demarcation Line was suppressed on Mach 1, 1943, and Gaby already seems to know that this is going to happen.

Gaby to Jean and Elisabeth Paris, February 23, 1943

Bien chers Lizou et Jean,

In a few days we will again be able to correspond by letter! It will certainly be nice, although a postcard is quickly done. This business of the Demarcation Line is not of much interest to me, because it seems that foreigners won't be able to travel anyway. But maybe Jean can, and anyway I do hope Lizou can come to spend a few days here soon. I am glad you didn't have any accidents while skiing and that you ate well. Did you get the card we sent on January 20th signed by Simone, Armande and me? ...

Kisses, Gaby

Elisabeth has gone to Switzerland again. She appears to be doing more than "having a few days' vacation" with her mother. In a long letter written feverishly as thoughts occur to him, Jean urges her to plead for aid for his clandestine enterprises and to do several other errands. He addresses her as "Mickey" (Mouse) or "la petite souris" ("the little mouse"). She calls him "Donald," because he quacks like Donald Duck when he gets angry or excited.

Jean to Elisabeth February 23, 1943

Ma bien chère Mickey,

I hope you had a good trip and that you got a chance to say hello to your Mom. Take time to enjoy your vacation. I think it might be best if you stay a little longer, but I won't try to influence you. If anything special happens on one side or the other I will let you know. I was very sad when I got back because of the departure of my Mickey, but still, I was happy for her that she was able to get a few days' vacation which will do her good. I forgot to tell you to ask your former boss to give you one or two letters of introduction if he can for people at Vichy who might be able to help Mrs. S [Sevenster, whose husband is in prison]. See what you can do about that. Don't forget to write a little note to Henri S. and tell him that we haven't forgotten him and give a few details of our recent life which will interest him. Your friend Na. could also give some suggestions. Go to see the Lamb's family. We hope to get him a visa to go to see his family. Could you get some information on who can go to Switzerland without being sent back by the authorities of that country? It would be useful also

AN ENGAGEMENT IN THE HAGUE 313

if our [Dutch] authorities take <u>urgent</u> steps with Swiss authorities to allow free entry for our citizens and if possible to furnish them with visas; there wouldn't be too many of them as there aren't very many left. The Gurs camp [concentration camp in Southern France] is going to be closed and we hope they will be transferred to Chateauneuf. ... Let's ask God to see that these efforts succeed because the situation of these unfortunate people is really terrible and we have to help them before it's too late. ...

Jean goes on to say that if "Fischer," (the Germans) organize the territory like the Occupied zone, those refugees having legal papers will have nothing to fear, but the 1500-2000 Jews will be left with absolutely no material or moral support. Only somebody who has a lot of money can help them somehow. Jean says it is imperative that the (Dutch) Government help "with all its strength" and it must send a minimum of 350,000 francs. His letter ends at the bottom of the second side of the page with:

... My dearest treasure, I'll leave you now. ... Let's have confidence in our celestial father and let's ask Him to shorten these difficult days. I don't ever forget you even for one minute. ... Kiss your maman for me and remember me to all our friends. I hope you will receive these few lines very quickly. Affectionate kisses from your Donald.

Gaby is unaware that Elisabeth is in Switzerland when she writes a postcard

Gaby to Jean and Elisabeth   Paris, February 24, 1943

Bien chers Lizou et Jean,
    I just received a letter from Mama with the good news that Annette was able to take her exam on Friday the 12th, and that she passed! So now she has her diploma. She has to make up 3 weeks of work she missed when she was sick, and then she is free to work where she wants. I am so glad. Annette offers you her services in case you need them sometime soon! We have a lot of fog these days. I feel much better and the work has calmed down in the office. Best thoughts from your
        Gaby

Papa writes in Dutch for Jean, "so you won't forget the language," and adds a note in French for Lizou. In the Dutch letter (March 8, 1942), he comments on the Allied bombing raids and again uses the analogy of the bowling game: "It's not such a bad idea that your friend is playing that bowling game. The way you describe it, he is getting more experience every time. I think it is kind of a rough game, but to each his own taste. Congratulate him for me."

Gaby gets her suitcase back.

Gaby to Jean and Elisabeth   Paris, March 10, 1943

Bien chère Elisabeth et bien cher Jean,

... Yesterday was a joyful day for me, as I finally got my suitcase back which had been at Sister Marie's. About a month ago Sister Marie's friend who was to inherit the house and the furniture it contained, telephoned me to say that everything would be settled on February 24th, and that the seals would be removed and that I would do well to be there in order to be sure to get my suitcase. I had written to the notary to inform him about it, and all he said was that he would inform the inheritors of my letter. Then I telephoned to see if the thing had been settled, but they were not helpful. They said that the inheritors weren't in Paris, and that all I could do was wait. When the friend telephoned me he told me that he could only have the house itself, and that he had no papers to prove that the furniture was supposed to come to him, even though at least a dozen people could certify to that. It just goes to show that everything should be done according to the rules. Then I telephoned to the notary to tell him that I had heard that the business was going to be settled and ask if I should be there. The clerk answered that I had absolutely no business being there and that if this suitcase really existed, which was yet to be proven, they would keep me informed. He was so insolent that I called the friend again and also Mr. Thibaut. I was advised to make an opposition to the sale or distribution of the contents of the suitcase. It wouldn't be an infallible solution, but I would have more of a chance to get it back. Maybe they would have returned it to me without that, but I preferred to take all possible precautions. Yesterday morning Mr. Thibaut called me to say that I could pick up the suitcase at a certain Paris address. I went immediately with Brother Meyer, as the suitcase was too heavy for me. You can imagine how happy I was to get it and to see that everything in it was in perfect shape. But now I will be more careful and it will serve as a lesson. ...

Sunday afternoon we went to have tea at Ragueneaud's across from the Louvre. They still make wonderful buckwheat crepes there, but you have to stand in line. We had to wait a half hour. But it's worth it because we have so few good things to eat now. ...

The weather is splendid now that the winter is over. But if we were to have another winter during the war, it would be terrible. Everybody is getting very agitated. According to Mama's letter, I see it's the same with Papa. He can never stay very long in one place, and it must be hard on him. But I wonder if it will really be over this year. We will certainly know in two or three months how things are going to happen. ...

I hope to hear from you soon, and especially I hope to be reassured about Lizou's return. Kisses to both of you, and all my affection.
Gaby

Gaby to Elisabeth and Jean   Paris, March 15, 1943

... Thursday morning I received a letter from Mama saying that Annette would get engaged the next day, the 12th, on her birthday. I quickly telephoned Gisèle, who was leaving that evening for Collonges, asking her to telegraph or phone you so that you could join in Annette's joy and be present in thought at the little family celebration. I thought of her a lot. Now I hope we will be able to go to her wedding, which won't be right away. I especially hope that neither Annette nor her fiancé will have to leave for Germany. ...

While I think of it, Mama's birthday is April 9. I hope you will send her a little note. It would make her very happy.

Still, don't you think Annette could have chosen a fiancé with a different name? What are we going to look like with a brother-in-law named Lykele? ...

Mama gives a few more details of Annette's engagement in letters in March. Annette and Lykele exchanged rings on Annette's birthday, March 12, and on Sunday, March 14 there was an open house for family and friends. Annette received many beautiful flowers, and "the whole house smells of it, I believe there were at least 10 bouquets." At the celebration there were home baked cookies and pastries, and getting supplies for this was tricky:

Mama to the children   March, 1943

... We had to give the baker butter and sugar, and that way we got some fine things. Lykele was able to get sugar, some butter and a couple of bottles of syrup. It is quite difficult to give people anything if there is a celebration. Most people's supplies are exhausted, and we can't buy things on the black market because the prices are so high, but the ice cream Annette was able to purchase was delicious. ...

Lykele really is a nice boy, and he would be happy to get to know all three of you. He talks about Mies, Jopie [Jean] and Lizbeth, as he calls Lizou, as if he has known them for more than 20 years. But that is because Annette always talks about you all. Yes, dear children, if we ever missed you more, it was yesterday when the whole family was here. ...

According to Mama, new regulations concerning the mail complicate things, but she looks on the bright side:

Mama to the children   March 21, 1943

... from now on we must bring letters that are still open to the Post Office. The Post Office worker then reads the letter, places a stamp on it himself, seals it and sends it. So it is not as simple as dropping it in the mailbox as we did before, and it's more time consuming. Sometimes we must wait a long time in line in the Post Office before being waited on. But we should not complain and we should be grateful that we are still allowed to write to each other.

Papa to Gaby   The Hague, March 23, 1943

Our dear, dear Mies,
... We are about to go to Amsterdam to get better acquainted with the Faber family [Annette's fiancé's family]. They are very friendly people, but we won't accept their invitation to spend the night with them. That would be too busy for them and for us. We will sleep in a hotel, because we are in a better position to do so now than when we were in Paris. ...

Did you know the piano had been taken away about a half a year ago? Since we were thinking we would be evacuated, and the piano was not ours, we had it taken away. Now it seems there was no need for that. The owner of the piano must pay a monthly storage fee, so it is better for her to place it back in our house. Yesterday we had the tuner come, and now all we are waiting for is for you to come and play it.

The weather is so nice now, and spring is in the air. Better this than the bitter cold. We have some coal now for next winter. Right now we are burning peat; it gives us enough heat, and if a bomb hits the house this summer, it won't burn as quickly as coal would. The peat will be gone by that time. Of course we hope that our house will not be hit. …

I once told you about a certain Mr. Trabski here, he is a virtuoso violinist. He was in trouble and he feared that with the closing of many businesses, his turn would come also. And he cannot live without his violin. Well now, all his troubles have disappeared, because he has been hired by the resident orchestra of The Hague, a very high distinction. He was very glad when he told us yesterday. He also gave us three egg coupons; now we can buy an egg for each of us next week. We have not eaten one since I don't know how long. That's why we are glad it is not too hard for you to get them.

… Bye, dear child, keep your spirits up. Every day is a day that will bring us closer to seeing each other again. Many greetings to all our acquaintances. Kisses from us.

    Papa

12   Escapes

Jean is becoming more involved in the rescue of refugees and has less time for his business affairs. In her letter to him Gaby writes, "I hope that later all those whom you have helped won't forget it immediately. But alas, gratitude is not of this world." Gaby encloses a photo of Annette's fiancé, Lykele. "I think he looks very nice," she writes, "It's true he doesn't look very Dutch."

Gaby thinks about a trip to Belgium to see her aunt and uncle, but wonders if it wouldn't be better "not to get too far from home," as things in the war "will start moving soon."

Mama, writing in Dutch, has some good news about mail service. She tells of a visit from "Erna," who brought them first-hand news of Jean. "Erna" is Suzy Kraay's Resistance name. Suzy Kraay is a member of Jean's team of rescuers.

Mama to Jean and Elisabeth   The Hague, April 4, 1943

My dear Lizou and Joop,

Now it really must be true. At the Post Office we were told that now we can send mail to the whole of France and we are so glad to be able to do it. Dear Lizou and Joop, the first letter is from your mother, who can now reach you directly from The Hague. We are thankful and glad to know that you are still doing well. Nice that Lizou was able to visit her mother, and we hope, Joop, that you could also take a few days' vacation. You are working so hard and you must rest sometimes. We know that you are not sitting still, and that your business requires you to run from early morning to late in the evening.

We spoke to Erna the other day, you know her, the dark-haired girl, and she said you always work so hard. Well, she did not have to tell us that; we already knew it when you were still living at home with us. However, you still have to watch you health and don't overdo it, Joop. You need your strength for later. We are all doing well. Pa has the flu and has to stay in bed for a few days, but today he is better already, and I think he will get up tomorrow or the day after. Pa is still teaching, but he can't do as much as he used to, but he wants to, and then he runs and gallops and forgets he is going to be 62 years old. Now that Jean Henri is helping us so much, he should be more at ease without the financial worries. You can be sure that when you come to Holland later on that all will be well and you will find some Dutch money here. The other day Jean gave us 1500 Guilders. We did not really need that, but we live in such miserable times that it can always become necessary and useful. Annette hopes to write you soon, and directly to you. Oh, she can't wait to visit you with Lykele. But Pa longs to see his son and daughter most of all. I better not speak for myself, because when I start thinking about that I get nervous and sad. I am glad that I am healthy enough to do my work and run the errands. That way I forget for a while the greatest wish that I have in my heart. You know I like my home very much and I could be happy and at ease in my home. But Pa, on the contrary, needs to be flying about. Holland is too small for him. He would like to travel and visit his children in France... He will be getting a good son-in-law, because Lykele really seems to be a good son-in-law... Lykele loves Pa and can have good conversations with him, and thinks that Pa is very educated. He has a lot of respect for Pa, which is nice. ...

Dear Lizou and Joop, I'll leave you now, and I hope you will send me a card when you get this letter. ... A thousand kisses from your parents and Annette.

There has been more bombing in the Paris area.

Gaby to Lizou and Jean   Tuesday, April 6, 1943

Bien chère Lizou and bien cher Jean,
... There was an enormous amount of damage in the bombing on Sunday, but it only lasted a few minutes. No deaths among our members. I didn't even hear a thing. When they gave the alert, I did hear what I

thought was the D.C.A. [anti-aircraft guns], but I thought it wasn't anything, and I was completely surprised to find out that there had been a heavy bombing raid. I'm writing you a few lines immediately so that you won't worry about me. I hope nothing happened to Uncle and Aunt in Antwerp.

Best kisses from your

Gaby

I wonder if it is safe for Lizou to come now, as there might be a landing (everyone is talking about it), and she might be stranded here.

Since the mail to France can go directly now, Papa writes in Dutch to Joop and Mies on the same day. After Erna's visit, the parents now know a good deal more about what Jean is doing beyond his business affairs.

Papa to Jean and Gaby   The Hague, April 20, 1943

Dear Monkey-head,

It is so nice to write directly to your home. It would be even nicer to hear that Lizou is there also, and that you are not there by yourself when you get this letter.

Before I forget, I must write you something that will give you great pleasure, and it is about Annette. You know she is engaged, and of course she does not want to stay engaged for long. She wants to get married. Well now, as things stand, one seems to need money when one gets married. The young couple are of course thinking about that also. But one does not find money in the street, not even the one-thousand-guilder notes which were recently invalidated. But here is the most interesting part. You should be glad for your sister. Of course you know this friend Hendrik ["Henri" or Jean]. Well, he seems to like us a lot, because you know what he sent us through Suzy? I mean for Annette's trousseau. Guess how much? Fifteen hundred and fifty guilders!!! We thought it was so much that we did it this way. We gave Annette two hundred guilders. Later on we want to give her some more. That seems more than if we give her everything at once. What do you think of our way of doing things? Annette feels she is almost in heaven, she is so happy. Lykele just came home also, as he has been on vacation for a week. They are both extremely happy with that money. We want to hear your opinion first before Ma and I give her more money. You know that Lykele would like to do business with you after the war, and I could go two ways with that money. One way is to give Annette the money when she gets married, and the other way might be to give 1000 guilders to start up a business with Joop. Let me know honestly what you think of it. Typical, right? A father asking his son for advice. However, I consider that my best days are behind me and that my son is going to be in charge. Forgive me for bothering you with this, but you will be doing me a great favor by answering. ...

Lykele is a very nice boy and very active also. I don't think he is going to stay with the Post Office. A life behind a desk is not for him. ... He would be better off going into business. Don't you think so? He has successfully completed the four-year business course and has worked in business a little in the past. But it seems his father did not understand him. He also left home once, just as a certain young man did. My impression is that he is willing and ready to learn and take on anything. I am planning to have his handwriting examined thoroughly. I will compare that with Ma's and my own observations.

We were glad to get your letter of April 2. Glad your business is good. Erna [Suzy Kraay] told us that also. She just visited us. Her information was precious to us and reminded us how much we love our children! She came in the morning. Ma was home alone. Annette and Lykele came home an hour later and after that I came home.

She was here with a girlfriend and they stayed for dinner. She informed us about a lot of things we had never heard from you, and we were almost jealous. Be careful and don't let her know so much without telling us. After all, we are your parents. But now we know, and that is the main thing. We are glad when Erna visits us and admire her because she is such an entrepreneur. Mama thinks she is pretty, but Annette thinks she wears too much make up.

Well, to each her own opinion. She seems artistically inclined.

Joop, you know what I am going to do next week? Make a trip around Holland. You can get 8-day trips for 18 1/2 guilders in third class and 26 guilders in second class. Third class is extremely crowded. I actually got sick returning from Amsterdam, because people opened the windows so they would not suffocate, with the result that I had to go to bed for several days. I am better. Ma took good care of me and we have an excellent female doctor. I also eat a lot of malt extract. But I will take 2nd class, so I won't be standing for those 8 days and will not catch a cold. I will also go to the south of the country and see the imitation of the catacombs of Rome. In anticipation of seeing the real ones. Don't think this is to be only a pleasure trip. No, I want to visit young preachers here and there and find out if they want to take a course in practical psychology. Not theoretical stuff, but to help them differentiate characters. So, you can see, it is work combined with pleasure. Well, dear fellow, E. [Elisabeth] claims you do not want me to tire myself with teaching, but I promise you, I will not overdo it. However, what to do? Last week two young preachers came to visit me. They wanted to learn Greek. I know how useful that can be. Should I refuse? I would be helping spread the Gospel if they can learn to interpret the New Testament better. But I promise you I will be careful and not do too much. …

Well, dear boy, I am going to stop. I will send a copy of this letter to Mies, and will enclose a copy of my letter to Mies for you.

I just heard that Lizou's mother has had a small accident again. It's too bad, and I will try to send her a note. Lizou, my sympathy, and we hope your dear mother will get better soon. Hugs for both of you from the three of us.

       Papa

My dear, dear Mies,

This is your father again, writing to his daughter after having been silent for some time. But you probably won't mind, because I was ill and weak for a while. Ma has taken good care of me and I have eaten very well since. … All three of us are well.

We are so glad, dear Mies, that you have friends that take good care of you. It is reassuring to know that you have plenty of food. But don't forget that next winter could be severe and people can get sick if they do not eat well.

I have not had time to answer your questions, but I'll get to that. I have been very busy with the preparation of lessons for the Sabbath school for the third quarter. I finished them three days ago. They are about forming character. There are twelve lessons: Respect, Thankfulness, Sympathy, Tact, Trustworthiness, Conscientiousness, Gladness, Peacefulness, Helpfulness, Humility. This actually makes ten but the last one, Humility, is divided into three lessons. …

I am being paid for these, but even if that weren't the case, I would still give it to them, because I know these lessons will do a lot of good.

They have partially been checked and approved, so I trust they will be printed. That will be a great satisfaction to me of course, since I cannot preach any more. I have trouble concentrating on my subject, while speaking in public, since I am so easily distracted. So this way I can still be useful. And without being useful, life is not worth much or nothing at all. ...

Education is not always as easy as many think it is, and later one sometimes discovers that big mistakes have been made. I can see that I made some by doing things my way. If I had to start life over, I would do many things differently. Yet I am thankful to God that He blessed Ma and me in the education of our four children, and that Lykele can now be influenced, too, because Lykele listens closely to us and is willing to accept it. I don't doubt that Lizou would also listen if I had to make something clear to her. So, looked at from that point of view, we did well. ...

We are glad that Annette is relieved of her greatest worries. She has her diploma now, and there is no shortage of work. ... She just made an agreement with a lady who expects her baby in June. She will go there three times a day to care for the baby and the mother. She will earn two and a half guilders a day and the rest of the day will be free to go to others or study or whatever. She has already made agreements with people for a full day, and in that case she asks three and a half guilders including meals. But of course she won't be able to do that for another month, because women do not time their babies exactly according to Annette's schedule. That would be exceptional. We are glad the doctors are satisfied with her and recommend her.

We were glad to hear that you were far away from the bombing, and I knew it already, because I could tell just where it was. But it is always good to hear from you.

Dear Mies, don't worry if you can't make the Tuesday night meetings. They don't even have them here, and there is no commandment from God about them. If we work six days and then rest on the seventh day, then we are following the commands. If we want to do something else, even if someone wants to get together every night or even at 4 or 5 in the morning, there is no objection. However, they have to let others decide what they want to do, according to their conscience. ... The Salvation Army have some meetings every night and the Mormons several nights a week. The Catholics have quite a few holidays in honor of this and that. ... Let the Sabbath be a day of refreshment, not of doing nothing, but calm activity which is in harmony with the spirit of the Sabbath. One should take it easy on Friday evening, so that one is not too tired to go to the meetings, and one should avoid conversations that disturb the spirit of the Sabbath, and take time to be calm and read something good, and being out in the open is best.

So someone has suggested that you go to Collonges. That might be fine after the war, because that would be a nice change for you and you would have fresh air and be close to Joop and Lizou. But we'll see how everything goes after the war.

Now, dear Child, I'll have to stop. ... God is love, and if we make that love known to others by word and deed, then our life is worth something in the eyes of God, no matter what people think of us.

Many kisses from Ma, Annette and Lykele! But mostly from your always-praying-for-you Papa

The Grand Rabbi and General Chaplain of the Israelites of France in Marseille tells Jean Weidner what can be done for Dutch refugees confined to camps in Southern France.

Rabbi Michel to Jean   Marseille, May 6, 1943

Consistoire des Israelites de France
General Chaplainship
65, Bd. Des Vosges
Marseille

                                                              Mr. Weidner
                                                                      Lyon

Sir,

Thank you for your letter of the third of this month and I am grateful for all the trouble you take in favor of your compatriots.

In the future I will continue to take care of Van Dam. Although he is not very important, he nevertheless finds himself in a cruel situation and is worthy of compassion.

Concerning your offer to come to the aid of other Dutch people, let me call your attention to the fact that there are a certain number of them in the camp at Gurs to whom your help would be of great service. I am writing by the same mail to the chaplain in Gurs so that he can give me a list of these, essentially those who are in need.

I will send you this list. Of course you can't help all of them, but perhaps you can find among your associates some people who would agree to adopt these unfortunates.

Among them are Dutch women whose husbands have been deported. If it were possible for you to deliver certificates of lodging to these women, I could probably get them liberated.

Certificates of lodging can be issued by any persons able to shelter at their home one or several of these internees, hotel keepers not excluded. Foreigners can also deliver these certificates. The only formality required is to have them checked by the Prefecture as to their place of residence.

I hope that you will be able to find persons who would be willing to come to the aid of these poor women in this manner. I don't need to tell you what an immense service you would be doing them.

In the hope of hearing from you, Sir, I am sending you the assurance of my devoted sentiments.

General Chaplain
R. Michel
Grand Rabbi

Gaby has made a sudden visit to Jean in Annecy. Gérard Blitz helped her get a travel pass.* Gabrielle is now getting more involved in Jean's rescue work. Raymonde Pillot, Jean's secretary, during the war, says in an interview in 1992, that she transferred Jewish families for Jean's network and that she went to get them from Gabrielle Weidner in Paris.†

On May 13, German forces in Tunisia were defeated by the Allies.

Gaby to Jean Paris, May 10, 1943

Mon bien cher Jean,

I wonder if I should address this letter to you only or if you are at last together again, you and Lizou. I hope so for both your sakes, especially now that new events could be happening; it would be better if you were together. Still, I would never have thought that the Tunisia business would happen so quickly.

---

* After the war, Gérard Blitz (1912-1990) founded Club Med, the worldwide system of resort communities.

† VHS Interview, Centre d'Histoire de la Résistance et de la Déportation, Lyon, France.

It has been ten days since I got home and I still think of the joy I felt when I saw you. I came back the way Mr. Blitz's father advised me to in order to try to prolong the travel pass. They were very nice to me, but they told me I had to make a new application which would be studied. I hope that won't cause any problems for Mr. Blitz. Anyway, thank him again for me. Now I am encouraged. And I don't think we should wait three years again before we see each other.

On the Sabbath I saw Guyennot, who said, "The war is going to be over this year." And I answered, "How do you know?" he said, "It's in the Bible, in Isaiah 42, where it says: they will eat their harvest in the third year." I pointed out to him that we're in our 4th year of war. But he answered that France was invaded three years ago. There's a way around everything...

On Friday I saw Mr. and Mrs. T. They seem to feel they need a change of scene. They would like to go Nice where they have a lot of friends. But isn't it illegal to go to Nice now that there is the forbidden zone? Wouldn't Haute Savoie be a better place for them?

I haven't been able to go and see the others whose addresses you gave me. I have to go personally to do those. But toward the end of the week, I plan to go and to give you the results of my visit.

... Ganty told me he couldn't make crackers anymore. So don't leave the packages too long in your armoire at the hotel, because I'm afraid they'll taste like mothballs. When Lizou gets back, tell her she should air out the armoire so you won't have that problem.

Thank you for the good chocolates you gave me when I left. They are delicious and it was such a big package. You really did everything to make my visit pleasant.

I am going to stop and get to work. So I'll leave you in the hope of hearing from you soon telling me that you are well. I forwarded to the parents your letter that came last Wednesday. Thank you for the note that came with it.

Greetings to everyone, and for you, dearest Jean, my most affectionate thoughts.

Gaby

Jean to Gaby   Friday, May 14, 1943

Ma bien chère Gaby,

   Very quickly a few lines to tell you I am fine.

   Lizou isn't back yet. The Berthelots [Gestapo in Lyon] are kind of a pain at the moment, and the Monniers [in Switzerland] advised Lizou to stay until she had a good opportunity to come back, and I agree, and I suppose that opportunity will come up soon. I was at Vichy last Friday. Then in Annecy, and I went through Collonges the day before yesterday and Annemasse. Business is good. Suzy saw the parents and she came here. I was glad. ... In Annecy I got your letter of May 10, just before I left and found the carbon copy of it here. Do I have to answer both of them separately? ... The present events prove that I wasn't wrong to hope that we would see each other before the end of the year, and the same with the parents. As for Guyennot's prediction, you can tell him that we had a little argument in the garden once when he claimed that it said in the prophecy that the Germans would not come to Paris. I believe Guyennot's new prophecy, but not for the same reasons! ... The line between the Haute Savoie and here is momentarily suspended, which won't get any complaint from me. Got a good letter from Mama dated May 2. I will send it to you as soon as I get back and when I have answered it. Received the crackers from Brother Ganty, and I'll write him again to thank him. ... Greetings to everyone. Affectionately, Jean

Gaby knows more about Jean's clandestine work since her visit to him.

Gaby to Jean   Paris, May 17, 1943

Mon bien cher Jean,

   ... I got your letter of Sunday the 9th. I sent the parents' letter and the one which was returned to you. I wonder if the censor will let it go through the way it is. We'll see, I guess. And today I got the Friday one. You are so good to write me such long letters, because now that I know how busy you are, I forgive you if you write only a few lines.

   This morning, I had a telephone call from a Mr. Guebel, I think it was, who wanted to know about a Miss Odette Molan or Molins, I didn't quite get the name, who is studying at the Beaux Arts in Lyon and who had told him she was going to come here, and he would find out through me where he could find her. I told him I didn't know this person at all, but that I would let him know if she came to see me. He gave me his telephone number. I wonder if it wasn't Suzy. [Perhaps it was Suzy. In the margin of this page this paragraph is bracketed with a curved pencil line presumably by Weidner, and "Suzy" is boldly handwritten next to it. The phrase "who is also studying at the Beaux Arts in Lyon" is underlined in pencil. Suzy was a student of art.] Anyway, I'm telling you about it, as it may be useful.

Sabbath afternoon I was stranded in the Métro because of a bombing alert, as they are enjoying giving us those all the time, and I stayed there for an hour, as the Métro only gets going again a half hour after an alert. I went to see Mlle Okhuysen. She works in an aid office which is either mostly or entirely for Dutch people. … [Catherine Okhuysen was a courier in Jean's rescue organization and a hostess for fugitives.]*

I am glad for you that the demarcation line hasn't been set up with Haute Savoie. That would require more red tape for you and will certainly complicate things for the Seminary.

You told me that Mr. Blitz was in Paris. I'm sure he was given the message but I wonder if he will want to get involved with my case [getting a travel pass] again. I'll see. It's much less important now that I have been able to go once [to see you]. I'm sure that in a few months it will be easier. Maybe he doesn't remember the address, but he must remember that it is the Adventist Church. Let's wait.

The other day, Mr. Desmet told me that it was strictly forbidden to give money to someone in Belgium or Holland, for example, and to give the equivalent here. I didn't know it was so dangerous. Fortunately it is of no interest to me! I'm not in business.

Did I tell you we got our bonus? I got 1200 francs. It's not to be sneezed at.

Herewith a sample of the silk twill that you once sent me and which I would like another meter of if possible. If you ever get more, you could put a meter of it aside. I'm putting the sample in the letter I'm sending to Annecy. That way you will not have to risk losing it by bringing it from Lyon to Annecy.

Yesterday there was an outing of the youth group to the Chevreuse Valley. There were only 13 of us but the weather was beautiful, and

---

* See Megan Koreman, *The Escape Line* (Oxford: Oxford University Press, 2018), p.101.

Armande and I had permission to go also. It always does one good to breathe good air for a few hours. We're having magnificent weather now. Thursday and Friday it was too hot, but since the Sabbath there's a little breeze, so it's perfect.

The young lady I saw this afternoon told me that it has been their experience that the personnel of the office where Mr. L. [Laatsman] works is entirely trustworthy. According to what she told me, they believe he is in Paris. ... [Mr. Laatsman is now working with Jean's escape line for refugees.]

I can understand that Lizou prefers to rest a little longer. She will see herself when she is strong enough to make the trip. The main thing is that she doesn't forget you or that you don't neglect yourself as far as clothes and food go. Who mends your socks during her absence? Kiss her for me when you write to her. Excuse my errors. I'm writing very fast, and I'm going to be competition for you! I'll leave you, with many kisses and sending my most affectionate thoughts.

Gaby

Jean moves about very quickly.

Jean to Gaby   Sunday, May 23, 1943

Ma bien chère Gaby,

Thank you for your good letter of the 17th of this month. So on Sunday I was in Toulouse and arrived Monday morning in Grenoble where I had business and then in the evening in Annecy. On Wednesday and Thursday I went to Annemasse for my business and returned here Thursday evening. Tomorrow morning at 5, I will leave for Moutiers and in the evening I will be in Annecy. And then I think I'll be back here on Wednesday evening. Next week I think I'll be in Anduze to get my papers renewed, and at the same time I think I'll change my legal residence to Annecy. As you can see, I don't stay in one place long.

Heard from Lizou who is waiting for the right moment to return by car, and I think that will be within the next two weeks. She has a lot of pain with her sinuses, and I think that treatment she is getting now will end up sooner or later in an operation. Try to find out from Dr. Albaric if an operation would be a permanent solution or if it is his opinion that it would be only temporary. Moreover, I wonder if it doesn't come from her general condition. Anyway, when we are in the mountains, she has hardly any pain.

In Toulouse I happened to meet Mémé Girou who hasn't changed physically in my opinion. We talked together for quite a while, but this time, he wasn't putting on his little act for me as he used to do. He told me he had to stay in Toulouse for another year and that he had had pneumonia and that he had to have his lungs inflated constantly. He is at the military hospital and has a very good doctor. But I told him that it seemed to me that the mountains would be better for him. He is bored, because he is not supposed to do anything but rest, but I think he gets around a lot anyway.

You are right, the Italians are putting barbed wire along the border. It won't matter. [This last sentence is in Dutch.] Suzy had to go back up to Paris, and maybe you have seen her. I hope to see her one of these days. I suppose that this Odette Maulan is Suzy, but I'm not sure, and as soon as I see her I will talk to her about it.

Thank you for the errand to Okluysen. This person is very nice to get the information. At what stage is the question of Troo's baggage? [At this point the rest of the page is neatly torn off along a straight edge.] ...

Yes, fortunately the demarcation line between Haute Savoie and here doesn't exist, as that would make a whole lot of complications. You said that in the enclosed letter you were sending a sample of silk twill, but it wasn't there. Maybe you forgot it. Remind me in your next letter, because otherwise I'll forget it again, but this time add the sample. Lizou wrote me that I should give you her affectionate greetings.

Herewith is a little letter for the parents. My greetings to all the friends.

Arthur and his uncle are well and will come to see us soon. They will probably visit first with Mme Girou and Berthelot [Gestapo Headquarters in Lyon]. The latter is very ill and I think he won't last long... Don't worry about Ganty's crackers. Most of them have been eaten, and they really didn't have time to pick up the taste of moth balls.

Gaby writes to Jean on May 26. Penciled at the top of the page is the word "répondu", "answered".

Gaby to Jean   Paris, May 26, 1943

Mon bien cher Jean,

Every time I receive a letter from you I wonder if I'm going to hear that Lizou is back at last. You must both have had enough of this separation which goes on and on, but it is better that Lizou is careful and waits a while so that all will go well. I hope that the reunion will be soon. ...

That would be great if your friend's sister could get me an extension [on the travel pass]. If I got it before Pentecôte, I would come to see you.* It would be short, of course, and in a way it would be better to wait until summer. As the trip is expensive, it would be too bad to do it for only 4 days. Besides, it is very possible that the sister can't do the travel pass. It's very wonderful that I was able to come once and that gave me immense joy. The pretty taffeta bag you gave me in Annecy is much admired here; everyone thinks it's pretty. Next Sabbath I'm going to use it with my suit which should be ready tomorrow. ...

Last week I sent a package to De Vos. I wanted to ask you something about that. Should I count the exact price, or should I figure it on a wider basis? For example, I put in some melba toasts. I bought them with my ration coupons, so they were a reasonable price. But if I had had to buy that at the black-market price, it would be much more expensive, and the same goes for the other things I put in. It all depends on when the 1000 francs are used up, as you are the one who has to pay, or if the people who have money are the ones to pay. I don't care one way or the other, and I can't take advantage of anyone's misfortune to cheat them.

Since you are making up packages, maybe you could ask Odette to give you one of those round cheeses from time to time (the crème de gruyère), the kind they have at Collonges. She gave me one when I was there. I gave some to several people in the house and I put a piece in the package also. ...

The weather has gone bad in the last few days, and there is a lot of wind. But as soon as there's a little sun, it's warm again.

It's really too bad that Lizou still suffers with that sinusitis. She would do well to see a specialist. I'll talk to Dr. Albaric about it and also my

---

* In the Jewish calendar, Pentecôte memorializes the day when God put the tablet of the Law into the hands of Moses. Among Christians, it is celebrated fifty days after Easter, in memory of the descent of the Holy Spirit to the apostles.

doctor when I see him. It's terrible to suffer all the time from headaches. That poisons one's life. ...

I'll leave you now, my dear Jean; sending you my most affectionate greetings. Kisses to Lizou also when you write to her.

Gaby

Gaby forgot to mention an errand for Lizou when she wrote the previous day.

Gaby to Jean Paris, May 27, 1943

Mon bien cher Jean,

You'll be surprised to receive another note from me since I wrote yesterday. It's because I forgot to ask you a favor, or rather I wanted to ask Lizou to do me a favor. As you asked me when I saw you if I needed shoes, because she could perhaps get me some, I am taking the liberty of writing her to get me some little canvas shoes. Read the letter I sent to her, that way you'll know what it's about and I won't need to tell you the same thing.

I just heard that the Doctor [Nussbaum] is leaving for Switzerland next week; he at last got his travel pass. I hope you didn't write too many bad things about him to the Division, because they will surely tell him! Fortunately you won't have to suffer for it...

While I'm writing you this, someone just brought me a letter from Mama at last. So I'll stop to read it.

Everything is still fine there. Yes, Mama is still asking when we'll see each other, But I am sure it will be at the end of the year. Anyway, we still have to have patience and courage.

... A Miss Koch came during the lunch hour, and do you know what she brought Armande and me? She brought us each an orange. I haven't even seen one this winter. We were very happy.

I'll send you Mama's letter when I have answered it. So I'll leave you now with many kisses,

Gaby

I wonder if you could find me a mountain back pack, not too big. Like the one Mme Molet made for us at the time of the exodus [from Paris to Anduze, June, 1940].

Dr. Van Tricht, a member of Jean's aid team in Monte Carlo, carefully answers a plea from Jean for advice about Elisabeth's sinus condition.

Van Tricht to Jean   May 27, 1943

... I hasten to answer your questions about your dear wife's health. Unfortunately there are several question marks for me! First, you spoke of a "rather acute" sinusitis. An acute sinusitis is never treated with surgery. Probably it is a chronic sinusitis with recurring pain. If so, and they are trying to cure it with surgical intervention, there must be an accumulation of pus in one of the facial sinuses, that is, either the right or left maxillary sinus or else the frontal sinus. The maxillary sinuses, which are alongside the nose are usually treated by puncture and repeated flushing out, just a small nasal intervention. But if the result of this method doesn't help, we operate, that is we open the sinus that is ill by going in between the cheek and the upper teeth, thus avoiding a scar. As for the frontal sinus, a cavity which is located above the eyebrows and the nose, the problem is more painful, and operation is only a last resort, as it often leaves a disfiguring scar. ... It is thus necessary to engage a specialist with experience and an unquestionable reputation. ... Unfortunately Reymond, the great sinus specialist of Freibourg [Switzerland] died a few years ago. He cured all frontal sinuses through the nose, so there was no possibility of a scar, a rather slow and difficult procedure, but much preferable...it is possible that his successor may use the Master's method. ...

Mama to the children   The Hague, May 29, 1943

Dear Children,

Last week I was about to mail you the letter, but I had not closed the envelope yet, just when your letter came, the one from May 15. ... I notice you say that you receive my letters at irregular times, yet I send them every Monday. But I am glad that you do get them so you can keep up to date with us. ...

This Saturday we had Lykele's parents for dinner and they were very satisfied. It was everything we could get with coupons, but I had saved up for this occasion, especially the butter. I was able to bake some oatmeal cookies, and they liked them very much. It was like eating meat, they said. There were mashed potatoes, cauliflower, salad and pudding for dessert. Not the very fine pudding, but made with skim milk, but still, it was tasty. It is now a big problem when you have visitors to feed them well. But with a bit of goodwill, one can succeed. I was so happy to be able to get a cauliflower. ...

We have not had another visit from Erna [Suzy Kraay] yet. We do regret that. We would have liked to see her. I think we will see her soon. Lykele has spoken to her and as soon as she has time, she will visit us and bring the tea Hermine got from Gaby. ...

Did Lizou get home again? It would be nice if she could go to Paris. In this troubled time it is good when family can come together now and then. It will be almost 4 years since we have seen each other. ...

It is sad that Lizou has so many sinus headaches. Maybe it is a sinus infection. Perhaps it would be a good idea to go to Gland and have Dr. Muller examine her. She will be treated well there, and having headaches all the time is not good. ...

Papa has had a little problem with the authorities, which will be further explained in later letters.

Jean to Gaby   Monday evening, May 31, 1943

Ma bien chère Gaby,

Tomorrow morning at 7 o'clock, I'm leaving for Anduze and will return Friday evening. This time I'll change my address to live definitively in Annecy. That will make it easier to renew my authorization to travel.

You can go to the secretary who gave you your pass last time and ask to have it renewed. She will probably do it for you. Anyway, we'll see each other before the end of the year, as the international situation is improving. ...

From Suzy, I heard that Papa had fortunately come out of the clinic where Fischer had put him. It seems that when he tried to come and visit us, he went via Rancy and Fischer didn't want him there, and put him in the clinic for a forced stay...but fortunately after a week he was able to get out as the doctor said that if he had to spend another week there that would be the end for him. It's terrible. Luckily it ended well. I don't understand why Papa isn't more reasonable. But we have to learn how to be patient. It is true that Papa is sick and can't control himself like a normal person.

Lizou is still at her mother's. Her frontal sinusitis is a little better but she still has a lot of pain. I passed on your note about shoes. ...

Greetings to everyone, and best kisses from your brother, ...

Papa's visit to "the clinic where Fischer had put him" was actually a week's imprisonment. Jean's letter to Mrs. Sevenster is written the same day (May 31) as Jean's letter to Gaby above.

Mrs. Sevenster's husband, as was noted earlier, had been imprisoned since December 9, 1942. Until his arrest, he was Dutch Consul, first in Paris, then in Vichy, then in Toulouse. Mrs. Sevenster will easily understand that Jean is telling her that his father has been arrested and imprisoned.

Jean to Mrs. Sevenster   May 31, 1943

... I had some bad news from home. My father is in the clinic like your husband, but under Dr. Moffe's orders. I don't know what was wrong, but I am very worried, and I am thinking of going to see how he is in a few days. I'm still waiting to hear more, as maybe everything will be all right. ...

In a handwritten letter from Gaby to Jean on June 4, Gaby says she is worried about their father's imprisonment.

Gaby to Jean   June 4, 1943

... It's strange, Mama certainly says Papa has returned, but doesn't say anything about his adventures. Maybe she preferred to pass over those in silence. I hope that there won't be any other repercussions. ...

One sentence in your letter worried me a little. You said: "The Dr. had said that if he were to spend another week there, that would be the end of him." Is his health really that bad, or were you just saying it like that? ...

ESCAPES   337

Papa's letter in Dutch to Jean brings an explanation at last, but not until the second page of his letter. And here he calls a prison a prison. Papa continues, however, to use the guise of being pro-German to hide his real opinion from the censors.

Papa to Jean   Friday, June 11, 1943

... You probably know I spent a week in prison in Den Bosch. Since I was innocent, and I was dealing with a decent person, I was let go after an investigation. We have so-called black soldiers here; they are Dutch people who are working for the Germans. I do not like to deal with them, even less than with Germans, as those black ones are less educated. Every German or almost every German is somewhat civilized, but some of those Dutchmen are not civilized at all. And it shows. I was walking in the beautiful wooded southern part of Holland. I was enjoying it tremendously, when all of a sudden one of those "black soldiers" stopped me. I did have my identity papers, but it seems that one must have a border pass when one is within a one and a half hour's walking distance from the Belgian border. In The Hague, of course, we would never have heard of that. So this one now came to the easy conclusion that I was going to cross the border. Of course he didn't have any evidence of that at all. He took me to a post where a "Feldwebel" [Sergeant] was in charge. He was somewhat embarrassed with this case, but he did not dare to make a decision. I was transported to another post where an officer was in charge. However that officer was not present at the time, and after he did not show up for two days (maybe he thought this was a good time for a vacation) I was transported first to Breda. It was too full there, so we went to Tilburg. No room there either. Then to the prison in Den Bosch. I shared a cell with somebody else. After a couple of days a third one joined us. The crisis became so bad that the doctor, who heard I was innocent, told my case to the director of German police. The German who was supposed to handle my case interrogated me immediately. He was then convinced that I was innocent and gave me my freedom. When I thanked him, he said, "Das ist ja mein Pflicht als Mensch." (That is my duty as a human being.) If everyone would think the way he did, there probably would not be a war.

In her 1994 interview with Alberto Sbacchi, Annette remembers a different cause for Papa's arrest. "He was on a bus," she says, "and there was an old Jewish man who was trying to hide his star, and an SS officer saw him and made the bus stop. The officer dragged the poor man off the bus and made him get down on his hands and knees, and hit him with his rifle butt. My father was very upset and protested that it was a shame, a terrible thing what he was doing to a poor old man. The officer took my father to the police station and arrested him. For a week we did not know where he was."

It is hard to say which of these two stories is the true one, but perhaps it was Annette's. In his letter to Gaby and Jean, Papa might have wanted to hide what could be considered reckless behavior on his part. Annette's version gives us an endearing glimpse of Papa's impulsiveness and his hatred of injustice.

Papa's letter of June 11 continues:

... We are in the final days of our T.S.F. [télégraphie sans fil, or "Wireless", a radio]. Soon perhaps, within a week our neighborhood has to submit these forms. It is actually understandable, because people lose their heads with all the propaganda that England broadcasts. One is not allowed to listen [to British radio] but from left and right we hear that there are some who do, and that they tell their stories in trams and cafés, or they say what they thought they heard. If everyone was more intellectual, it would not be harmful to listen to two different sides. However, this is not the case, so it is understandable that it is for the people's own good that they are being protected from those crazy rumors; all radios will have to be confiscated. By saying "all" that is not completely true. The Germans are allowed to keep them. However, they are more disciplined than the Dutch. I fear, however, that there are those Dutchmen who will get around the rules, because Ma read in the paper that there were many who submitted real old radios [when radios were called in by the Occupation authorities], possibly an obsolete radio that had been replaced by a second one. That's the way it goes if not everyone cooperates. It would be so nice if everyone cooperated to construct a new Europe. There are some people here who seem to be so stubborn, that I believe that they have to be hammered flat before they will cooperate. Where will it go from here? Stricter rules, of course, and those who obey the rules will be suffering along with those who don't.

Willy Hijmanns, a member of the Weidner Foundation Board who knew the Weidner family, tells a further story about Papa (as told to Megan Koreman), this time saving his bicycle from confiscation. Just as they called in radios, the Germans in The Netherlands confiscated men's bicycles. When Papa was asked by a German officer if he had

ESCAPES   339

any cycles, he answered, "My wife's bicycle is upstairs." He neglected to mention that his own bike was upstairs, too, but since the officer was not interested in women's bicycles, he did not investigate.

Mama to Jean and Elisabeth   June 13, 1943

As soon as we get a letter from you we shout through the house, "A letter from Joop," and Annette and Pa rush in and together we read the letter. ...

Pa is somewhat nervous lately. High blood pressure and his heart is not as strong. I spoke to the doctor who examined Pa, and it is not bad news, but he has to have better food. I am therefore grateful that dear Henri [Jean] made it possible for me to give Pa what he needs. We don't get enough with coupons alone. Pa needs extra food. But all the extra food costs 6 to 8 times as much, and I would never have been able to pay for that, but now I can give it to Pa. ... Pa was used to drinking a lot of milk, and for a while he did not get any, but now things are getting better. You should never write about the fact that Papa was not well, because he never wanted you or Mies to know about that. ...

The next day Mama writes to "My dear Children."

... Pa has gone to Nijmegan for a couple of days. His cousin lives there and he can have some good conversations with her. I could have gone also, but Lykele is here now and Annette has a painful boil on her hand. She got it from a lady that she nursed. She cannot go to work for a couple of days and she has to be taken care of herself. Compresses all the time and Lykele is a good help for her. ... Today it was a little better, but the hand was swelled up because she had a second infection, but she did go with Lykele to dinner at his married sister's house. I also stayed home because I expect a visit from Erna. I am somewhat worried about her, as she has been promising to visit for a long time, but I never see her show up. Is she sick or is she too busy? I don't know. I could write to her, but I really don't know how to reach her, because she is always traveling for her work. This week a friend of hers came to ask if we had seen her. So I stay home as much as possible, so that when she gets here someone is at home. Each day I think, "Will she come and surprise me today?" I hope so with all my heart. ... You also wrote that Suzy is coming to see you. That will be nice for you. Give her our regards and tell her we look forward to seeing her also at some time. Also give her regards from Erna and tell her if Erna brings me some tea, there will be a cup waiting for her. ... [Erna and Suzy are the same person.]

Please let this war end soon. We are now in the fourth year, and a wave of misery is going over the world. ... Many kisses from all of us. Your loving parents, and Annette and Lykele.

Mama's letter to Joop was returned, so she forwards it to Gaby, and at the same time she has the opportunity to send some small gifts to her.

Mama to Gaby   Thursday, June 17, 1943

Dear Miesje,

On Monday I sent the enclosed letter to Joop and Lizou, but today it was returned, because letters to that region are not accepted anymore. ...

Did you get a visit from Brother v. d. Hoven? He was so kind to take things for you. ... The package of cherry twists had been here in the house already for 2 or 3 years, and Pa had kept the can of spread for your bread for several years. I did not have any cheese, but Brother v. d. H had a couple of cheese coupons and he managed to buy the cheese. Then Annette said, "A pity we don't have any apple syrup, Mies likes that so much." That's when the Brother said, "You can still get it with a coupon. I will get it for you if you have a coupon." I gave him one and the Brother got the apple syrup. The container was supposed to last us a month, but I don't like apple syrup that much and was glad to please you with it... Dear Mies, my writing is bad, because I am writing without my glasses, as they broke in half and are being repaired now. I feel very uncomfortable without my glasses. But I'll get them back soon. ...

Pa has recovered well from his illness. We were all very worried after Pa got his nervous break-down [his imprisonment]. Fortunately everything is normal again, and we don't see any consequences.

Many kisses, dear Miesje, Bye, much love from all of us, Pa, Ma and Annette.

Gaby sends Jean several people in need of his help.

Gaby to Jean   Paris, June 19, 1943

Mon bien cher Jean,

    I was kind of hoping to hear from you this week, but I think you have probably been busy. I've had a lot to do, too. Since Tuesday morning there has been a Dutch Brother here who returned to The Hague a few months ago and who took along your wedding photos. He brought me a letter written the day before by Mama. I was very happy about that. There were also two photos of which one is for you and is enclosed. Mama also sent a few photos for me and I'll enclose a sampling for you.

    I wonder if you had a visit from two of Annette's friends who want to work for Arthur [who want to escape to England, probably because of their imminent call-up for obligatory work in Germany]. They were thinking of coming to Lyon to see you. I'm a little worried about them and would like to know if they are all right. They came to say hello to me on Tuesday.

    I have a lot to do this week, because I had to take care of the Dutch Brother. He slept in the small room and had breakfast and one other meal per day with me. Right now it's a big problem to put together a decent menu. Fortunately he had been given enough ration coupons for ten days. If you see him tomorrow night, you will certainly have to buy him some bread for his trip with the coupons he has left, because I can't buy any this evening, and he is leaving too early tomorrow morning. He has only 3 pounds of bread left, and he will buy some in Marseille.

    Two friends of Miss Okhuysen were also to go to Lyon this week and she asked me if you could take care of them. I said they could go to see you in any case. All this will give you a lot of work. I don't think you will find the time to come and see me any time soon. But if all goes well, I hope to come to see you this summer. Maybe between now and then Lizou will be back, unless she's asking for a divorce! One might think she is getting enough of you!

    The weather isn't at all nice this week. It pours rain constantly. But today the sun is shining. We had a baptism this morning.

    My dearest Jean, I'll leave you now. I don't remember the address of your hotel. I told this Brother to go to Brother P. Meyer's. Maybe you'll be having dinner there tomorrow evening and so you would see this Brother. If you don't see him, he will leave everything at Brother Meyer's.

...

The cocoa is a gift from this Brother; I took half and the other half is for you.

From The Hague on June 22, 1943, Papa chides Gaby for spending too much of her own resources to send packages to Dutch refugees, just as her brother does in Lyon. Papa includes an account of his latest trip, undertaken very soon after his release from prison in Den Bosch.

Papa to Gaby   June 22, 1943

... First, about your efforts with money and packages. You outdid yourself for those friends. But what did I hear: you have to contribute so much every week, and even give up some of your own food? You must not do this any longer, dear child. You yourself need the time, food, money and more of your strength than you can give. ...

... Last week I made a tour through Holland again. I went to see Aunt Hermien, as she was evacuated far from here. I went by train to where nature is really beautiful, and then I traveled further on my bicycle. And guess what I ate there? Bread with bacon and ham. [Papa is a vegetarian and eating any form of pig meat is strictly forbidden among Seventh-day Adventists, who observe the same dietary restrictions as Jews.] But it did me some good. Also whole milk, several glasses. I also bought some cherries, freshly picked from the trees, much cheaper than in the city. Nice, isn't it?

I went to a concert in Nijmegan where my niece and nephew live. It was Beethoven's 9th Symphony. There were 250 in the orchestra. How beautiful it was. It was expensive, however: 2 and a half guilders per person. ...

Just now a lady came in for a visit. Beautiful! Ma and Annette had just left to go shopping and the doorbell rang. This lady who has a four-week-old baby rang the doorbell with tears in her eyes. Annette has been taking care of her and now the mother had dropped her baby accidentally, not too far from here. She asked if she could wait here a few minutes. Right now it seems things are already better and she is tending to the baby and letting it drink some. I just picked her up from the cradle and gave her to her mother. It seems so long ago that I carried such a small human being.

...

Annette's energetic letter from Amsterdam confirms that Gaby has recently visited Jean and Collonges. Annette also warns that her fiancé Lykele Faber may be in danger of being called up for forced labor in Germany, and will need help from Jean and his team.

Annette to Jean   Amsterdam, June 22, 1943

Ma chère petite Gaby,

Your letter pleased me immensely. If you only knew how happy it makes me to receive a letter personally from my big sister. I am always happy to hear news of you, but when it's a letter in French for me, I am doubly happy. I was also agreeably surprised to see a letter from Mr. Meyer. I thought he had forgotten me as it has been a long time since he wrote to me.

If you only knew how happy I was for you that you had seen Jean. Has he changed much? And just imagine, you saw Collonges. I can't think about Collonges without being terribly homesick for it. How I would love to see my mountains. Here everything is so flat. Four weeks ago I got a week's rail pass and I traveled all over Holland. The countryside is pretty, but so monotonous. Switzerland, with its lakes and glaciers, is so beautiful in comparison with Holland. I really hope I can go to Switzerland for my honeymoon. It's my beautiful dream. Will it come true? Oh, I hope we can see each other this year. What a joy that will be, right Gaby?

I love my work. ... I think Jean and Elisabeth are waiting for the war to be over, until I can come and help Lizou [with a baby]. Of course I also think they are right. I wouldn't want to have a baby in the first two years of marriage either. Lykele agrees, fortunately. Here in Holland, all my friends are getting married. I think it's contagious. But it isn't much fun right now with all the restrictions and the ration tickets. It's a real trick to prepare a meal nowadays. We haven't seen any eggs for two years, and I love them so much!

I have more work than I can take on. My last caretaking job was very pleasant, a couple, still young, he 25 years old and she 20, with their first baby. Everything went very well and on the 11th day she was on her feet and active around the house. They were so happy to have a little girl. As a gift from them I received an electric tea kettle. How happy I was, as you can't find those anymore, and they are so practical. Right away I wrapped it up. I already have a lot of things for my kitchen. I also have a very pretty modern tea set, a breakfast set and a dinner set. But it will be a while before we have any furniture. It's so expensive here. You have to be a capitalist to be able to buy any! So for the time being, it is out of the question. But anyway we will wait until the war is over to get married.

Do you know my pal Faber? [Here Annette is being careful to mention her fiancé covertly.] He wrote me that in a few weeks he might go to see Jopie [Jean]. He wants to ask his advice, because he doesn't like Fischer at all and doesn't want to do what the latter tells him to do.

Right now I am in Amsterdam at my fiancé's for a few days. I can't work for ten days or so, because I have a boil on my wrist. I also had an abscess in my hand last week which gave me a lot of pain. I got the boil from one of my patients who had one on her buttock. After a few days my whole hand and my arm were swollen so that I had to see the doctor. He was afraid there was blood poisoning and that my arm had to have compresses immediately and to rest. Last week the doctors made a deep incision. There was an incredible amount of pus. And what a lot of pain. Well, the worst is over, and now all I have to do is wait for the wound to close.

Now all the young men have to leave for "arbeidsinzet" [hard work] in Germany. In France, too? My fiancé is in the Post Office, and so until now he could stay quietly in Holland. But now he thinks he will have to go to Germany. It will be hard to be separated, but nothing can be done about it. We should be grateful that we have been able to be together this long, when all the other young men had to leave several months ago, even newly married men.

But we must trust in God, right? …

Now I'll leave. Greetings to my friends and affectionate kisses to you.
  Annette

At the end of the letter above, Annette doesn't name her fiancé as she did earlier in the letter when she was telling Gaby that Faber would try to escape so as to avoid going to Germany. Here, putting a positive note on the obligation, she doesn't need to use the code.

A postcard from Mama to Gaby, written in Dutch, expresses her gratitude for the presents from Gaby and confirms that Lykele must escape from The Netherlands.

Mama to the children   The Hague, June 23, 1943

Dear Children,

This morning Brother v. d. Hoven visited us. He works for the armed forces and gives you his regards. Miesje, what did you do? You have hardly enough to sustain yourself and you give us butter and eggs. We almost cried about it. A half hour after the Brother had gone I was making pancakes with your butter, because somebody gave me a small bag of flour the day before. And how glad we were to have the tea, thanks a thousand times for that. I just hope you are not short of butter. The Brother said that you were so kind and praised you very much. He said there was a shortage of food in Lyon and we thought it was better than in Paris. But it is the same everywhere. Poor Lizou and Joop, you'll also have some hard times. We hope your friends will help you.

The Brother brought so many goods with him. I am so glad to have the towels. I needed them and we cannot buy them anymore. Pa is so glad to have the undershirts, they probably came from Henri. ... On Friday the 25th two letters were sent to you, one from Pa and one from Annette, so I am just writing you a card. Next week a long letter from me. Lizou could not return yet? Annemarie's [Annette] fiancé must also leave. For the rest, everything is OK here.

Many kisses, Pa, Ma and Annette.

Johanna Gertrude Weidner-Linschoten,
Columbusstraat 13, The Hague.

On the same day that Mama writes to the children, Gaby is writing to Jean. She mentions that Suzy Kraay may cause problems for Jean. She does not explain what the problems might be, but in June Suzy had been arrested. In her postwar report of October 23, 1945, she wrote: "In June, 1943, I went to Oloran... at the Spanish border, despite the fact that Mr. Weidner didn't want me to. At Oloron, I was arrested in bed by the Germans and interrogated. After 4 hours I was released, but I had to present myself to the French Police. The latter claimed that my papers were false. I was arrested and sentenced to a month in prison. From the prison I was transported to the camp in Guers [Gurs] as an undesirable foreigner and there I stayed from the month of June until November 1, 1943."

As for funding for his own rescue work Jean Weidner had reported on June 20, 1943, "We are totally without funds."

Gaby to Jean   Paris, June 23, 1943

Mon bien cher Jean,

According to your little note of Friday, which came Monday, I think you must not have seen Brother v. d. Hoven, the Dutch man who spent a few days here. He doubtless went to Brother Meyer's since I didn't give him your address at the office, thinking that you wouldn't be there on a Sunday.

I see that you don't stay long in one place. You are so good to write me so regularly despite your having to run all the time. Yesterday afternoon I received your typed letter, also written on Friday. I was very glad to get it but on the other hand, it worries me a lot that because of Suzy, you might have some problems? If I were in your shoes, and all those people came to ask for help, I would send them packing. It seems to me you have already done your part. And you are so good-hearted, that you would spend everything you earn to help this one and that one. You mustn't let yourself be taken advantage of.

Yes, I received the money that Brother P. Meyer gave me from you, and thank you so much. I think you are going to bankrupt yourself for me and the parents, because you need to buy furniture, especially if you are thinking of getting an apartment in Annecy soon. That would be nice for Lizou. I think you did the right thing by insisting that she return home. Of course the trip is a little tiring, but that situation cannot go on forever. When she is there she can take care of the store and that will unburden you a little. But you have to tell her kindly, because as you know, she is very sensitive, and you must not order her to do it. Anyway, I think you must know what approach to take with her. ...

I would be sorry to terminate the packages for the Trabskis, as they really need them. What I dislike about it is that every week they write to me and give me a lot of errands for this one and that one, either to friends who have to do things for them, or to friends who might send them packages. I'm getting tired of it, as it takes an enormous amount of time. When they ask for things to be sent in their packages, they are really demanding. They ask for candy, pain d'épices [gingerbread], sugar, butter, everything that we already have so much trouble getting, or that we can't get at all.

I send one package about every two weeks to De Vos. Each package comes to around 100 francs, as I count the minimum, without taking a loss on it, of course. I got a card from him last week in which he tells me that he is very grateful for what I do for him. I was very pleased about that. He shares everything with a girl who is there and who never receives any packages. When I have used up all the money, I'll let you know so you can tell me if I should continue.

About the silk twill, you don't have to send me any. I decided to make a smock with what I have and an apron with what is left over. ... So don't send the extra meter I asked you for. No, thank you, I don't need any other fabrics, I have everything I need for the summer.

I think you may have seen the Droz family who are in Annecy for two weeks. I think that Mme Droz will have bought some things at your store. But anyway, don't give her too much, because she is well supplied, she gets a lot of fabric. They must earn piles of money and can buy things on the black market if necessary.

That's fine about the back pack, I'll remind you from time to time.

About my travel pass, I haven't looked into it because I thought that foreigners didn't need them anymore. But it seems they are necessary after all. Anyway, I'll go a little later, as I plan to take my vacation in the second two weeks in August. Is that all right with you? If another date is more convenient for you, let me know so I can make arrangements, as we can't all be out of the office at the same time. At that time I'll start applying for my travel pass and will go back to see the girl in question. But will we still be able to travel by then?

I am in good spirits but sometimes I get nervous seeing we are not making progress. As for the spiritual side, you must not worry about me, Jean. Of course when one is in the Work and particularly in the offices, we see a lot of things that are shocking and even scandalous. I don't worry about it as much as I did as far as work goes, but when it's about serious things, I put in all the devotion and seriousness I am capable of. I don't forget that it's the work of God. I know we all have faults and I know I mustn't look too closely at what the men do. I would never leave Adventism because of anything some Brother or other has said. I remain faithful, but I don't have narrow ideas either. I try to act on my conscience and according to the principles I was brought up with. I don't let myself be influenced by anything Brother Oscar Meyer might have said. When he talks sometimes about the attitude of the Doctor, I think of all Papa used to say when he tells over and over again the business about his retirement and all the trouble they gave him, and I tell myself that when these people begin to get beyond fifty years old, they all have fixed ideas, and you have to forgive them. ...

Thursday, June 24

I had just finished my letter when I got your postcard of the 21st. I am very happy to know that Annette's two friends had a good trip, something I hadn't dared to hope for. You are really spoiling me these days, because I have heard from you for 3 days in a row. Don't get too tired helping Juliana's friends as there seems to be no end to that.

I'll leave you. Kisses, Gaby

Juliana was the daughter of Queen Wilhelmina of The Netherlands, so in the letter above, "friends of Juliana" is Gaby's code for Dutch people.

Jean writes concerning his wife to someone who has connections in Switzerland.

Jean to a Swiss contact   Wednesday morning, June 23, 1943

Dear Sir,

Once again I take the liberty of presuming on your good will, and in advance, I thank you for your kindness.

Please find herewith a letter for Elisabeth, and I would be very grateful if you could get it to her immediately, as it is very urgent.

I hope she can come home soon (I mean Elisabeth, not my letter). I would have come to see you, but I am very busy at the moment, but I think I will have that pleasure next week. Instead I am sending my secretary to you to ask you to give her any letters Elisabeth may have written to me. Perhaps if she comes back with a letter this evening, I will send her back again tomorrow with the answer, as I am leaving tomorrow for Lyon.

I am adding a little package for Elisabeth also, containing some items she asked me for. ...

A few days later Jean writes to Dr. Van Tricht in Monte Carlo about his efforts to help some more of "Juliana's friends."

Jean to Van Tricht Lyon, June 28, 1943

... I will try to come and see you soon, but I can't yet give you specific date, as I am assailed from all sides. It's incredible. Sometimes I feel at the end of my strength, but as everyone knows, a Dutchman hangs in there all the way. ...

According to recent news from my wife, the treatment she received was a success. She now has much less sinus pain. As soon as she gets here, we will go to see you and I will be very glad to introduce you to her. I have the honor of having met your charming wife, and I will be glad to have you meet mine. ...

At the moment there are dozens of young people arriving who are leaving their country as a result of all the miseries being imposed upon them. We must help them materially and morally, and get their situations regularized with the French authorities. Right now the department of Haute Savoie is particularly crowded because of the arrival of our young people who want to get to Switzerland and who are sent back. Thank God we have so far been able to regularize their situations, and we think we can hold out as long as necessary, thanks to the help of those like you who want to help our unfortunates, legally, of course. ...

13 "Serious Things Could Happen to Us"

Now Annette's fiancé must follow the escape route. Gaby discusses his options in a letter to Jean.

Gaby to Jean   Paris, July 3, 1943

Mon bien cher Jean,

    Last Monday I received your letter of June 25 and then I heard from Brother Meyer that you are sick. I was extremely sad to hear it but I won't worry too much as I know you sometimes have trouble with your tonsils, although in the last few years it has been a lot better. You get a high temperature from it, but I hope you are better now. I think Brother Meyer will write to his brother and that he will let us know your news, until you can do so yourself. I really don't want you to get too tired. I think you must be traveling a lot. Please be careful.

    For the last few days I have been a bit preoccupied, because I had a visit from Lykele. He would like to spend his vacation with either Monnier [Switzerland] or Sanz [who is in England]. Maybe you can advise him there on what would be best.

    What you told me about Suzy is quite worrisome. Let's hope that everything is going to be all right for you.

    I saw Mlle Ok. [Okhuysen] and gave her the message. Did I tell you I had received a postcard from Trabski a week ago saying that they were going to be deported? So no need to send me the 5000 francs for them that I asked you for. …

I hope to hear very soon that you are completely well again. But please take care of your health. ...

Mama writes from The Hague that Annette is very sad about the sudden departure of her fiancé Lykele. She disguises the event and the young man, so as not to endanger him or Annette or any of the people on Jean's team who will have helped him escape.

Mama to the children   The Hague, July 4, 1943

My dear children,

 This is my regular Sunday hour to write to you. Last week I wrote you a card because Pa and Annette had already written you and we hope you received it. I am writing this to all of you, because we are not able to get in contact with Joop. The letter we sent to Lyon was returned. I hope that Lizou and Joop will be able to read this letter. Did Lizou return or is she still at her mother's? ... We are expecting a letter from Joop and also from you, little Mies. We have not heard from you since June 8th. In Joop's last note he said he would write us in 3 or 4 days, but we have not heard anything yet. ...

 Thank you again Mies for all the things you sent... I would have given the undershirts to Lykele, but unfortunately he wasn't here anymore. Annette was somewhat down. She did not look well, pale and blue under the eyes. She was sad, everything happened so quickly and unexpectedly. She said she is glad to have a busy nursing job at the moment so that she has little time to think about it.

 We got a nice letter from Aunt and Uncle in Antwerp. Annemarie was very happy to get it. Everything is going well in Antwerp and Annemarie, who always longs to go to Paris and Germany, dreams of that more than anything because the war is lasting so long. [The inclusion of Germany in the list of Annette's dreams may be to satisfy the censor.] She asks you, Mies, to send all her friends her regards and most of all the young friend, Jeanne and To's brother [Lykele]. He might visit you at your office. Tell him that his old girlfriend has not forgotten him and will write him soon.

 ... Times are getting worse and things are getting nastier. But we must not lose courage. Fortunately we are still able to work and we can forget the awful things. Yesterday I went to visit Annette at the house where she is working. The people were extremely satisfied with her and said she is excellent. From all sides people come to ask her to work for them; however, she can take only one at a time. Joop and Lizou must write her 5 months in advance when they need her, or she will already be occupied. Her boil is almost healed but not quite yet. She is wearing gloves when working as a nurse. Fortunately she was still able to buy them. Those things are not available now. Where she is working now, the people are very friendly and nice to her because Annette was so discouraged this week by all the awful things that occurred. There is hardly any family that is not touched by the terrible war.

Papa is traveling again for a few days, and that does him some good as he cannot come to see you. He thinks of that often and we all long for that day. We have not seen Erna [Suzy Kraay] for weeks now. She is not ill though, as a friend of hers wrote us, but she is probably too busy. We do hope to see her again soon. Has Suzy stopped by, Mies? Or at Lizou and Joop's? Annette would like to know. Suzy would probably have seen Jeanne's brother [Lykele] and that would have been nice. Are you thinking to go to Lizou and Joop for a vacation, Mies? As long as nothing will interfere, as this is such a terrible time. It is hard to plan anything in advance. Annette was also thinking she would take a couple of weeks' vacation time at the end of this month. But that will not happen now. She plans to keep working now. Li's [Lykele's] family is doing well, we got a card from his parents with good news, and his sister has gone to Friesland. His married sister here in The Hague is also doing well as are her children. Annette went there yesterday to tell them about Aunt and Uncle W. Yes, visiting family is consoling in these days of sorrow and despair. However the Lord rules. We hope to see our dear children again God willing.

Our best regards to all three of you and many kisses, your always thinking of you and loving parents and Annette

Jean must go to Switzerland and asks His Excellency J. J. Bosch van Rosenthal to help him get the necessary papers.

Jean to J.J. Bosch van Rosenthal July 5, 1943

Excellency,
Mr. Loudon and the consuls of this region have given me an important mission which would take me to Switzerland for about 10 days. These

persons have asked me to talk with you and also with several personal friends in order to assure the maximum of success concerning the whole situation here and especially the financial situation. I must ask you to help me get a visa for a stay in Switzerland of about 10 days to 2 weeks. Unfortunately I will have to leave and re-enter France illegally, but I am willing to run the risk of illegal passage on the French side. The questions to be discussed are urgent…

As well as being worried about Lykele's escape, Papa is concerned about the practice of passing the same Communion cup to all those taking Communion in church. He would prefer individual cups for sanitary reasons.

Papa to Gaby   The Hague, July 9, 1943

Gaby chérie,

Yesterday I mailed Annette's letter to Lykele and at the Post Office they told me that A's page to you was too much, so I'm sending it to you separately. Impossible to do that without sending you a few lines.

What a relief for us to know that L. isn't ill anymore [that Lykele is safe]. It's lucky it went so fast, because it can drag on as it did with me [Papa was in prison for a week], but even with me it could have lasted longer. Oh, how grateful those who are in good health can be.

You wrote us that Jean has tonsillitis and a high temperature. Write us immediately as soon as you know anything more, right? I like to think that Lykele can help him. But above all Jean must not tire himself all out. May God grant him a prompt return to good health. We are praying for him.

It's too bad Elisabeth is not with him. No one can take care of a husband better than a wife can. But that's the way it is! We have to wait patiently.

I went to let Erna's parents know of her illness [imprisonment]. They hadn't heard about it yet, but I find it is always better to tell the truth. I hope God will not let there be any complications.

Thank you for the information concerning the question of the individual cup. I had asked for the Doctor's [Nussbaum] address, because I thought I remembered that it was he that had written a few articles about that in 1921 in the Revue [Revue Adventiste]. … Here they are stubborn (not the members, but certain pastors); it seems there's no way to make them see the reasons behind this way of doing things. It's really fanatical literalism. We don't pass the whole loaf of bread either, so why the wine? And anyway in the largest churches, they use several cups to save time. So why not let those who wish it take the cup individually?

It's really nice of the Meyers to take such good care of Jean. I hope to be able to thank them in person later on. ...

I was traveling toward the North of the country and I drank good milk there and ate eggs. What a delicacy! I will probably return there in a few days, as it does me good.

We are all eager to see what this summer will bring, because a change of one kind or other (sorry, I think I made an error: of one kind or another) must come about. It can't go on forever. Clothing wears out, food is so scarce, tension grinds us down. Let it be over soon! But not so that it will happen again in ten years. So it's better to suffer a while longer. ...

Mama and I send our kisses, hoping to bring them in person some day. We think of you every minute. Our greetings to Jean and Lykele.

Papa

Gaby to Jean   Paris, July 11, 1943

Mon bien cher Jean,

It is Sunday morning. I should be at the meeting, but Brother Charpiot told me I had to type the program for the committee meeting this afternoon. I am waiting for him and as he hasn't arrived, I suppose he is still correcting it, and so I'll take the opportunity to write a few words. I have been so busy this week that I haven't had time. Really, these past few weeks I have had so many people here and it is such a problem to prepare meals. For the conference I also had a lot of people, but now it's over. We can go to bed earlier and get up a little later.

It was such a joy yesterday morning, just before church, when I met the Fasnachts and they gave me your message. I was so happy. In the afternoon I slipped out for a moment to go quickly to mail a registered letter to Annette. Yesterday evening I had received the enclosed letter from Mama, so she will be reassured. Poor kid. I was so nervous myself, so it must have been much worse for her.

I was so glad to meet Li [Lykele]. He is a charming boy and the week he spent here allowed me to really appreciate him. Already he seems like a member of the family. He absolutely does not want to be dependent on anyone, and I can understand him.

I haven't had time to answer your note that I received on Monday, it was the first one you sent after your illness. Poor Jean. So it wasn't just the tonsils, it was also overwork. Be careful. You won't get ahead of the game any better if you get really sick. And you have to think of your wife. I can understand that you are sad that she hasn't returned. You asked Papa to write to her, and I am going to tell him this afternoon as I'm going to write to the parents. Mme Droz told me you were a little depressed. But I am sure that if you told Lizou nicely that you are beginning to have had enough of being alone, that she will do everything in her power to return. According to a letter from Odette, you heard that the fact of not having an apartment is what is keeping her with her mother. That could be true. For a young bride, it is of course hard not be able to set up in an apartment. Wouldn't there be a way to rent one in Annecy, even if it's not in a new building, since you intended to do that at Easter, when I saw you. Of course that would be much nicer for Lizou, and after the war you can come to Paris. You have to try to make concessions on both sides. And maybe you should pay more attention to her. I don't want to preach to you, Jean, as you are old enough to know what you have to do. But it certainly isn't very interesting to her to see you running around for this one and that one, and why? Only to be met with ingratitude, most of the time. One has to help out, but within limits. What you told me about those Dutch people amazes me because they seem to have been well brought up. Really, those who helped them must not be about to do it again. It seems to me that you have done your duty and that you can rest a little now and think about your own affairs a little more. I hope you won't be angry with me for saying this. You know how much I want you and Lizou to be happy and so I am taking the liberty of saying this in your own interests.

Please tell your friend that I didn't receive a telegram. ...

Now I want to talk a bit about vacation. I was counting on taking mine in the second two weeks in August, but I am told that in Haute Savoie it already gets cold by then, and I would like to take it sooner, say from August 6 to 21. Do you think you will be a little bit free at that time? I'm writing a note to Lizou, telling her that I hope very much to see her then. You can read it. I'm going to go to the Consulate this week, because it appears that all foreigners, and not just the Swiss, can cross the line with a valid passport. I would like to have your answer as soon as possible,

"SERIOUS THINGS COULD HAPPEN TO US"

because I have to get my ticket a week in advance. We can't get them earlier, but if we go any later, there might not by any seats left. Anyway if I see I can't get one, I'll go to the gentleman who got me one at Easter. If I need anything other than a passport I'll take steps to get a pass. On the other hand I would like to know if I should get a ticket for Lyon to arrive there Friday afternoon, August 6, or get a ticket to Annecy to arrive there on Friday morning, as there is only a night train. That will depend on your plans, as I think Lizou will be back by then. I'm told you have to have a special permit to visit Haute Savoie. Can you arrange that? I could also go to Annecy and go immediately to Collonges if that would be better for you. Think about it and tell me what would be best for you. The time will go quickly and I have to start thinking about it seriously, unless events prevent us from traveling at that time. We never know. ...

Brother Charpiot still hasn't brought me the work I was to do. So I'll go to the meeting and do the work later. I'll mail this letter tomorrow, because perhaps there'll be a note from you in the mail. Be of good courage, mon cher Jean, and take care of yourself, and don't get too tired. Are you really all well now?

Je t'embrasse très fort.
    Gaby

Just when this letter was about to leave, one came for Li which I'll enclose immediately.

Mama to the children   The Hague, July 12, 1943

My dear children,

... Miesje, our regards to A's friend. We are glad that he has not forgotten us. Annette wants to write him regularly now, and we hope that when he is fully recovered, he will write us too. Nice of him to go and see Joop, too. He has probably done so already. We look forward to hearing from him and hope to see him after the war. It is so sad that he has been so ill [in danger]. Fortunately he has withstood the crisis and hopefully he will have no complications from it. Now you also write that Erna has fallen ill [is in prison]. We are deeply sorry about it as she had such a busy life. It must be awful for her to lie in bed quietly. And Joop has taken such good care of her. He is sorry also that she has not recovered from it yet. Her family will also be very sad about it. Let us hope she will recover soon, as she is young and will have strength. ...

Annette is still a bit down. She had hoped to be able to go and visit you. The war is lasting such a long time, and sometimes she is homesick for the country she was born in [Switzerland], and she has days when she really wants to go back. Some time ago I said to Pa that I really wanted to go to the cemetery in Gland again. It is eleven years this week that our François passed away, and I would really have liked to visit his grave. ...

In church I just can't get used to sharing a cup. Having only one cup is not hygienic, and I despise it. Here in Holland they still hold onto the old customs. ... I am also a bit skeptical about X-rays. One photograph alone is not enough to explain anything, I think. ...

Annette is healthy, and her lungs are fine. ... She needs a lot of rest and good food... Papa does not eat meat at home but when traveling he does; if he doesn't get enough, he eats everything when he is hungry. ... Nice, Joop, that you still want to buy an automobile after the war. We would be so happy to go somewhere together. ... Well, dear children, our thoughts are always with you. ...

Your loving parents and Annette.

Gaby is still using the formal form "vous" to address Elisabeth.

Gaby to Elisabeth   Paris, July 13, 1943

Bien chère Elisabeth,

I was so sad not to have had the pleasure of seeing you when I went through Annecy at Easter. Jean told me then that you would be back soon and that you would probably come to see me in Paris. Alas, time passes and not only have you not yet come to see me but you're still not back in Annecy.

Once again I am making plans to go into the other zone. I am thinking of taking my vacation from August 6th to the 22th, or else the 13th to the 29th. I would be very sorry not to see you this time, and I hope you will do all you can to be there. It would make me very happy, but I think it would make Jean even happier, as he thinks it has been a long time that he has spent far from you, which is understandable as he loves his little wife so much.

Annette is very sad to have been obliged to separate from her fiancé. But I hope she will be brave. She doesn't even want to take a vacation, because being busy helps her forget her sorrow. Let's hope that their separation won't be very long. Fortunately I saw Jean again at Easter. That was a very great encouragement for me.

My dear Lizou, I'll leave you with the firm hope of seeing you soon. Please give my greetings to your mother and I'm sending you my affectionate kisses.

    Gabrielle

Despite Mama's conviction voiced in her letter of July 9 that "it is always better to tell the truth," Gaby wishes Mama hadn't told Suzy's parents that their daughter was in prison.

Lykele has joined Jean, and Gaby is expecting to hear more about him from Jean. Gaby refers to Lykele as Jean's "brother-in-law," to avoid using his name in a letter to The Hague from which Lykele has so recently escaped.

In her letter in Dutch to her parents, Gaby reminds them that she will soon go on vacation but for safety reasons does not mention what they already know: that she will cross the Demarkation Line again and meet with Jean and hopefully Lizou.

Gaby to parents   Paris, July 19, 1943

Dear Mama, Papa and Annette,

The letters are coming very quickly these days. …

I thank Papa heartily for his dear letter. I can't go back to it anymore because I have sent it to Jopie [Jean]. Jopie is very well again according to what he wrote this week. … I hope he takes a vacation this summer, as that will do him good. If Lizou gets home again, he will be calmer. It was making him nervous. …

Did Brother v. d. Hoven give you the 500 francs he owes me? Most likely. You should give it to Annette. I can't send her anything for her engagement, but she should buy something with it and consider this her engagement present from me.

Jopie says to tell you that you should not have told Suzy's parents that she wasn't able to write for the last couple of weeks, but that she will do so soon. He thought it would have been better if you had not told them she was ill [in prison] because from far away, one always worries more if one does not see that person. But her case does not seem to be too serious, because she will be able to write again soon. [Suzy's month in prison will be over soon.]

Jopie will most likely tell me about his brother-in-law in a few days. He says he likes him very much.

I also hope that Lizou comes home soon, because if Jean is neglected, he'll feel lonely, having meals by himself and having to take care of his clothes.

I hope that you can all stay healthy. Buy everything you need, even if it's more expensive. ...

I can certainly understand that you want to go to François's grave this month. I am sure that this will soon be possible. You just have to have patience for a little while longer. ...

I am looking forward to vacation because I feel rather tired. It is the same every year in July. Another three weeks and I'll be on my way.

Dear Papa, Mama and Annette, I send you many kisses.
   Miesje.

Gaby is having difficulty getting travel documents

Gaby to Jean   July 20, 1943

Mon bien cher Jean,
   ... I'm writing a few lines as I have a letter from Mama to forward and a letter from Annette for Ly. I am anxious to hear from you about the latter and to know if everything went all right.

I hope to hear from you also about vacation dates. ... I am a little worried because when I went to the Consulate on Friday to renew my passport, they told me it would take two months. Now it's the Germans who handle that and the passport has to go to Holland. It's really annoying, and moreover, the people at the Commissariat won't validate foreigners' identity cards. They say you have to go to the Prefecture to get a pass for the other zone. As soon as I know the date of my vacation, I'll go where I got a pass the last time, and I'll probably get one. I'd prefer that to the risk of being sent back from the Demarcation Line. My vacation would be ruined. ...

I'll leave you now, my dear Jean, sending you my best kisses. Greetings to Ly. Tell him that Mme Droz and Gisèle thought he was charming!
    Gaby

Another side of Jean's financial situation is revealed in his letter to Dr. Van Tricht on July 23.

Jean to Dr. Van Tricht   July 23, 1943

… I must tell you that as I have been making loans and donations for the past two years, my financial situation has not improved. … I have just about abandoned my business in order to devote myself to our unfortunate countrymen, and the money goes out faster than it comes in. …

Jean to Elisabeth (no address or location for either, only a date)   July 21, 1943

Chère Elisabeth,
    Foreseeing that serious things could happen to us, I would like the Juliana [Dutch] authorities to intervene with the Monnier [Swiss] authorities, so that in case of danger I could go there and be accepted. Also act quickly with Claparède about Lykele Faber, Annette's fiancé. Also ask Nico's boss if he knows the entry permit number for Mr. de Schotten. Madeleine B. wrote that the authorization had been issued, but they didn't have the number yet.

Gaby to Jean   Paris, July 28, 1943

Mon bien cher Jean,
    Yesterday a letter for Ly arrived and I'm sending it to you in Lyon, because I think you'll have it sooner than if I send it to Annecy. If I was sure that Ly opens your letters (at least those coming from me) I would have sent it there because then he would have it sooner. But if he doesn't it's better that I send it to Lyon.
    According to your card of the 19th of this month, which I received a few days ago, I see that you are still very busy. But take care of your health,

Jean, you mustn't do anything rash. I suppose that you are completely well again, as your card said everything was fine.

In my last few letters, I asked you for some information about vacation, and I'm concerned about not having received any. First, about my stay in Haute Savoie. Do you think you could get the authorization or should I apply for it here? It isn't worthwhile making travel plans if it is going to be refused. On the other hand, I am invited to the Workers' meeting in Collonges which takes place from September 1 to 8. For this conference, we are all asking for a group permit. So it would be from August 16 to 31 that I need an authorization. But are those dates convenient for you for a vacation? I was thinking of leaving Sunday evening August 15, and arriving Monday morning in Annecy. I could stay the rest of the week and leave Friday for Collonges. I wrote to Brother Evard to ask if they would accept me as a boarder at the Seminary for about a week. If you are in Annecy again during the following week, I could come and spend two or three days. What do you think? I do not at all want to bother you, but I think they will accept me as a boarder at the Seminary, and if not I'll have to find lodging elsewhere. I would like to have your answer as soon as possible, so I can reserve a seat. ...

I'll get second class reservations, especially since I will get reimbursed for a 3rd class ticket, as I am invited to the Workers' meeting. That comes to several hundred francs, which will allow me to spend an even pleasanter vacation.

I am enclosing the letter Annette wrote to me. About Lizou, do you think that it's because she doesn't love you anymore that she doesn't want to come back, or is it because of material difficulties. I hope I will see her. Of course you can tell by her letters if she is a little detached from you. It bothers me to talk to you about it, but lately I have thought about it a lot, and like Annette, I am very surprised that she didn't come home when you were sick. Well, it's probably better not to talk to you about it, as it must bother you. But I would like to hear what you think sometime.

When I come, do you want me to bring anything? If you are in Annecy on Monday, I will make a few pastries which we can eat together, especially since Tuesday will be my birthday. For the first time in 4 years I'll be celebrating it with family, since you and Ly will be there at least. August 10 is Papa's birthday. If you have time, write him a little note, that will make him happy. A registered letter from here takes only 4 or 5 days maximum. So you still have time to do it. ...

"SERIOUS THINGS COULD HAPPEN TO US"

I am so happy at the thought of seeing you again. I hope there won't be a landing while I'm there and I would be stranded; that would not be fun. ...

Ask Ly if he wants me to bring the Dutch Bible that Sister Dethier lent to him, or were you able to give him one? Is there anything else he would like me to bring? ...

A handwritten letter from Gaby to Annette's fiancé Lykele, who is in Annecy. For Ly, Gaby writes in Dutch.

Gaby to Lykele   Paris, August 2, 1943

Beste Ly,

This Friday your letter arrived, and I sent the two letters to Annette right away. The one that came this morning will be mailed shortly. If at any time you want me to send a letter first class to Annette, you must leave the envelope open, because the letters we take to the Post Office have to be open. You have to put your full address on it. You can write your full name, but also put with it: 130 Bd. de l'Hôpital, Paris, 13. The normal mail which is not first class can be closed and a full address is not necessary.

You can read the letter that I am writing to Joop. In about two weeks we will see each other again. Nice. It could have been very different. Thank you for your letters. I was so eager to hear how everything had gone on the trip. You must have been so tired standing all night long. I think I will have a seat reserved by friends.

The letters to Holland go much faster now.

On Friday I got a letter from Mama which was written on Monday. I want to answer that tonight and mail it tomorrow, and both of you will be able to read it then.

I will leave you now, see you soon, many greetings.
    Gaby

Gaby to Jean   Paris, August 2, 1943

Mon bien cher Jean,

    This morning I got your letter of July 23 and I thank you for the information. I had indeed asked you for the pass for Collonges. I went Thursday and got it. But there was also a paper that said that for Haute Savoie I would also have to have an authorization from the Prefecture. ... I can't go to the Prefecture this afternoon, as I am alone in the office and the concierges aren't even there. But I'll go tomorrow first thing, and I will write you immediately to tell you what the answer is. I am a little afraid I won't have the authorization before August 15. Moreover, it could happen that I will be asked for a paper signed by you to prove that I am going to family. Well, I'll see. Anyway, even if I don't get this paper, I will still leave, hoping that you will be able to get me the visitor's authorization. Or should I not leave? That would be too bad.

    I am terribly sorry that you are going to be absent the first week I am there. I had made plans for making a few pastries which we would have eaten together on my birthday. But on the other hand, I am certainly glad that you can go and see Lizou. I hope you will persuade her to return. In any case, you will be able to talk and to look at the situation clearly from all angles. I can't make any pastries that would keep a week, but I think you will have some at Lizou's that will be much better. Ganty gave me 2 kilos of crackers for your packages, as I asked him if he had something since I was going in two weeks. So I will bring you those. ...

    I'm sending this letter both to Lyon and Annecy. I'll send you another tomorrow when I will have been to the Prefecture. Dr. Nussbaum just telephoned me. He is going to apply to the Prefecture for the visitors' permits for all the Paris Workers as a group, because even the French who want to stay more than 5 days in Haute Savoie have to apply for the permit. He said that for all foreigners, except the Swiss, you first have to have a permit from the Germans. Luckily I have it. ... Since I have to go to the Prefecture tomorrow, I will take the application for everybody, and I will specify that I want to stay beginning August 15. I'll see what they say. ...

    I thought I might do this: I'll arrive Monday, August 16, and will stay probably until Tuesday in Annecy, then I'll go to Collonges. ... If I can't stay there I'll change my plans. I'll stay until the following Monday, and then I'll go and stay several days in Annecy, as you will be there then. Maybe Ly could come to Collonges from Friday the 27th to Sunday the

29th. Well, we can arrange all that. But I can see that we won't see much of each other, especially since you will have to go to Lyon after a ten-day absence. Poor Jean, you are so busy. But I hope you are becoming reasonable and that you are no longer running around so much for this one and that one. ...

You said you wouldn't have time to write me a long letter before Friday. But, my dear Jean, don't take that much trouble. We will see each other soon and, God willing, you will be able to answer all my letters when we talk as we did at Easter. I'd prefer you write a little note to the parents; it makes them so happy.

Lately the weather has been so hot. I need a vacation; fortunately I'll soon have one. I'm so glad you like Ly. I like him too, and I think Annette could have done worse.

Je t'embrasse bien fort, mon cher Jean. Friendly greetings to Lizou when you see her and try to bring her back, as I would like so much to see her. We don't know each other very well, and I would like to know her better. But most of all, try to get some rest, as it would do you good.

Affectionately,
Gaby

Gaby to Jean   August 5, 1943

Mon bien cher Jean,

Yesterday afternoon Mademoiselle Milès went to the prefecture to submit my application for safe passage to Haute Savoie. I will have the answer at the end of next week, before I leave. I don't know if it will be favorable. But it's worrisome that you won't be there when I arrive and if my permit was refused, which seems to me to be improbable, you won't be there to make the request directly at the Annecy prefecture. Maybe you could leave me a note that I could show them if I was obliged to go without authorization. That would spare you having to take a step that might be useless, but at least I wouldn't risk having problems when I get there, as I must stay in a hotel. At a private home that would be less serious. ...

I wish you a good trip as you are leaving Saturday. I think you must be happy at the thought of seeing Lizou again. I hope you will bring her back with you, and most of all I hope she won't keep you until the end of the month because then I wouldn't see you at all, which would really upset me. Be nice to her so that she won't want to stay over there. ...

Get some rest. Looking forward to seeing you in two weeks. I'm sending you, my dear Jean, my best thoughts.
       Gaby

Gaby has taken her vacation in Annecy and Collonges as planned, and attended the Workers' Conference in Collonges in the first week in September.

Jean's escape line may have met some temporary curtailment in the face of danger, as suggested by a note to him which Ernestine Dubois wrote on August 24, asking him not to send any more "merchandise" for the time being:

Ernestine Dubois to Jean   August 24, 1943

... as it is very hard, if not impossible, to dispose of your merchandise. When things are going better and maybe from time to time by chance, I could accept, but otherwise I would like you to understand and not be angry with me. As soon as I can, or when there is a possibility, I would ask you in a little note or in a visit to begin sending me things again.

One can imagine that Ernestine is not referring to textile merchandise here, but people being passed along the rescue route.

In his own attestation of June 29, 1948, Jean Weidner reports that his three forms of Resistance activity continued until September, 1943: helping Dutch refugees residing in France, many of whom were Jews; helping many of these and other refugees from Allied countries to escape to Switzerland; and transmitting information for the Resistance and the Dutch Government.

Weidner reports that after the arrest of the acting Dutch Consul in Lyon, his address was found among the consular papers, and "the Gestapo came to arrest me. But I had been warned by friends and never returned to that address and went into hiding."

In October Jean made his "first trip to Paris and Brussels and made contact with Mr. Laatsman and several others."

Herman Laatsman had been at the Dutch Consulate in Paris and it was he who had carried many things to the Weidner parents in The Hague for Gaby. In Laatsman's postwar report on his activities he gives a vivid account of his first meeting with Jean in Paris on a street near Place d'Italie. Gabrielle had walked with Laatsman there from nearby "130" and pointed out Jean coming toward them on the street. Laatsman tells in detail the clandestine trip to Annecy and Lyon he subsequently took to learn from Jean first-hand about the work of which they were both now to be a part.

There was at least one more surprise for Jean on that visit to Paris: Annette was there, too. In the 1994 interview with Alberto Sbacchi, she reveals that she began to help Jean in his clandestine activity soon after she turned 21 (which happened in 1942) and could do as she wished! "I wanted to help my brother, but he said no. My sister was already involved, but he did not let me do it. So one day, all by myself, as a clandestine, I crossed the borders of Holland, then Belgium, and I got to Paris. In Paris I went to see my sister, and she was very surprised to see me, and when Jean realized that I did this trip all by myself, and also because I spoke French fluently, he let me help him."

Mama, writing to the "children" on November 1, 1943, reflects her pleasure that they have all been together, and that Jean has even seen the aunt and uncle in Belgium. She identifies Annette as "Annemarie," who used to live on the Rue Thomire. This was the Weidner family's address when they lived in Paris.

Mama to the children   November 1, 1943

... I was so glad that you saw the aunt and uncle still in good health. ... Naturally Mies was glad to see you and you met that girl Annemarie from the rue Thomire at the same time, Mies told me. You have not seen her for a long time. Did you still recognize her? She had not met with Mies for a long time either, and all of a sudden there she was right in front of her. Anyway, you know how you always teased her in the old days, but you probably did not do that this time. She has also become a lot older now. I haven't seen her in a while either, and I'd be happy to see her again, myself.

In November, 1943, Gaby is planning her next trip, this time to see the family in The Hague for the first time in over four and a half years. Jean may have been planning to join her for at least part of the trip, but then apparently his plans change.

Gaby to Jean   Paris, November 28, 1943

Mon bien cher Jean,

A few lines to tell you that I saw your friend on Friday morning. He gave me your letter and those which I was supposed to transport. I had a few errands to do Friday and this afternoon, Sunday, I would have taken them if it had been absolutely necessary. I saw Brother Meyer and he told me that he was going to take the messages himself tomorrow, Monday, which spares me the errands. I hope it is all right with you that he is the one to do it. ...

The gentleman who took care of the travel passes isn't there anymore. At least he isn't at the entrance where he used to be, and I don't know his name. I asked the parents to send me a certificate saying that Papa was sick. Maybe that way I can go. But I'm afraid Papa isn't sick enough for that.

I got a letter from the parents and I concluded that Papa wanted to go and see Aunt Hermien again in December. Are you thinking of going? I'm going to write them in the next few days to tell them that Papa would do well to do a little less traveling.

Mama says also that she can't find colored shirts for Papa, size 40, collar 41 or 42. Do you think you could get some? If not, I will ask for some ration coupons and maybe find some here.

Papa would very much like to have some real rubber suspenders. Do you think you could find some?

Would there be any way to get a nightdress for Annette, size 46. She would be very happy to get one.

So I'll see you in two weeks. But I can imagine that you won't stay long as you are probably going to spend the holidays with Lizou. Don't forget to bring money, it's important.

When you left, I had just 7000 francs left which I gave to Mlle Ok and I had a lot of expenses just then. There's always the office, but I don't like to ask for money. So I'm counting on you. Mr. L [Laatsman] is very happy about his trip. He told me that I could be very proud of you.

See you soon, kisses, Gaby

A note from Gaby to Jean with no salutation:

Wednesday, December 23, 1943

I don't have time to write you today, but you can let me know when you receive this letter. I'm sending kisses to both of you, as I certainly hope Lizou is back. Have a good holiday. Greetings from Mr. Meyer also.

Gaby

14 Gaby

Gaby returned to Paris after her dream-come-true holiday visit to her parents and Annette in The Hague. Annette managed to reach Paris to visit her, and Jean was there too, perhaps intermittently in January and February of 1944, so there was little need for letters between them.

On February 11, 1944, Suzy Kraay, "Erna," the member of Jean's Resistance group who had visited the Weidner parents in April, 1943, was arrested by French police in the Café Arc-en-Ciel ("Rainbow") at Place des Fêtes in Paris. She was carrying packages of food for Dutch-Paris refugees for their journey south from Paris to Toulouse. According to her own account, she was carrying an address book containing the names of many Dutch-Paris agents,[*] a highly irresponsible thing to do. When she and her captors left the café and went onto the street, she divested herself of the address book by dropping it onto the pavement. And, a helpful passer-by picked it up and handed to her, "You dropped this, Miss."

Suzy later testified that she was interrogated at Gestapo headquarters and threatened with torture by "bathtub". Mr. Laatsman described this torture in detail, as it was applied to him: "I was frequently plunged into the bathtub nude with my hands and feet tied, head underwater until I was blue with cold and on the point of drowning, after which they pulled me out and struck me on the chest with both hands to get the water out of my lungs. This was repeated several times. ..."[†] Suzy was also threatened,

---

[*] Deposition of Suzy Kraay, October 23, 1945, in the Weidner Collection of the John Henry Weidner Foundation for Altruism.

[†] Laatsman Report, 1945, in the Weidner Collection of the John Henry Weidner Foundation for Altruism.

she reported, with mistreatment for her father who was already imprisoned in Amsterdam. She then "confessed" and gave the names of many more Dutch-Paris agents, including that of Gabrielle Weidner.

A letter in Dutch from Gabrielle to her parents on February 24 confirms that Annette is with her and nothing is amiss. Gaby's letters in Dutch are a little less expansive than her French ones. Dutch is a struggle for her, but it pleases her father that she writes in her "native" language.

Gaby to Mama and Papa (in Dutch) Paris, February 24, 1944

Dear Mama and Papa,

You probably think I have forgotten you lately. It is true that I have hardly written since Anne Marie got here. But time flies. I'll probably feel lonely after she goes home again, but thankfully she is going to be here a little longer.

This morning we were so happy to get your letter dated the 20th. This evening Jopie will read it, too. I haven't read it all yet, because it came this morning. My friend gave it to me.

We are all going to dinner at Brother Meyer's this evening. Joop is very busy, but he stays healthy. If there were anything wrong we would write you about it. He coughs a little, but says he doesn't have time to worry about it. But it is not that bad.

Yesterday morning he saw Lizou briefly.

It has been very cold here for the last ten days. I hear the same thing is true where you are. Fortunately Papa does not have to sleep in the attic room. He would not be warm enough there. I was sorry to hear last week that he had been sick again. Thankfully he is doing better now. If possible, make sure that he eats well to get stronger. But you must eat well, too, dear Mama; don't give it all to your husband. Can't the doctor do anything for your leg? Do you still have that support hose?

Thanks for the pasta and the apple syrup. The friend who brought it will give it to us this morning. It is very sweet of you to always think of us. But we aren't that badly off. The only thing is, one has to have the money to buy extra supplies, or we wouldn't be able to survive. I have not had an apple for over a month. But just now I was able to buy 30 kilos of them, and I'm so glad. Anne Marie will eat some as well.

Tonight Brother Nussbaum will be leaving for Switzerland. He is so lucky to get a visa every time. He is also making preparations to go to Spain in March. It seems that some of our churches are being closed. But I don't know if he will get a visa for that.

Many kisses from your Miesje.

Just two days later Gabrielle was arrested by two Gestapo agents in the foyer of her church at 130 Boulevard de l'Hôpital in Paris. More than fifty years later, M. Calcia, a former member of the church at "130" told of the arrest in his own way in a letter to Jean Weidner in 1990.

... It was the Sabbath. At that time my sister Pauline was secretary of the Sabbath School; when she came out into the hall to pick up the collecting briefcase which was behind the plank which separated the vestibule and the entrance to the concierges' booth, which you remember well (as it's all changed now); when she saw two men come in dressed in black coats and hats, and she recognized right away that it was the police; then she heard them say the name of Gabrielle Weidner. She went up to them and said: Gabrielle Weidner just went out to do an errand. She realized right away that it was about you, but then, a member of the church came out and said to them, "No, she is in a group; she's listening to the lesson." And someone went to get her. I was in my group, led by the church treasurer. Someone came to get him. I had no idea what was happening; when he came back a few minutes later, very upset, he tried to take up the lesson again, but he couldn't even remember what the subject was; and he said to us, "Excuse me, something just happened..." and that was all. He went on with the lesson. It was only after the church service, that my sister told me what I am writing to you. I forgot to tell you, that they allowed Gabrielle to go and get her coat in her room, and then all three of them left.

In a 1994 interview with Alberto Sbacchi, Annette gave her own recollection of those events. Because she has lived most of her married life in Italian Switzerland, she speaks mainly in Italian, but slips back into her beloved language of French a few times.

... It was a Saturday morning and we were in church. My sister was expecting two agents from Jean, "Moen" Chait and Veerman. They should have been there already on Friday. They were one day late. We were in Sabbath school, and Brother Desmet, my sister's boss, came in and said two men wanted to talk to her. She thought that they could be the people she was waiting for and she told me to wait there and come out ten minutes later so we would not disrupt the class. I waited 10 minutes and then I went to her room, and as I opened the door, I saw that her face was very pale, and that two strangers were there. I knew these were not the people she was expecting.

When she saw me, she had a strange reaction. She asked why I hadn't knocked. 'Qu'est-ce que c'est que ces manières, à ne pas frapper à la porte?' [What kind of behavior is this, not knocking on the door?], and speaking to them, she said "I keep telling her how to behave, and that she must knock before she enters." It was very strange what she was saying, and soon after I realized that she was pretending that I was her maid, and that she was trying to teach me good manners. She wanted them to think that, and it worked well. Besides, my sister and I did not look alike. She was a brunette and I was blond. She slammed the door, and I soon realized that the two men, dressed in civilian clothes but wearing boots, were from the Gestapo.

It was terrible for me. I felt torn between two feelings. I wanted to warn Brother Desmet that the Gestapo had arrived, but on the other hand, I had sworn to my brother that I would never say that my sister had worked for him, and I had to keep that promise. So I hid under a porch on the Boulevard de l'Hôpital, where our church was, and 20 minutes later I saw Gabrielle walking with two strangers, and I never saw her again. I ran back to her room and my picture in its frame was on the bed upside down. I interpreted that as a sign of warning from my sister of a dangerous situation.

At that point I wanted John to know that she was captured, but I did not know how to find him or where he was. I went to my sister's colleague saying that if two men came in, they would find me at the usual café; I did not mention any name. I went around looking for John. I looked in many places where he could be, many different cafés, but he was nowhere. Finally, I went to a café where I knew he had met some people before and waited. At around 7pm Moen and Veerman showed up. I told them what had happened, and they gave me the name of a café where John had a meeting room. As I walked in I saw that he was upset to see me entering that place. But when I told him what happened to Gabrielle, he started to make phone calls. Everything was useless at that point. It was too late.

Pastor Meyer was arrested [in Lyon] as were many other people whose names were found in Suzy Kraay's address book...

The day after my sister's arrest, my brother asked me to go back to Gaby's room because he had given her a very important microfilm and a fake French ID for me. I thought she would probably have hidden the ID in a book, but there were so many books in the room, how could I find it? I felt just as if my hand was guided by an invisible force to a book. I opened it, and my ID was there. Then for the microfilm, the same thing happened, and let me tell you, I am not the kind of person to imagine things, but I had the concrete feeling that my hand was pulled to the gramophone. There was a rag in the horn to deaden the sound. I took out the rag and the microfilm was there, hidden in a pen. I thanked God immediately, because I knew that it was He who had pointed me to exactly where I would find them.

The next day I had an appointment at the station Gare du Nord with Oscar Meyer and my brother. ... All of a sudden my brother said that the Gestapo was there and we had to break up and each of us go in a different direction. ...

The day after that my brother told me I had to go to Switzerland. It was too dangerous to go back to Holland now that they would have found out that I also worked for him.

Both Annette and Jean were quickly routed to Switzerland separately. In the 1994 interview, Annette describes her escape via the Dutch-Paris escape line through which had passed so many of the others whom Jean's network had saved.

... It was very difficult, because the snow was so deep in February. I passed through with Veerman. At a certain moment I was too tired to go on, and I dropped to the ground. I didn't care anymore if they would catch me, and I said, "That's it. I can't take anymore." Veerman got very angry. He reminded me that my sister got caught and that my brother was in continual danger, so how could I surrender like that? That was the only way to keep me going. So I went on like an automaton, almost unconsciously. We passed through between Collonges and St. Julien. I remember, I slipped under the wire, and Veerman passed above me, and my coat tore from top to bottom completely. When I got to the other side, I thought, "now it is all over, and they're going to arrest me." The Swiss uniforms were almost like the German ones. I was so exhausted at that point, that it was too difficult to think that I was finally safe and on the right side. It was early in the morning, around 5 AM. We had passed the Salève during the night.

Gaby was taken to the prison of Fresnes. Armande Raimbault, the young bookstore secretary at the Paris church, received a note from Gaby. The letter, on two sides of a half sheet, is undated, but was probably written at the prison shortly after her arrest. Gaby asks for the things she needs and she knows exactly where everything is in her room at "130." She says that whoever brings her the package must get off the train at La Croix de Berny, a small town just a few kilometers north of Fresnes. Gaby is not at liberty to write about the prison, and her letter was probably taken out secretly.

Gaby to Armande Raimbault

Mlle Raimbault
130, Bd. de l'Hôpital
Paris 13

Ma chère Armande,

Since it is likely that I will have to be here for a while longer, I would like you if possible to send me a sleeping bag, if you haven't already, or if that isn't possible, then the gray blanket on my bed, a piece of laundry soap, a cake of bath soap, and some tweezers, which you'll find in a cardboard box beside the washstand, a bra, a pair of pajamas, a pair of socks, a tube of Sanogyl [toothpaste], two pairs of stockings; Tuesday is package day. We're allowed one food package a month. Send what you can. You get off the train at La Croix de Berny. Maybe someone who doesn't work could bring the packages. Ask Brother Desmet for the money. I will reimburse him later, as I have already spent all my money from the office here. Thanks so much. Greetings to everyone.

   Gabrielle

Also some darning cotton, in the sewing kit in the drawer of the sewing table, but not the scissors, and my glasses.

There are no more letters from Gaby. On March 13, just over two weeks after Gaby's arrest, the most anguished letter of all comes from Papa in The Hague. For fear of the censors, Papa dares not speak of the awful event he is actually talking about. At the top of the letter is the censor's stamp: "CENSURÉ" in letters a quarter of an inch high, and surrounded by a box.

Papa to Jean, Elisabeth, and Annette   The Hague, March 13, 1944

Our dear All Three,

As we are not sure where two thirds of the trio are, we are simply addressing all three of you as a group; so it's up to one of you to be the benevolent mailman, if necessary. Thanks in advance.

I really don't know how to begin, because what would you consider the most important? Forgive me if I make an error on that score.

And first, I hope you have been all together for a few days, so that you could celebrate Annette's birthday yesterday: Yesterday Miss Aimiable and the children of the lady in Wateringse Street (the name escapes me), Kover, I think. The children brought a cake and flowers. Of course today is their mother's birthday, so today my wife went to bring her candy. And a little while ago the Mulders sent one of their sons to commemorate the birth of the prodigal daughter (!) [Annette] and asked forgiveness for having treated us in the way you know about.

Madame Dumont [Papa's code for Annette may have been chosen because of her love of the mountains of her childhood] wrote to some neighbors who were nice enough to let us read the letter, which was so interesting. That lady really knows how to express her thoughts in a most wonderful way. But what saddened my wife and me so much was the news concerning her sister, a former student at Collonges, who was taken to the hospital [prison], it seems. We are anxiously awaiting her release, because she is really such a nice girl, always ready to render service. It's doubly sad as she had a lot of work ahead of her. Who will do that work now?

Madame Dumont loves her native city of Lausanne [in Switzerland, where Annette was born] so much, that she tried (or is going to try, I don't know exactly) to get closer to that city. If so, she will probably live with her sister-in-law [Elisabeth] who is also a charming person and wife of a very active businessman, who is often away from home. So the two ladies will keep each other company very nicely.

We received a card from our son dated February 23 saying that he was well, but that his wife had to stay at home because of a cold. We are awaiting news that will reassure us, as we are a little worried. In times like these, it is so easy to catch something which can get more serious. He also wrote me that he had bought two beautiful stamps for me. So, you understand that my philatelic heart beats faster right now, as I am consumed by the desire to see them and to possess them.

Old people are sometimes very stubborn; we saw that recently about Berend's father [Papa himself. "Berend" is a name that occurs frequently in the Weidner family genealogy]. He had been advised to rest for two weeks. He really needed that after his recent illness [imprisonment]. But do you think he wanted to do that? No way! And the man has his finger in everything just as if he were a young man like his son. Incorrigible people.

I am glad I could take up my lessons again. It seems Oscar is ill, so I haven't seen him for a few days. But I don't think it will be serious; he has a good constitution.

Fischer is crazy about visits these days. And he is also very curious; at least according to Sister Marie, the assistant midwife [Annemarie, Annette], whose correspondence he had the gall to open. And she was telling me that Fischer intends to visit us as well. Of course he can come, and we'll have a little chat, but as for reading his correspondence, I wouldn't even think about it. But I can't hold it against him, because after all one is the product of the upbringing provided by the parents.

But we have a beautiful prospect in that we will also have a visit from Arthur, the former sailor. He'll be able to tell us such interesting things (of course I don't dare guarantee that everything he claims to have experienced is 100% true, but anyway) and, in spite of the fact that we have little to give him, we will do our best to welcome him like a prince. When he is here, we will talk with him about you all. It is so good that he sees everything the way we do. For that he is quite admirable.

My wife is at the doctor's this morning because of her leg where one of her veins opened six weeks ago. She is in a lot of pain. The doctor says not much can be done other than keeping it very clean, that's the main thing. She doesn't sleep much at night.

It's terrible, what you wrote about that sick girl [Annette] who was delirious in the way you describe. If what she was saying were to be taken seriously, that would make trouble between husband and wife in any marriage, but you shouldn't pay any attention to it. Intelligent people don't judge anyone on the basis of what another says, but according to what they see with their own eyes. So, don't worry, OK?

My wife and I are going to hear St. Matthew's Passion in a little while. We have our tickets already. We have heard so little music since radios got so rare.

The day before yesterday I was in Amsterdam, at Ly's parents' house. They were so sad because their son's fiancée has a sister [Gabrielle] who had a rather serious accident, but I told them not to be too sad because a broken leg can be cured, and it isn't certain that the accident was even as bad as that. Let's always look at the sunny side and not the dark side, and I am sure that the doctor will do everything he can for her.

I think I told you that I am in charge of the effort; we will make for a home for abandoned children, through postage stamps. I wonder if it will have the hoped-for results.

Yesterday we had a visit from Jean's friend... But the uncle and aunt waited for him in vain, but he would still be very welcome...

Can you give me information about foreigners who come to Switzerland? I heard that they are confined. If so, is it by nationality, or by religion, or by some other system? I ask because it's always good during a conversation to be able to have something to say that they don't all know, something unpublished. And do you know how many camps and how many detainees the Swiss have? Do they work there and what kind of work do they do? How many men? How many women? Anyway, anything that can make a conversation interesting on this subject will be welcome. Thanks in advance.

Is Dr. Steiner still living? [Rudolf Steiner, founder of anthroposophy, died in Switzerland in 1925] ... and the stamp seller Clavel? Does he still have his store? Who is at the former Geneva church? Is the couple still there whose name escapes me but who sold antiques; they sold us our wooden bear which everyone here admires. Give them our greetings if you see them.

Say, just out of curiosity, how many florins are equal to a Swiss franc now? And how many French francs for a Swiss franc? I would like to know when I buy stamps for the collection. ...

I see I must stop my chatter. Greetings to mother Madame Cartier, you three, and all the friends. My wife sends a kiss to anyone who wants one.

       Your devoted,
       J.H. Weidner

At least 70 of Jean's Dutch-Paris team were arrested and imprisoned following Suzy's confession. Many were deported to concentration camps and some did not return.

Jean Weidner's secretary, Raymonde Pillot, was also arrested and imprisoned at Fresnes. She was then deported to Ravensbrück and then to Zwodau in the Sudetenland. After the war Raymonde reported that she had seen Gabrielle Weidner and Suzy Kraay at the Protestant church service in the prison at Fresnes:

... On Wednesday, March 15, I met Mlle Gabrielle Weidner and Suzie K. at the Protestant Service held at Fresnes. At that moment, Suzie K. swore before me to Mlle Weidner that she had never talked and she added herself that it would have been impossible because she had never been tortured. That was the last time I saw Mlle G. Weidner and Suzie K.

On March 21, Jean reports from Geneva, Switzerland, to his parents in The Hague on the situations of his two sisters. His letter is in Dutch.

Jean to Papa and Mama   Geneva, March 21, 1944

Dear Everyone,

Lizou, Annette, and I were so glad to receive your fine letter of March 9th. We are all doing fine. Henri came to visit us on Saturday evening. The Spring weather is nice, very sunny, and it's too bad there is a war, because it would have been nice to be together in this time of need, but keep your spirits high and trust in God, and it won't be long before we are all together again. Annette is going to go on a diet to lose weight. You can find everything you need for medication here.

I have good news about Henri's sister (the oldest) [Gaby]. She had confidence in the hospital [the prison at Fresnes] and was in good spirits. Of course it wasn't pleasant for her to be lying in a bed. But her illness is not severe, and the hospital is one of the best around, very clean and good food. (Of course it is not as good as being at home, but nothing too much to complain about, and we and our friends bring her a lot of goodies that she is allowed by her doctor.) And she is with 6 other patients whom she can talk to, so she is not bored, and the doctors allow her to do small jobs that don't tire her out, like sewing, knitting, etc. The doctors are very nice to her and treat her gently. As you can see, you don't have to worry about her. The doctors thought that it won't be long before she is completely recovered [released from prison]. Fortunately, she has nice women friends who are taking care of her and so you don't have to worry at all about her health. I am writing very honestly without hiding anything, because you might think that I am not writing the truth so as not to scare you, but I would rather explain the situation as it is, especially when it concerns health. We must pray to God that this accident does not have any dangerous consequences, and that she will soon be completely healthy again. I am convinced that it will happen.

Annette will probably go to work for a family to take care of the kids. She is very brave, but worries about her parents. She would rather have worked for them, but, alas, that is a little too far away. It seems that Ly is going to stay with Arthur, and he has a nice room and good food. Lizou always has a lot of work and she got some more with the visit of her sister-in-law [Annette] who, after a long journey, was happy to stay with her a couple of days. Her sister-in-law was just celebrating her birthday when she was there [Annette's birthday is March 12], and they had some good food, even chocolate and oranges, etc. She was happy and so were we.

Dear all of you, we often think of you and pray to God that He gives you the strength to get through these troubled times. Arthur's uncle [USA] is very courageous and we are getting good news about him; he wrote us that he he would come and pay us a short visit in about 6 weeks, and we would be happy to have him, but in this war, there is no certainty about traveling etc. We would be happy to send you food or clothing, but we will lay it away for the day when you'll be here.

Would you be able to visit a friend of mine? But I lost his address. I'll give it to you next time. His brother-in-law was a good friend of Mies. I would be happy if you could visit him some time and stay in touch with him. His name is Bekking and he lives in Amsterdam. He is a painter and is secretary of the association of independent painters. Perhaps you might be able to find his address at some bureau for addresses. Send him my best regards, also to his nephew who lives with him.

And now, au revoir, dear all, many, many kisses, and keep your spirits up. …

Jean writes to his parents again on March 29. He continues to use the codes, "Fischer," "hospital," "Henri," "Arthur," "Erna."

Jean to Papa and Mama   Geneva, March 29, 1944

Dear Everyone,

    We were happy to get your letter of March 13th. We were especially glad to hear that you are all well and that Ma and you are keeping your spirits high. Too bad that Mother is having so much trouble with her varicose veins. But we are happy to know that the rest of you are doing well and that you did not get a visit from Fischer, because I know how much Papa hates that guy. Ma must have been happy about that, too, but he may show up at some point, because he is always nosy, and he could cause lots of trouble for you. Madame Dumont, who was born in Lausanne, is going to stay another couple of days in the camp here. Yes, even when the Swiss return to their own country, they must be quarantined in a camp for 3 weeks, because the authorities are scared of diseases. Naturally, they are free to go after that. Madame Dumont came back because her brother is not in good health, and she thought it better to stay close to him. Also, her sister is not totally healthy, but we have heard nothing for the last two weeks. Henri is leaving tomorrow to visit her. He hopes the doctor will tell him she can leave the clinic, as she did not like it there at all. Let us pray for her. Arthur is coming to visit us shortly. Do you still remember him? You haven't seen him for a long time. He already has several nice children. I saw one of his sons a little while ago, a good student, he said his father's business is doing well, and that he is making money, but in a couple of months he plans to completely step out of the business by the end of the year [the war will be over by the end of the year].

    Elisabeth has an infected finger which was quite painful for a couple of days but is much better now; her husband is going on a trip tomorrow, but he'll be back in a few days. ...

    Business is going well for Joop, although he did have some setbacks last month. Joop is a little young to be conducting such big business deals, but he is learning to be more careful, and I am sure that he will overcome the difficulties without any more trouble.

    On the subject of family accounts, I am afraid that Erna told that idiot Fischer that Pa received money without accounting for it. Pa should just tell him that his son's clients or friends owed it to him but that Pa did know about these debts or what they were for, only that I sent money to Henri's father and mother who needed it and Erna [Suzy Kraay] handed it to you on our behalf. Anyway, all those accounts will be straightened out.

At the moment it is impossible to get on top of it. Banking is impossible, too, because the money can't be cleared.

Lizou sends you her regards. We hope that the war will end soon, and that we will see each other again. Have hope and faith in God.

We worry about Mies's parents' health and we hope that their daughter's accident did not sadden them too much. I am sure that their daughter will be cured soon.

Well, au revoir to all of you, many kisses and regards from us all, keep the spirit and I hope to send you more good news from us soon.

The letters from The Hague continue. Papa's handwritten letter bears the now-familiar blue censor's streak on all four sides. He is preoccupied not only with Gaby's "illness" (imprisonment), but that of Suzy Kraay and others as well. He also alludes to the fact that at the time she was arrested, Suzy was burdened with several large food packages destined for the refugees escaping from Paris by train that same evening. In this letter the "F's" are "Fischer" and "A's uncle" is again the USA.

Papa to Jean, Elisabeth, and Annette   The Hague, April 9, 1944

Our dear All Three,

Your kind letter of March 21 found us both in good health. My wife still has trouble with her varicose veins, and sometimes a lot of trouble, but she is happy to be able to think of all the blessings she still enjoys. So, you had a visit from Henri [Jean] and he celebrated Annette's birthday with you three. That's wonderful. We were happy to hear that his sister, despite her illness, is full of courage in the clinic. Let's hope she will soon be well, thanks to the good treatment and good food which can be added to what she gets.

It's charming that A's uncle wants to come visit you. You will see that he is a good pal. When he comes, you will give us news of him, right? Because I would like to know what you think of him. [The Allied landing in Normandy took place less than two months later, on June 6, 1944.] So Ly is staying with A? We are pleased to hear that he was given a good room and that he is eating well. The young should eat <u>well</u> if they can. We the elderly, can make do with less.

Do you remember the artist-painter Bekking and his 15-year-old nephew? Well, I was there the other day. He was in bed with the flu. I saw him anyway as well as the nephew who has been with his uncle for a few weeks. The last time he saw H's sister was, I think, February 26. She was well then. [Gaby was arrested on February 26th.] The boy made me laugh when he told about the things they did to keep warm, they burned everything they had. The heating question needs revision. At the same time I saw the nephew, I went to see Ly's father. I gave him Ly's greetings. Of course he returned the greetings.

You know Suzy, right? She had an accident and through her others did also. It was by carrying more than she could decently carry on the train that it happened. She will be a long time getting over it. You have to be careful when traveling. But we have to be careful all the time anyway.

Today the Mulders brought us two eggs and some flowers, because it is Mama's birthday. And I had forgotten it. So, after dinner, my wife put a magnificent cake on the table and reminded me. She said: "Gaby wouldn't have forgotten it, and maybe the others wouldn't have either." So I kissed her and she didn't want me to pay for the cake. The Mulders will come to visit tomorrow, Easter Monday.

The young De Jongs had their baby three weeks ago, Ineke, a big girl of almost 3 1/2 kilos. They were so happy. But then the nurse who was taking care of her caused her to catch diphtheria through another patient she was also caring for, and the child died a week ago. The parents are devastated. …

The F's are still good neighbors. They are always ready to be of help. The other day they even let us read an entire letter from a woman friend that we know also. The man is very helpful with the typesetting of the 4 Gospels. I also needed 4 illustrations. Well, not only did he get me the books but he even reproduced the engravings himself. He gave me a good address to get the copies done and I'll have them in a few days. Yesterday evening he helped me with the placement of the inscription on the cover.

You know our friend K., the coal merchant, right? Well, just like H's sister, he was taken sick, ten days ago. He won't get well soon, poor man, as he is badly taken with it. But there are people who aren't careful, just like me when I was young: in winter I sometimes went out without an overcoat.

Bubby's father was also taken sick. But in his case it isn't his fault. That's Bubby for you. But that didn't prevent him from catching it. Let's hope he will soon be well. I like him a lot; he is a pleasant conversationalist.

My wife has a good memory. The proof? She was telling me a little while ago that her birthday five years ago was also on a Sunday. But I'm very skeptical of that, because, although I don't have a good memory, I remember that only every <u>seven</u> years an anniversary can fall on the same day of the week. [Papa forgets about leap year, and there would have been two of them since Mama's birthday five years before—1940 and 1944—and April 9 did indeed fall on a Sunday in 1939.] But anyway, whether it was 5 years or 7 years ago, she remembers that day in Paris. What a busy day that was! Elisabeth was supposed to come, but she hadn't arrived, and then later the unforgettable telegram: "I'm coming." Complete emotional breakdown. And then the office apartment was taken, since the agreed-upon time had passed. Consternation! And yet later, in Eternity, we will see that even that disappointment had its good side.

Dear friends, I have copied a few lines for each of you. Each of you must choose your favorite. And don't fight over them. Sorry, I made a mistake: I'm not copying them, I'm translating them from Dutch. They are from Prof. Dr. J. Gunnin in "Christus Consolator":

1. Wherever you are and wherever you go, you have influence on others, and the latter can, through you, become better or become worse.

2. He who pursues happiness for himself never finds it, but he who searches for it for others' sake, finds it for himself like a happy surprise.

3. It is infinitely easier to be orthodox than to love.

N.B. Today is Wednesday, April 12. So it has been three days since I began this letter. All is well. Au revoir from both of us and from friends.

      J. H. Weidner

Jean thinks that the Allied bombing raids may be getting in the way of the Dutch-Paris escapes, as he writes to General Van Tricht in Berne on April 30, 1944. General Van Tricht is the brother of Dr. Van Tricht in Monte Carlo, who has been serving on the refugee committee.

Jean to Van Tricht   April 30, 1944

... at this time the trains are having a lot of trouble getting through after bombing raids, and the situation in France is very tense. I think it would be better if we could limit travel to Spain as much as possible, and the verifications in the Pyrenees seem to be more rigorous and more dangerous than last year. Of course we will keep our services entirely at your disposal to facilitate as much as possible the departure of people toward Spain, if you think it's necessary.

Through friends, Jean hears encouraging news about Gaby. He writes his parents in Dutch in early May. In his letter "Maryse" is Annette. The parents will understand because Annette's full name is "Annemarie."

Jean is not too far off in his calculations of "Arthur's uncle's" visit, as it will come in the form of the Allied landing in Normandy on June 6.

Jean to Papa, Mama, and Annette   Geneva, May 2, 1944

My dear All,

Coming home on Sunday evening, I was glad when Lizou handed me the letter that Joop Sr. [Pa] sent on April 9th, and his wife's letter from April 16th. I spent a couple of days visiting Sister Massange and I sent you a few words from her as well. I hope you received it. I am traveling a lot for my business, and my dear wife is not too happy about it, but of course I have to work hard to earn my bread and butter. Business is good, never the way one would like it, but I am happy nonetheless. In a few days I am going to visit my clients in order to make new contacts. If I have time I will visit Henri's wife [Jean's wife, Elisabeth] but that depends on how much time I have left. The word here is that it is very hard for you to travel, and it is the same in Belgium and France. The trains are working well and there are seats available. Of course it is not the same as before the war, it is more expensive, but that is the way it is. Charlotte [Belgium] is well, but her husband makes it hard for her, she is not even allowed to leave the house without permission. A real criminal, but anyway, the doctors think he is not going to live much longer, and I believe that in her heart Charlotte is hoping for that. She cannot go on living like that.

I have good news about Gaby. She is in good spirits, and good health, though of course she must stay in the clinic a bit longer, but the doctors told her that it is only for convalescence and that she did not have anything wrong with her lungs. I spoke to a friend of hers who was lying in the bed next to her for a month, and she said that the clinic was very good. In Switzerland the clinics are very good. Of course the food is not as good in all of them, but the one Mies is in is one of the best. She has a nice window and fresh air. I am glad that you have met the artist-painter. So sad for mother that she has those varicose veins. Lizou was happy with your letters and her finger is much better. Arthur is doing well and will come to visit us soon. I hope to be home when he comes, because I love to hear his stories. He also has such an eccentric uncle who can be very comical, but is a fine, very generous gentleman. He wrote me a nice letter with an invitation to come and visit him for a few days, but I don't have much time and within 3 weeks he is coming to visit us anyway.

I forgot Ma's birthday, but I think of her all the time and soon we will be together and I have a number of presents to give. Many kisses for Ma's birthday, keep up your spirits, we will soon be together. The 3 thoughts Pa wrote about were beautiful, but I am too shy to decide which is the most beautiful one, so I am taking all three, but that may be too selfish.

Maryse is doing well, but I haven't heard anything from Ly in a while. Maryse's sister [Gaby] is well and very patient; she reads the Bible often and busies herself doing jobs that her health allows. Her nurses appreciate her a lot, but that is understandable, because everyone who knows her loves her. But her doctors find that she does not look well. We always must have faith in God and pray for everyone we love. Everything is fine between Jean and Elisabeth. Of course they have a lot to learn about each other. Jean is very happy with his dear wife, she really has the gentle character that he appreciates a lot. Jean has changed a lot. He is much nicer to his wife and takes care not to get nervous. I believe that he has made much progress in that area and besides he does not have the financial worries that he had in the past. Jean's superiors appreciate him very much and as long as he stays healthy, I believe that he has a beautiful future ahead of him. He has a father and mother who gave him a good upbringing, and one can see their results. They have a nice apartment with telephone and a nice radio, the latest model Philips with 6 tubes. He doesn't like his mother-in-law much; she has a beautiful heart, but does not belong in the same category, she is uneducated, and not sociable, but that will all get better after the war is over. ... We are grateful to God that He has spared you in the bombing of The Hague. We pray for you every day in the morning and evening without skipping a day. Make sure you eat well, spend your last cent on food, don't save any money, spend it all on provisions so you are able to eat well, that is the main thing, and your family has money for you anyway after the war, so don't worry about it. Best regards to the whole family.

Au revoir, all of you have faith in God and many kisses from Lizou and me, and many thanks for all the letters from Ma and her husband. ...

A letter from Papa to "Our Three": Papa reassures his family about how "the Fransdonks' house" (where their apartment is on the second floor) fared in a recent bombing.

Papa to Jean, Elisabeth, and Annette   The Hague, May 15, 1944

Our dear Three,

Debts must be paid, so now to work, as I have before me a postcard dated April 26, and a letter of March 29, this last from Geneva where you all three live, and the card from the native city of one of you three [Lausanne]. ...

As for our accounts, you think the way we do: all that will be settled after the war. In the meantime we will do as circumstances require. We are very happy to be in very different financial circumstances than during the last war. We buy necessities without looking at the price—unless it is completely unaffordable. We have been doing this for a year, and we both feel much better. Otherwise I don't think I would have survived, and maybe neither of us would have. ...

Erna's [Suzy's] father is really unlucky. You know that he was taken sick [imprisoned] at the same time his daughter was, right? Or rather for a lot longer. After seven months he got out of the clinic. His wife was so happy and so was he. But then he had a relapse so that they had to take him back on the same day. We tried to console his poor wife, but her grief is deep. And then to have her daughter taken ill abroad, without being able to go to her or have her brought home, is also a cross for the unfortunate mother to bear. Everyone had his own cross to bear.

At last, I have the joy of finding someone interested in publishing one of my essays. Every day I expect to receive proofs from the printer. It will be a 72-page brochure entitled, "Why these four?", indicating the common goal as well as the particular goal of the four Gospels. It is divided into 16 small chapters. There are also a few illustrations. Of course it will be a very limited edition because of the paper shortage. But when the war is over, there will be other brochures to follow, God willing. ...

So you say that everybody is talking about upcoming events. It's the same here. I think that throughout the whole world, there is only one wish:

that the war ends. Many believe that everything will be over this year. I don't know, but I also hope so, if only to be able to see the three of you. What a wonderful day that will be! Where will it be? In Holland? In Switzerland? Elsewhere? What about our Gaby?

We are glad that Jean takes such good care of his sister who is ill. It is a great comfort to her and for those who love her. I know that the parents appreciate it enormously.

It's funny: every time we receive a letter from you and other friends, we are very happy for a time. But after a few days we begin to long for another missive. We are never satisfied.

You know, it's not true that the Fransdonks' house had a lot of damage. Don't believe it for a minute. They themselves were not hurt, and the inhabitants on the second floor weren't either. All that happened was that at a certain moment some cracks appeared in the ceiling in various places. That's all, and I can assure you of this positively. Besides the house is old. The important thing is that neither the inhabitants of the second nor the third floor were injured. The teacher's [Pa's] wife even stayed in bed the entire night and her husband was only up for two hours. So don't let people exaggerate when they write their "news" to you.

Annette, you are lucky to have a lot of invitations. Isn't that the same for all those who were born in Lausanne? ...

They're predicting the end of the war for the day after August 6. Why? Because when people think of that date they will say "C'est tout" ["That's all," and "C'est tout" sounds more or less the same as "Sept Août" or "August 7"].

My wife is taking free swimming lessons. We have a lot of opportunity for it now. But she doesn't know how to dive; and she doesn't know how to swim under water. ... Someday my wife and I will have a contest to see who can be the first to swim from here to Gouda.

I think it was two months ago that we heard that Oscar had the same illness as his brother [Paul Meyer was arrested when the Gestapo came to his home looking for Jean Weidner and didn't find him]. It was probably an error. If he is well, that's good. ...

Say, do you remember this boy from C. [Collonges, and the boy is Jean]? Have you heard from him? He is a boy who is very daring. His parents are always afraid that he risks too much. But we think he is careful not to buy merchandise that will ruin him. I think he likes traveling and climbing.

Arthur and his uncle send greetings. As soon as they can they will visit friends. Only right now it isn't very profitable to come to people's houses, as they have nothing left to give. You have to bring your own food. But let's hope that will soon change.

I'll stop my chatting. You can see by this letter that we are still alive and that we haven't forgotten you.

Many greetings from both of us.
          Papa

In his letters to Joop (in Dutch) and Elisabeth (in French) Papa foresees the possibility that he will not survive the war.

From Annette, Papa has learned that Jean has been imprisoned. Jean was arrested, along with two fellow agents, in Toulouse on May 20, as he was preparing to take some messages and information to England. One of the other agents managed to escape on his own. On May 29, Weidner succeeded in persuading one of his guards to transfer him and his remaining comrade to a lower floor in the prison, making it easier for them to escape through a window on the third floor and jump to the ground.*

Papa to Jean   The Hague, June 25, 1944

My dear Joop,

Received your interesting letter from the mountain area. We heard from A. already that you had left the clinic, but now we actually got something you sent yourself. We appreciated that tremendously. Joop and his parents live right next to each other, at least if one measures from the heart.

Yes, that must have moved you quite a bit when you came so close to the grocery store that so tempted you in the past. And all those memories from the past: the pink chalet and the school and the trips with your father to the Col des Mosses. It is true that we didn't have much money, but that's why you learned to cope and overcome the difficulties. That is more valuable in life than money, because it shapes one's character, and character is forever ...

---

* John Weidner's Deposition for the Defense in the trial of Inspector Brunner, June 21, 1948, in the Weidner Collection of the John Henry Weidner Foundation for Altruism.

We hope that your wife got her papers quickly and that you still had a good vacation. Perhaps it turned out to be a second honeymoon.

And now you want to know how things are with us? Well, now, dear fellow, everything here is just fine. We lack nothing. Ma is making progress with her foot. The hole is getting smaller and yesterday for the first time in seven months we took a walk together. How do you like that? And we did not use the chair I bought for Ma (a wheelchair) but walked the whole way and came back by tram, getting off close to the house. In the past we had to watch every dime we spent, but nowadays we are giving it out without even thinking about it.

I am grateful that I am still able to do a lot of work, even though I am starting to forget a lot of things, worse than before. I am doing some teaching, Dutch, French and English and also the Bible. The Head Deacon from Utrecht comes to take a double lesson here every week. He is also the one who bought and published my manuscript on the four Gospels. Too bad that the printer promised to do this months ago already but has not done so yet. However, he said he would do it this week. We'll see …

I mentioned that I bought a wheelchair for Ma. Why? It was not because I thought she would become an invalid, but for a different reason. Foresight is power, is it not? It is with a sudden forced exit in mind. Just imagine that we would be forced to evacuate the premises within two hours, then what? And if Ma were already tired from errands, then she would not be able to do that. After worrying about that a lot, and I saw the opportunity to buy that wheelchair for 125 guilders, I thought, "I'll take that." I'll be able to wheel Ma at any time it becomes necessary. Now I have peace of mind. I wanted to wheel her around yesterday, but she did not want that, only when it is really necessary. And we'll hope that will never happen. The chair is not idle however, for right now, while I am writing this letter, I am sitting in it, and it is very comfortable.

Listen, dear fellow, one never knows what will happen, so your mother and I have taken precautions, within our limits.

We rented a safe-deposit box, not to put our treasures in, because we have none. However, we did put stamps in it rather than keep them here. If something happens, they will be safer there than here at home. … The cost is 40 guilders until mid June next year. … Ma and I both have rights to it on any day, and if anything should happen, you have the right to act as you see fit and make arrangements with your little sisters. We know that you won't have any trouble with each other.

Dear boy, you know what I am thinking about right? Suppose this would be the last letter I would send you, what would I recommend the most? Here it is: First of all for yourself, that you would always live close to Jesus by not regarding Him as a hard master but as a close friend to whom you can tell everything, and who has infinite patience with you. ... He makes us go through all kinds of experiences to finally take us where we need to be. ...

Secondly, take care of all of those who are close to you, first of all the woman you have joined your life with. And just by taking care of her and others, family acquaintances, and finally everyone you are helping, you will see greater happiness yourself. ... Don't be impatient, but trust Jesus and you will get all the help you need. That does not mean that you will always conquer everything, but you will learn a lot more about how to conquer it the next time, and if you fall, learn to fall less often and not quite as deep.

I do not urge you to care for your mother or for your sisters, in case I am not there anymore, because I know that by nature you cannot refuse that. But never do anything that is not in harmony with the one who shares the secrets and bitternesses of life with you. Bye, dear fellow, let us hope that we will see each other soon in Geneva or elsewhere, ...

Also from Ma, many kisses, your always-thinking-of-you
 Pa

Papa to Elisabeth   The Hague, June 26, 1944

Our very dear Lizou,

Forgive me for having written to Jean in Dutch, as I cannot undo my tendency to watch over him as to what I taught him when he was still in my Dutch class in the old days. That way he can practice reading in Dutch as well as translating it. Maybe the letter can even serve as a "textbook" when you are filled with the desire to learn this widely spoken language.

Come to think of it, I could write you a textbook, but I fear that it would be too much of a good thing. But I beg for a little patience on your part for every time I make an error [in French]. Agreed? Thanks in advance.

All our congratulations now that Jean is entirely well. And yes, he must have suffered intensely from the uncertainty about where you might be. Your thoughts must have been with him constantly. And our thoughts and sympathy were with you constantly. How glad we were to get the news of his return to health, not only for us but also for you. We hope you were able to take a vacation with him, and that you are both trying to outdo each other in the effort to spoil each other. We followed you in our thoughts through your outings and excursions "High up high on the mountain, there is an old chalet." (As you can see I quote it in my own way.) I am just thinking of that passage from St. Paul and applying it to you: "Perhaps he was separated from you for a time so that you could get him back for all eternity." Philemon 13. ...

Do you want to know why particularly I am writing this letter to you? Here is the reason: We are on the eve of great events; everybody agrees. And as that will involve the sacrifice of thousands and thousands of men, that could also be our own destiny. True, we can count on the aid and protection of God's angels. But that does not necessarily imply that we won't die as victims of such and such an accident. Certainly, sometimes the children of God are protected materially in a really miraculous fashion, but it is not that which should interest us primarily. We should look at things from a higher point of view. And so we see material things as subordinate to definitive and eternal things. ... So I say to myself, "If you no longer had the privilege of seeing Lizou, what would you say as a last farewell?" And that is why I am writing the following. ...

I cannot think of you, dear Lizou, without thinking of him whom you have chosen as a travel companion. I know you are united with him in your heart and that he also loves you tenderly. And I can already see you both, when we have left you behind, trying to make each other happy, by completing each other. ...

I'm not going to ask you to be good to him, as that would be an offense since you are filled with tenderness for him. But this is what I think: the greatest happiness is when, besides affection, there is unity of thought and of goal.

When Jean felt drawn to you, I planned to give you instructions in the same principles I raised him on, but circumstances have prevented me from executing my plan. But I have seen your readiness to accept these principles, and I told Jean I was sure that you would let yourself be led in the right way. But for every type of person there are dangers, as there are for you also: a docile nature needs to be placed under a good influence, without which this docility and resignation may not bear fruit... Those who have a strong tendency toward docility must be careful not to let individuality be crushed. ... They must choose intelligently the ways they will be influenced...and that instrument is, above all, Jesus. ...

It is possible—and I wish it for you with all my heart—that sooner or later you will see in a tiny little being the reflection of yourself and of Jean. In that case, my dear Lizou, try to discover in him or her what are his or her character traits. He or she will have some tendencies that should be atrophied and others which must be fortified. But then, the danger will exist, as always, when the child needs modification, that the father or the mother will not see the necessity of it. May God preserve you both from such an error. And if the child has too much of a tendency toward docility, then develop very early a tendency toward independence, and if he has Jean's tendencies, develop his or her docility. If this is done in careful and constant way, later on the satisfaction will be great for you, for Jean and for no. 3.

If this were to be the last letter written to you by my hand, it will not win any prizes on the score of poetry or sentiment, but I am aiming especially at the practical side, and I have confidence that you will take it as such, am I right?

And above all, may we see each other again at the great meeting when the uncertainty of life and of death makes room for the happy reality and the unshakable certitude of eternal life with Jesus.

We both kiss you affectionately as one of our daughters, and ask you to give our greetings to your mother.

        Your Dutch Papa

Jean writes a long letter in Dutch to his parents on July 10. He has encouraging news about Gaby through friends who can gather such news safely. Jean is now a hunted man, and Gaby's captors hope to catch Jean by holding Gaby hostage.

Jean reveals that Annette's fiancé Lykele has reached England and that Elisabeth's mother is still a problem. Jean's own marriage is not going well.

Jean to his parents   Geneva, Monday July 10, 1944

My dear All,

We were so glad to receive 2 registered letters: one from Papa and one from Ma. That was worth celebrating. Lizou was also very happy to get a letter. Lizou likes getting letters, but she does not easily write one. Last week we got a letter on Monday, too, yet in the past it was always on Friday. As long as we get it, that's the main thing. Last week I wanted to write, but it got neglected because of all the work I had. But I am determined that this letter goes in the mail today. Annette is with her Aunt Vaucher. I'll send her the letters in a little while. She is also longing for news. I was so happy with the previous letters and read them carefully. I enjoyed them very much.

We are of course very worried about you in these special circumstances. We are however putting our faith in God that He may take care of us, that we may see each other soon, and as Papa said: if for some reason it's not here on earth, then it will be a while later in heaven. I am so convinced that we are living in a special period right now and that we can learn much from the Bible by studying the prophecies. What we are going through today will serve as an example for Christians later. But I have such a desire to see you again. I have so many questions to ask Papa about so many things, and to do that in a letter would make it too long.

This war confronted us with so many problems that we never thought about in the past, but Papa knows how to apply principles for whatever is happening and I would like to know his opinion about that. Also about my relations with Lizou's mother and Lizou herself, but it gets too long to explain everything in a letter. We will have many stories to tell and many questions to ask each other.

The latest news about Mies is that her health is good. She is still in the same hospital. That news came from around June 20th. I hope to get a letter one of these days, as well as one from a friend of mine who is able to get news of her. She is well taken care of, however, and her morale is good. Dr. Arthur [England] will be visiting her soon and he has a good treatment for her, so she will be cured within 2 months, he told me. She is surrounded by nice people; the other patients are very nice and they all encourage each other and if one of them gets a letter or news from home, they all read the letter, so you see that the spirit is good there. When sick persons are separated, they think right away that it is terrible, but when they are all together, they see that they are not the only ones. They can be cured, and they are well taken care of. I know that you love her very much and she often thinks of you. She is not able to write you in her condition, but her friends will write for her and will read our letters to her and when she gets stronger and her arm is not as weak any more, she will be able to sit up in bed and she will at once write to you herself. Yes, that accident she had was very sad, but luckily her life is not in danger. Her brother is doing well. On that day, God helped him in a miraculous way, so he was not in that same accident. I am so thankful to Ma that she writes regularly, so it is nice to hear news at regular times that everything is still all right. I was happy to hear that the varicose veins are healing. Yes, it is my opinion as well that to stay healthy you must eat the best food. It does not help to save money now and become sick later, for you would then spend the money on medical treatment. ...

Yes, it has already been five years since I have seen Ma. But be of good cheer, as I am sure I will see you soon. I have already taken steps to get a visa for my business and I hope to be able to leave shortly. Perhaps you'll be able to come here for a visit and return to Switzerland to visit little François's grave. ...

As for Maryse, on the outside she looks normal, but she says that she is very nervous and not able to sleep etc. It would not surprise me that her nervousness was caused by her treatment. In one month's time, she has lost a lot of weight by taking those extracts. It could very well be that her body went through a change or something, and that her nervous system has become weaker. It may get better when her body becomes more stabilized. She is with her aunt and does not have to do anything so she is able to rest and enjoy the care of La Lignière clinic. I am certain that she is going to do better after a while. I gave her money so she can eat well, as she needs that. So you do not have to try to send money to her, she has all she needs.

The health of Dr. Arthur's uncle is just fine. He is completely healed of the illness he had 3 years ago. Brother Deddike [Germany] fell down the stairs and tore his whole right side open. He had an operation, but there is not much hope. He is too old and lived a bad life. His blood is bad and his resistance is weak. The doctor told his wife that she should be prepared because he may only live to the end of the year at best. Sad, isn't it? Papa had lived with him for a couple of years and probably feels sad about it too. That Charlotte really is some woman, one day she acts this way, the next she acts differently, but she is nice. Her mood changes so often, that no one knows what her character is like. But she has some good qualities nevertheless. The divorce from her husband is almost settled and she will be able to marry again 2 months from now. She is already living with that man, but then she will marry him officially. Morally this is not quite right, but it is hard to talk to her about this subject. It is difficult when it's someone else's family business. We are trying to get some news from Ly. The last we heard was on January 21 when he left the Sanz-Loringham family …

That idea of a wheelchair for Ma is beautiful. That way you don't have to worry too much. But I had to laugh when Papa said he was sitting in it. Watch out! I can picture Pa sitting in it and Ma pushing it! It was a good idea to rent that safe deposit box. I will save the address in case I need it.

Pa, Lizou loved the letter you sent her, and of course I read it too. The encouragement you gave me made me stronger. I liked it that you gave us some advice as if it were the last time. I'll save those letters, and I'll read them again, because one can learn a lot from them. I am so convinced that we will see each other again. Yes, my biggest worry is to stay in touch with Jesus. Of course I won't get any help with that from Lizou. She is too much under her mother's influence, and that makes it difficult with her French character. But just because of the fact that she won't be any help in my spiritual life, I am being extra careful not to be drawn into that. I am sure that if I could be totally alone with Lizou without her mother, it would be much easier for me. The way I see it, I cannot live with Lizou when her mother is nearby. I keep telling myself that there is war on and that I must be patient. Lizou still has to learn a lot of things, but she is sincere and easily influenced. It may take years before she understands us. Her mother always criticizes everyone and is very unsophisticated. She never tried to educate Lizou more spiritually. That mother is a misanthrope and she planted a certain mistrust of others in Lizou's heart. Lizou never lived with her father or with brothers or sisters, so that is one whole side of her education that she missed out on. She does not understand a lot of things. But she wants to do well, and I can learn a lot from her, because in many ways her character seems closer to Jesus's than mine. But we must progress together. I find that she has progressed with a lot of things and she thinks that I have, too. I know nobody is perfect, and I thank God that I have such a good wife with a gentle character, because I certainly could not have been happy with anyone else, because of the character I have. But I must have patience. If her mother weren't there, everything would go smoother. There is always friction between the mother, whose daughter remains her daughter, and the husband, who keeps saying, "she is my wife." It's hardest on Lizou, caught between her mother whom she loves and me whom she also loves. Sometimes when the mother goes too far, I have to tell her to stop it. I don't want her to be the boss, and I don't want Lizou to forget that I am her husband and that she has obligations toward me. Fortunately she has done better with that lately. Anyway, I will be able to explain it better at a later time. I will tell you also what I had to endure from her mother. Though she is honest and good-hearted, she is not intelligent and does not compare to our standard of moral and intellectual life.

The main thing is that Lizou and I continue to love each other, pray often, and read the Bible. That way we are always prepared to go forward in life. As Pa described it, I have to learn to take the first step. I do that sometimes, but not as much as Lizou, whose character is better than mine, and also for another reason. If I am angry and am not talking to her, it touches her more than if I speak to her in a loud voice. Being French, she forgets quickly, and if I say something nice to her she thinks, "Oh, so it's not so bad," and she forgets easily, but if I don't let go immediately, it makes a deeper impression on her. Anyway, sometimes I don't know what to do and then I think, "If I do this, it will be an advantage, but it can also be a disadvantage and if I do it differently, the outcome is going to be the same." But when I see what trouble some of my friends are going through with their wives, then I am grateful to God that I have such a good Lizou. Of course it would be best if Lizou could talk with Papa. Papa could explain all those things to her. She has a lot of respect for Papa, and she thinks he is very impartial because of the fact that once he told me I was wrong.

You are never out of our thoughts and we are certain that we will see each other again. Keep up your spirits. Many thanks, Pa and Ma, for your letters. They strengthen our morale. Do not worry about us at all. I am definitely taking a vacation with Lizou at the end of the war. The business is not doing anything anymore, so you don't have to worry that I am overworking myself.

Best regards to the whole family.

Many, many kisses ...

It is almost two months after the Allied landing. When Jean writes to the Minister from The Netherlands about plans they must make for the eventual return of Dutch detainees from concentration camps, Gaby is still in prison in France.

Jean to the Minister from the Netherlands Geneva, July 31, 1944

... We must not forget those of our compatriots who are at this time in prisons and camps and day after day await their deliverance. Yet it is clear that the Allies will not free all those detained as soon as they arrive without first getting information on the reasons for their arrest. If one of our qualified representatives is present and activates the inquiry and gives information, those persons will be liberated that much more quickly. ...

To General Van Tricht in Berne, Switzerland, Jean writes about a disturbing message he heard on Radio London.

Jean to Van Tricht Geneva, August 14, 1944

... The day before yesterday, I heard on Radio London that the Germans have given the order that 1500 political prisoners from Paris should be transferred to Metz and massacred en route. I am very worried about my sister who is one of them.

Jean to Van Tricht August 17, 1944

... I hope to go home soon to take care of my compatriots in need and get those out of prison who are there for our cause... I am so happy that things are going so well. I can't wait to see if my sister can soon be freed in Paris if she has not been taken away from there. ...

But Gaby had been taken away, just three days before. On August 14, the day that Jean had written to General Van Tricht about his fears for Gaby, she was seen boarding a train, the last train to leave Paris with deportees headed for concentration camps in Germany.

This last train, "le dernier convoi," pulled out of Pantin Station in Paris just before midnight on August 15th, 1944, carrying prisoners from Fresnes and other detention points.* But in Nanteuil, only 100 kilometers northeast of Paris, a railroad bridge had been destroyed by Allied and Resistance bombing and the train could go no further. During the day of the 16th, the prisoners were forced to carry German baggage and booty through the village and around the destroyed bridge. For those at the end of the train (and this would have included Gaby, as the prisoners were placed in the railroad cars in alphabetical order) this was a foot journey of five to six kilometers. The inhabitants of the village, fearing to approach the guarded prisoners, left food and water on their doorsteps, and a few managed to put supplies into the hands of the prisoners, but most were brutally beaten back by the German guards who also "took pleasure in knocking over containers on the doorsteps." Several prisoners were able to escape with the help of the villagers. The over 2000 prisoners spent the night in a field guarded by the Germans near the railroad station on the other side of the Marne River. In the morning prisoners continued their journey to the concentration camps of Buchenwald and Ravensbrück.

On this train were also a number of other members of Dutch-Paris, Jean Weidner's escape network, including Herman Laatsman. Both of Christiane de Renty Beaujolin's parents were on this train. Since the men's and women's cars were widely separated, neither knew that the other was on the same train. Christiane's mother, the Countess de Renty, learned only after her liberation from Ravensbrück in 1945, that her husband had been on the train and died in Dora Buchenwald the previous December.

On August 25, 1944, just eleven days after the train bearing Gaby departed from Paris, the city was liberated.

"At last Paris is liberated," writes Charles Wehrli to Jean from Switzerland on August 27. "The sound of German boots will no longer be heard there."

Jean takes the clandestine route back to France in September. Elisabeth, who remains in Switzerland, still hopes for news of Gabrielle.

Elisabeth to Jean   Friday evening, August 15, 1944

Mon cher petit Donald,

Your letter came this evening. I thank you with all my heart. ... I'm giving this note to Armand [Lap] and I don't know when you will get it. ...

---

* Survivors' recollections of this final train journey from Paris have been published in *Le Dernier Convoi*, in the collection "Les Cahiers de la Résistance Seine-et-Marnaise," no. 1, Association National des Anciens Combattants de la Résistance. A commemoration of this day takes place annually at Nanteuil.

I think that your trip probably went well under the best conditions, and I want so much for you to get news of Gabrielle very quickly. I'll be waiting with great impatience for good news of you, and I would have liked to be a part of the convoy, but there is never room for the little mouse.

I'll write you again at the Maison du Coupon [Weidner fabric store in Annecy] and in Lyon so that you hear from me right away, and if I have the chance I will write you a note in the capital via Simone. Goodbye, my dear little Donald, think sometimes of your little Mickey who wonders when she will at last be with her little duck for good.

I'm sending you much tenderness and je t'embrasse de toute mon affection.

Gaby was taken to the women's concentration camp of Ravensbrück and transferred to its satellite camp of Konigsberg, a civilian work camp, where she arrived in mid-October. The winter of 1944-1945 in Europe was the coldest in many years. As the Russians approached, the Germans abandoned the camp on February 5, 1945. But with her weakened health, Gabrielle was not able to withstand concentration camp conditions. She died in the arms of a friend on February 15, 1945.

Afterword

In the tranquil and beautiful Dutch Cemetery north of Paris, Gabrielle Weidner's name appears on one of the bronze plaques in a small memorial structure at the back of the green lawn. In both French and Dutch, the plaque is dedicated "To the memory of the Dutch Resistants in France who died for the liberty of their country and its allies during the war of 1940-1945." Gabrielle Weidner is the thirteenth and last name on the list. On another plaque in both Dutch and French is inscribed: "The land for this cemetery is a gift of the people of France."

Jean Weidner made a number of unsuccessful attempts to have Gabrielle's remains repatriated. In 1947, he was still making appeals for information from anyone who had been in the Petit Konigsberg concentration camp. One answer came from M.Th. (probably Marie-Thérèse) Henry, hospitalized with tuberculosis of the bone since her release from the camp. The letter is translated from French. It was handwritten and dated November 24, 1947.

"I knew Gaby rather well in the camp. We were a part of the same barrack in Block 8. Then later I joined her in the work detail where we shared the same bunk structure. We stayed together more than six weeks, six long weeks during which I watched helplessly the wasting away of her strength and her fight to hold on until the victory. And she came very close. When we were freed by the Russians, we had to depart from the camp, leaving in a mass grave eighteen of our comrades.

"… With all my heart, I will try to do whatever I can for the brother of Gaby for whom I had not only a sincere affection, but also a very great admiration."

Jean traveled to Poland in March, 1977, hoping to visit Gabrielle's final resting place. He was shown only the field where the prison camp had been.*

Suzy Kraay, whose arrest resulted in the detainment and deportation of many members of Jean Weidner's rescue network, married a concentration camp survivor and had two sons. She lived in Amsterdam and denied being Suzy Kraay until 2017, when two Simon brothers whom she had successfully rescued as children tried to find her. They had read the Dutch edition of Megan Koreman's book, *The Escape Line* (published under the title *Gewone Holden*) and hoped to thank Suzy Kraay for saving their lives. Maarten Eliasar was approached by Mr. Simon in January 2017, and the brothers met with Suzy in April of that year. It was then that she admitted for the first time who she was. "She felt re-habilitated," writes Maarten, and getting in touch with the Simon brothers had, in her own words, "shed some light on the end of her largely ruined life." Suzy Kraay died in May, 2019.

Annette remained in Switzerland where she had escaped after Gabrielle's arrest. She was hospitalized for some time and under a doctor's care for several years. In 1950, for a change of scene, she spent a semester at Pacific Union College, a Seventh-day Adventist college in California. Her then fiancé, Charles Hipleh, was awaiting the finalization of his divorce from his first wife during this time. On her return from California, Annette married Charles, who was a dentist in Ascona, in the Italian part of Switzerland. So her yearnings to live again in a French-speaking country were somewhat realized, though in her interview with Alberto Sbacchi in 1994, she speaks almost entirely in Italian.

Annette and "Charly" had two children, a son Carlo, born in 1951, and a daughter Ariane, born in 1953. Charly died in 1979. Daughter Ariane, trained as a children's nurse in Geneva, had been trying to free herself from a drug dependency for at least two years when she died in 1984. Carlo had some difficulty finding his way in life, and, like his sister, struggled with drug addiction. He became ill and died in 2004 at the age of 43. His death ended the descendancy of "Papa" and "Mama" Weidner.

Annette lived in Ascona until her death in August, 2004.

Lykele Faber, Annette's fiancé at the time of his escape from The Netherlands in 1943, worked for a time with Jean in Annecy. Lykele then

---

* Naomi Weidner in an interview with Megan Koreman, Las Vegas, October 13, 2009.

went to England via Spain. He was parachuted into The Netherlands and was a part of the Battle of Arnhem in September, 1944. He survived this ill-fated operation and was later parachuted again into the north of The Netherlands.

Curiously, Annette says in her interview with Alberto Sbacchi in 1994, that Lykele died at the battle of Arnhem, but he actually survived the war, married another woman in 1946, and lived in Canada until he died in 2009.

Annette must have known, however, that Lykele did not die at Arnhem. On June 13, 1945 (more than a month after the end of the war and nine months after the battle of Arnhem) Annette wrote to her brother Jean: I have heard from Ly [Lykele] … Last week I received a letter dated May 13 from London, and he said he was leaving for Germany for three months. Yesterday I got a telegram sent June 7 in which he says he went to Holland, that all is well and that he found an apartment for us in The Hague."

Papa and Mama Weidner remained in The Hague at war's end. In his first visit to them after the war, Jean brought them the terrible news that Gabrielle had not survived deportation.

In 1946, with Jean's help, Papa was able to realize his dream of visiting the United States, where he attended the Adventist conference in Washington D.C. In 1947, while he and Mama Weidner were visiting Annette in Switzerland, he was taken ill and died at the Adventist clinic in Gland.

Mama's last years were lonely and sad. She lived in The Hague for a few years and then came to live with Annette and Charly and baby grandson Carlo, but the relationship was a fractious and difficult one, according to Annette's letters to Jean. Mama died in 1960, in Switzerland.

Elisabeth Cartier Weidner, Jean's first wife, never returned to her husband for any length of time. She spent most of her time with her possessive mother in Switzerland, and Jean divorced her on the grounds of desertion in 1955. When interviewed by Alberto Sbacchi in 1994, Simon Rudi, a Weidner business associate after the war, said, "Jean told me he was not married to Elisabeth but to her mother." Rudi added that Jean did not have the patience to deal with this. Gisèle Sevenster-Dominicus observes during her interview with Sbacchi that Elisabeth's mother would say to her daughter: "You are too beautiful to wait for a boy who is doing these things and not making any money at it."

In her own interview with Sbacchi in 1994, Elisabeth expresses surprise that Jean Weidner's accounts of his wartime activities mention her work only briefly and do not reveal that she had been his wife. Sbacchi speculates that this may have been because divorce was frowned upon in Adventist circles, but Elisabeth believes that Jean's refusal to acknowledge her role was out of bitterness on his part.

Yet, when Jean Weidner talked with Alberto Sbacchi in 1994 about the latter's upcoming travels to interview Dutch-Paris agents in Europe, he encouraged Sbacchi to go and see Elisabeth as "she was my right arm. I could not have done this work without her."*

After the war Jean Weidner served for a time as investigator for the "Bureau de Recensement," with the rank of Captain in the Dutch Army. He was delegated by the Dutch Government to distinguish the true Dutch Resistance heroes working in France, from former collaborators trying to whitewash their records. This was a difficult if not impossible task, and he offended a number of prominent Dutch people by coming too close to the truth as it concerned them. He returned to his textile business in Paris.

In the years immediately after the war, Jean received the highest civilian awards of several countries for his wartime bravery and leadership of the Dutch-Paris escape line. In 1946, he was bestowed both the French Legion of Honor, and the United States Medal of Freedom with Gold Palm. In 1947, he was awarded the Dutch Order of Orange-Nassau by Queen Wilhelmina. He was made an Honorary Officer of the Order of the British Empire, and an Officer of the Order of Leopold by the Belgium Government. Yet in peacetime, Jean remained a relatively unknown man with few means, struggling to resume ordinary life and find opportunities for work amid the ashes of post-war Europe.

It was not long before he closed down his business and moved definitively to the United States to make a new start in the health food business. He arrived in Southern California in 1955 where he began modestly with a van full of products which he sold door to door or took orders for later delivery. His business grew to three stores in the Pasadena area.

At the Adventist Church he met Naomi, a beautiful, vivacious and life-loving operating room nurse. They were married in 1957. Jean's lifelong correspondence, still in French, with friends in France, Belgium, Switzerland and Italy, gives a full account of his life after the war.

---

* Tape recorded interview of John Weidner by Alberto Sbacchi in the Weidner Collection of the John Henry Weidner Foundation for Altruism.

AFTERWORD 405

Jean's public life included giving presentations in churches, synagogues, and lecture halls throughout the United States about the Dutch-Paris escape line. Working with author Herbert Ford, he co-published *Flee the Captor* in 1966, about his clandestine activities during World War II. The book is told in the style of an adventure story and personal memoir, and was translated into French as *Le Passeur* ("the border crossing guide") and Dutch as *Vlucht Narr de Vrijheid* ("flight to freedom").

History continued to follow Jean Weidner, as he and Naomi employed as their delivery person one Sirhan Sirhan, later the convicted assassin of Robert Kennedy as the latter campaigned in California for the nomination as Democratic candidate for President in 1968. Jean and Naomi had not kept Sirhan in their service for long, as the young man did not find it important to follow the prescribed order of deliveries to the Weidner clients. The Weidners were obliged to testify at Sirhan's trial where Jean discovered that "I along with five others was on the list in his notebook of those to be killed. Charming" [letter to the Beaujolins, December 14, 1969].

In 1978, Jean was honored as one of the Righteous Among the Nations at Israel's Holocaust Memorial, Yad Vashem. In 1984, he received a Scroll of Honor from the Simon Wiesenthal Center. In 1993, he was one of seven people chosen to light candles recognizing rescuers at the opening of the United States Holocaust Museum in Washington D.C.

Re Koster, an opera singer and voice teacher, and her husband were the first people led by Jean Weidner over the Salève mountain to Geneva. In her interview with Alberto Sbacchi more than fifty years later, she gives a harrowing account of their hazardous climb over the rocky cliffs and the descent into Switzerland. Of Jean Weidner, she said, "He was absolutely marvelous. The moment you met him, you felt he was a unique person. He was humanity itself. With his cleverness, his intelligence, his charisma, helping others became his life's credo."

Jean Weidner died on May 21, 1994.

Historical Timeline

In legal correspondence the Weidner family members could not discuss events of the war, and in non-legal correspondence, it was even more dangerous to do so. Their letters make only veiled or coded allusions to war news, and virtually none to Jean's clandestine work as leader of the Dutch-Paris escape line. The following selected events of the War, and from Jean's rescue operations (in italics), form some of the background of the Weidner family letters.

May 9, 1936	Italian forces invade Ethiopia
August 23, 1939	Nazi-Soviet Non-Aggression pact signed
September 1, 1939	Nazi invasion of Poland
September 3, 1939	Britain and France declare war on Germany; "The Phony War" begins; French troops are moved to the Maginot Line
May 10, 1940	German invasion of France, Belgium, Luxemburg, The Netherlands
May 13, 1940	Dutch Government in exile established in London
May 15, 1940	Holland surrenders to Germany
May 28, 1940	Belgium surrenders to Germany
June 3, 1940	German *Luftwaffe* bombs Paris
June 16, 1940	Marshal Pétain becomes French Prime Minister
June 22, 1940	France signs armistice with Nazi Germany
November 10-11, 1940	Bombing raid cripples Italian fleet at Taranto, Italy
December 9-10, 1940	British offensive against Italians in North Africa
January-February, 1941	British successes against Italian forces in North Africa
March 11, 1941	President Roosevelt sings Lend Lease Act; the United States, which has not yet entered the war, will supply war materiel to Europe

June 22, 1941	Germany attacks Soviet Union, rupturing Non-Aggression Act
July 26, 1941	Roosevelt suspends relations with Japan
August 21, 1941	Siege of Leningrad begins
December 7, 1941	The Japanese bomb Pearl Harbor
December 8, 1941	US and Britain declare war on Japan
December 11, 1941	Hitler declares war on the United States
January 20, 1942	Wannsee Conference organizes the "Final Solution of The Jewish Problem"
January 26, 1942	First US forces arrive in Britain
May 29, 1942	Jews in France ordered to wear the yellow star
July 4, 1942	First US bombing missions on Europe
July 16-17, 1942	Paris Jews are rounded up and imprisoned in the Vel d'Hiv
July-August, 1942	*Jean escorts first Jewish refugees down the Salève mountain to safety in Switzerland*
September 13, 1942	Battle of Stalingrad begins.
October 14-16, 1942	*Jean is captured by a French border patrol, held for two days, and severely beaten*
November 11, 1942	Germans and Italians invade Unoccupied Zone in France
February 2, 1943	Germans surrender at Stalingrad
March, 1943	*Jean travels to Geneva to seek financing for his clandestine rescue work; he secures major support with the help of World Council of Churches Secretary General, Willem Vissser 't Hooft*
March 3-4, 1943	British Royal Air Force bombs Renault factory at Boulogne-Billancourt, in Paris
July 9/10, 1943	Allies land in Sicily
July 19, 1943	Italian Fascist Government Falls
September 1943	*The Gestapo attempts to arrest Jean at his home in Lyon but he eludes capture and continues his rescue operations as a fugitive under false identities*
September 9, 1943	Italian surrender to Allies is announced

HISTORICAL TIMELINE

October, 1943	*Jean makes his first trip to Paris and Brussels to expand rescue operations; in the coming months, he estimates, the escape line transports as many as 100 downed American and British pilots to safety via Paris and across the Pyrenees Mountains into Spain*
February 18, 1944	Plans confirmed for the Allied invasion of France
February 26-28, 1944	*The Gestapo arrests Gaby and dozens of other Dutch-Paris members*
May 8, 1944	Date for landing in Normandy set for June 5
May 20-29, 1944	*Jean is captured by French paramilitary police while preparing to deliver messages to Allied intelligence in England; he escapes by leaping from a three-story building before they can hand him over to the Nazis*
June 4, 1944	Landing is postponed for 24 hours due to bad weather
June 6, 1944	"D Day" Allied landing in Normandy
August 25, 1944	Liberation of Paris
September 17, 1944	Allied bombing assault on The Netherlands
April 12, 1945	Allies liberate Buchenwald concentration camp; death of US President Roosevelt
April 29-30, 1945	Soviet army liberates Ravensbrück
April 30, 1945	Hitler commits suicide
May 7, 1945	Germany surrenders

Sources

All but four of the letters and documents cited in this book are selected from the correspondence of the Weidner family contained in the Weidner Collection of the John Henry Weidner Foundation for Altruism. The Weidner Collection was first located at Atlantic Union College in South Lancaster, Massachusetts. From 2013 to 2023, it was housed in the Hoover Institution at Stanford University. Inquiries about the Collection should be directed to the Foundation. All permissions for publication of Weidner Collection materials and photographs are by the Weidner Foundation.

The originals of four of Gabrielle's letters (March 6, 1940; July 19, 1943; February 24, 1944; and Undated) are from the Archives Historiques de l'Adventisme en Europe, Section Collonges-Sous-Salève (France), Weidner Collection, Box 10CP1, File 7. Archivist Guido Delameillieure and the Archives Board (Conseil des Archives) have kindly given permission for their use in *The Weidners in Wartime*.

The letters, documents and interviews in French were translated by Janet Carper of Cornish, Maine. Anthony Sluis of Toms River, New Jersey, is the translator of the letters in Dutch.

Recorded interviews by Alberto Sbacchi in 1994, also in the Weidner Collection, furnished additional information and clarification, notably his interviews with: Christiane Beaujolin, Elisabeth Cartier Jolivet, Re Koster, Gisèle Sevenster Dominicus, Jean Weidner, and Annette Weidner Hipleh. Anna Rein, Senior Lecturer of Italian at Bowdoin College, is the translator from the Italian of the interview with Annette Hipleh.

Acknowledgments

So many people have helped along the way to bring this book to life. From the beginning Kurt Ganter, former Executive Director and present member of the Board of the Weidner Foundation, has encouraged and supported this project. Kurt stood ready to help at all times and was an early reader of the manuscript.

I want to thank Naomi Weidner for her early encouragement for "the letters book."

For five years while I was translator of documents, Stan Tozeski, archivist at the Weidner Center, shipped boxes of pages and recordings for me to translate from French. He advised me about dealing with crumbling paper, rusted paper clips and difficult handwriting. During the evolution of this book of Weidner family letters, Stan constantly made available to me whatever I needed. His expert cataloguing, filing and preserving of all the Weidner documents has been indispensable to this project and will continue to serve future researchers.

Without the steady and ever-willing help of the Weidner Foundation's Dutch translator Anthony "Tony" Sluis of Toms River, New Jersey, the book of Weidner family letters could not have been completed. Tony translated hundreds of documents in the Weidner archives and was always available to help with the family letters, returning fully translated ones in a few days' time. A memorable moment was when Tony and my poet husband Tom worked to transform the spirited Christmas gift poem written for Annette from a rhymed and metered Dutch poem into a similarly rhymed and metered English one. The Dutch and English versions flew back and forth between New Jersey and Maine across cyberspace evolving into its final form within a day and a half.

A big thank you goes to Anna Rein, Senior Lecturer in Italian at Bowdoin College, for her translation from Italian of the recorded 1994 interview with Annette Weidner Hipleh.

Catherine Ronchi, Town Council member and First Assistant to the Mayor of Orry-la-Ville, France, responded to a noontime phone call from a complete stranger (me) about the location of the Dutch cemetery and memorial to the Dutch Resistance in France. Catherine drove to the cemetery during her lunch break, took photos, and mailed them back to me by mid-afternoon. A few weeks later, when Tom and I came to Orry-la-Ville, a short train ride from Paris, Catherine met us at the train station and drove us to the Dutch cemetery and showed us the memorial to Dutch Resistance. After picking up her daughter at her job in nearby Senlis, Catherine delivered us back to the train station. During the ride she showed lively interest in the Weidner project, suggesting resources, and citing local historians of the Second World War period. It seemed as if we had always been friends with Catherine, and as an elected official of her town, she is a superior ambassador for Orry-la-Ville.

Pastor Gilles Georges welcomed us one steaming July day in 2009, when we came to visit "130", the Adventist Church in Paris. After recounting the World War II experiences of his parents and expressing his interest in the events of that period, he told us that the structural layout of the building was exactly as it had been in Gabrielle Weidner's time, and he remembered some of the people who had been Gabrielle's associates. Since an extensive renovation and restructuring was planned, we felt lucky to visit the rooms along the sunny corridor on the top floor unchanged from when Gaby and her friends lived there, except that they now serve as offices instead of dwellings. Pastor Georges showed us the kitchen nearby where Gaby and her colleagues prepared meals for themselves or for their guests, and we descended the curving staircase by which they came down to work each morning. It is thanks to Pastor Georges that we have a real sense of her surroundings as she wrote her wartime letters to her family.

I am grateful to Rozemaryn van der Horst of Captain Cook, Hawaii, for her interest in the Weidner letters book and for helping me with the Dutch language. Rozemaryn died in 2018.

My thanks go to readers Ancy Morse of Rochester, Minnesota, Meredith Harding of Cornish, Maine, and Marie-Claire Rolland of Paris,

France, for their thoughtful reading of the manuscript and their helpful suggestions.

I want to thank my niece, science writer Hannah Holmes, and her literary agent Michelle Tessler for their reality check and for their advice about publishing today.

I am grateful to Guido Delameilleure, archivist at the Collonges Seminary for his interest in the project and for securing permission for the use of four of Gabrielle's letters, including her last ones, which are in the Seminary archives in Collonges, France.

When I wrote to Christiane Beaujolin to ask whether Julien Beaujolin and her late husband Gilbert Beaujolin were one and the same person, she responded immediately to explain that her husband was born Julien Louis Beaujolin, but that his friends later decided to call him Gilbert! Christiane welcomed Tom and me to her home the following summer and spent many hours in the years afterward recalling for us her own Resistance work during the war and her service to her country in the postwar recovery period. In the summer of 2011, she drove us to Nanteuil-Saacy to visit the site where the 2000 deportees on the Last Convoy, including Gabrielle Weidner and both of Christiane Beaujolin's parents, were held in an open field awaiting a backup train to carry them to concentration camps in Germany. We are grateful to Christiane Beaujolin for her friendship and her interest in the Weidner book projects. Christiane Beaujolin died in 2015.

Maarten Eliasar has always been ready and willing to share his recollections of Jean Weidner. I am grateful for his insights into daily life in The Netherlands in wartime.

Megan Koreman, skilled researcher and author of *The Escape Line* (Oxford University Press, 2018), detailing the work of Jean Weidner's Resistance network, has been a wonderful colleague and friend and source of information and support. She has shared many findings with me for this book in the course of her research for her own.

Ron Osborn, who serves as Executive Director of the Weidner Foundation on a voluntary basis and is a full-time professor of ethics and philosophy at La Sierra University, has also been the editor of this book. His suggestions are invaluable and insightful and he has undertaken all the tasks of publishing a book with patience, good humor and tolerance for the author's whims.

Lastly but truly first and foremost my husband Tom Carper, first reader, computer problem solver, editor, layout advisor, patient and tolerant colleague, overall supporter and best friend for life, has made the completion of this project possible.

Janet Holmes Carper

Janet Holmes Carper is a teacher of French at all levels and to all ages. Her teaching career began as an English assistant in the Ecole Normale d'Institutrices in Châteauroux, France, for two years. In a rural Maine high school she was the entire French department. She has also been an editor of French and German textbooks at Holt, Rinehart and Winston. Though French is her second language it is on an equal footing with her first. Janet resides with her husband Tom in Cornish, Maine. Nearly every summer finds them in their 14th-century stone farmhouse in the Loire Valley in France.

www.ingramcontent.com/pod-product-compliance
Lightning Source LLC
Chambersburg PA
CBHW020512080526
44583CB00013B/577